CITIES
OF
LIGHTNING

CITIES
OF
LIGHTNING

THE ICONOGRAPHY OF
THUNDER-BEINGS
IN THE ORIENTAL TRADITIONS

SAMUDRANATH

Lightning Bolt Press

Published by Lightning Bolt Press

Distributed to the trade by
Blue Dolphin Publishing, Inc.
P. O. Box 8, Nevada City, CA 95959
Orders: 1-800-643-0765
Web site: www.bluedolphinpublishing.com

ISBN: 0-9660203-0-8

Library of Congress Cataloging-in-Publication Data

Samudranath, 1971–
    Cities of lightning : the iconography of thunder-beings in the oriental traditions / Samudranath.
        p. cm.
    Includes bibliographical references.
    ISBN 0-9660203-0-8 (alk. paper)
    1. Spiritual life. 2. Spiritual life—Hinduism. 3. Spiritual life—Tantric Buddhism. 4. Spiritual
life—Taoism I. Title.

    BL624 .S228 1999
    291.2'11—dc21
                                                                            99-050176

Cover art: Jampa Tsomo
Cover design: Lito Castro
Back cover photo: Judith Edoff

Printed in the United States of America

10   9   8   7   6   5   4   3   2   1

Dedication

I dedicate Cities of Lightning to all Thunder-beings.
They dedicate it to the enlightenment of all sentient beings,
to the complete eradication of ignorance, suffering, disease, famine,
warfare in this world and all realms.
May all beings abide in peace.

Contents

Acknowledgments

I want to thank the Thunder-beings first and foremost, without whom this work would not have been undertaken, without whom there would be no sacred wisdom-paths, no excellence or self-illumination, without whom there would be no beauty and true compassion in the world. Without this Mystery there would be no transmission-vessels leading us back to it, and no inherent goodness to speak of. The Mystery is our consciousness and a profound wisdom which is thoroughly beyond all minds.

I give thanks especially to Lord Shiva who created, assigned and guided Cities of Lightning. I thank Primordial Rudra for his grace and transmission, and his sacred revenue of dwarves, skeletons, etc., who constitute his body. I thank Shri Mahadurga Kalike Paremeshvari Mata, Kalbhairav, and dakini retinue. I give heart-felt thanks to Mahavatar Shri 1008 Sambasadashiv Haidakhan Wale Babaji, Shri Muniraj-Dattatreya and Haidakhan kula. I give thanks to Goraknath, Thirumular and the Nava Nath lineage, to Kriya Babaji Nagaraj, the Trikasara lineage of Kashmir for extending the Non-dual Shaiva Tantra unblemished. Omnamahshivaya.

I want to thank venerable Lei Kung, my godfather, and Yuan-Shih T'ien Tsun, Celestial Venerable of the Primordial Beginning. I give thanks to the Immortals of the Thunder-method, Bo Yang (Lao Tzu) and master Hua-Ching Ni for bringing the ancient tradition of the feather-men to our hearts.

I want to thank Chakrasamvara and Vajra-yogini the origin of Buddhist Tantra, and the Vajra Family Buddhas for their profound blessings, namely Vajradhara, Vajrapani, Hevajra, the Vajra-Lady Kalike, and Simhamukha dakini. I want to thank Guru Rinpoche and his emanation of Barway Dorje Choktrul Rinpoche for initiating me into Vajrayana. I thank Machig Labdron, mother of the Chod rites. I want to thank Sangye Tenzin Rinpoche. I want to thank those which, unseen have guided Cities of Lightning who travel in rainbow-clouds clothed in complete Enjoyment bodies. I give thanks to Gyaltsen the great Kalachakra master for his blessings, Geshela Tenzin at Namgyal Institute, venerable Khenpo Karthar Rinpoche, the Karmapa and unbroken Mahamudra lineage. Lastly I thank Jetsun Milarepa and retinue for his profound blessings, and for awakening heart-felt devotion.

I want to thank Ehyeh Asher Ehyah from whom my family lineage of the 77 derives its love and secret essence. I give thanks to my mother, Rikpay Drolma who is a face of the Mysterious Mother, my father, also my aunt and uncle, for their unexcelled patience and encouragement. I thank Melchezedek.

I thank Lord Osiris and Isis and the distant Starthunders. I give thanks to the seen and unseen vajra-brothers and sisters of the vast living-place for their luminosity and guidance. I give thanks to all Thunder-people and children of the Mystery, particularly the heyokas, one in front, one in back, one who dances while still, the others while moving counter-clockwise.

I give deepest thanks to Tunkashila, Wakinyan Tanka, the Crescent-Moon Eyed, their egg and voice-born and Blue Lightning Mother. I thank the Chanunpa and its bearer Grandfather Wanbli Gekaya for his immeasurable love, wisdom, voice and activity.

I thank the Blue Star behind the sun, the infinite Mind-ocean and its inhabitants of dolphin and whale people for guarding sublime wisdom-treasure with unimpeded power.

I give thanks to all Thunder-beings who anonymously guided this exposition visiting in thunder-dreams in wisdom bodies of Thunder-clouds, lightningbolts, rain, rainbows, rolling thunder, sacred stone, space-ship geometries, self-appearing light, etc. May they guide all minds back to the Omniscient Mystery space.

Thanks to my close vajra-brothers and sisters at KTD, to Narayani at Haidhakandi, to Kathy, an unexcelled teacher, yogini and lady of lightning.

Thanks to Jampa Tsomo for the cover design of Lord Shiva, Garuda. Thanks to Dr. Judy Edoff for the back cover photo.

And finally, thanks to Blue Dolphin Press for the printing of this text.

BOOK ONE

Cities of Lightning

Opening Verses

Om Namah Shivaya
Before the Glorious Wisdom Wheel whose spokes
    are Lightning flashing in space, I bow.
Before the Heart of all Cities of Lightning, I bow.
Before the Father-Mother Dancing in Bliss of
    Union, I bow.
Before the Mandala of Indestructible Space and
    Primordial Luminosity, I bow.
Before the Jeweled Lamp of Infinite Consciousness
    and His display, I bow.
Before the Ancient One of Lightning, moving-
    through-all-things, I bow.
Before the Lightning branching in space-womb,
    I bow.
Before the Dancing Blue Star, Stellar Chakra, I bow.
Before the Wisdom Thunder-bird, I bow.
Before the Stainless Wisdom Dakini of Lightning,
    I bow.
Before the Lotus-Feet of Haidhakan Sambasadashiv,
    I bow
Before the Lightningbolt of Compassion, Sampa
    Lhundrupma, born on the Mt. of Meteoric Iron,
    I bow.

There is no greater Source of Refuge than the Thunder-beings; their Lightning-Tree protects those who come under its branches from inner and outer obstructions; their rain-bow tent protects those who seek refuge from the hail storm of today-world disease.

There is no greater, more worthy vessel than that constructed by Thunder-beings, to take us across the Flood-sea of degenerate views and activity. They are the thunder-storm of the Mystery which is over us, guiding us to love, and they are the pilot-light in our hearts which sails the vessel of the body-mind to the shore of Luminous Perfection.

There is no more precious Source of Enlightenment than the Thunder-beings throughout infinite space. They are a wisdom-sky filled with the thunder and lightning of loving grace; their fiery clouds cracking to liberate all sentient beings from suffering.

There is no greater ornament which falls than the thunder and lightning of Mysterious Divinity. Because they are stainless purity, Thunder-beings are beyond material incarnation. Because their jeweled hearts overflow with love they produce emanations and activity. They produce imagery and Cities of Lightning. They produce wisdom tradition, the essence of which are the means that sentient beings can use to attain Divinity.

Through thunder and lightning they capture our minds and enlighten us. Through outer light we are physically awakened, returned to the beginning or dawn of our existence. Each day countless beings wake up to begin a new cycle. Through inner wisdom-light sentient beings are mentally awakened, they are returned to the beginning and dawn of their mind. When our mind is spontaneously illuminated by the radiant-bliss of an Enlightened Mind, we see our true nature, we are awakened to our blissful Divinity, our Enlightened Mind.

Through thunder and lightning, Deity connects sky to earth, vast inner space to the ground of our present awareness. There is no greater blessing than the mixing of minds through the medium of lightning and thunder. Deity's wisdom reflects itself in the atmosphere and in the mind-sphere in the form of thunder, lightning, clouds, rain, rainbows, sparks, and clear-light imagery. When we recollect Deity's theophany, we recollect our enlightened nature. We do so through visualization of imagery and recitation of sacred sound. We echo the wisdom and luminous blessings of Omniscient Deity, so that we're spontaneously awakened. We turn the mirror of our mind to Omniscient Deity to reflect his wisdom and blessings into the universe to liberate all sentient beings from suffering.

We might see Thunder-beings in the clouds and in our dreams—they are seen through inherent wisdom. When the senses are pervaded with wisdom they can perceive the wisdom of the Spirit. When ones practice reaches its peak, and one becomes a Deity, then ones body becomes the union of awareness and subtle light, so one perceives Deity's as everyone, as all sounds, forms, and thoughts. This is not a fabricated illusion, it is Truth—we each are a Deity, and the Deity is a collection of Deity's. Nature is a Deity and it is a collection of Deity's. It is a fabricated illusion to not perceive things as they are. The aim of our training is to realize things as they are. Natural means "as it is." When the mind rests "as it is" without elaboration, without fixation, without fear and doubt—the natural state within dawns, and the nature of things (Truth) can be perceived. This is the dawn of the sacred day that the Wisdom Deities cause in all minds. So we awaken to begin a new cycle in which our hearts are one.

Thunder-beings bring us back to the spring of our life, when we came forth as stars from the fountainhead of Infinite Space. The whole idea or motivation behind the Oriental traditions is to return our mind to the state of bliss and tranquility—the state of naturalness and unity we possessed before we were born. This is the state of perfect inner freedom in which the mind possesses the power of unlimited expression and immeasurable compassion. Thunder-beings create storms with their mind, they weave them out of sky-like awareness with perfect ease. In the same way, our minds, when liberated from afflictive states, attachment and revulsion, will be free to express enlightened Self-nature. Through hot and cold, positive and negative charges, Thunder-beings control the universe and all minds, weaving storm-phenomena within liberated Self-nature. In the same way, when our attachment and revulsion is liberated, there is simply natural luminos-

ity, whose friction weaves all internal phenomena like blissful lightning.

There is no more sublime dance than this Dance of thunder and lightning. It is the configuration, the very Wisdom-mind of one and all Thunder-beings. Through it they bring all minds to dance in radiant majestic clear-light Mind; through it they cause all minds to speak from Universal Mind with one voice; through it they cause all hearts to live from Universal Mind with one pulse; through it they bring all minds to peace and bliss beyond suffering.

An Introduction to the Thunder-beings

Quite often when people hear about the Thunder-beings it is in the context of shamanic traditions, the traditions of indigenous peoples who supplicated Deities of the Storm to sustain their crops, to bring beneficial rains and avert harmful storms, to heal and drive away negative forces. Since beginningless time people have worshiped Thunder-beings. The early cultures were initiated by Thunder-beings, and their belief systems were established by Thunder-beings. Thunder-beings created the universe, the world and all life; they gave people food, shelter, fire, the first language, law, wisdom, the arts, spiritual sciences, and all knowledge. They cared for the people as parents care for their children. And the people worshiped them with jeweled hearts, as Father-Mother, as creator, sustainer and destroyer, not through primitive rites, but in simple yet sophisticated and Holy ways.

The Thunder-beings are behind all pure religious transmission, both ancient and new. If you look into the worlds religious traditions, if you look into their origins, you will discover that the tradition, the view or set of beliefs about the universe, spirit, nature, life, etc., come from Thunder-beings. We know this because tradition relates it, that Omniscient Wisdom-beings taught the early people, either directly or in profound dreams and mystical visions of thunder and lightning.

The God of virtually all God-centered traditions across the globe is a Thunder-being, or multiple Thunder-beings. It is a universal belief that the God and Goddess, the Omniscient Wisdom-beings who stand as the Crown Jewel of all wisdom-traditions, are Thunder-beings. Their theophany or mystical visitation is universally one of storm-display. This means not only that he-she functions this way in the atmosphere, but that everything they do, all activity, manifestation, revelation, has Wisdom-thunder-power behind it. It means that all people are related to Thunder-beings, that the most sacred beliefs of all traditions come from the hearts of Thunder-beings. If we pray to them we might experience the truth of this as perfected masters of the past did, we might prove the existence of sublime Wisdom-beings for ourself. They are invisible, yet out of compassion they reveal themselves; everyone can experience them in nature; they are manifest in the storms, lightning, rainbows, in the stars, the sky, stones, oceans, animals, people, and elements. We live with them. We participate in their majestic dance or play. They are within the body-mind-heart of all beings. They manifest as creative thoughts. We know them through love within our hearts. They are our inherent perfection, our pure positive qualities and activities, our health and harmony. Know this is how close Thunder-beings are to us. Because they are within our mind we might experience them directly and instantaneously, like lightning, to receive guidance, inspiration, insight, wisdom, love—to help self and others.

They are perfect and free of suffering; there is no more sublime Source of Refuge. Because they are fully within our mind we can attain the same state free of suffering. We can achieve this while on earth in this body. In fact in Oriental traditions, this body is imperative, this life is taken to provide a means of attaining the highest wisdom and perfection. Thunder-beings have provided the perfect means to attain perfection for all beings.

They are behind all integral wisdom traditions. They are the roots of all pure religion across the globe, throughout the multi-universe and innumerable realms. For example the Ancient Thunder Lord(s) known as Shiva, originated tradition in India, Nepal, Siberia, China, Kumari Kandan (Lemuria), South East Asia, in Judea, South America, Atlantis, and Egypt. The Thunder-beings Lei Kung and Yuan-shih T'ien-tsun, Celestial Venerable of the Primordial Beginning, originated all spiritual sciences that originated in ancient China that became known as Taoism. The Thunder-being known as Chakrasamvara (Wheel of Supreme Bliss) originated Buddha Dharma in India (through Shakyamuni Buddha's heart), the Thunder-being Vajrapani protects it, and the Thunder-master Guru Rinpoche brought it to Tibet, Nepal and the West. The Thunder-beings known as Yahveh-Ehyeh-Asher-Ehyeh originated all pure Occidental traditions of Judaism, Christianity and Islam. The Thunder-beings known as Wandjina originated Australian shamanic tradition. The Thunder-beings known as Tengeri originated Mongolian shamanic tradition. The Thunder-beings known as Tunkashila, Animiki, Katchinas, originated Native American traditions. The Thunder-beings known as Tlaloc originated tradition in Meso-America. The Thunder-beings known as Osiris and Isis originated tradition in Egypt. The Thunder-beings known as Zeus and Dionysius originated tradition in ancient Europe. Thunder-beings known as Jinn originated tradition throughout the Middle East. In Africa Thunder-beings originated traditions as well. In short, just as the Thunder-beings' magnificent storms blanket the earth throughout the year, so does their wisdom pervade the cultural traditions of the earth.

The traditions were transmitted from Thunder-beings through the pure and clear mind of human representatives. Their wisdom flashes like lightning in the clear sky-mind of their human messengers. The Thunder-beings developed all transmissions based on culture and time; the beliefs and practices they developed are suitable to the people within that culture. The beliefs they developed are the Truth, and the practices are the ways for humans to adhere to the Truth—to return to unity. The Thunder-beings developed tradition out of compassion for suffering beings, for their illumination.

Thunder-beings are the cause of real love, peace, justice, beauty and goodness in the world, because they are the cause of these pure ambrosial qualities within our individual lives, within our hearts and minds. They control what happens in the human world through the hearts of people. They control what happens in nature through the hearts of natural-deities, angelic-spirits, animals, and electro-magnetic fields. There is harmony in nature because Thunder-beings control it directly through open-hearted beings. The cycles of universes, galaxies, constellations, planets, of seasons, of individual lives of all beings, of cells and atoms, of everything, is controlled or governed by Thunder-beings. They are all-pervasive, so work invisibly through the heart of all beings and phenomena.

There is considerably less harmony in human society because the hearts of the people are closed. We have free will, freedom to choose, and have made imperfect choices which have clouded our minds, which have not resulted in peace, but in turmoil. Essentially, because we have chosen to cherish ourselves and ignore others, the Source of Harmony in our lives cannot act clearly to maintain peace in the human world. It lives in the world through our love of others, through wise activity. One might argue that nature is equally or more chaotic than our society, but nature flows beautifully with great stillness and cyclic grace; what calamity and natural disaster we see in the world is the response primarily of degenerate human activity. Everything is interdependent or related. The collective negative emotions of a nation at war are sufficient to cause natural disasters like earthquakes years later. The toxic pollution of the oceans during Nagasaki and Hiroshima is sufficient to cause massive storms years later. The present misuse of crystals to broadcast chaotic electro-magnetic frequencies carrying messages of violence and non-virtue in T.V.'s and radios will bring natural disaster in the near future. The present misuse of electricity directly causes a negative response which alters weather patterns, and brain waves. The present misuse of fuels and atom energies will bring natural cataclysm unless such activity is ceased. The present misuse of body and mind will bring the demise and suffering of innumerable sentient beings, unless such activity is ceased.

Our own negativity contributes to the degeneration of human culture. Our positive, creative activity, our virtue or Dharma contributes to the harmonious balance of the earth. If we live this sacred way, then we will be blessed with wisdom and bliss. We become a part of the Life and Dance of the Thunder-beings who are the Source of all things. If we live out our lives according to their way, we will become inseparable from them, the Source of peace, harmony, love, perfection, wisdom in the universe.

If we want peace for ourselves and others we simply must choose it. We choose it by working to establish inner peace, clarity and wisdom, through meditation, and by working to help others through kindness, generosity, virtue, compassion, and so on. We can practice religion as a sure means of establishing inner and outer peace. Dharma means humanitarianism, and the practice of wisdom or meditation. Dharma means following the ways of the Thunder-beings, God or Enlightened Ones. This way always results in harmony and peace immediately. We always feel it instantaneously when we offer ourselves to help others, when we share, when we work for the welfare of others. What we feel is the blissful heart of the Spirit-moving-through-all things. It moved us, and is moved by us, so encourages us to continue in our path

of virtue. The more we give of their love, the more we're given, until we become sacred—until we have sacrificed everything and there's nothing left but wisdom and love. This is the fruit of religion, the goal or heart-treasure of human existence. Self-sacrifice provides continuous bliss. It is continuous or unbroken bliss that every being seeks. The general teaching in Oriental tradition is that this state is achieved by going within, through meditation. The special teaching or Tantra, which enhances meditation and bestows the ultimate goal, is the use of a personal enlightened Wisdom-deity.

Our positive alignment with Thunder-beings results in the fruit of continuous bliss and tranquility— because this fruit is what they are. When we pray to them, the luminous blessings we receive are the wisdom-nectar of the Deity. The sacrament is the Deity. It is likened to precious divine nectar and wine because it intoxicates, it is likened to blood because it is alive, it is likened to medicine because it puts things back together. The blessings are the enlightened quality of the Deity which remove suffering and awaken the quality of enlightenment within us. Our positive relationship with them results in upliftment, internal transformation, protection now and in the future. Just hearing the names of Omniscient Thunder-beings, or seeing their sacred images is sufficient cause to encounter them in the future, to follow their Holy Way to enlightenment. This is so because their images, names and instructions are profoundly blessed. They have made aspirations that anyone who encounters them, their wisdom, in images, names, masters, scriptures and so on, will be released from suffering. So that when we do encounter them, we attract an instant blessing from their all-pervasive Mind. If we're clear then we'll feel it and use it to generate devotion. If we're not clear then it'll make us clear. Through such blessing power the Thunder-beings inspire and guide all beings to their blissful state. With this in mind we might understand the efficacy of divine-imagery. It is literally created out of love or blessings; it is the intention to help beings, it is the intention to release those who see it (image) and hear it (name) from suffering. Sacred art is created by Deities with this kind of magnanimous love and wisdom.

Religion, which we call wisdom-tradition, is the Mind-transmission of Sublime Wisdom-deities, and is likewise developed out of their love and perfect insight to guide all beings to them. The Thunder-beings are formless Sublime Wisdom-beings, who, in the Oriental traditions are responsible for originating or expressing the subtle Truth of spiritual reality, guarding it and disseminating it for the benefit of sentient beings. Like a wisdom wheel of lightnings, they send their light of Truth across the earth. Wherever this Eye with its lightning-cornea looks, they put their harmonious enlightened vision. This activity is proven throughout the scriptures of every religion which relate how this body of wisdom spontaneously manifested. For example the Torah scripture arose out of a thunder-storm of Deities gathering over Mt. Sinai. Ancient Shaiva scriptures arose directly from the five-faces of Lord Shiva, some of these were given to his consorts, others were transmitted under the sea, some arose as letters in space, others were written in stone. Ancient Taoist scriptures arose out of heaven realms were they were transmitted to Deities, then written on jade tablets and given to the sages. The Buddhist scriptures were transmitted from Lord Buddha and the Dakinis to the mahasiddhas. Innumerable Tantras have been concealed as sacred treasures (terma) inside rocks, lakes, sky, and the minds of treasure finders.

* * *

Every spring the Cities of Lightning arise in the sky, as a collection of ever-darkening clouds, pregnant with high-voltage luminosity and subtle wisdom. They envelope the sky in wisdom-flames, rays of lightning and crackling fire, cracks of thunder and nourishing rains. They are the enlightened revelation, the mind and vision of invisible Thunder-beings. These Cities of Lightning are controlled by a singular Wisdom-being at their center, a Thunder Lord or Lady of Lightning. He arises out of vast inner space and adorns himself in cloud, lightning, thunder, rain, hail, a funnel or other non-dual living phenomena, like thunder-stone. He travels in the lightnings and clouds and speaks through the thunder. The lightning is his vehicle of light, the thunder his vehicle of sound. He gives revelation in wordless speech and invisible form. He dances as intangible light and weaves music with instruments that don't exist. Out of liberated energy he creates magical wisdom-display, he creates reality—nature.

Zig zagging in front of Thunder Lord is an emanation of himself, the Thunder-bird, the shield-bird and great tuning angel who flashes lightning from his eyes and cracks thunder from the flapping of his wings. Around the Lord and his Thunder-bird are their children or emanations, their messengers, who are an assemblage of wise spirits which constitute the unseen body of the Lord, the unified Spirit which controls nature. This family we call the Cities of Lightning. It is one Wisdom circle of the Spirit and retinue, one Enlightened Mind of multiple transformation-bodies. It is the Thunder-spirit appearing in nature, as nature.

The Thunder-beings are manifesting their enlightened minds as nature, and yet they are beyond the universe. They are everywhere, but since they abide within and above us, we can establish an intimate relationship with them in order that they will reveal themselves within us. They are the Self or Mind within us, our perfect tranquility and bliss. We can relate to them in the storms and stars, but primarily we must seek them within. We supplicate them continuously and their blessings enlighten us, as the lightning enlightens the earth. When they make a light within our awareness, we will be able to see our own enlightenment. Their light dispels the darkness of ignorance in all minds, which prevents us from seeing our infinity, our tranquil space and compassionate-bliss. All of our difficulties and suffering arise from this lack of sight (insight) or knowledge, therefore it follows that the solution to all of our difficulties, and the antidote to all of our suffering, is the light of knowledge. Within all traditions we supplicate the Thunder-beings, the Lords of Enlightenment to bestow this light upon us, and to dispel the darkness which is the very root of all our suffering. This universal antidote or medicine is depicted in many ways in iconography. Lord Shiva bestows what is known as amrita or wisdom-nectar which he culls from the inexhaustible ocean of his compassion, and pours down into his devotees. The Buddha Shakyamuni holds within his begging bowl the plant known as myrobalen—(a universal cure) symbolizing that the Dharma is the universal cure for all suffering and its root. The image of medicine is a universal symbol of the wisdom of the Thunder-beings.

Nature and universe are not arbitrary. It is governed by these Thunder-beings through the force of their all-pervasive Mind, (we call this force wind or energy, electro-magnetic energy). Just as a person has an essence which expresses itself through energy, activity and speech, so also the thunder-storms we see in nature, the stars and so on, have an essence which cannot be seen but expresses itself through its energy, activity and speech. Just as our own wisdom-essence has existed since long before this body and will exist forever after it, so also these Thunder-beings have existed since long before the present display of the universe, and will remain forever after it. In most traditions it is the Thunder-beings who are responsible for creating and destroying the universe.

The Thunder-beings are a related family of divine beings who bring about weather changes such as wind, rain, thunder-lightning, snow, mist, hail. With their mind they control the hot and cold elements, or you could say positive and negative charges, to cause all weather changes, and to control the universe and minds of all beings. Through their power abiding in the atmosphere they nourish the earth and protect the people. The Thunder-beings sustain the life on earth. Thunder-beings use water and wind to cleanse the earths surface. They penetrate to cleanse the soil through lightning, and in winter send down a glorious electric blanket after the whiteness of the Absolute, to totally neutralize the harmful causes of disease. They make the earth pliant and fresh, suitable for spontaneous gentle life explosion and balanced transformation. Growth is radiance, the flow of divine iridescence. Thunders have been worshiped since ancient times as inseparable from the earth, as Lords and Mothers of fertility. Through lightning they cause rain. Rain nourishes all beings. It recycles polluted waters, by purifying them in the charged clouds. Through lightning they directly purify or enlighten the air we breath, water we drink, the earth we cultivate. The electricity purifies the domain of all beings, invisible and visible. Indirectly Thunder-beings put nitrates in the soil; the lightning burns the air, the burnt air falls in the rain to assist plant growth. The electricity of lightning touching down is a vitality which helps the seeds and plants to grow and which destroys harmful influences, such as diseases that choke off life. The lightning also provides ozone which keeps the ozone layer from dissolving due to human endeavors. In the ancient tradition of India, called Sanatan Dharma, this life-force was called pranas or "breaths" and is the living essence of lightning. Through the lightning all life has been initiated or created, is sustained, and will be destroyed. In all traditions it is Thunder-beings who govern nature and all life; they are the creators. They sustain balanced life, and destroy imbalance, the cause of suffering.

Even though there is great noise and seeming chaos, destructive rage in storms, in truth this is merely a means of ushering in peace, of clearing great obstructions. Because there are strong obstructions to peace in the world, there need to be stronger means to destroy or clear those obstructions. (This is why Thunder-beings appear fierce and wrathful). Everything Thunder-beings do has the effect of bringing about peace. Because so many beings are ignorant, have made poor choices, there is much turmoil in the world. Thunder-beings are perfect and beyond suffering, nature is their manifestation; it is quite beautiful and harmonious. Where there is calamity, the cause is poor human activity, such as war and pollution. Nature is controlled by Thunder-beings through wisdom and love, through Enlightened Minds. It is tranquil and ebullient within, the Spirit shines through it. On the surface it is impermanent, and therefore suffering. In its heart, in the heart of all beings, it is beyond suffering. This is our potential. The Spirit shines through us, works on us by working through us, blesses us by working through us. Through a clear mind it works to establish peace and harmony in the world. It works through our compassionate endeavor. We merely have to choose it. If we choose it, to help others, to live for others, to make others happy, and if we abstain from harming others, there will be true lasting peace on earth. There is little peace on earth because there is little peace in our hearts. In order to establish it we must work for it diligently, through meditating, and through compassionate activity. Meditating increases our wisdom or insight, our capacity to be of true help to others. Wisdom is the light of the Thunder-beings shining through our heart. When it becomes activity it is compassion. It is the wish to help others and the actual ability to help. We have to put our hearts together. If we have difficulties getting along with each other then we need to practice patience, generosity, kindness, equanimity and so on. We need to practice Dharma. There is inherent beauty in nature. This beauty is the result of Dharma, of Thunder-beings, of their invisible Cities of Lightning. There is little beauty in human cities because the city of our body-mind obscures the City of Wisdom in our heart, our stainless heart of natural beauty. The Cities of Lightning are free of suffering and rebirth, because they are free of its cause—ignorance, lack of awareness and love. The gate to these Cities is liberation. The Thunder-beings are the cause of liberation from suffering for all beings who choose to live according to their way. The Cities of Lightning are nature, but we do not see them. We fail to see them because our activity has degenerated. Degenerate activity has clouded the mind in a veil of darkness. We require religion, wisdom, Dharma, the blessings of the Thunder-beings to dispel this darkness with the power of enlightenment, the crystal clear Lightningbolt of the Thunder-beings.

The Thunder-beings are the Lords and Mothers of Enlightenment. The essence of Oriental wisdom traditions is the experience of enlightenment. This experience is attained through Thunder-beings, or Wisdom-Deities. They bestow this experience upon us. It is depicted through lightning and storm phenomena, rainbow-light, stellar-light. It is the awareness-sound and awareness-light of the Deities, manifesting according to the needs of the individuals. For some people, the Deities actually appear as a storm, in dreams, visions, and afterlife. Deity's intangible blessings appear to wisdom-eye as a lightningbolt. The Thunder-beings use storm-display to awaken all minds. Beings that cannot perceive Thunder-beings internally, are aroused during atmospheric storms; the thunder and lightning awakens the Deity's in our body, the experience of enlightenment, our true Deity-nature which we possessed before we were born. Our Deity-nature is our intrinsic freedom, our minds free creative expression. Because we think that our mind is limited by this body in space and time, our natural freedom and bliss become limited. As a result, we develop fear, doubt, desire, hatred and so on. Out of these states we create our future; negative states yield suffering. By cultivating divine states, we create a future of peace. So the aim of Oriental traditions is recognizing or remembering that our nature is free, unlimited, blissful, loving, wise, clear, luminous, tranquil, and training to establish these qualities in our mind. We seek the experience of enlightenment in the Lords of Enlightenment—the Thunder-beings. In the precious secret systems known as Tantra we achieve our aim through invoking the blessings of fully enlightened Wisdom-deity's to purify the negative habits that we developed. The power of Thunder-beings destroys the snakes of bad habits that afflict our mind and cause disease. If we remove all impurity, all self-cherishing, from our mind, it becomes the natural abode of Thunder-beings, it becomes like the sky, it becomes the realm or circle of enlightenment—the City of Lightning. We administer the medicine of their blessings to the afflictions of attachment, fear and hatred, to heal the wounded heart. We ingest the alchemical pill of their blessings, concentrated in mantra and image, to attain deathless life and perfect enlightenment. We mix the elixir of their blessings in the crucible of our own mind to transform base metal negative states into pure soft sublime gold of spiritual heart-qualities.

The Thunder-beings literally bestow enlightenment upon those who live virtuously or naturally and practice spiritual cultivation as a method of destroying suffering in the world. The Thunder-beings awaken us with thunder and lightning both in nature and on the subtle level of mind. This is one way they manifest their blessings. It clears our mind, leaves a light in it. For this reason we visualize or think of it. We're attracted to it because it attracts us. Only love can do this. It attracts us then opens our heart, makes an empty space so that love can shine through. It dispels the clouds from the moon-crested crown of our soul; it opens the hidden treasure-casket of our Consciousness, and lights the jeweled lamp of our heart. Just as the blessing of lightning touching down causes seed germination in the earth, the subtle clear-light blessing of Thunder-beings touching down on the ground of our awareness causes the seed germination of future enlightenment.

When we're given wisdom, there is an inherent responsibility to act compassionately. The Thunder-beings bestow enlightenment and wisdom so that they can benefit the earth and human society. They very often work through artists and spiritual teachers, healers and weather-makers, yogis and sacred clowns. They are in everyone's creative endeavors, even the smallest and humblest good deeds. They are in our Truth or righteousness, our virtue and lightheartedness, our integrity, sweetness and outrageous creativity, they are subtly behind our heart, as its essence, they're within our consciousness which is infinite, they are in all self-less activity. To contact them through our mind is to know them, to know them is to realize we're one with them in self-illuminated awareness.

Thunder-beings are concerned not only with such things as nourishing the earth and sustaining the lives of all beings who've created the condition for taking material form, but they are equally concerned with transmitting subtle wisdom and inspiring love so that the cause of suffering will be liberated or transformed into the cause and root of joyous exaltation. Thunder-beings awaken within us the clear vision of our mind, they assist our purification or spiritual cultivation which culminates in the view of our true nature as unchanging wisdom and bliss. All Oriental traditions affirm that our ultimate nature is unchanging, so when we refer to the Absolute, we definitely don't mean something "out there," but we mean the state of eternal tranquility, perfect equilibrium, indestructible awareness. Thunder-beings provide both the paths to this state and the light by which to attain it. We call this subtle wisdom—grace or blessing-light, and in Tantric traditions worship it as shakti or dakini (with a blissful female form).

At present we are in need of wisdom which restores the mind and can be applied to healing the substance of the body and the earth. The methods given by Thunder-beings for contacting them are powerful tools for liberating negativity, for healing broken hearts, for enhancing mental clarity and joy, and gathering positive energy for the alchemical process of transforming the coppery mind into golden Spirit. Their methods are tools for preventing or stopping wars and violence in the world and in the mind. They are means of ending famine, and nourishing the hearts of all beings with the elixir of inner calm and joy. Their effectiveness has been demonstrated throughout history. The precious Tantric master, Guru Rinpoche used the Thunder-beings and their methods to subdue obstructing forces to the Dharma in Tibet. My Thunder-master Haidhakan Shiva assigned a small group of devotees in India to chant Om Namah Shivaya for 24 hours. The next day the government of India changed (for the better). Certain masters, by working together have prevented atomic warfare, and through means like Om Namah Shivaya will completely transform the hearts of people, to annihilate warfare at its root.

Because the Thunder-beings are inseparable from nature, their practices have a very beneficial effect on the environment. The electric radiance which such methods evoke is of great benefit to the earth, rivers, lakes, oceans and atmosphere, and therefore all beings. The practices which Thunder-beings have developed for humanity purify the mind-body and atmosphere. They balance our individual electric field, inner energy, and the electro-magnetic field of the earth.

In ancient times people used to do particular practices with Thunder-beings, like Indra and Shiva every day and this caused the crops to flourish, and the people to be happy, free of famine, warfare and disease. This continues to be true in some places. When my master Haidhakan Babaji practiced (Om Namah Shivaya) it would very often rain wherever he was. By doing fire ceremonies throughout India he alleviated famine and caused world peace. He was Shiva on earth, so his practice would arouse all the Thunder Deity's (Shiva) in the atmosphere, who would rain invisible and visible blessings on earth. Practice of Thunder-beings purifies the atmosphere just as lightning purifies it, so the air is good to breath, so the rains are clean and nourishing. Now more than ever we need to pray aloud to our personal Deity's; that they will arise to purify our inner and outer climate is for certain. The secret of this is in the breath. Clear-light comes through our heart, and the vehicle of the breath carries it throughout the body and then sends it into the atmosphere. Deity also arises as subtle-light before us when we call him aloud. This is what Thunder-beings want. The benefit that Dharma has on all life cannot even be hinted at. We each must taste the nectar for ourselves.

Wherever thunder-methods are used, the spring, the primordial radiant state of life is re-established. When the light of the Thunder-beings shines through ones own body of consciousness, the clear-light of wisdom abides on the earth, amongst the people and nature . Therefore I cannot stress enough the efficacy of utilizing the simplest methods transmitted by the Thunder-beings, such as virtue and repetition of Deity's mantra (name). It is our responsibility to learn of their way—that of Truth. It is our responsibility to adhere to this way. The fact is it will return us to the omniscient state we arose from . The fact is it will bring us to rest in the unbroken bliss of tranquility which is our integral heart-nature.

One of the outstanding characteristics of all traditions derived from Thunder-beings is the reliance on blessings and grace to dispel ignorance and suffering. If we want to transform our mind it must be blessed. If we're incapable of this, we supplicate Deity's and masters to bless us.

Through thunder and lightning Thunder-beings give freely of themselves, they bless the earth with the outpouring of their immeasurable qualities. Wherever it rains, there is the blessing of Thunder Lord. Wherever lightning touches down, there is the love-light of Thunder Deity. Whenever you hear thunder, there is the sound-blessing of Thunder Deity. The Thunderbird issues rain from his wings, lightning from his eyes and thunder from his beak. Thunder Lord holds and hurls lightningbolts and shoots them from his eyes. He reveals that these blessings originate from him. His activity is very often beyond our awareness. Who today can understand what is said in the thunder ? Who today can see the result of the thunder, clearing out negative energy and subduing spirits ? Who can hear the thunder before it arrives rumbling in the earth, dreaming and electrifying us ? Who feels the throb when the lightning falls ? Who knows intimacy with Thunder Lord expressing their compassionate heart in pure wisdom-display ? The Spirit is a nourishment to all beings, the rain, lightning trail, clouds, thunder, imagery and imperceptible grace-waves are some of its modes of nourishing beings. Storms are nourishment to beings, we live off their breath. (Go out after the storms and drink the clean air, the negative ions, it's healthy and good). To love is to nourish. Anything which is nourished has been loved. We nourish ourselves by loving one another. The greatest way to nourish others is to feed them the elixir of spirituality, of Deity's sound (name) and light (image). We can take this example from Thunder-beings, whose love is everywhere in the universe, as sound and light. We fail to see it because we have trained or created the habit of not seeing it. To see or live with it as we once had (prior to birth) we must train in the habit of loving one another. We have not appeared here for another reason but to love and serve one another. Every person comes here originally because he-she has an intention to help, to express Self through loving activity. Every heart embodies love, the wisdom-light of the Mystery. Each heart is the golden heart of Wisdom-Deity. Instead of there being one distant or separate heart as we might suppose, there are simply many hearts to a Wisdom Deity, and there are many Wisdom Deities to the Mystery.

The Thunder-beings awaken the earth through sound and light (thunder and lightning). Likewise, through sound and light (name and image) they extend themselves to awaken the mind. Their names and images form the basis of the Oriental traditions (Tantra). The image is both the instruction of immutable wisdom, and when used by the practitioner, the conduit through which clear-light awakens the mind. Through the image and sound the adept aligns with the Deity to attain the enlightened state, to attain the immutable state of the Deity. The image and name method is both the vehicle, like a chariot or bird-mount, as well as the ultimate goal as City of Lightning.

Through the practice of invocation (and image-visualization), the Thunder-beings rain their blessing-lights upon us. Their grace comes into our life and transforms our life. By thinking of our Lord, our Lord thinks of us. Because he is everywhere, he arises

within as awareness-light, as blessing or medicine. It sets the mind at peace by removing negativity, the causes of inner turmoil, illness of the mind and body. At the same time their unique energy lights up our awareness, so that in the glow we can see the nature of our mind and reality.

Cities of Lightning is about plugging into the unlimited electric-blessing circuit of the Thunder-beings to attain inner perfection, to become a lamp for their wisdom-light. Cities of Lightning is about ingesting the ambrosial clear-light Mind of Enlightened-Wisdom-beings to seal off the root of spiritual thirst and desire in our lives. Cities of Lightning is an exposition on the clear-light imagery and its use in the Oriental traditions.

Thunder-beings are sublime crying Deities. They look upon all sentient beings and because they see all minds at once, perceive the sufferings of all minds. Out of their boundless compassion their hearts are pricked in mad bliss and sadness, the same sadness that all suffering beings experience at once. Their tears are the rain which literally nourishes the earth, and symbolically it is the blessing-light, the gentle pouring rain of their heart, intent upon washing away the sufferings of all beings. Secretly, their tears are the melting love of every heart, the wisdom-essence which trickles in the positive endeavors of all beings. They arise unseen from the limitless space of the heart, and, upon our choosing, washes away the roots of suffering. Their tears are the light which takes the numerous forms of spiritual practices, the skillful methods which we use to attain the enlightened state, free of suffering, ebullient with the light of wisdom and bliss intoxication. Their tears are the indestructible light of wisdom that takes the form of numerous intangible Deity's. They can be seen as pure vision when we invoke and pray to them, the rain of wisdom-light falls onto ones crown in the form of billions of tiny Deity images.

The Thunder-beings' mind is cognizant space and ocean of wisdom-light. Through its luminosity it takes an intangible light-display, a mystical form or image, and arises amongst thunder and lightning. These are the Deity and signal the awakened and indestructible nature of its mind, and they are the compassionate motivation to awaken all sentient beings who fill space. Luminous Mind and compassionate motivation are one, and this is the lightning, or activity of enlightenment. To symbolize the unity of wisdom and compassion, the lightning is depicted as winged, or the

Thunder-being reveals himself as Thunder-bird. His heart is winged, the two wings represent the inseparable unity of wisdom and love. Lightning is the wisdom-light of pure intention, intention to awaken minds of sentient beings. Thunder is the wisdom-sound of pure intention to awaken minds of sentient beings. Where the intention is the same as the manifestation—there is Truth. Thunder-beings are Lords and Mothers of Truth.

The Origin of the Crystal Vision Known as Cities of Lightning

Five years ago I used the thunder-method and supplicated the Thunder-beings during a storm to heal an illness I'd been suffering from for some time, an illness which modern medicine could not treat or solve. I knew the Thunder-beings were the greatest healers in the universe, as many people have been healed by their power, either by being struck by lightning or through visitation in the spirit. The Thunder-beings healed me, completing my request, and within a series of visionary experiences or visitations they revealed that I would set down their guiding wisdom for publication as a book. Over three years or so they provided the instructional wisdom to achieve this work. They buried it in my mind as sparks of their own awareness-bliss, which is transmitted in the lightning. For this reason Cities of Lightning is like a mind-terma or "revealed treasure" given by the Thunder-beings. Usually terma refers to specific mystical texts of the Buddhist Tantra buried and revealed by Guru Rinpoche and the Buddhas in minds or geography. Cities of Lightning was revealed as a symbol-treasure, the whole of which was seen in my mind as a Pure Vision prior to writing it.

We often think we're greatly responsible for creative endeavors, whereas the truth is, the Wisdom-beings are responsible. A Shaivite poet known as Kalidas had once composed a poem of immeasurable beauty, after which he took great pride. One night Shiva appeared as Nandi the Bull and revealed to Kalidas the letters of his poem which were inscribed on Nandi's teeth all along. We should feel ecstatic that we're worthy to receive subtle wisdom and the transmission of creative ideas through our hearts. That we're extensions (incarnations) of Wisdom-beings on earth should cause us much joy and peace.

Many Thunder-beings revealed themselves and together guided the exposition of Cities of Lightning.

When they healed and put me back together they left some of their wisdom. This Thunder Mind is spontaneously present, and is either concealed or revealed, it is always there as the transformative power of the universe, the light of consciousness and life. The creative theophanies or revelations of this Mind are the Cities of Lightning. They are the methods which the enlightened Minds use to reveal themselves. They are the vehicles which we use to awaken or reveal the spontaneously Enlightened Mind within.

I am a student and practitioner of the Thunder-method which includes work with all Thunder-beings regardless of cultural distinctions. The method of contacting them is universal—the Tantrikas use the same method as the shamans, Chinese Immortals, Hebrew and Sufi mystics, the only difference is in language. There is only one Spirit and this reality is expressed in multiple ways according to cultural lineage. The symbols themselves arise as expressions of the subtlest Consciousness of the universe. The Consciousness is the reality, while the symbol is merely the husk or adornment developed for expression within a particular place and time. Iconography is the interpretation of these wisdom-symbols, the interpretation of Gods visual theophany and the interpretation of their revelation as Truth which includes both the accurate view of the universe, and the path to the enlightened state. Distinction among the traditions merely rests upon the various interpretations of the symbols transmitted by the Primordial Wisdom Mind. All symbols of spiritual reality arise from the same living-place or state of dynamic, ebullient silence. The symbolic image-bodies of Cities of Lightning are interpreted according to lineages of masters who make up the spine of their respective traditions, and according to the all-pervasive wisdom of the Thunder-beings. The images themselves have all come directly from the Thunder-beings, the interpretation of the symbol-bodies is according to the tradition within which the Thunder Deity gave the imagery and transmission.

Lineage is very important in the wisdom traditions. Wisdom is always transmitted through lineage, from the heart of master to that of the disciple. Each of the Thunder-beings herein has come forward to provide the necessary initiations and wisdom to interpret their iconographies as they are centered in the Tantra (oral transmission) of their respective traditions. My spiritual lineage is a chain of lightning in three branches. The first extends from the Buddha's such as Guru Rinpoche, Vajrapani, Chakrasamvara and the Wisdom-Dakinis. I am an initiate and student of the

Mahamudra lineage. The second branch extends from Shiva through Mahavatar Haidhakan Babaji. I am an initiate, teacher and student of Shiva's Non-dual stream of Sanatan Dharma. The third branch extends directly from the venerable Immortal Lei Kung, the Primordial Thunder-bird. I am a child of his, student and teacher of Tao. These Thunder-beings represent the immutable wisdom that originates the spiritual Truth of the three Oriental traditions—Buddhist Tantra (Vajrayana), Shaiva Tantra (Sanatan Dharma) and Taoist Tantra (Fou Jou), respectively. These paths are set down in this text to elucidate the specific methods utilizing iconography of Thunder-beings.

The Buddhas transmitted their path during this civilization in India and Tibet through Buddhas like Vajradhara, the mystical appearance of Shakyamuni Buddha, and Guru Rinpoche, the embodied Tantric Buddha. Shiva originated his system billions of years ago, and has since transmitted it in India at the beginning of this civilization and continues to renew the system through incarnations like Haidhakan Shiva. Lei Kung transmitted his path initially in ancient China of 12,000-4,000 B.C. through the shamanic tradition and continues to renew it through the tradition of Immortals known as Taoism, through masters like Lao Tzu.

Cities of Lightning is the expression of the Thunder-beings' Infinite Vision of Reality. The iconography of seven Thunder-beings will be presented. These Thunder-beings are the root-Sources of the Oriental traditions. With this in mind we can see the efficacy of presenting their iconography and their view. Each has come forward to point out which images appear as a thunder-lightning revelation, and throughout they have provided the wisdom to interpret the sacred language of their symbolic vision.

Within the Buddhist Tantric vehicle the iconography of five Thunder-beings will be presented, these are Guru Rinpoche (Sampa Lhundrupma), Lion-faced Dakini, Vajrapani-Hayagriva-Garuda, Chakrasamvara, and his Wisdom-Dakinis (Vajra-varahi). Each of them originated profound Tantric practices and is responsible for disseminating, protecting and keeping Buddha Dharma alive on earth. The methods which they protect are secret mantra vehicle, utilizing sound and light, invokation and visualization to effect the enlightened state of Buddha-hood. Within the Shaiva Tantric vehicle Lord Shiva will be presented in peaceful, fierce and wrathful guise, and as Mother Durga. Shiva is the originator and protector of Tantric wisdom, responsible for disseminating it and keeping it

alive on earth. The methods which he transmits consist of many sciences, primary among which is his Mantra vehicle utilizing image and name to effect the self-illuminated state of Shiva-hood. Among the ancient twelve wisdom-sciences of China, later called Taoism, the Science of Invocations and Talismans (Fou Jou) is originated, transmitted and protected by the Thunder Lord known as Lei Kung. His vehicle is a Tantric path by definition, utilizing name and image to effect the undecaying state of shenhood—immortality or Deity-hood.

Cities of Lightning is the efflorescence of the unique and compassionate nature of the Thunder-beings. It is their ideation or vision of reality and illumines the path which the Thunder-beings have displayed for human spiritual achievement. Cities of Lightning is an exposition on the three Oriental traditions and the Thunder-beings who originated their Truth. Cities of Lightning is the first full and accurate exposition on the mystical revelation, view and method of the Thunder-beings in the Oriental traditions. Another text of this nature does not exist in this realm. Cities of Lightning is dedicated to the awakenment of the hearts of all beings and serves as a vessel for the wisdom of the Thunder-beings.

* * *

The paths illuminated in this text are sacred beyond words. I chose to expound deeply on each one to show that they are immeasurably profound and not shallow, in hopes that this will inspire faith and devotion in the path and the Omniscient Wisdom-Sources. I pray that this elaboration serves to inspire hearts to pursue the Thunder-beings and enlightenment.

The paths herein are the precious heart-teachings of the Thunder-beings. They are based on secret oral teachings transmitted from Deity's Mind, and are therefore extremely sacred. The Wisdom-beings bestow the practices in visitation. These visitations initiate the masters return to the City of Lightning as well as function to transmit methods by which the diverse human family can gain initiation and attain enlightenment. The images of the Thunder-beings are revealed in dreams and visions, as the arising of the Cities of Lightning in the mind-stream of their earthly messengers. Through these means and through the light of daily practice we return to the City of Lightning, the inner and outer pure realm of Thunder-beings.

The images and names of Thunder-beings and their methods of accomplishment are a secret, nevertheless the Thunder-beings want their heart-essence amongst the people, so they asked me to present them. Their intention is that, having a glimpse of the Mystery—the treasure—will inspire people to pursue it at the end of the rainbow, that, having a taste of their wisdom-light will cause one to thirst for it, and to pursue it at its Source. A metaphor which expresses this is the Ganges river in India. While it is holy and clean at any place, it is holiest and clearest at its outer source in the Himalayas. (The stream of blessings that releases those who drink from suffering is the inner Ganges—whose Source is Shiva). Another example we can use to describe this is in the thunder-storms. They're a beautiful expression of the minds of Thunder-beings, they express their enlightenment, they display their qualities to all beings. They inspire and move our hearts to pursue their invisible Source, to actually become this Source, to practice to enlighten our minds.

Through practice with these Thunder-beings I am able to write about them and their traditions. I do not recommend this activity (of practicing multiple traditions) to anyone. It is the skillful means of the Deity's to keep disciples in one path. It is very difficult to realize one path let alone multiple paths. If you attempt to take many paths you run the risk of having to take more lives to realize the goal. Spiritual materialism, so rampant in this country nowadays does not lead to any realization, it just creates confusion. Practice one thing with devotion, and be open-minded and aware of many things. Do not nurture pride that any one tradition or Deity is the only tradition and Deity. This causes clouds of doubt to accumulate in people, and has caused war in the past. By adhering to one practice with devotion, the goal is achieved in one life. This causes clouds of wisdom to accumulate in people, and is a cause for harmony in the world. Devotion is what causes Deity to consume or saturate us, to turn us into intrinsic freedom. Open-mindedness or faith is what allows this to take place. Open-mindedness is what allows people to embrace one another's culture, and religious ideals. Open-mindedness is compassion. Open-mindedness is conducive to peace and harmony on earth. All Dharma has this goal.

Thunder-beings and Sublime Dharma

Dharma essentially means Truth, wisdom, clarity, realization, compassion. Because people in the present times ignore Dharma, inherent goodness or wisdom, they have created all kinds of troubles and harm for themselves and others. The earth and universe mirrors perfectly our activity. So the response is going to be natural purification, overt revolution. We're beginning to see the beginning of this at present, with disasters, land-slides, floods, incurable diseases, twisters, droughts, famines. This is now. Earthquakes and volcanoes will come. We might see warfare and then a complete purification of nature ushered in by Thunder-beings, in which no-one can escape, only those who pray and practice with their personal Wisdom-divinity will be protected. All the things which people are working for, unless it is Dharma will be useless in the future. When we practice Dharma we're building a solid foundation for our future lives, and for the future of the world.

The purification cannot be averted unless everyone puts their hearts together. We are inherently related, one family, but within this family people are ignoring one another, because they ignore themselves, because they prefer to cherish and take for themselves as opposed to cherishing others.

The only antidote for poisonous activity is Dharma. Dharma means cherishing others and bettering ourselves. Dharma will protect us individually from calamity and overt revolution, and if we all practice the religion of our heart then we will all be protected. Thunder-beings have complete control. If they see us living good lives, trying to do our best to live together in peace, then they will not allow natural disaster. You see, the negativity which people have generated must be destroyed otherwise it will destroy us all. The negative habits we have generated must be reversed, their cycle broken. Negative intentions are what causes negative results both on an individual level and a collective one. Unless we practice to reverse or purify this activity, it will devour us like a black serpent. Warfare causes natural disaster. The root of warfare and all troubles in the world is lack of compassion and wisdom. We may not immediately see the relationship, but it is there. It is natural for beings to practice wisdom and compassion, or humanitarianism. We don't need to be harming one another and committing wrong-doing—we're potential Enlightened Ones. We are supposed to live in peace and harmony here. Because we may feel helpless to nurture true compassion for others, we practice wisdom: meditation, worship, prayer, ritual. This frees us from suffering so that we can truly help others. It frees our mind from limitation, so it can express itself through insight and creative activity. Through the perfection of wisdom, one might become faultless, so that the results of all of ones actions have vast benefits to beings. This perfection of our nature is enlightenment. The experience of enlightenment is what we seek. It is characterized by tranquility, bliss, joy, equilibrium, fearlessness, intrinsic freedom. All traditions tell us this is our ultimate aim, Oriental traditions tell us this is our ultimate nature. It is not something outside us we're seeking. We might use an external approach to a Wisdom Source (God or Enlightened Being) to realize it is internal, what we are, and what is beyond us. We know the Source if we have practiced religion, prayer, recitation of Deity's name, etc., we have tasted their mind of enlightenment. And perhaps now we're ready to begin feeding others.

If we truly want to be this freedom from suffering we need to work for it. Thunder-beings will judge us based upon whether we've given or taken. We are not with their family if we're living for ourselves, so we are forced to take rebirth, seemingly separate from the Source of well-being and love. If we live to benefit others, then they will be happy with us, for living the truth, the way of the universe, so they take us into their midst, into their luminous cloud; in short, they fill us with happiness. Cherishing others is the root of happiness, and the way of life. All life must give of itself to fulfill its Dharma, to live its Way (Tao). Only beings which fail to cherish others, to give of themselves are reborn into great suffering.

If we follow this Holy way, we will eventually be reborn beyond the universe, we will return to the state from which we arose. Our aim is to reverse the present way of mundane living, which is clockwise, and to fly counter-clockwise, to reverse bad habits of body, speech and mind, to cultivate excellent wise habits of body, speech, mind. This will cause us to remember the exquisite state from which we arose, the state of unity beyond duality, of unagitated stillness, of unchanging wisdom, of unquenchable intoxication, of unexcelled perfection.

There is a beautiful story which demonstrates this point—that without self-sacrifice one cannot reach the enlightened state. Long ago there were giant monsters on the earth, and giant wise Deities. The wise Deities came to subdue the monsters, since the monsters caused much harm to beings. This is very real, the petrified bones still exist on the earth. This one monster was wreaking havoc and destruction, so Lord

Shiva opened his third-eye and a lightningbolt shot forth. Out of the smoke where it touched down arose a wrathful Lion-headed Deity. He was projected to subdue the monster. Thunder-beings often subdue malevolent beings by eating them and digesting them with the force of concentration and love. So this Bhairava (wrathful Shiva) was hungry, baring his fangs, roaring. The monster was really scared and pleaded with Shiva. Shiva, who is also mercy and love, gave in. The threat was enough to turn the monsters heart to the Dharma. But the Lion-headed Deity was still hungry, Shiva made him hungry to devour this monster. So Shiva told him to eat himself. He started with his feet and ended with his neck, so that what remained was a lion-face. Shiva was very pleased, and said that he'd never seen a better display of what life is all about. He called the Lion-face Kirtimukha, "Face of Glory," and said whoever did not bow to this Face could not reach Shiva. A Kirtimukha is hung at the entrance to Shiva temples, to which people bow before entering. Because the temple is a reflection of the body with its Shiva (heart) in the center, chakras, subtle nerves and so on, the meaning of this story is as follows: whoever does not practice self-control or self-sacrifice cannot reach the state of Shiva—eternal tranquility and bliss. This high realization is characterized by a vision of an infinite ocean of blue light (Shiva), which is called the "Face of Glory." So whoever does not live by the way of the light within, that expresses itself in self-sacrifice, self-control and love cannot embody this ocean of wisdom and its beatific qualities.

The blessings which Thunder-beings give to us make us like them, totally free of any suffering. Thunder-power awakens the mind of complete enlightenment since it arises from a completely enlightened Mind. It awakens in us the impeccable qualities inherent in the Thunder-deities that bestow it. The main difference between us and Wisdom-deities is that the qualities of their mind are fully awakened. Their mind is like the full moon, while ours is like the moon obscured by clouds (our nature is obscured by negative states). So we supplicate the Wisdom-deities to purify our mind, to become like them. Thunder-beings tell us we can achieve this heavenly state here in this body. It is known as the experience of enlightenment, the aim of Oriental tradition. It is said that all beings have this potential, this Mind, we just need to be awakened to it. It means awakening pure qualities within, of wisdom and compassionate bliss, it means awakening our inherent goodness, our sense of genuineness and perfection. Different religions have different names for this state, and unique practices for attaining it, but it is the same highest level of realization. You can call it Shiva or God, Tao or Great Ultimate, Buddha or Awakened Mind. The traditions view and depict it as one or multiple Wisdom-deities. All the Wisdom Thunder-deity's abide in this state—so they represent it.

Deity's preceded us on earth, and established tradition or Dharma wherever they happened to be. Examples include the Tradition stemming from Shiva in India, from shen (Deity's) in China, from the Buddhas of this world-system, the shamanic lineages transmitted from Thunder Lords in mountain abodes, the Kabbalah of Yahveh, and so on. These Wisdom-beings started lineages which have come down directly to us. Each lineage, its wisdom and blessings is sustained by the accomplishment of each lineage holder up to the present. In this way Deity's continue to walk the earth to sustain the Dharma and to originate new approaches and practices suitable to the changing times.

The view or wisdom of the Deities is perpetuated based on our attainment of the Deity through the practice transmitted to us. We become Sublime Beings on earth by aligning with a lineage of masters and practicing to accomplish their level. In this way, lineage is perpetuated and remains an unbreakable link to the Deity. Like a lightningbolt on the earth, the stream of blessings of the Deity is perpetuated in the hearts of the lineage holders to establish beings on the path of liberation from suffering. The light of the Wisdom-sphere is a blissful vision. This vision begins in the heart merged or saturated by the Deity, and spontaneously emanates grace-waves which transform the environment. The Deities chain of enlightened activity is self-manifesting within the masters intangible light-field. Light radiates and is attractive, so draws people of a similar resonance together. The resonance is wisdom, so it is view, therefore the minds of master and disciples are very often alike. Because the view is light, it awakens the mind. This has been demonstrated in Tantric traditions where disciples would gain enlightenment simply upon hearing the teachings. In the Kagyu or "whispered lineage" of Tibetan Tantra these teachings are referred to as "dakinis breath" by virtue of the sublime emptiness of inspiring wisdom that has come down to us from Lord Buddha. It is transmitted directly, there is no sensory medium, the ear of ones heart receives the light of wisdom directly. This is possible because Deity and master's all-pervasive heart is never separate from our own. There is no space between the two, so there is no time, so there is nothing lost. There are not two things, but One. When Lord Buddha taught Dharma, all beings of different languages and cultures understood because at his level all beings are endlessly connected. When Lord Shiva taught Tantra, the hearers were instantly enlightened. This is only possible where you have a fully enlightened Source teaching a perfect doctrine to clear-minded students. For us nowadays, because our minds are unclear, we cannot perceive the Wisdom-source to receive full enlightenment from the transmission. Even though the power of the lineage has maintained the stream of blessings unbroken and undefiled from its Source, our own obscuration prevents us from receiving the same blessing that the Source bestowed.

Fortunately there are masters who continue to attain enlightenment on earth, so are capable of maintaining the lamp of the lineage blessings so that it does not die out. We therefore have access to the Enlightened Ones and their secret teachings as they are cloaked in symbols. The teachings are the same as the enlightened Source of the teachings, so they are able to bring us to enlightenment if we practice them with faith, devotion and diligence. The languages that Wisdom Deity's spoke in became sacred, so that even repeating what the Deity has uttered enlightens our mind—this is the reason why Deity's names and liturgies are so powerful, this is the reason why certain languages (like Sanskrit, Tibetan, Chinese and Hebrew) are inherently sacred and others (like English) are not—the Lords of Enlightenment spoke them and made them enlightened, imbued them with wisdom. So a mantra like Om Namah Shivaya, which Shiva spoke, even when learned from a book like this one, can bring immense benefits and enlightenment. Used diligently it will attract Shiva's blessings and his initiation so that one can attain his state. Any of the practices given in this text will attract blessings and is a cause for full enlightenment if engaged in diligently. This is the blessing of the Thunder-beings.

Thunder-beings establish the Truth in all realms of existence—they transmit Dharma directly to clear high beings who are messengers, who are inseparable from them. It is broadcast in wisdom-sound, such as speech, thunder and subtle-resonance music. It is broadcast in wisdom-light such as imagery, lightning, letters, rays of coloration and geometries. For those who are unable to receive direct transmission they transmit it through signs, indications, and symbols—

through language, through oral teaching and scripture. These scriptures are considered very sacred, they contain the awareness-light of the Deity. When we repeat the language of the scripture the Deity arises. This is the case with the Tantric scriptures. So that when we read the liturgy describing the image to be visualized, and when we recite the invocation that we've been empowered for, the Deity actually comes there.

The conduit for the transmission of tradition on earth is a human representative of the Thunder-beings, known as a Thunder-specialist. The patriarchs, mystics and shamans of most ancient and new traditions are Thunder-masters. They are chosen to speak for Thunder-beings on earth, to sustain lineage of pure ancient tradition or originate new pure tradition. Some examples include Gorakhnath, Haidhakan Sambasadashiv, the Buddha, Guru Rinpoche, Lao Tzu, Moses and Christ.

All wisdom-tradition comes about because beings call out and request it, because they request some means of achieving well-being, and because enlightened beings respond by providing such a means. Wisdom-beings respond by incarnating on the earth, they make a choice to come here which is born out of their magnanimous love for beings. They may take the form of angelic-beings or Deities to visit and bestow blessings. They may take the form of any being, including animals.

They developed the Oriental wisdom-traditions out of their accomplishment and transmitted the various practices through earthly messengers or emanations. The traditions elucidate as the quickest methods to our goal, practices which utilize the images and names of Wisdom-beings; the methods we use are the Cities of Lightning, the mandala and the profound instruction. Inherent in these is intangible blessings.

Thunder-beings transcend limited tradition, culture, pantheon, hierarchy. The Truth or Dharma is the spiritual reality which arises as symbol. Multiple interpretations of those symbols creates religions. The Thunder-beings bear the Truth as wisdom. It is the integral view of reality, the all-pervasive view which threads all hearts and yolks us to a common Source. The living-image is the Truth because it serves this function, of yolking us to a common Source. The Truth is like a magnet, a power of luminous attraction— love. It suggests we're primordially related to Lord because it appears as a man or woman, God and Goddess. It means we're primordially related (to one another) because it unifies distinct minds. Because

there is one light-thread weaving the varied quilt of Reality, this is how we know that there is unity amongst all beings. Because we strive toward virtue and kindness, this is how we know there is unity amongst all beings.

The view of Sublime Thunder-beings is like that of an eagle, vulture or falcon; since these are the highest flying birds they have the broadest, deepest view. This is one reason Thunder Deity's imagery has attributes of eagle, this is why all Buddhas take Garuda ("Great Eagle") form. This is why in most cultures eagle and falcon are associated with Thunder-beings. But the actual view of Thunder-beings exceeds this, it is all-encompassing. It is said that the eagle flies to the height of the firmament, becoming "great eagle" which departs for space. Thunder-bird flies through space, navigates the stars, soars through infinity. Because the minds of Thunder-beings are all-pervasive, they're omniscient. Their eyes are everywhere. To look through Thunder-birds eyes is to possess infinite wisdom and compassion. These might be depicted by a moon and sun, which you encounter in iconography as the eyes of Thunder-beings or over the heads of the Deities. It means the enlightened state is wisdom and compassion and the way to achieve it is wisdom and compassion.

Thunder-beings transmit the view to people, and give us the practices for realizing this Truth. All religion which comes from Thunder-beings have two components—wisdom and compassion. The essence of all religion is humanitarianism. Primitive barbaric religions like ancient Tibetan Bon-po and modern Western occult, witchcraft, and voodoo are not from Thunder-beings because they possess neither wisdom nor compassion. They are also harmful to others. If this were not so Thunder-beings would not work to abolish them. Such religions arise for brief periods because people fail to understand the way of the universe—cause and effect, and to follow this way. Dharma is the means of adhering to this way.

From the outset we need to have some understanding of the law of cause and effect. The universe and all beings are a mirror. Our minds are mirrors. So whatever we choose, we choose to live with. If we're for ourselves and all others, then the reflection of our face of love in the universe and mind will smile back at us and nurture us. If we reflect a heap of negativity then we can only expect the same face looking back at us. Cause and effect are the same in essence. Because we have acted harmfully to others in the past we create the condition for having to enter the universe again and again, to take a body to experience the results of our actions. This is the cause of rebirth. In Oriental traditions this belief is fluent. The aim of Oriental tradition is breaking the cycle of rebirths. The result of practicing Oriental tradition is that we bring the incessant chain of rebirths to an end and destroy the root of rebirth forever. Dharma is the view and method of achieving the state free of suffering and rebirth, the state of the Thunder-beings, our natural state. All Dharma comes from the natural state which Thunder-beings embody. It arises from a clear heart spontaneously—it is already present, so one experiences its limitless inexhaustible qualities. We participate in it and seek to recollect it within our heart, for this reason the heart is called Dharmachakra—wheel of Dharma. We may not see it clearly so we rely on those who do, the Enlightened Ones, to enhance our clarity. The way to break the cycle of suffering and rebirth is to live by the wheel of Dharma. Both Buddha, Shiva and Tao can be thought of as a wheel, a wheel of pure wisdom. Before the Buddha was worshiped in images he was represented by a wheel. The wheel is the way of the universe, the way of wisdom, simplicity, harmony and love. To follow this wheel brings the greatest bliss and enlightenment. Thunder-beings are the Wisdom Wheel of Lightning, their blessings emanating into the directions of space, into the hearts of all beings.

Wisdom and compassion are the mind of all Thunder-beings, so their practices concern cultivating these together. The traditions emphasize the cultivation of meditative awareness with devotion. Good meditation awakens wisdom and devotion awakens love. Because we individually suffer, we wish to be free of suffering. What we practice to alleviate this suffering is wisdom or awareness. Because all beings suffer we wish them to be free of suffering, we refer to this as the cultivation of compassion. Thunder-beings provide the methods for achieving ourselves through the cultivation of wisdom and compassion together. There are many approaches to cultivating these together. In Tibetan Buddhism, when you engage in meditation, study, prayer, the cultivation of wisdom, you do so with the intention to benefit all beings, you actually dedicate the merit of what you're doing to help others. In Sanatan Dharma, one combines meditation on mantra (and image) with self-less service. In wisdom traditions, all that we do is offered to help others. If our motivation is immeasurable, the result of our practice will be immeasurable—the benefit it has will reach all beings and will enlighten us.

We develop wisdom through meditation because it is the actual ability to know how to help beings. Wisdom is the solution to all affliction. Wisdom is love, they're not different. Wisdom is always directed toward helping others. It is the perfect insight into reality and mind—it simply knows how to help. Compassionate motivation alone might lack this sight, so it might harm others. We have all witnessed or been a cause of discomfort to others because our good intentions lacked sight. Wanting for others is not enough, we have to want what they want and what is truly good for them. To know what is truly good for others, what brings true well-being, what heals, means we must be wise, all-knowing. Compassion means suffering with, this implies that our mind is awake and open to suffer with others, to see what they're going through in order to help them. Compassionate intention is the wish for others' well-being, and it is implementation of this wish through our activity. Our activity will be imperfect, it will turn to dust and cause a measure of harm until it is imbued with actual wisdom-light, until a Wisdom-being is the doer and Lord of our heart. This light comes through spiritual practice or the cultivation of wisdom and love, it comes through our connection to Sublime Perfected Beings, through such acts as prayer, meditation, repetition of sacred wisdom-sounds, etc. When there is wisdom in our motivations, they will be vast and all-accomplishing, our wish to help beings will accomplish its aim. Wisdom-light alone liberates beings from suffering. It is its own activity. For example a realized master or sage, one who has spent his entire life sacrificing his limitations so that Omniscient Mind could dawn, emanates light continuously from his spiritualized body of splendor—so that his climate, the atmosphere in which he lives is spontaneously and mysteriously free of suffering and disease, the crops are good, there is no crime, people are happy and full of love. The Thunder-beings activity works through such a person around the clock, and yet seemingly nothing is done.

The practice of wisdom tradition for us not only clears our mind—so that insight or omniscient vision is clear, but it also awakens love in our hearts. When we invoke Wisdom-deities blessings, we invoke a clear-light which is both wisdom and love. We have invoked a Deity which is wisdom and pure love—so the result will be the gathering of wisdom and love. This gathering can be likened to the accumulation of rainbow-clouds amassing in the sky and radiating their five-light splendor to awaken the minds of countless beings.

In Tibetan Buddhism and Sanatan Dharma and most schools of Taoism it is taught that enlightenment is only possible through venerating and invoking Wisdom-beings. It is possible to attain a deep samadhi, absorption or rest through meditation without Deity's, but the highest realization cannot be attained otherwise. Perhaps the sleep of Brahma and Vishnu represent this unenlightened rest, the state of Sravaka and Pratyekabuddhas also designate it. These beings have, according to scriptures, not attained the highest state, so the Enlightened Ones radiate light and sound to them, telling them that there is a greater achievement, awakening them to the need for further cultivation. The light and sound manifestation of Thunder-deity reminds us of this need to attain enlightenment in order to liberate countless suffering beings. Since Thunder-beings embody this state, only they can introduce us to it. At present we have not had this experience of enlightenment (because for eons we've been obscuring it with negative states, with self-cherishing), so we need the Wisdom-beings to show us this experience, to awaken us to it. We therefore supplicate them for blessings, for vision, for wisdom. What we may receive is a thunder-storm, what we definitely receive is an unconditional grace.

In Tantric traditions we rely on beings who are totally free of suffering to attain the state free of suffering. We rely on beings who are free of suffering to free us from suffering. They embody our natural state, so we supplicate them to attain this state. Because Thunder-beings are completely free of suffering, because they are inherently perfect and omniscient, they are perfect Sources of Refuge. As a perfect Source of refuge, we can have faith in their transmission, in their view, as an ideal means of attaining liberation. We should supplicate our Lord for blessings. Achieving the same state of absorption depends upon our personal motivation to attain it (devotion) and their impartial blessings (compassion).

The Thunder-beings of this text were the greatest yogis on earth because their minds remained like lightningbolts, totally without barriers of fear, doubt, totally natural, open and clear. So they were and are responsible for originating yogic traditions, and for maintaining the integrity or pureness of these traditions. Lord Shiva established Yoga on earth and continues to renew these paths through his appearance as perfected yogis. Yoga means union, it is the recognition of the primordially unified state. It is ones union with all minds, because at the level of the Absolute there is no duality, no I and you. Another supreme master of yogic tradition presented herein is Lord Buddha who is responsible for bringing precious Dharma to us. He originated and established several classes of yoga for the varying achievements of diverse minds.

Lao Tzu was also a supreme Yogi, who collected and disseminated the 12 major Taoist sciences. Yoga, no matter the practice, is for awakening wisdom or clearing the mind. We know that wisdom frees us from suffering and brings us bliss, since we have tasted it from having prayed. The idea is to recognize that its not something outside us, coming from some sky-god, but is entirely within our heart, and we must be awakened to see it clearly. The mind must be free of fear and confusion which distort our vision of mind. So yoga is about purifying negativity, fear and emotional distraction which are the causes of suffering.

The Thunder-beings want their children to be enlightened warriors for truth and righteousness. Just because their traditions teach yogic means, this does not imply passive arm-chair philosophizing. It's easy to talk about the view and spirituality, but the highest yogis talk little and practice much. Even during talk and activity there is continuous practice. Thunder-beings want people to stand up for what is good, to fight against what causes harm to beings. These traditions are the way of the solitary warriors, yogis and powerful mystics. Thunder-beings give war-power to those who demonstrate that they will use it to help others. Shaman Crazy Horse was such an example. The power he received from Thunder-beings made him impervious to bullets and gave him the power to conquer enemies. This was thunder-power. The same power for us conquers our recalcitrant self-cherishing. Peace is the outcome of this war. Because people have strayed so far from Dharma, fierce means, thunder and lightning are necessary to bring about harmony. So the Deity-means elucidated in this text are especially appropriate methods of accomplishment for people in these times.

The more degenerate minds become, the more force is needed to cause recognition of the original self-less state. This force is embodied in Thunder-beings across the world. Most stories you read about them concern their activity of subduing the most fiercely incorrigible minds—demons, of turning enemies of the Dharma to dust. For example in Vajra-yana, it is taught that the origin of wrathful Deity phenomenon started when there was a demon known as Rudra wreaking havoc in the universe (this is not the same as Lord Rudra-Shiva, Melter of Diseases). The

Primordial Buddha, Ever-Perfect (Samantabhadra), to subdue this being, needed to manifest immense power and great wrath because wrathful beings are closed, their minds are unclear they cannot feel the peaceful Wisdom, they won't respond to it in a positive way. So Samantabhadra became Chakrasamvara and overwhelmed the demon with power, thus subduing him. When anyone meets the all pervasive Wisdom-Mind of all enlightened beings in the form of Thunder Deity you are overwhelmed, he is a Thunder-storm that envelopes universes, and is totally concentrated power. In many instances demonic beings, such as spirits and sorcerers are subdued by actually being struck by lightning. It forcefully changes their mind, brings them back into balance, makes them realize their sense of smallness, it enlightens them to see the force of their bad habits. Their ego-trip was based on being able to constantly conquer weaker beings, so their personal power, their power of darkness of cold energies rose to a great extent. The Wisdom-beings never let such demons and sorcerers get too strong, they allow them to exist for a time, then at a certain point, because they care deeply for our welfare, for the welfare of the kind-hearted, they subdue the demonic. Often in the cries of sentient beings, directed toward Wisdom-deities, they respond, and the response is the manifestation of a fierce Thunder-deity. This is a fluent theme in the Vajrayana scriptures.

Because the Thunder-beings are supreme warriors, they all bear a warriors weapons and the look of a warrior, their marrow is warrior and their power is war-power. Their path is about cultivating or becoming a warrior. They want their children to be true enlightened warriors (Bodhisattvas), Heroes and Heroines (Dakas and Dakinis), especially in the present time. This means that we fight the inner battle against self-cherishing, fear, desire, negativity first— these are the enemies of our own well-being and the causes of suffering for those around us. We fight this battle through continual self-sacrifice, through continual austerity. Since we are imperfect and limited we supplicate and make offerings to All-pervasive Unstoppable Wisdom-Deity. The best offering is self-sacrifice, our sense or belief in our own limitation. This belief or doubt is a real energy that obstructs our limitless vision and our ability to accomplish our hearts intent. So we do all that we can to gain victory over this sense of limitedness. We generate doubt and fear by choice, so now we do the opposite, we generate love and kindness—this is the sense of our unlimited

ness. By generating or choosing to help beings in our heart, our choice makes a light, this light lifts us out of suffering, this light is our warriors shield, this love-light is the weapon which defeats all inner enemies. In Vajrayana this light of intention is called bodhicitta, "enlightened mind," without it, tradition says, we cannot attain enlightenment. Becoming wise means choosing to love. These are again the warriors weapons. All the weapons of the Thunder-beings that you will encounter in the imagery denote enlightened qualities of wisdom and love inseparable.

The way to wage the battle of injustice in the world, to dispel the darkness of ignorance of all beings is by instructing people in wisdom tradition, in view and practice, and dedicating our virtuous activity to benefit all beings. We can teach people whatever we know about wisdom and compassion—since these are the essence of all traditions, we might come to agreement with whoever we're speaking to. Once we're skilled in administering the antidote through speech, then our activity might be deepened, to include actual thunder rites, working with Thunder-beings, directing their bolt to heal, exorcisize, pacify, redeem, subdue, purify, cause weather changes and so on. There are eight or more special powers (siddhis) which can be developed and applied to helping others. It is really only incarnations of Thunder-beings who can perform these with proficiency. But Thunder-beings provide power in times of war to assist the good people of the earth to keep peace. (I think now is an appropriate time to supplicate and pray to Thunder-beings to bring about peace and understanding in the hearts of all people). Tunkashila, the Ancient Lightning God has been supplicated in ancient times for war-power. Indra was supplicated for war-power in ancient times. And there is a strong tradition of warriors in the Shaiva tradition of siddhas. When the peoples liberty was being jeopardized by unjust government, by imperialists, they fought. The trident and weapons which yogis bare became not only reminders of spiritual accomplishment but were implements of external victory. Shiva used them to fight external battle—they symbolized his victory against demonic forces in the universe, so for the yogi they became perfect symbols of victory over all obstacles. Generally the Deity's weapons symbolize perfection of wisdom and skillful ways of helping beings. The Thunder-beings used them when they walked the earth to destroy harmful obstructors, causes of disease, evil spirits and actual monsters. When Guru Rinpoche brought Buddhism to Tibet he needed to subdue local demons, gods and sorcerers who were against the Dharma, so his Deity implements, his vajra (thunder-bolt), trident, and skull-cup became weapons.

The enlightened and wise activity of Thunder-beings is the expression of the subtle law which preserves the natural balanced working of the universe. They achieve their function by controlling the elements of fire and water, positive and negative, to control the weather. They function through the elements to assist in growth, the birth of the new and removal of the old. They express the nature of the transformation of energy in the universe. They are the activity of creation and destruction concentrated into one moment and place as a lightning. They are the subtle essence of nature, at the root of the five elements. Electrically they connect their Wisdom-mind to the elements to restore form to its youthful state. The bolt is the image of this connection. By electrifying things they bring them back to their beginning, when they were new born—embryonic. When life is newly born, it is radiant, fresh, vital, flexible, responsive, harmonious, awake, because it just came from the Unborn and these are the attributes of the Unborn state. So the Thunder-beings bring nature back to its dawn again and again through their "powers of reversal." After every storm there is a sense of clarity and freshness, of new birth within the earth, of returning to the dawn of time. The great light of the Thunder Creator has just touched the earth, in such a way it is renewed and sustained—recreated. Lord Shiva takes the form of a blue-baby to represent this state—to represent the Undifferentiated, to represent our non-difference, our true nature.

Thunder-beings achieve their function in the mind sphere by returning us to wholeness and balance. They attract us into their sphere by guiding us through the light of their nature to act creatively through compassion and to refine and balance our inner energy, our mind. They assist us magically, invisibly, to live natural lives, to follow the subtle law or Dharma. They are our intuition!! They assist our spiritual evolution which is a process of reversal, of reversing the negative effects of ignorant thought and action (karma). Their light electrifies our karmically generated inner winds (subtle energy) which support the pure spark of the mind. They clear out obstructions between the Wisdom-Source and its extensions (people) wishing to express themselves through pure positive qualities of mind, speech and action.

The power of reversal is the natural vitality or will-power of the Thunder-beings. To make storms they gather and radiate energy. Their gathering is denoted by the Thunder-spirit gathering clouds around an energy body as a cloak. They gather charges of hot and cold which collect around a nuclear center (heart). The powers clash above the clouds, one from the sun the other from vaporized water, producing lightning. The lightning in turn triggers the rain. The storm is governed and controlled by Thunder Lord or Mother at its center and his Thunder-bird which zigzags out front. The power which they radiate can be absorbed from the atmosphere to produce positive effects in nature and the mind. The subtle essence of the Thunder-beings can be gathered and absorbed at any time. It awakens our Deity nature, it awakens the Thunder Deity's in our body. The power exists within our psycho-physical organism by virtue of the fact that the thread of Universal Consciousness is mirrored perfectly in the human body and heart. Such is why in Tantra it is taught that the human body contains the universe, and why the cycles of the universe are mirrored perfectly in the body. Such is why it is possible to align ourselves with the Deities wisdom-spheres and gather their energy to refine our own into its subtlest spiritual expression.

All Thunder-beings function through enlightened compassion. Because people die occasionally from lightning or twisters, hurricanes or floods, that does not in any way imply that retribution is being practiced or that Thunder-beings are malevolent destroyers. They're unquestionably, profoundly good. They are impeccable examples of universal law and virtue. Their power is the greatest protector, and it is a great destroyer. If we connect with it (the universe) through creative, protective activity then we will be protected and our negativity will be destroyed. If we connect with it through destructive activity then we will be destroyed, because our energy becomes darkened or clouded. When things become disconnected from their Wisdom-source they die, the life-force exhausts itself. To be struck by lightning isn't an accident or mistake of some clumnsey being. The universe responds to everything we do. We are drops in this vast ocean of the universe, so everything is stored in the cellular-memory or mind-stream which magnetically produces an effect upon reality. Our relationship with the universe happens at this deep level. It is based on the electro-magnetic quality of energy. We're fully responsible for our thought and activity. Reality is a mirror. Inner darkness will eventually attract its counterpart, it will attract calamity. Sorcerers and truly malevolent beings are destroyed by the sheer compassionate intention of the Thunder-beings to protect the decent people and animals of the earth from injustice, illness and death. Nevertheless, those sorcerers attracted their own demise.

There is a true story concerning Mahavatar Shiva Babaji which illustrates the perfect working of the universal law. He would often take long fasts after which his devotees would offer him milk. One jealous and avaricious man gave him lime to drink instead, which appears like milk. Certainly Babaji was aware of this, but to affect wisdom, accepted the offering and drank it down all at once. Immediately the ignorant man received the negative effects of his action. He just gave the lime to himself so he fell to the ground writhing in pain and begging Babaji to put a stop to it. Eventually Babaji did after reminding the man of the inescapable law of the universe.

So the lightning can work in such a way as to cause negative karma to be worked out like a knot. But one should not imply that the lightning always works in this way, it might as easily be a burning vessel of divine blessings. Thunder-beings might give lightning-initiation through it. When a person is initiated by lightning they're imbued with pure wisdom-power which remains in the psycho-physical circuit. He or she lights up like a lamp and leads people out of darkness. Another way they might use lightning-tools is to heal an illness which modern medicine could not. A person with an illness who learns that the Thunders are the greatest healers, supplicates them, magnetizing the pure positive energy of the mind, wishing to return to harmony, with the pure positive energy of the Thunder-mind wishing to see people happy. So there is a healing charge from the Spirit. Anything is possible ! In every event it is a blessing; it might be as a gentle kiss from God, and if it causes some suffering then it releases one from suffering.

Occasionally mischievous spirits, like nagas (invisible serpents of the animal realm, who are under the government of Thunder-beings) can cause thunderstorm phenomenon at various times, and can wreak havoc by creating a hail storm or an atmospheric imbalance. Some lamas feel that El Nino is a result of the nagas, who are angry at people for polluting their home—the oceans and water sources. If we live according to the Thunder-beings road there would not be such problems. We need to be aware that everything on earth is related, that what we do to earth we do to

ourself. We should be compassionate to all beings and their home. Many winged-ones visible and invisible live in the sky, so we should not pollute their home in order to make ours a greater comfort. In the end our own homes will be destroyed. Many animals visible and invisible live in the waters and earth, so we should not pollute their home in order to make ours a greater comfort. The end of such activity is calamity.

Within every storm Thunder-beings can be invoked. Thunder-beings are behind all thunder and lightning, even if it appears otherwise. Again, the nagas and other spirits are under their control—this is depicted in imagery where Thunder-beings, like Shiva and Thunder-birds control snakes to encircle wrist, ankle and neck. If there is an overly destructive storm, Thunder Lord can be invoked to arise in the center of it to correct the imbalance or avert the storm and subdue the spirit that caused it. But this is a rare case, usually black spirits never get this far, they're subdued long before. The infinity of Thunder Lord implies that he has eyes that are everywhere and unstoppable power which overwhelms the incorrigible minds. When you hear a thunder-clap that splits the air for miles in every direction, you know this strength, this ability to achieve anything. Thunder-beings wisdom, if invoked in the storm can be rapidly assembled to fly out to the four directions bearing the power to awaken the minds of all beings, the medicine to heal all minds to bring them back to the harmonious state. We call them Sublime because they are the inherent cause of beauty in the universe. If you disbelieve in their all pervasive essence as the cause of beauty and magnificence underlying all phenomenon from thoughts and internal musings to trees, rocks, rivers, clouds, stars, space, plants, animals, rain, then at least you might see the beauty in the freshness that comes after a storm, the healing that many people have received from Thunder-beings, the real beauty that comes through prayer that millions upon millions of people have experienced and which leads people to truly embrace the essence of religion.

One of the functions of wisdom is to have the solutions to any problems and the means to dissolve those problems. Wisdom is necessary to sustain spiritual beings and to restore those who fall out of balance. I cannot help but see that we have fallen vastly out of balance, that wisdom is required now more than ever, so the Thunder-beings are pouring forth their hearts into all domains of human activity and are secretly behind everyone's heart, prompting us to choose goodness. A loss of balance constitutes loss of control over the mind, which causes suffering. To set polarities in balance is to regain control over the mind, yielding the spontaneously abiding natural wisdom.

A balanced mind expresses itself through moderation, therefore moderation becomes the path to attain inner balance. This was a key teaching derived from Lord Buddha's experience. The balance of polarities is the primordially unified state of non-duality or Truth embodied by Wisdom-beings. They appear as contraries because they unify what to us seems broken and opposite, like positive and negative, hot and cold, dark-light and white-light, creation and destruction, tranquil and fierce, emptiness and form, spacious and solid, open and closed, absence and presence, sacred and profane, gentle and fierce. . . . It expresses their non-dual nature, their state of non-fixation which perceives one substance and energy weaving reality. This nature colors the activity of enlightened minds in the embodiment of the Thunder people from the sky of our inner vision to the context of the human society.

There's a good story which depicts the light-hearted presence of the Non-dual awareness. (And it echoes the ancient function of the Thunder Lords on earth). In Mathurai in South India long ago, Lord Shiva created a flood. The district gathered together to build dikes. Everyone was rallied to participate. But an elderly woman could not, so prayed to Shiva for some help. Soon after she gets a knock on her door. It was Shiva. He ate alot of rice cakes and went out to join the work. He spent the whole time clowning around, dancing and singing. He would just fill his bucket and dump it out, singing and dancing. After a short while he returned to the woman and said he was hungry, so she made more rice cakes. He ate up all she had, then went back out to carry on his antics. Finally he got caught by the government official who was organizing the project. This man had a problem with Shiva's behavior so the man smacked him. Because Shiva is everyone's nature, everyone felt the slap. At the very same moment the dike flew up into the sky, completed. Shiva is the display of the universe and the true nature of this display. The Dancing Shiva Nataraj depicts this dance of all things, which tells us that nature and its Source are one, which tells us that reality is electrified, brought to life by the Spirit and force behind it. For example our body is brought to life by a subtle Spirit which neither changes nor dies. When the connection is broken, a corpse remains, and the subtle spirit and its life-force leaves for another place.

We might not recognize this sacred essence in our life because we don't spend our lives paying attention to it, cultivating it. We have to relax into it, meditate to experience this true nature. We have to view it properly and learn how to become aware of it. We think if sacred essence does exist it must be a certain fixed way, which is an incomplete view taught as religious dogma. The Wisdom-being very often will take the opposite view to smash our conventional interpretations, of spiritual reality, human nature, whatever. For example, Oriental Thunder-beings appear in cremation grounds, wearing garlands of skulls, ashes and bone ornaments, holding skull cup full of contrary substances. There are no more holy beings in the cosmos. Even God is one of them. They are iconoclasts, they break stale, concrete views of reality as being one way or another. If the mind which perceives things is impure, unclear, ignorant, then reality appears this way and one develops attraction (for what is good) and aversion (for what appears bad). This produces suffering, because everything we're attracted to turns to dust, and everything we're revolted by cannot be avoided. So we must cut this ignorance off at its root with the flaying knife of skillful means and wisdom. The Wisdom-holder is called an iconoclast or crazy-wise clown by mundane standards and is placed on the edge of society. Later I'll talk extensively about Thunder-specialists and Crazy-wisdom.

By thinking that the Wisdom-being is only peaceful, gentle and joyously sweet we close down to nature and wisdom within our nature, and so fail to respect God and nature. We might find it hard to forgive ourselves and others and impossible to see God throughout nature. We might close down to what we are and forget that the source of our creative bliss and love is all around us. It is there whether we connect with it or not. It shines on us, through us and as us; in our hearts we will know it as blissful-love. It is never remote from us as long as we're not remote from it. By thinking that the Spirit is remote or transcendent we feel it must be a chore to gain a response from it. But since that Consciousness is actually displaying us, the illusion of separateness can fold at the moment the heart turns in sincerity to look into its Source. We can only see the complete picture by realizing we're a part of it, by training ourself to live this view of ourself and reality. We can only experience divine energy through ourself, through a calm and open mind. The training entails viewing ourself from the start as divine, Buddha or Shiva, our highest divine ideal. And then living that ideal. Such a view is the natural state of the mind when it relaxes into itself. It releases us from self-cherishing and opens the heart to the bliss which impels us to reach out to one another in compassion.

Letting go of duality, notions of good-bad, pure-impure is necessary to being open to the subtle grace of Wisdom-mind. It is so subtle it's called emptiness, and can only be proven through meditation. The erroneous view of self and reality is the maker of opposition or the inner turbulence which obscures our vision of subtle reality and our comprehension of its ultimate non-dual nature. Ideas are just empty shells, symbolic displays for communication. If you think the idea is reality you are being deceived. For example the Deities sometimes clown around (do things backwards) or appear in violent guise to symbolize they're actively destroying negativity, compassion in action. If you just see their image or antics without experiencing their nature, you might be inclined to reject them. The Deity transmits his nature when he reveals his image, so in the transmission by human lineage (Abisheka initiation), the master must be able to arise as the Deity and transmit the Deity's wisdom-quality to the disciple(s), and the disciple for his part must be open and present-minded. The state of openness and awareness is the door to the non-dual state of the Deities. Openness is required to return to our true abode because Openness is that abode. Presence or clear awareness is required to return to our abode because Presence is that abode. This Wisdom-deity-sphere of limitless openness and spontaneous presence is the City of Lightning. The mandala of the Deity of the pure enjoyment realm is the mind-emanation of the Deity projected within its unlimited space. Whatever you see there is the Deity, likewise whatever you see here is the Deity. This is so because Deity is within our awareness, and without. This is so because the mind creates reality. If the mind has diffused into Deity's ocean, it easily perceives the reality-display of Deity's wisdom or non-dual energy, because this Wisdom-deity is the reality. The achieved ones know that the Deity is actually revealing himself in the atmosphere and on the screen of the mind (in lightning). The achieved ones know that our nature is that of a luminous Deity, not different in essence than Wisdom Deity. We are working to recognize our luminosity, our lightning-like indestructible diamond-Mind, our jeweled treasure chest of brilliant qualities. The vajra diamond-lightning is the revealed heart of existence, which is concealed as light in our potential energy and revealed upon awakening with great sound and light, with great truth, insight, love. So our awakening can be symbolized by thunder and lightning. Practically what this means is our obscurations or emotional afflictions, our ignorance and bewilderment are none other than wisdom-light. We simply fail to recognize it by having trained our minds to ignore it. Therefore our mind-training and Deity practice is designed to liberate obscured energy so that it manifests as it should, as luminous clarity and bliss, insight and compassion.

The Thunder-beings generate thunder-storms and control the weather, they sustain the existence of all beings on earth and they keep the earth fresh and strong. They travel in the thunder-clouds, the upper sky, and space, they descend and ascend in the lightning which they create as a trail. They are above us and they are within us as our spiritual inheritance which they brought out of their own. They help those who are in need and they give us assistance to return to our divine abode or state, the place from which we arise as creative, blissful rays of the Spirit. They are the living Dharma, Unlimited Source of Blessing. In order to give us the assistance we need to fulfill ourselves, to be harmonious, joyous and tranquil, they give us methods for contacting them, taking refuge, for invoking their blessing-lights and applying that grace towards our transmutation. In Oriental traditions we call these methods Tantra. In virtually all traditions there is a division between the exoteric and the esoteric, the outer and the inner. The inner teachings are the secret, mystical teachings. All teachings arise from the Wisdom-source according to varying dispositions of people. The Tantric method is not suitable for all classes of beings, but only those of excellent virtue and clear awareness. Therefore Wisdom-deities gave a full spectrum of teachings to suite every disposition. In the Sanatan Dharma tradition, Lord Shiva gave the exoteric tradition in the body of Vedas. This stream became known as Hinduism. He gave the profound secret teachings in the Tantras. Similarly, Lord Buddha gave exoteric teachings in what are known as Sutras. This stream became known as Sutrayana, Hinayana or Theravada Buddhism. He gave the secret teachings in Tantras. This stream is known as Vajrayana Buddhism. You have the same division in the Taoist tradition, in which the Deities's supreme secret vehicle is known as Tantra.

Tantra is a system of mind-training which predominantly is characterized by methods of purifying body, speech and mind together. It embraces the exoteric tradition by including virtuous and moderate activity as a path of natural living. It is an esoteric tradition in that it is a path to enlightenment which engages body, speech and mind to attain full enlightenment. Tantra is the cultivation of the heart of primordial wakefulness.

Tantra as Thunder-Method

Thunder-beings are the Lords and Mothers of Tantra. The paths to enlightenment, to recognize in one life our omniscient nature of inherent wakefulness are the Oriental traditions known as Tantra. (Although Tantra has existed in other cultures, such as amongst the Native Americans, it is primarily a phenomenon of Oriental traditions). The oral history of Tantra from the perspective of Tantric traditions like Sanatan Dharma, Vajrayana and Taoism is incredibly vast, it encompasses eons, billions of years. But it has a certain limited time frame within which it appears during the present civilization. Shaiva Tantra was the first to appear. It arose 432 million years ago (according to Tantra), died out and was renewed by Shiva in the time between 30,000 B.C. and 5,000 B.C. It was written in the first scriptures around 3,000 B.C. It flourished in pure form in the present yuga, but degenerate views and motivation has caused some Tantric practice to degenerate. Even though there is great interest by Westerners, the Hindu Tantra portrayed in many books is not pure, it is the residual teachings of self-serving people and cannot even be traced through lineage to Shiva. What is being taught in "Tantra camps" and books cannot ensure enlightenment because the warmth of Shiva's breath cannot be felt in it. Shaiva Tantra does continue to exist in pure form—in particular the lineage of Naths has kept it from being adulterated, as well as the Trikasara of Kashmir, the Siddha Yoga lineage and lineage of Mahavatar Babaji Nagaraj.

Buddhist Tantra first appeared on earth (in this eon) during the life of Buddha, around the time of Christ. Although, like Shaiva Tantra, according to oral Tantric history, it has existed for eons. Taoist Tantra in essence has been on earth for multiple eons as well. During this civilization it arose around 12,000 B.C. Something distinct known as "Taoist Tantra" arose around the same time that Buddhist Tantra arose.

While Taoist Tantra has nearly died out completely, the Buddhist Tantra flourishes in all parts of the world. It is my express desire and I feel that of the Thunder-beings that the essence of their Tantra be preserved, so that people can continue to contact the Wisdom-Source to attain the Wisdom-Source. Therefore I dedicate Cities of Lightning toward the preservation of pure Oriental Wisdom-tradition to return all minds to luminous tranquil wisdom Space as rapidly as lightning.

The practices which the Thunder-beings develop out of sound and light arise from the fully enlightened mind of beings who wish to see people living good, natural lives. The Truth or Dharma which they espouse, and these practices, are together called the Tantra or "extension" of the Wisdom-beings. Tantra refers to the extension of blessings and grace by the Wisdom-beings, embodying the Truth of the universe. Tantra is the key to our own inherent wisdom-nature (goodness or excellence) which is not different in essence than the wisdom-nature of the Deities. Tantra provides the keys to bliss, to the state of the naturally enlightened mind. Tantra presents the methods whereby the Deity's wisdom-mind and subtle creative energy of bliss are mixed with our own mind and energy, producing enlightenment. The Tantra of the Thunder-beings provides the keys to enter their Cities of Lightning, their state of wisdom, bliss, freedom, power, tranquility and love. This is not the (Left-hand) Tantra known commonly in the West as a system solely of sexual practices advocating unnatural use of the body, advocating destructive behavior. It is the way of the middle, of natural, moderate activity. It is the way which views our psycho-physical person as transformable into a blissful angelic being, as transmutable into a subtle blissful substance, radiant-wisdom or spirit. It is the way which views our mind as space, and returns us to Infinity. It is the way by which we spiritualize ourselves to become a Wisdom-being of a similar caliber as those we refer to as Thunder-beings, Awareness-deities, Buddhas. The fact is, through our positive aspiration to benefit the earth and guide all beings to liberation from sorrow, and through spiritual cultivation, we can give birth to ourselves as Wisdom-beings. The fact is we are extensions of them on the earth, therefore it is our aim and duty to work towards this goal, to awaken our hearts and give birth to ourselves into the incomprehensible, the omniscient state of "profundity and immensity."

Tantra refers to the result of the path, the Absolute, the mind of beginningless enlightenment, and it refers to the practices which lead to spontaneous realization of this nature. It is therefore called in Buddhist Tantra, "training in the result," and in Shaiva Tantra—"identification." Because we have identified with limitedness, with a finite material body, we have made this condition our home. If we identify with unlimitedness, Infinity, unlimited bliss, freedom, space, then we will awaken this true state within. We identify with Infinite Consciousness as Wisdom-deities in order to achieve this. The image is an integral part in this process of transformation. It is the symbol of our Mind. It is given for use as a method of awakening the mind through the joint practice of visualization of the image and repetition of the name (and often includes mudra or gestures as well).

Even Christ said in secret, "the Kingdom of God is within and without . . . it is here now, only people do not see it." The multi-universe, all of reality composed of innumerable realms is one sphere of Infinite Space, out of it all minds arise, and all internal phenomena such as thoughts, and all external phenomena, such as planets, stones, things composed of five elements. This sphere of Space is the Primordial Thunder-beings, the deepest nature of our mind and the universe. This is also Tantra—the continuum of Mind that remains undefiled throughout countless lives, through all mental states. It is the root of the universe. Every Omniscient Wisdom-being represents this Infinite space, the Absolute nature of all things, and every Wisdom-being represents the energy of enlightenment—the means to attain this state. Through them, their blessings, their paths, we might attain the same state, we might become Omniscient. We might realize our unity, our inter-connectedness to all things through this deep all-pervasive nature. We are extensions of this all-pervasive Primordial Wisdom-being, like waves on the surface of an ocean. Because we do not pay attention within, our nature becomes unclear to us. We think we are our thoughts, our feelings, so we say "I am an angry person, a sad person, a fearful person with many thoughts and a chemical imbalance." So we experience what we think we are. We become what we think. If we think of our limitedness, we create limited states. But this is not the truth, we have to start training in the truth. This means seeking to recognize who we really are. Religion used to be about this, cultivating inner peace though truth. The truth of our nature is We're perfect inner peace, equilibrium, bliss, unlimited. So if we identify with an Unlimited inner Consciousness, then we become that. It is who we are. We might identify with Thunderbeings because they are who we are, our true nature, our potential enlightened Mind.

The idea behind Tantra is to stop imagining our world and our experience in a negative light, colored by poor habits of thinking, but instead to shift our view and begin imagining Reality to be as it is. So instead of telling ourselves that we're afraid in this situation, angry in that one, instead of getting depressed when things don't go as planned, instead of desiring more pleasure from experience, we simply must learn to rest into the natural inherent beauty and delight of Reality and our mind.

The Deities are an excellent means of bringing this about. We imagine ourselves as a perfect Deity who lives in a boundless Pure Realm, whose experience is quite naturally one of pure delight and peace. We invoke this experience through recitation of Deity's mantra or name which causes the natural experience of the Deity, which is our natural mind and the nature of Reality, to become totally present. We use our full capacity of visualization—our imagination—to recognize the wisdom-Deity within and all around. We visualize imagery, light, color, sound, touch, taste and emotion or feeling quality. We think that our surroundings are Deity's abode (like the house of God), that those beings inhabiting it are Deity's children. We think that our body is also the palace of the divine. We think that our mind is the Lord, and its thoughts, musings and feelings are Lord's creations or play. We think that all things are the play of our Lord. Eventually this kind of training causes the true nature of mind and Reality to dawn.

We must train in enlightenment, that it is now, at our fingertips. We simply do not recognize it. So we train our minds, we practice methods of clarifying or purifying our minds, of becoming more aware, so we can see who we are within, and what it is that really exists without. We use the Wisdom-beings to achieve this. They are three things: they are the nature of all minds and the universe. They are our perfect stillness within, and our pure bliss. They are our wise love, compassion with sight or insight. Just as we are manifesting this body, this vehicle of activity, so also, the Thunder-beings are manifesting a vehicle for their enlightened activity, they appear out of space through changing energy, through the elements, as a body, as clouds, lightning, rain, rainbows, stars, and as wise people. These manifestations are the distillation of all-pervasive Wisdom-Deity's love. We use these manifestations as means to recognize our Omniscient state. We use their loving energy to purify and clarify our minds. We call this energy wisdom-fire. So when we thank them for giving us fire, we mean both outer fire and inner fire-light. This inner wisdom-fire is the Light that all religions talk about. It is the first tangible appearance of the Wisdom-deity, who is beyond us. Because he-she feels like utter space, like nothing, they manifest a Light. This light manifests the subtle experience of enlightenment. It flashes and lights up our mind when we pray to invoke it, and it shows us our true Deity-nature, it shows us our present enlightenment when it enters our mind. The imagery, the Cities of Lightning, is the form of this clear-light, this wisdom-fire that purifies our mind, that brings us to enlightenment. Nature and our guru is also this clear-light, they manifest the stream of wise blessings of Omniscient Thunder Deity, to set us on the path, to instruct us, to guide us to enlightenment.

The iconography is transmitted from the highest level of realization. The expression of this level of attainment is known as Tantra. The Imagery and symbols arise in the clear mind in vision and dreams as the manifestation of primordial wisdom. This state or mind of wisdom and its luminous manifestation as Imagery, as Deities, is Tantra. So Tantra is this pure mind and its clear-light manifestation. When this wisdom is promulgated in scriptures we call them Tantra. Most cultures have examples of this manifestation of Primordial wisdom. The most essential form is the circle, the most elaborate is a circle containing Deities, retinue, gates and so on. Because the primordial state of all beings is the same interdependent continuum, this accounts for the vast similarities in imagery and religious symbolism. Because of cultural differences, this accounts for the minute differences between religions.

Tantra is all-pervasive view, and the supreme methods of accomplishment, the self-perfected state and the practices to attain this state. Tantra is like thunder. Thunder happens when two sparks connect, one rising up from the earth and one descending from the heavens. The spark of a yogi's mind rises up and receives a revelation by the influx of super-luminal transmission coming down. The yogi is consumed by the Deity, by the lamp of non-dual energy. The Deity has arisen in form and transmits his or her guiding light as view and method. The Deity is mantramurti, mantra-image; the description of his image is an invocation of the image. (Like in the Kabbalah when Yahveh wanted the universe to appear, he spoke it into existence. Those words were then transmitted as the Torah scripture).

The Thunder-beings are Lords of the Tantra. Tantra is Lord's pure light vision and speech. Tantra was originated by the Thunder-beings; their lightning is the spark of the Tantra. Tantra is developed to suit all natures. Tantra is the compassionate expression of the wisdom-mind, or the mind in primordial union with the Absolute. It is the mind relaxed into its state of naturalness, the non-fixated, undistorted state of its beginningless enlightenment. Tantra means "continuum," "warp and woof" and "extension," the unobstructed, all-pervasive, Omniscient Mind. Tantra is the expression of the fully enlightened Mind wishing to benefit all beings.

The Tantra has poured forth from a peaceful, joyous and compassionate heart; they teach us how to cultivate our mind, to rise to the same state as the Deity. Tantra is the overflowing of the creative energy of the Universal Mind which tickles the heart with bliss. Tantra is the enlightened heart-continuum, symbolized by the diamond, the clear, indestructible jewel, which held up to the Sun of Dharma, filters and focuses light of primordial luminosity to a point which slices ignorant views and awakens wisdom. Enlightened thoughts arise like sparks, like tiny diamonds, the indestructible children of our heart, the diamond womb of all Buddhas. In the space womb, the mind reveals itself in its emanations, its diamond-thoughts. It hatches with thunder, and lightnings arise. Such thoughts are rapid in their achievement, they never miss the target or fail to liberate it. This describes the emanation of thoughts and of emanation-bodies of clear-light manifestation. The indestructible space focuses or concentrates into lightnings, into revelation of Enlightened Minds. Deity's mystical appearance is a means of communication. Wisdom Thunder-birds utterance is lightning-bolts and they instantly become manifest as Wisdom-children. Thunder Deities easily appear out of lightningbolts which descend to earth, Vajra master Guru Rinpoche appeared this way to spread Tantric Buddhism to Tibet, to subdue babaric peoples and incorrigible spirits. In the mind sphere Thunder Lord uses the lightning to subdue our mind, we visualize lightning to enhance clarity and subdue negativity, inner demons. Through lightning we make an elegant transition to Dharma activity, we move from self-centered behavior based on ignorance, to self-less behavior based on a clear view of our nature.

The practice Tantra is actually the mind-energy of the Deity Tantra. The image, mantra, inner and outer mudra are the method of achievement. (Inner mudra means the inner gesture of calm and openness, inner connection to Deity; the outer mudra is a gesture which connects us to outer Deity). Thunder-beings express the methods that are efficacious to achieve our potential for full enlightenment or union with spiritual reality. Thunder-beings protect these vehicles and disseminate them. They are Lords and guardians of Tantra. The vehicles are constructed out of their light of wisdom and represent their skillful means of assisting us to the goal. Wisdom is essentially the ability to become aware of the causes of suffering and in doing so become liberated from them. Once liberated from the cause, we are instantly liberated from the effect. Wisdom is clear awareness, it is the solution to the multiplicity of world problems because it is the solution to the mind's erroneous view of itself and reality. Many Thunder-beings achieved themselves in previous eons; they incarnated, endured life, pleasure and pain, refined themselves and gave birth to themselves above the clouds and before space. So in some sense they constructed practices out of their accomplishment. They set the foundation for our achievement. They are not remotely different than we are, not even the primordial or unborn ones, but always are transmitting creative ideas to benefit us. They are responsible for all true creative endeavors, their power is the fertility that breaths revelation into the earth and inspires or pricks the heart, causing it to overflow in creative bliss. They are responsible for all positive behavior on earth, for the small humble good deed and the miraculous feat. It is the spontaneous flash which comes into the mind; every thought is a revelation of the Light, every sprout of the earth, every newborn chickadee, every movement in the dance of a butterfly. No one is exempt from this revelation, the only requisite is that the mind become clear and present, free of fear and doubt. Freedom from fear and doubt means our natural wisdom can shine and love can fill the heart like a wine-skin of undiminishing nectar. The way to liberate doubt and fear is, 1. Not to choose them, to choose positive thoughts instead, and 2. To train in awareness. By choice we let fear and doubt in. By choice we let peace and joy in. Since this is the case, that one energy must replace the other, it follows that the more positive energy we bring in through our good intentions, the less limiting energy will govern the mind and the less suffering we will have. So we seek always and everywhere to nurture good intention, to cultivate the mind of bodhicitta, and we seek to discipline ourselves and to absorb creative energy to replace negative energy.

The Eastern traditions do not advocate anything but positive behavior and the generation of creative subtle energy, since Wisdom-beings are responsible for transmitting these vehicles. If there are any subnormal practices which cause the mind to become darkened, it is based on misunderstanding and misapplication by people, and is the reason for closely guarded secrets, for strong protectors to guard these practices. It has more to do with how the practice is applied, than the practice itself. For example the chakra pujas (of which there are five) include the 5-m's (panchamakara): sex and the ingesting of substances like liquor, wine, fish, meat, things religiously forbidden—which is engaged in to break our sense of duality, and rigidness about things. Sexual yoga is another major part of Oriental Tantra that is greatly misunderstood. Religious fanatics take it as sinful even when it is sacred, and fools take it as license to indulge in all of ones grossest desires. The practices of vajroli mudra and karma mudra (sexual yogas) are designed to awaken the mind (as opposed to indulging in base pleasures which cloud the mind). All three Tantric traditions utilize sexual yoga as a means of identifying ourselves and our consort with Divinity, and as means of awakening this Divinity within.

The practices gather natural luminosity, what is in the directions, the stars and the pure omnipresent Wisdom-deities, to awaken our mind. The power can be used creatively or destructively, to heal or to kill. It is like uranium, it attracts lightning to a place and the rain which follows—such is its natural function. Thunder-beings use it to benefit the earth. Fools take such power and twist it for their own intentions and its bound to blow up in their faces.

The Truth is the wisdom that governs the harmonious order of beings on earth, as a subtle guidance behind and within our life it secretly causes all positive transformation. When our mind is clear it follows this way quite naturally, it acts from this center spontaneously. Just as one doesn't see where clouds come from, one doesn't quite see where good activity comes from, one becomes free of the egotistical belief that one is causing good to occur. We are each part of something much more expansive which originates our thought and witnesses the mind. This is really the description of Tantra as well, as the deepest level of the mind, or the Infinity focusing itself as a ray or bundle of rays (shaktis) into one point—our awareness. The wisdom-sphere depicts it as a diamond, which comes to a sharp point, which contains light, which is totally clear. The method Tantra arises from clear spacious wisdom, from the omniscient state. So Tantra is totally organic, totally natural in essence, like the Tree of Life. This Truth of spiritual reality has been on earth for millions of years along with humans. It has taken multiple forms suitable to the time and circumstances of its arising, like the way vegetation and animals arise as a development of the geography and climate.

Mind-training is the path of Tantra. It presents a way to restore our nature of pristine qualities, to awaken the heart of Infinity whose center is every-where and circumference no-where, to build some-thing ever-lasting out of psycho-physical existence, to refine the alloy of existence into the beautiful gold of spiritual essence, the condition for sustaining life in-definitely in subtle inner space, ones future self.

The methods of training are written in scriptures known as Tantras, composed of teachings as well as the direct practices for merging with the Deity who originates the Tantra, for entering the mandala of the Tantra. All Tantra of Shaiva, Buddhist and Taoist origin utilizes three components to purify ones com-plete being of body, speech and mind. These are mudra, mantra and samadhi. Mudra is a ritual gesture which is made which causes the body to be purified. In some Tantra it is used to manipulate internal energy. It can also be used to supplicate Deity's blessing, and to make symbolic offerings to the Deity's. In any case it causes body to be purified. Mantra refers to the recita-tion of wisdom-sound to purify the speech and invoke the Deity to give blessings. There are millions of mantras with scores of uses, but in this text on Deity yoga the mantras I will discuss are called name-mantras, they are simply the sound of a Deity's wis-dom—they invoke his clear-light mind to descend so that we can mix it with our own.

Samadhi refers to the clear focus of ones mind during practice. It can be focus on an image, a letter or seed-syllable, or focus on an intention, like healing someone, changing the weather, stopping a war, etc. This causes the purification of the mind, making the mind a clear and open vessel to receive the blessings invoked during practice. In the Tantra mudra, mantra and samadhi are applied toward the attainment of ourselves and all beings. They are a component of most Tantric practices of the three traditions. Once a yogi has attained mind-control, then he is able to engage in enlightened activity. So he applies the Tantra to skillfully benefitting beings. He might practice exorcisms and weather making, healing and pacifying spirits. He has become Deity on the earth so reflects the activity of the Wisdom-deity's. They have given

transmissions where you see them in the clouds or in their palacial realm engaged in a particular practice, with mudras, mantras and samadhi. A simple example of this is the origin of the weather making dance of most traditions. A person sees the Thunder-deity per-forming a dance (and song) in the clouds which causes rain, then you arise as the Deity through the Tantra, do the dance and song and, if ones virtue is excellent, ones motivation is clear and strong, then it rains.

Those who attain enlightenment through Tantra are called mahasiddhas or great perfected ones. They are those who attain both immortality and full en-lightenment. Those who work toward this attainment are called siddhas and yoginis, practitioners who work to attain enlightenment through abandonment (of non-virtue) and realization (of the perfected state). The wisdom traditions are founded by immortal mas-ters. The Oriental traditions are founded by immortal and enlightened masters. Shiva's great incarnations and innumerable disciples attained both immortality and realization, they transmitted Sanatan Dharma. When they were on the earth they demonstrated mi-raculous powers to guide people onto the path and when they left, if they left, there would be weather changes or other signs of achievement. Innumerable Buddhist yogis also attained immortality and enlight-enment, displayed miraculous power and departed in rainbows, sparks, etc. Sometimes, even though mas-ters have the capacity to depart this way, they will leave the body to give the devotees relics. The body may be burned and what remains are drops of solidi-fied wisdom (rig sal) as happened frequently with Buddhist masters. The body may be buried, and then disappears later, as happened frequently with Taoist and Hindu masters.

There is a reason for writing about such things. It demonstrates the pure qualities of the guru, so that we can easily generate devotion and confidence in our master and the path he embodies. Without these no attainment is possible. It also demonstrates the extent of spiritual cultivation, the goal. Our master demon-strates the two siddhis to guide us to his state of enlightenment. Through mundane siddhis he per-forms miracles to guide beings who need to see such tangible demonstrations. They demonstrate a certain degree of mind control. Through clarity and bliss the master attracts beings and establishes them on the path. Through perfect insight the master demonstrates super-mundane siddhi to guide beings perfectly to enlightenment. Through his bliss he focuses the Bud-dhas blessings to transform our minds.

In Tantra we worship Wisdom-deities by identifying ourselves with them. They realize their enlightened nature and are all-pervasive, our mind is their mind, its "extension" into time and space through material form. The practice of Tantra puts our enlightenment right now, not at some future time. We are enlightened now, our internal experience of thoughts and emotional states are merely adornments of this natural state. Our natural state remains unchanged behind them all. Our nature is timeless, undecaying and indestructible. This form-body is only the way or means that unchanging Wisdom-mind, Buddha, Shiva, God or Tao, has taken for helping beings. So we don't really need to figure it all out, to create elaborate technologies for looking at what we are and what extends beyond us, we just need to practice to realize this view. We need to live this view of Wisdom-deity on earth. To attain realization of this view means to realize ones activity as perfect, unflawed. Because we fail to realize this, our activity is imperfect, we make mistakes, we harm ourself and others, we create suffering for this precious deity in future, we create the conditions for future bewilderment and rebirth. To realize our natural state as Wisdom-deity, implies to be free of bewilderment, clear, controlled. To control the mind means to be able to control rebirth, since it is mind which travels from here to there and back, from one life to the next. So the essence of Tantra is practicing mind-control and acting as Wisdom-deity on earth—compassionately.

The Tantric traditions are yogic paths, that is they use yoga practice as a means of attaining internal harmony, the natural open unified state. Yoga practice contains two components, self-control and awareness. Through yoga the yogi practices awareness, and simultaneously learns to control the mind. The mind creates its condition on earth, through lack of self-control and awareness it creates a hell of suffering for itself. Through presence of mind and self-control, the mind can totally liberate itself from suffering.

Because these yogic traditions use subtle energy or wisdom-light to enlighten the mind and transform its state into wisdom and bliss, they are regarded as internal alchemy. Alchemy seeks to transform a mind burdened by gross or heavy emotional states into a mind of subtle wisdom and luminous compassionate bliss, and a body burdened by gross elements into a body of subtle blissful wisdom and rainbow splendor. Essentially this is achieved through purifying, dissolving, awakening the gross energy of mind-body.

The yogic practices utilize Thunder-beings' wisdom-clear-light to achieve this. The light is invoked upon reciting Deity's name or mantra, and fully absorbed upon visualizing Deity's light-image. The immediacy of Tantra comes about through lightning-like flashes of realization where awareness is awakened to its natural state adorned with its pure qualities.

Tantric view and practice brings all seemingly mundane activity onto the path. In truth, nature and life is imbued with Deity wisdom. Even in oral tradition of Judaism the masters taught this when they said "there is no-where that God is not" (this ought to be the foundation of Western tradition). Our body and the body of the universe are Wisdom-Deity's, or God. They are the root-essence of beauty in our life. Through them we perceive beauty and goodness all around and within us.

The essence of joy that we receive from mundane acts comes from the beatitude of the Deities inside our body meeting Deities outside our body. It comes from within. In Shaiva Tantra, Shiva's beatitude in our body, heart and spine is responsible for the enjoyment we derive from the experience of mundane activities, from eating to sex. Because we think happiness comes from without, we are searching continuously outside ourselves for it. This causes us to forget others, to create attachment to things, people, our bodies. This attachment or desire brings us back here continuously, it causes rebirth and is the root of suffering. Therefore we seek to break this attachment, and to cherish others. This ends the cycle of rebirth and suffering.

We should derive delight from nature and seek to help others overcome bewilderment and self-cherishing. Nature in its nature is inherently good, and a cause of delight. There is nothing we do that does not participate in and include this goodness, wisdom, beauty, and auspiciousness. There is no situation which is not inherently auspicious. Our limited impure perception causes us to see something other than beauty, our impure mind causes us to experience something other than delight and bliss. Our impure mind prevents us from participating directly in this field or circle of wisdom and bliss—nature, and from deriving delight from it. Even though we do not see this circle fully, we do not see its wholeness and emptiness, its bliss and tranquility, nevertheless, there is no act which does not arise from it. There is no person, thing, thought or idea which does not arise magically from this circle or realm of wisdom. This makes everything in essence good, truthful. We just need to realize this by purifying our mind and perception. If we purify our mind our experience of reality as it is will be one of calm and bliss. If we purify our perception we will actually see the wisdom of nature (as Wisdom-Deity). We seek to increase our inherent beatitude by invoking its Source in the universe, by ingesting it's light.

The Tantra contains means of bringing all activity onto the path. So whatever we're doing will bring benefit to all beings. The easiest way to do this in the beginning is to offer up all that we do to our personal divinity in order to liberate beings from suffering. We offer up virtue to establish virtue, and we offer wrong-doings to end wrong-doing, we offer positive states of enjoyment to enhance bliss of all beings, and negative states to burn up the negativity in all beings. On a more elaborate level we can arise in the form of Deity to do whatever we're doing, from bathing to putting on clothes, from sleeping to working, from eating to excreting, from meditating to having sex. This will cause wisdom and bliss to arise in our mind and activity.

In Tantra we use outwardly mundane acts to awaken super-mundane wisdom-mind within. All we do must have a positive motivation to benefit all beings. This results in a positive outcome. Then we apply the means of achieving our aim to benefit all beings—the Deity yoga. We are an Awareness-deity, an emanation. This emanation arose to benefit beings, to achieve the enlightened activity of the Deity in the universe. By meditating and acting as the Deity (through compassion) we can achieve realization of our Deity-nature, our limitless Mind.

Tantra is a tradition of embrace as opposed to one of denial. This doesn't mean "anything goes" as some have mistakenly critiqued. It means that instead of shrinking away from reality, from nature, we embrace it to see that it is inherently good. The most disgusting things are wisdom in essence. But our revulsion has caused the illusion of impurity to cloud our minds.

The craziest thoughts are wisdom in essence. We must embrace ourselves in order to transform ourselves. This doesn't mean we should act to harm others. We renounce the activity that causes suffering, and then we embrace the suffering, and use it to grow and help others who suffer. We own our negative states, we embrace them instead of allowing them to sting others. By doing so they're liberated. By embracing ourselves we're liberated.

The Tantra exists in many traditions and realms. Among realms it is fluent in the highest pure realms, such as those of Shiva and Chakrasamvara, among traditions it has existed with certain Native American traditions, but is most fluent in the Orient. It seems that the link between the Native American traditions of the Hopi and Navajo with the Tibetans is the Tantra. The Tantra has also linked the culture of ancient India with Egypt, Judea, South and Meso American cultures. These traditions have many commonalities in terms of rites and iconography. These similarities in traditions can be likened to the fact that the Wisdom-deities who originate the traditions transcend culture and time. They do not appear as cultural beings, but have been represented by some artists in this way. For example the Buddhas do not appear Indian, Chinese or Tibetan, but some artists have portrayed them this way. Long ago in Tibet a painter of sacred imagery would engage in the Deity's practice for 10 years in order to see a vision of the Deity to paint the Deity most accurately. This was very effective, because the power of Deity's blessing in such works is capable of liberating upon seeing. In addition, the closer the icon is to its actual mystical form the more intense the devotion will arise in the seer. When devotion arises in the heart, the Deity arises spontaneously and we're enlightened. Thus one can see the efficacy such imagery has toward our enlightenment. The imagery is a vehicle of Deity's wisdom, a crystalization of His blessings.

Elaborate Reflections on the Thunder-beings of Universal Pantheon

The Thunder-beings are the greatest protectors in the universe. Some people however, looking upon the atrocities and slaughter of the devout Buddhists in Tibet, the religious Taoists in China (by Chinese government), the persecution of Native Americans by Euro-trash, and so on, have had reason to doubt the protective capacity of the Lords of Enlightenment. But we are told that the Wisdom-deities allowed these atrocities to take place in order that the wisdom-traditions would spread, so that, for example Tibetan Buddhism would spread to the West to help turn people's hearts. The wisdom-traditions grew up in great secrecy and the Western world, dominated by ego-centric beliefs, was in dire need of their wisdom. So the Thunder-beings warned the wisdom-holders, the sages and masters, who embody the tradition. In Tibet the protectors filled the sky with black-clouds and Thunder-storms—they were warning the people.

The masters heard them and received dreams—the masters being the voice of Thunder-beings, spread the message as far as they could. The masters protected the precious teachings with their life. In China the sages took the Taoist teachings deep into secluded mountains abodes; in Tibet the masters took the teachings into exile in the Himalayas and India. All of us who practice these traditions are indepted to these people for bringing the treasure, the antidote, to the West.

To think of the Thunder-beings with a sincere heart, to carry their name with us is to receive some of their protective grace and to be transformed in its fire. Because they're unconditionally loving, their light or secret essence pervades the universe, like the pure scent of sandalwood. Out of their love, the Thunder-beings manifest in the form of imagery, sacred music and mantra.

Primordial Thunder Lord spontaneously generates an intention to assist sentient beings, so to fulfill it, he-she branches out, enters the universe and the atmosphere and the ocean of suffering beings. He puts his wisdom, his ability to liberate beings amidst those beings. The idea of Shiva or God as transcendent, sleeping, a static corpse, is totally misleading (this image is meant to suggest perfect immovable tranquility). His superluminal grace or activity is everywhere. Because it is generally imperceptible, it makes itself known, graspable, it takes the form of wise teachers, to tell us how to contact the imperceptible grace which destroys suffering. It takes the form of mantras and images. It takes the form of benevolent thoughts or intentions, to destroy suffering in the heart and world.

Thunder-beings control the power of life, thus they live undiminishing lives in subtle inner space and have the ability to create and restore life, or take it away. They give birth to themselves as a revelation which emanates into subtle existence at the edge of the sky and space. From this abode they control the elements, causing storms and healing hearts; they also protect the earth and its inhabitants. They are situated in the five directions of space, around the earth, around a person, within the atmosphere and within our minds. Thunder Lord emanates as lightningbolts into the four directions of space, and each emanation gives birth out of love to innumerable emanations. Each directional emanation symbolizes a dimension of awareness, an expression and function of wisdom in the mind and thunder-power on the earth. The Thunder Mind is all-pervasive space and is revealed through its five-di-

mensional emanation. Each directional emanation expresses a unique flavor of Deity's wisdom and activity. The Thunder-heart becomes thunder-bolts going into the four directions. The East (spring, dawn) is the dimension of awakening, the dawning of the clear-light of the mind. The power can appear white or blue (rain). The South (summer, noon) is the dimension of rapid, unobstructed growth; the power can appear yellow or red. The West (fall, sunset) is the dimension of fruition and movement into dissolution and can appear red or blue. The North (winter, night) is the dimension of absorption, return to the Unborn, which is like space so is black, or dark green.

Thunder-beings are born with the thunder and lightning of mysterious divinity, they are born from it. They are born from an egg cracking, cracking lightning-thunder. Yet they are Unborn, Unoriginated, Uncreated; they arise spontaneously to bestow blessings. Before Thunder Lord could be perceived by the senses, he appeared in subtle space, the unseen subtle aspect of nature, a vast realm transcendent to time and space. Though Thunder-deity appears visible in nature only occasionally, he exists continuously in the subtle realm where he has his first revelation. These mystical forms will exist continuously until there is no more need for them. Because beings are fixated on form, we cannot perceive the formless—so we concentrate on the light-form in order to receive blessings and enhance our awareness so that we can perceive the formless Absolute.

The subtle, unseen existence is the immutable life and mystical appearance of the Thunder-beings called Cities of Lightning. These clear-light-bodies arise into visionary form as thunder-clouds, thunder, lightning, rain and a real image-body of the Mysterious Source. This arising constitutes the unique and beautiful picture of their Minds, which, pervading space, contract to manifest in a particular place and time for the benefit of all beings. They arise out of the formless state through creative-light. The revelation into the sphere of our mind or atmosphere is called the mandala, Wheel or City of Lightning. This Wheel has four spokes and a hub, four lightningbolts going out to the directions, and a center or heart. The heart is the Heart of the universe, depicted in mystical symbols as the Thunder-deity's palace or mountain abode, as Mt. Meru, and the Tree of Life. This mandala exists in outer space and sky, in the geography and in the inner space of our body-mind. Wherever we invoke Thunder-deity, his mandala or City arises. We seek to realize this City within our heart—it is the liberated state. When we do so we will be able to enter the outer City of Lightning, we will become a Thunder-being.

Thunder-beings live with the thunder and lightning in vast inner space, in miraculous Cities of unparalleled majestic beauty, they are surrounded by their various mind-emanated retinue in this mandala situation. The nucleus is a drop of wisdom, a distillation of an all-pervasive Spirit. The Spirit moves these drops South or North, East or West signaling seasonal transition. They live somewhere else, and they live right where we are. Thunder-beings live where we can see them, and they live in the deep nature of our mind-wheel. Until we are able to see their subtle existence, we believe that we can become one with them, that we can realize our inherent oneness with them. So we practice to purify our perception, to see what is naturally there. They are not confined to functioning in the atmosphere, but in truth control the universe and emanate into the atmosphere to control the weather.

The power of thunder is always with them, cloaked in different forms, shapes and colors, or no particular form but its own—lightning. The Thunder Mind arises out of the urge to awaken beings, to liberate them from suffering. Therefore every rain-spell and thunder-storm is a blessing upon the universe. The Thunder Mind arises through pure creative energy, it branches into sound and light and expressions of enlightened speech and activity. It spontaneously takes the image of a lightning-bolt, signifying revelation. It spontaneously takes the form of a god or goddess, Wisdom-being or Dakini, to signify that a living wise Spirit is responsible for nourishing the earth by coming and going in the clouds, bursting forth in the rains, sporting in the lightnings, speaking in the thunders, stretching out in rainbows and Tantra. With the appearance of a man or woman the formless Deity instructs us by transmitting wisdom. The image is a key, a method by which we might absorb the ocean of wisdom behind it, to fulfill our aim. Accompanied by devotion we might absorb the positive qualities inherent in the imagery-light of wisdom, so that we might quickly attain the formless state of the Wisdom-deity.

The Thunder-beings reveal themselves through our minds in profound mystical experiences and the display of natural phenomena. The Cities of Lightning are the specific revelations projected to enlighten or awaken nature and the mind, to pacify suffering, to destroy the roots of suffering. Whether you see them in the atmosphere or the mind, stellar-chakra or mind-chakra, they are woven from this singular non-dual substance—wisdom-light.

Thunder-beings can appear before us, they can descend out of the storm on the lightning, appearing visibly to us in a tangible form or in a gossamer-light-form. Because most of us are not worthy of such an experience, our mind is impure, we are only capable of feeling them and seeing their gross atmospheric play. If we're somewhat more open then we can receive dreams of the Deities. These are real in the sense that wisdom is visiting us, the substance of what we experience appears only to inner sense. Within the context of these dreams the Deity projects something like a film or play in our mind. He mixes his mind with our own, and we receive wisdom, we're enlightened. The images we see are the actual Deity. Many people have seen them, sometimes groups of people witness them in a collective vision.

Our world is a realm of Wisdom-display, Thunder-beings are everywhere, sacred is in the profane, every mind is potentially Enlightened-mind and every act and thing is inherently beautiful and magnificent. Life is magical. We practice profound magic of awareness-spell and mystical diagram, Tantra of Mantra, in order to realize that there is much more here than meets the eye. There are mandalas in our pours, there are Pure Wisdom-spheres right before our eyes. Because this is the case, by invoking the all-pervasive Deity, they appear immediately—they are beyond space and time, but are not outside of our immediate perception. Deity's sphere is not outside our lives, it extends well beyond them, but includes or envelopes them like space. If we think the magical sacred enlightened state happens somewhere else we're vastly mistaken and just postpone our pure exaltation . If we think it will happen after death it will. If we have faith in the enlightened state here and now, then we cause it to dawn here and now.

Thunder-beings are the Self of the universe or the self-less heart of the universe. In our mind they arise through natural wisdom or intuition. They arise in a self-less heart, such is the heart of the Cities of Lightning. We have to begin with some clarity and train in the fact that Deity's Wisdom-sphere is the palace of our body, its contents and all external appearances. Even if we begin with little clarity, the work of the Wisdom-being is miraculous—they have developed vehicles for every single disposition, for every single mind. In Tantra this includes animals and all other beings; the Deities take the form of the specific being to guide them to the enlightened state. For gods, the Deity will take the form of a god. For example Shiva takes the form of Brahma, Vishnu, Rudra, Indra to teach gods. For garudas, the Deity will take the form of a Wisdom-Garuda to teach the garudas. For nagas, the Deity will take the form of a Naga-King to teach nagas. For dolphins and whales the Deity will take the form of a dolphin or whale. For people, the Deity will take the form of a wise person. For example, Lord Chenrezig has taken the form of Buddha Shakyamuni, Guru Rinpoche, the Karmapa and the Dalai Lama.

The Thunder-beings are the power of wisdom, whose mind is perfect clarity and unimpeded accomplishment. They can advance us as fast as lightning if we're willing to offer ourselves, our self-cherishing, to serve the Dharma. They are the creative power of illumination which produces awakening wherever it shines and strikes. They appear mystically as a lightning and a limitless wheel of radiance. The lightning being the revelation of the limitless light, the thunder the revelation of its unimpeded power through sound. The Wheel is the shape of wisdom. Their essential nature is blissful, so often they appear as dancing Gods and Goddesses. They dance as the lightning and the lightning dances within them. They can move anywhere within limitless openness very quickly, like lightning. Lightning in the shape of a bird is their vehicle. So they appear most often as flying Deities and Thunder-birds. Their moving is a function of the wisdom of emptiness in which there is no movement, only the revelation of the omnipresent. They are Eternal and therefore immutable, unclouded and therefore impersonal, unimpeded and therefore autonomous. They are unstained emptiness and therefore indestructible. They are spontaneously self-renewing and therefore supportless. Their heart is the essence of love, therefore they are protective, compassionate and giving. They are like wise grandparents to us, they give us freedom and space to learn by response from reality, to have fun and make mistakes. They shelter us from ill fortune with their wings. Their natural virtues are selflessness and kindness which they awaken in all beings as the golden elixir of the heart of heaven and earth. Even though they make thunder and lightning with the greatest power in the universe they are perfectly still, abiding in the deep calm nature of their mind. Because we have arisen from the very same continuum of Consciousness, our essential nature is not different than theirs. Many Thunder-beings evolved through the universe by taking bodies and

achieving themselves spiritually. They represent our greatest potential as fully enlightened spiritual beings. We have the potential to give birth to ourselves as Thunder-beings or Wisdom-beings.

We go through the practice of establishing a positive connection to the Wisdom-being and attuning our mind to his or her Mind. We establish a positive connection with the Wisdom-beings, as opposed to a negative one, because our attainment will be quicker. We establish a positive connection with the Thunder Lords, opposed to a negative one, so that we do not invite calamity or get struck by the bolt of immutable wrath. The Thunder-being literally reflects his wisdom clear-light in the heart of the practitioner who invites him to abide there. He reveals that he already exists there. Because our heart is infinite, all Deities exist there. Our awareness is the abode of Wisdom-deity.

When we visualize the image, because image is the Deity, our mind takes the Deity's form and absorbs the Deity's qualities through light. Simultaneously we repeat the name of our Deity. When we repeat the mantra, because mantra is the Deity, our mind takes the form of the Deity and absorbs the Deity's qualities through sound. He manifests within and before us. Our Deity yearns to free us from suffering, and so gives freely or unconditionally of his mind of bliss. We yearn to melt into our Deity, so with this we're magnetically drawn together. When we think of Deity, he thinks of us . . . and so on until there's only one thinker, one doer. From the beginning we identify with a new expansive consciousness as our own. We identify with the Truth, with Infinite Consciousness as our mind, with mind as it is, instead of mind as we've been mistakenly taught to view it—as limited. This is the view of Tantra, that, from the beginning we identify our mind with the Wisdom-mind of the Deity, and practice to awaken Thunder-mind within us. Thunder-beings are our natural luminous state of intrinsic freedom. Thunder-mind is our indestructible or immovable nature. This is the secret symbol of the lightning.

To make contact with their light, which is always shining, to work with their power of transmutation means our energy must be of the same frequency as theirs. When our energy is pure our hearts are clear, their light can shine freely. Therefore a preliminary for all methods is virtuous behavior, which is naturally purifying based on the mirror-like nature of universal manifestation. In addition there are simple practices which can be embraced in order to speed up the process of purification, so that we can come to shine with their subtle light. These processes are preliminaries or initiation practices which prepare the mind through gradual refinement for the practices which rapidly transmute the mind.

Thunder-beings are the creative energy of the path, the means or electricity by which the spiritual body can be given birth to. In Shaiva and Buddhist Tantra this energy-aspect or grace of Father Deity is the Mother consort. She is invoked as Mother-shakti or Wisdom-Dakini. The Deity or Dakini's wisdom-energy is the power to dissolve all negative states, to purify the mind-stream so that it can arise as stainless clarity colored with pure joy.

The Deity imagery is the clear-light-vision of the unseen, a tangible way of connecting with intangible energy. We clear our minds so first we can experience light, then emptiness. We experience subtle wisdom-light by mixing awareness-light with it. By mixing emptiness-Mind with mind, progressively we refine our awareness into subtler states of emptiness—until we're absorbed in the Undifferentiated Absolute, pure indestructible emptiness.

Their thunder-power comes from the Blue Star behind the sun and universe, and is total Spirit, beautiful Wisdom. Subtly they control the universe through electro-magnetic fields. Since mind is subtle energy, through it Thunder-beings control minds. They control mind through the individual person, spirit or animals' self-control. They arise through drops of light at our crown, forehead and heart. We choose and allow this power to take control because it provides instant medicine to the poison of mundane existence, of mental afflictions. When we feel this energy it is inspiration. Before we could feel it, it is wisdom of emptiness.

Their unseen grace is responsible for returning us to the Omniscient state or heavenly abode. In the mind sphere it awakens wisdom and in the atmosphere it awakens the thunder to awaken the earth. In the mind sphere it awakens primordial wisdom, the integral state of wakeful intrinsic freedom. In the earth it arouses the primordially free state of health, joy and wholeness.

By praying to Thunder-beings our aim is not to be struck by lightning, and the result is not to be struck by lightning. The result is grace of peace and inspiration. If we take the Winged-one to completion, the height of Thunder Mountain (the crown), to the "Nest of the Highest," highest enlightenment, rebirth, the material

universe is transcended, one becomes a Celestial, a part of our Lords body of Luminous Space. As a rain of tranquil bliss, a natural peaceful mind is pacified and awakened, as a rain of lightningbolts a heavily burdened mind is pacified, freed of suffering and its root. (Whenever you come across stories where thunder and lightning are used to subdue spirits or where Deity uses wrath or where someone is struck by lightning, dies and returns, the theme is very often that a fiercely recalcitrant being or person, one with a heap of sins is turned into a protector, a spicy and powerful person who has witnessed quite intimately the power of the Deity and converts beings to Dharma based on this encounter. In Vajrayana many Dharma protectors are such beings—they were once unruly demons who caused disease and death, so the Thunder-beings came along and subdued them.)

One of the most intimate connections you can have with the Deity is to be enveloped in the wisdom-light that comes out of their grace-empowerment. Everyone can become intimate with Wisdom-deities for as long as we have the keys to their mind. These are the mantra of the Deity, and the image. Name and image are the nectar of the Wisdom-beings. Through them we ingest the samadhi-essence of their minds. When we're full then we feed everyone to make them happy. We give them the means of creating wine, of sampling Deity's intoxicating bliss for themselves. We introduce them to the taste of enlightenment, then provide the means to sustain bliss-body, a body created and sustained by Deity's celestial vitality. This idea of ingesting bliss is a strong Tantric theme which appears in the Shaiva and Buddhist Tantras, the mystery cults of Thunder-beings like Osiris and Isis and Dionysius-Bacchus, and the sacred mushroom shamanism of Thunder Lord (Tlaloc) in Meso-america. From one perspective the idea of sacred intoxication is a metaphor (such as with Dakshina Tantra, or right-hand approach), from another it is a means of enhancing the experience of the Deity (as in Vama, or left-hand approach).

Our creation of spiritual-body is by a death, a dissolution of our gross-vision body. The Deity, through its light ingests us, dissolves us, kills our sense of limitation, the root of our suffering. They eat us as long as we're tasty, the tastier we are the more quickly and intensely we're devoured. We're tasty if we're sweet. Wisdom-deity's like heavenly sweets, flowers, lights, pure incense, pure intoxicants, beautiful jewels. This is a commentary on our minds which we offer. So from the start we need to cultivate heavenly sweetness. Then our practice will be full of Deity's exaltation. (This is not to say that our defects are not good offerings, but they must be transformed in our view first. We have to be able to view fear, desire, anger as actually beneficial to others before they should be offered. Until then we offer virtue, and our mind-stream. This liberates the mind stream so that eventually everything can be seen as inherently good, and therefore offered. Tantra even contains secret practices for transforming the five-meats and five-nectars into amrita, they will change outward appearance when they change inward essence.) Tantra is a means of bringing all activity onto the path, so that there is no profane activity which must be excluded from practice, that all life is what it is in truth—sacred. Yogis are able to see the things we take to be dirty and bad to be in actuality, beneficial, wisdom. Life becomes sacred when it is offered. When offered it becomes transformed into light, through ingestion by Wisdom-deity. While Deity transforms through blessings, it is our faith and devotion which allows this transformation to take place, which allows Deity to really envelope us.

* * *

Thunder-beings are the spiritual and physical manifestations of the Spirit. Nature is their field and wisdom-display, not their limitation. Nature is the expression, adornment or symbol of their Mind. We call this Consciousness a Supreme Being or multiple supreme beings by virtue of the response we gain from it, as well as the visionary experience that it bestows upon us. In truth there are many Wisdom-beings, many mystical images, many Cities of Lightning, but all together they function as one, one unity, one Wheel. They are one unified body because they work together harmoniously, because they are governed purely by wisdom and love.

Thunder-beings are related to one another by virtue of their energy formation, as embodiments of wisdom and power, and their activity of displaying thunder and lightning in the inner field of mind and the outer field of existence. For this reason they appear similar from tradition to tradition, and we're inclined to think they are identical image-bodies. But this is not the case. One must receive the visionary transmission in order to know if they're the same beings, because along with the body of vision, one feels the profound nature of the Deity.

They are the spiritual body of the universe, while what we perceive through our senses is the manifest body of the universe. The two are actually one continuum of emptiness-appearance. Through our inner sense, our consciousness, we perceive the subtle inner working of the universe, the spiritual kingdom of Wisdom-beings at the root of things. Through our heart we might know the reality, the Non-dual state of the universe, the Absolute Truth, the primordial Origin of all things. Non-dual actually means that our heart of spacious awareness is not distinct from the Absolute and all things. Through the same consciousness functioning through the doors of eyes, ears, nose etc., we perceive the outer working of the universe, the effect of things. We feel cut off because we're always living through our senses. We must begin paying attention within, to live through our wise-heart of pure Consciousness.

The universe manifests through diverse minds, from stars to storms, stones to plants, fish to birds to people. Within they're unified, on the surface they appear separate. The state of all Wisdom-beings is unity, there is no disharmony between them because their minds are harmonious, so they perceive each other as one substance or wisdom-light with infinite variations. Their view is the highest omniscient view like that of an eagle and their is no disagreement amongst them. There is one Wheel of Dharma. It has multiple paths or methods of attaining perfection. With this understanding, there should be no religious disagreement amongst people, since the Origin of religions are the same, whether revealed by a human embodiment of Wisdom-being or a visionary revelation of Wisdom-being.

Because there is no duality, there is certainly not any opposition between Wisdom-deities like Lord Buddha and Shiva, or Buddha and Yahveh. And there is no opposition between cultures and people, except what we create from closed-mindedness. I've heard lamas speak of such things as Yahveh and Shiva as mundane gods. I've heard of many Westerners speaking negatively of Buddhas. This kind of religious pride stems from misunderstanding. Fear comes from misunderstanding which comes from closed-mindedness. If people want to cast judgement upon something or someone they need to really know what it is they're judging, and to really know you must become an insider, you must become intimate with the person or doctrine, you must actually take the perspective of the person or view.

All Wisdom-deities deemed God or Buddhas represent the Non-dual Wisdom sphere, they are simply its various manifestations, and they communicate its essence through the masters, through a particular culture and language. (Mind, Self, Logos, God are different words in different languages which mean the same thing!!) What the masters are describing is the same, but the language creates a net of symbols for alluding to the Absolute. Where language is the same and view appears to differ sometimes it is simply a matter of focus. For example Buddhist Tantra and Shaiva Tantra were both initially transmitted in Sanskrit, and they are transmitted from the same level of highest realization; Buddhist Tantra embraces the symbol of Samantabhadra to describe the ocean of Wisdom Mind, Shaivites use Shiva to designate it. Although each communicates a unique feeling quality which expresses the view, one Buddha, one Shiva, they nevertheless represent the same level of highest unchanging Non-dual wisdom. Masters place emphasis on one aspect of the enlightened state as a skillful way of helping beings to attain this experience within. The various traditions simply use different skillful means to attract their children who are transmigrating in the universe back into their wisdom-spheres. If we cannot hold such openness then we can at least agree on the efficacy of humanitarianism.

Living as a true-human is living as a child of Thunder-beings. The children of the Thunder-beings reflect their Father-Mother Deity in the clear ocean of their mind. Inwardly this means embodying their ambrosial qualities and receiving their powers and sovereignty from them. Some people arise out of thunder and lightning and so dream about it as a precious reminder, this makes all thunder-people related by the lightning.

There exists one great Lightning-bolt and we are among its branches. The spark of our life in our hearts, the mind distilled in essence drops (of awareness) throughout our being, are the sparks of divine reality. For example, in Vajrayana the mandala of peaceful Deities is in our chest, the mandala of wrathful Deities is in our head. In Shaiva Tantra, Shiva is distilled in drops within wheels situated on the central fire channel inside spinal column, within lunar and solar channels, within the crown, head, heart. Shiva is all the Deities in the body, the organs etc.. In Taoist Tantra you find similar diagrams; the mind is made up of pieces of energy like stars. In all Tantra the body is the microcosm of the Deity, the universe the macro-

cosm. This makes a direct correlation of stars, constellations, universes, to the body-mind's internal lights, viscera, and so on. Thunder-beings are distilled in the universe as stars, in the atmosphere as the root of storms, in geography, and in the body. The cycles which they govern, also correlate the system of constellations to that of internal workings in our body-mind circuit.

The lightningbolt designates inner and outer forces which are controlled by Thunder-beings to destroy the causes of suffering in all minds, to make the earth clear and fresh via tangible electrical lightning vajra, and to make our mind clear and fresh via intangible electrical light vajra. In the outer universe, the directional powers of thunder correspond to the pure creative-destructive energy currents of the four directions. These energies can be aligned with by aligning with their Source-deity, the Deity who controls them, to bring rain, snow, avert hail, perform exorcisms, heal and generate energy for inner transformation. In the inner universe the dimensional powers correspond with the pure energies which we receive as our divine inheritance, which are concentrated in the heart, head and torso primarily as drops, wheels and energy-flows.

There is a lightning-tree branching above the sky; it is the nervous system of the earth. Our own nervous system mirrors it. As the awareness-light of Thunder-deity connects sky to earth, so also our nervous system connects sky-mind to the body and material realm through electronic impulses. The healthy functioning of the nervous systems of all beings is precipitated through the lightning. Our nervous system is gateway to the subtle mind and realm of spirit. This is really the basis of Tantric systems, especially the Kundalini tradition of Shaiva Tantra. When Thunder-beings reflect their wisdom in the atmosphere, there is enlightenment. When Thunder-beings reflect their wisdom in the mind-sphere there is enlightenment.

We're a Deity in essence, so within our body we can experience enlightenment, within our nervous system. Generally in Tantra we use Deity's wisdom-light to achieve this enlightening experience, in the kundalini practices one might use the Deity Shiva, his mantra(s) and grace to awaken the inner lightning (or one may have this experience simply by bringing the mind to rest). The Wisdom-beings exist within us as our divine inheritance, our true essence. We are much more like them than we've been conditioned to believe. The Cities of light and sound, wisdom and bliss exist within us as our inherent wisdom-nature enfolded in the depth of the mind. They are interpenetrating at the level of Infinity. They cannot be pinpointed in a space, because this subtle root of our mind is beyond space, it is our dimension of pristine awareness. The Wisdom-deity is the creator of inner worlds and the witness to them, the display and the mirror reflecting it. Our positive qualities and creative activity come from this inner place.

Meditation causes these qualities to dawn within, they have no external cause or support. The root of all our activity is within, in our thought. If we truly want to help others, and we want our activity to be flawless, then we need to do some meditation. If we want to create perfect unmoving tranquility, then we need to do some meditation. Formless meditation is excellent, and can create good inner stillness, and thus become a foundation and aid for Deity meditation. Meditation on immeasurable Wisdom Source is unsurpassable. The reason is because the Wisdom Deity who we meditate on is infinite and perfect. So if we have devotion we can become just like them.

Through this form of meditation we receive wisdom from Thunder-beings which manifests in two forms: mundane siddhi—the ability to transform reality (our body into the Deity or any form) and cause miraculous feats, and supermundane siddhi—the omniscient state. The mundane siddhis (of the master) which communicate the accomplishment of practice with Sublime Thunder-beings are the same abilities as the Thunder-beings, such as rain-making, exorcism, subduing spirits, emanating countless forms, etc. Accomplished thunder-masters are able to control the pure power of life in order revive a life-less corpse (or to take life), and in secret traditions there is evidence of practices for actually creating life. Wisdom-deities, it is said, used certain words, or mantras to cause life, so when a master who has accomplished the same state as Wisdom-deity uses that mantra and practice, life is created. (A well-known example of this includes the Golem of the Kabbalah).

A beautiful story comes to mind which demonstrates the siddhi of a Thunder master. It concerns a high Dzogchen master known as Dzong Dzung Rinpoche. One day he walked to the top of this mountain, his disciples following. During his vajra-dance a thunder storm arose. Thunder Deity began to rain lightningbolts, so his students kept their distance. They described what they saw. Their master was struck by lightning several times while he danced. He kept dancing. His foot prints were seared indelibly into the rock where he danced.

The supermundane siddhi of a master which communicates accomplishment of practice with Sublime Thunder-beings is the same capacity as the Thunder-beings—infinite consciousness, unmoving tranquility, unquenchable intoxication, Eternal Space.

The realization or state of Thunder-beings is not an impossible achievement. But it is a very high achievement which few can be said to have attained. Some teachers nowadays think they have got it, while all they have done is attained some inner relaxation. But this is not it. It cannot be attained on our own through meditation. Those who attain absorption through meditation will be called or urged by the Wisdom-beings (through light-sound) to higher attainment, they will have to enter the path of wisdom and compassion.

It is difficult to understand omniscience since we're not omniscient and all-pervasive. Essentially it means the mind is totally free to express itself as it chooses. The Absolute can be alluded to by alluding to its sovereignty, the ability to express itself freely. A master of some achievement, who has freed his mind from great limitations of bewilderment, fear, etc., gains the ability to be in multiple places at once, teaching different students different things. A master of somewhat greater achievement, has greater freedom to express his mind, more intense love, will be able to be in a hundred more places at once, perhaps even other realms. He may be in animal form, spirit form, natural-deity form, human form, all at once. He may be on the other side of the universe. He got there through concentration and the realization of his mind as free and all-pervasive. Sun, moon, stars, all realms are within his mind. At the speed of thought he can manifest wherever he wishes. As the mind becomes increasingly free to express itself, it's ability to help beings in many places increases. Eventually the master attains the highest state, of the Thunder-beings, and is in the minds of all beings simultaneously. He is able to emanate in a billion realms and places simultaneously. He is able to act flawlessly in all emanations, and so on. The ability to do this is both one's realization of unlimitedness, intrinsic freedom, and one's compassionate intention to help beings. Limitations and obstacles are destroyed by wisdom, by Deity's blessing, leaving the mind free to express itself. Through compassion the mind utilizes its freedom to achieve the aims of all beings.

Siddhis of Lightning: The Secret Accomplishment of Primordial Thunder-beings

The highest degree of accomplishment is to have complete control over mind, and therefore to demonstrate complete control over the universe. The Thunder-beings who are primordially achieved, who never strayed from their nature, created the multi-universe. Their power of thunder and lightning was instrumental in this activity. Through it they create, sustain and destroy universes, through it they signal the transition of seasons on the earth, through it they bring beings out of space and return them thereto.

Those who have a superficial knowledge of Buddhist Tantra may contend that this doesn't include Buddha activity, and is irrelevant to this text. But it does. In Buddhist Tantra, The Buddha Vairochana creates the universe as a field within which Bodhisattvas practice skillful means of helping beings who must incarnate in material form (to work out karma from previous lives in previous universes). In the Shaiva Tantra, Lord Shiva creates, maintains and dissolves universes, and in fact takes the form of all beings at this moment.

Long ago, Thunder-beings created out of mind (wisdom) and light (love), plants, animals, all beings. They arose on the earth out of the storm-clouds or out of lightning. Because lightning is thunder, we might say they sung beings into existence. Thunder was the first speech or language. Turtle, lizard, frog fell from the clouds. While others arose out of the lightning touching down on the elements, like earth and ocean. The essence of life comes from the Thunder-beings through the lightning, the form comes through the combination of electrified elements. It's like the conception of a fetus, there's a minute spark (bindu) from the joining of elements which attracts a spirit of the same frequency as the combined resonance of the parents. So parents bodies are creator microcosms in which lightning sparks elements to conceive life.

Creation of life out of lightning is controlled by the Thunder-deity, it is not a chance event. The forms that beings take often bear signs inwardly and outwardly to ancient Thunder-beings. Inwardly they are extraordinary minds, outwardly they bear marks and move in ways indicative of the movement of Thunder-beings. For example lizards have three eyes; dragonfly, butterfly and bumble bee have wings and move like lightning. All birds are related to Thunder-beings—they live close to them and resemble them inwardly and outwardly. Animals like antelope, deer and moose have antlers signifying lightning. Bull, buffalo, horse, lion, tiger are strong, fearless and courageous. Dog is impartial lover and knows his way home. Beaver builds a good home. Cow nourishes well. Humans can manifest excellent visions. First wise people arose as Thunder Deity's forms on earth. Thunder-deity continues to come to earth in this way; by stepping out of a lightningbolt. (The imagery of one such being will be presented below: Guru Rinpoche).

Most people with some exposure to mystical traditions and Tantra believe that highly realized masters and yogis could do many feats, that they could create a crystal palace out of air, or multiply one fish to feed a thousand, cause great storms, cause it to thunder in a clear blue sky, split the clouds, walk through stone, fly through space, be in 18 places at once, be minute or vast in size, catch lightnbolts in their coat, hang clothes on sunbeams, or fly. Many teachers and practitioners do not think it is possible that the universe was created by Wisdom-deities. But if our masters can materialize miraculous appearances, and this power or siddhi comes from Wisdom-deities, then why shouldn't Wisdom-deities be able to miraculously create the multi-universe like a crystal palace or rainbow??

Siddhi is developed naturally out of perfect mind-control of yogis. They control their internal elements (energy), so are able to display control over the overt elements. Siddhi is the natural self-display of Thunder-beings—they are subtle wisdom-mind and subtle energy. Through their energy they are able to control the universe with their mind. For them it is as spontaneous as creating a mental image is for us. When the entire scope of the universe is considered, creating winds, rains and storms is magical display done with great ease—that is why in Shaiva tradition the universe and all life is known as a "play" or lila of Lord Shiva.

The Thunder-beings are primordially achieved, they control the multi-universe through all minds. They are certainly responsible for initiating life on the planet. They did so with the lightning, the pure power of life, that comes from the Blue Sun behind the sun. The sun sustains the overt form of life which presently exists here, the Blue Star sustains the inner life-star which lives through the form.

All life was initiated billions of years ago by them. We existed within them as well, in their belly or egg, in their mind. Our mind never departs from theirs. We never loose our potential Deity-nature. The lightning contains the power to take life-less elements and bring about life. But behind it is a real Spirit or wisdom and a real live intention to cause something miraculous. The thunder-dream of Frakinstein demonstrates this possibility. I'm sure scientists have set upon this idea and sought to prove it. Although Frakinstein also demonstrates the necessity of wisdom behind ones intention. Thunder-beings are omniscient. The golem which Kabbalist mystics created with the magic of holy names, the electrical cables of the Lightning-spirit, resulted in causing chaos as well. What Thunder-beings created out of pure compassionate motivation has the measure of perfection of those Deities. What they created embodies their wisdom. There is wisdom in the hearts of all sentient beings, in the plants, in the earth, air, fire, water, space, stars, and so on. Thunder-beings are creating nature as their glorious Vision of Reality. They have arisen as the minds of sentient beings, and they are displaying the universe within Infinite Space Mind. All minds at their deepest level are Uncreated, Unoriginated, Unborn. This primordially enlightened nature of our consciousness is symbolized by the imagery of Wisdom Deity.

We exist in timeless unity with our Wisdom parents who are emanating us into the field of existence. We are changing extensions of the mass of unchanging wisdom-clear-light, and from this view are actually a collection of light fibers projected from empty space, we are luminous space congealed and woven into various shapes. We are a dance of light and sound emptiness, insubstantial like space. This Cosmic and microcosmic Dance can be depicted as Shiva, Chakrasamvara or the Wisdom-Dakini.

The space that does not appear is changeless, the light which does appear is impermanent, shifting, dancing, subject to arise, remain for a time and dissolve. What is tangible is light. Electricity is light. Light is a tangible state of cognitive space. This space is the nature of wisdom—totally conscious. Everyone sees light in our heart, mostly as sound or thought. To think is to see our own consciousness taking shape through sound and light. Because we're not aware of what is beyond thought and feeling and sensory experience, we're not aware of the true nature of reality, which is the same as our true nature—space and clear light. Our mind projects our limited view of nature onto reality, we're unable to see beyond it unless we train to do so. So the reality we live with is a mixture of pleasure and pain, whereas the actual state of awareness and reality is bliss. When the mind is free of the barriers of conceptual thinking, when we train to be fully aware of ourself and our environment, then we experience the true nature of Reality, and experience infinite realm of Pure Enjoyment, instead of finite realm of desire.

Sublime Wisdom-beings are in our love for one another, our love for anything. They are in our blissful enjoyment we gain from any experience. Objects that evoke such feelings are not the direct cause of our bliss, such as the sound of rain, the sight of the ocean or a flower, dew on the grass, baby birds, stellar chakra. The cause is within. Our unceasing mind-stream is the Wisdom-being. For as long as we mistake the true cause of bliss by forgetting Wisdom-nature, we will be lost in the realm of sensory experience, clinging, attraction-revulsion, seeking joyous exaltation in the objects we desire. The cause of pure enjoyment is love. Love is what is attractive in us which makes all things attractive. Love is the bliss of experience. If we want to be happy we just learn to love. It is through the inner luminosity generated from compassion that we experience the beauty of pure enjoyment—that is desireless joy. We practice meditation on compassion to increase this joy, and we practice meditation on tranquility to enhance this joy, we practice devotional meditation on Wisdom deities to unfold this joy like a lotus. The essence of Oriental traditions is the movement inward, meditation. Our supreme masters point to this by their earthly activity; Buddha and Shiva, Guru Rinpoche and Lao Tzu, are supreme yogis. All excellent spiritual teachers used meditation and taught it. Prayer, dance, music, art, poetry, architecture, science, creative activity are forms of meditation, as long as we concentrate, become absorbed.

The Dream of existence is staged and projected by these ancient Minds, by Thunder-beings. First aspects of the universe were emanated, such as stone, space and star-lights. Similarly, upon the young earth Thunder Lords walked and initiated human civilization. The essences existed in unity with their all-pervasive Mind. We existed in them first, so they brought our essences out of them, out of the subtle state before time and space, out of the non-dual state. To symbolize this we might speak of our perfected-masters as being born of the hair, bones or eye of the Deity, such as with

Shiva and the Nath siddhas, or as being emanations of the body-speech-mind aspects of the Deity. Out of Mind they brought the first lives into space and substance. The Infinite Consciousness differentiates and creates the condition for taking gross vision bodies on earth. Awareness-silence arises as a creative sound, the sound becomes a homogeneous luminosity which organizes into distinct luminous essence, a Vision, and the Vision becomes an actuality. Poetically you could say, the Deities conjured a Vision and sung it into existence. Through sound Wisdom-deity's intention achieves its goal. The intention and the sound are the same. Thunder we hear is the intention to enlighten our minds. Tantra or the essence of Dharma teachings is like pure intention. Vajrayana teachings appear to Buddhas of Complete Enjoyment bodies in Pure Realms as light shining from the mouths of the Wisdom Buddhas. Shiva transmitted all (Veda) and Tantra through his five mouths in a similar fasion. When our hearts intention and prayer or mantra is unified, then whatever goal we set out to achieve will be achieved. The simplest examples include praying for someone who becomes well as a result.

We are all related as if by lightning zig-zagging through space connecting all hearts. Because we're endlessly connected we're able to know one another on a deep level. In Buddhism this is called "Interdependence." Our mind is able to know things by merging with the object of knowledge through light. We're inherently unified by love. We're able to effect one another in a very positive way with intention through light (thought) and sound (prayer). Whatever intentions we have—they reach their goal. Because we're part of an interdependent indestructible web, our prayers work, they come true. Our love is the motivating power behind them.

The Ancient Thunder Lords: Their Remarkable History, Function and Ascent

The Oriental traditions teach that most Wisdom-beings gave birth to themselves into the Spirit through the physical realm. Having reached the highest achievement and served selflessly to benefit sentient beings, they ascended into subtlest reality. The process or way of the universe is cyclic, it arises from its Unmanifest Source, becomes manifest for a time, then returns to its Source.

During the young life of the earth, Thunder-beings descended from the subtle space. They combined themselves with the pure elements, taking bodies as giants. Their bodies were a reflection of spiritual emanation. In the Spirit, they gather subtle atoms to take form as an image of the formless Absolute. In the physical realm they gather physical atoms to form a body perhaps after the original image of the Spirit. A manifest form arises directly out of spiritual substance. Mystics and shamans have seen the Thunder Lords on earth, and at the same time have a notion of their function. It can be seen because to the Omniscient Mind everything is known simultaneously.

These giants were among the first beings on earth. They generally lived inside huge mountain caves. Wherever they lived or stayed became sanctified, so even today we consider these places sacred and holy, places for spiritual practice. Among them are the five Mt. Kailash in Himalaya where Shiva and his retinue dwelt. When Thunder-beings walked the earth there was no thunder or lightning, only rain. The Thunders controlled the power of the Source to bring forth thunder and lightning. They possessed the spark which originally illuminated the earth. Our mind is self-illuminated by the light of the Unmanifest, space is illuminated by the same light in its manifest form, from the sun and stars. As the manifest mirrors the Unmanifest that spark might be said to initiate the tree of earthly development.

One function of the embodied Thunder Lords was to carve out geographical features like river beds and canyons. They moved earth with their thunder-bolt scepters. Their strength was clearly a manifestation of their inner strength, the power of the Mystery. They were not alone on earth. There were giant serpents who are the nemesis of the Thunder-beings. Thunder-beings are the power of universal good, of love, while the serpents are degenerate beings who serve only themselves. They are dark, clouded energy-beings that chose avarice over kindness. They were poison on the earth, so they caused disharmony and suffering to beings on the earth. Their radiation could cause insanity, the poisoning of the waters of the mind, and death, the poisoning of the waters of the earth. Since Thunder-beings are in charge of maintaining universal harmony they had to subdue these beings. That makes them the first warriors and exorcists. Their protective-destructive power is fully in harmony with the subtle universal law. Their protectiveness is destructive of negativity. They are always loving, it is the nature of their heart—the heart of life.

So Thunder Lords battled these serpents fiercely. Niagara Falls was produced from a battle in which the Thunder Lord Hino pronged a serpent causing its tail to crash down hard, the result of which is the giant falls. Myths abound which recount the battle between Thunder Lords and serpents. Some examples are Yahveh's battle eluded to in several places in Hebrew scripture, Indra's slaying of Vritra, Shiva's activity of subduing or controlling naga serpents, and the numerous Native American accounts (which tell us that the petrified bones and bodies of the Thunders and serpents still exist as a testament).

Myths abound in ancient cultures of this time when the Deities, our ancestors, walked the earth, long before the present civilization. Being our creator ancestors, they are not something remotely different from humans in their purity today. These earliest giants gave birth to people and the first animals, birds and plants as well. The Hebrew Kabbalah or whispered tradition, which stretches back 70,000 years, speaks of Elohim (Gods) who walked the earth and created other giants known as Nefilim and man and woman. Elohim likewise figures as a destroyer of one or more giant serpent beings. In the Vajrayana secret oral teachings, originally people were seven times larger than we are, much wiser and more balanced in terms of male-female energies. Our obscurations or strong habitual tendencies have caused our present bodies, our present circumstances, to appear the way they do. The primordial Thunder-beings embody the enlightened state, they never departed from it, so they never had anything to attain. They had duties to fulfill, which was their enlightened activity.

In India, Shiva was on earth in various forms who were the ancient Deities, some of which bore tridents, controlled serpents and lived on mountain abodes. So too he initiated human civilization. There was a creator called Purusha who walked the earth as a giant and spoke the thunder, "DA, DA, DA." Mother Durga was on earth before the previous civilization. In China there are written records interspersed with visionary accounts (mythologies) of earliest people as giants who ascended to populate the Three Highest Realms of Divinity. Some examples are Yuan-shih, Pan Ku, and Ti. Throughout millions of years and numerous civilizations, humans have walked the earth and those that remained pure in their nature ascended to become Wisdom-beings, many of whom form the diverse imagery and deity pantheons of the world traditions. Since some or many failed to remain pure, the Wisdom-beings transmitted spiritual practices so that people could adhere to the Dharma or natural subtle law, so that people could continue to achieve divinity. That wisdom was originally natural living and has become what we know to be the ancient spiritual traditions. I think we are very fortunate to be able to learn spiritual reality and practice from the Wisdom-beings in the midst of these degenerate times.

When the Thunder-beings were on earth, they very often lived on high mountains. Some examples are Lord Shiva who dwelt on five Mt. Kailash, Yahveh who dwelt on Mt. Sinai, and families of Thunder-beings who dwelt on mountains in America like Mt. Katahdin in Maine. The mountains remained the sacred seat of the Deity even after they left their bodies or dematerialized, at least this is true in the Oriental traditions where sacred geography is deeply respected. Mt. Kailash is venerated by Shaivite, Vajrayana and Bon po practitioners. Many places have been sanctified by the Thunder-deities' pure presence, some places are recognized as secret lands. Within them pure beings continue to live. Some examples include Shambhala, Sikkim, Pema kod, The Valley of Parvathi, the 5 Mt. Kailash. Everything within these lands is totally sacred. For example all beings, people and animals are holy and when they die exhibit weather changes and rainbows. Many global myths relate how individuals stumble upon such places, live for a time in great bliss, then return after a few days to find everyone old while they have not aged. Generally with the Thunder-beings these lands are within mountains. There is an entire land within a mountain. Here in the Americas, these sacred sites and their Deities have been disrespected. Stories exist which tell of the Thunder-beings leaving their earthly abodes. Mt. Katahdin is one such example, another will be recounted later. The families left these abodes and went to the Western Wisdom Abode.

When the Thunder Lords died after living long, long lives, they left their bodies on earth while their spirits went up into the clouds, to an adjacent realm. This realm is often depicted as a mountain abode where the Deity has a mandala palace, throne, seat, or nest of dried bones and a huge egg from which baby Thunders are hatched amidst crackling lightning. They might also be seen dwelling within a cavern in a mountain summit, or at the edge of the sky in a cloud dwelling, or in a nest in the Tree of Life, the point of which is to show that they dwell in a subtle state, the resonance of which is depicted through height. The height of Thunder Mt. and the Tree of Life reveal high spiritual attainment. From the height, root and center of reality they control the universe and work with the pure creative light of life. When they ascended they were able to bring about atmospheric thunder and lightning by converging their spirit and gathering the hot and cold energies of the directions corresponding to fire and water. They took on the attributes of the angelic Bird because they were ascending to live in the sky and vast inner space. They also retained something of the original image of giant man weilding thunder-bolt scepter. In doing so they set the stage for the ascent of earth people into the subtle realms to become angelic birds of sound and power. The Thunder Lords were demonstrating the way of the universe, its crystallization into form and remergence into formlessness.

Thunder-beings, once they ascended, reflected their earthly function; they would maintain the balance between light and dark, positive and negative, heaven and earth, good and evil. They had already subdued the serpents bodies, now it was necessary to subdue their spirits. The serpents are dark energy rays, causes of illness and death. They are mostly unseen and live in deep waters and earth, where cold energy collects. Those that have been subdued are cousins to the dragons, who use the same wealth (electro-magnetic energy) to cause thunder. Sometimes the position of dragons and serpents has been confused. Dragons are benevolent beings who assist humans, they are protective Thunder-beings. So are the subdued serpents, who are guardians of earthly wealth, waters and spiritual teachings. Some examples are the Naga Kings and the Rainbow Lightning Serpents of Australia and Quetzalcoatl of Meso-America. The unsubdued serpents poison waters and are attracted to peoples inner and outer filth. They cause illness and insanity and are sometimes manipulated by sorcerers. Thunder-beings subdue these beings, either putting them in prison realm or making them into Dharma protectors. (A black dragon I know ate and digested 3 such evil spirits at once). The function of the Thunder-beings is always to preserve the young, harmonious nature of nature. When some energy of the earth falls out of harmony with the whole, Thunder-birds bring that energy back into harmony. This is certainly the case with serpents and monsters, people and animals who disrupt harmony, the unobstructed flow of life. Most Thunder-beings adorn themselves with serpents to symbolize their victory over forces that cause suf-

fering, obstruct growth of the mind and crops, the reharmonization of dark with light, the transformation from dark to light, ignorance to wisdom. Some of these wild beings are struck by lightning and return to their original nature as protectors and lightnings.

In Vajrayana teachings, it is said that in ancient times nagas were causing incurable diseases, so Vajrapani requested that Buddha take Garuda form to subdue them—which he did. Many stories relate how nagas were subdued and bound by commitment to serve Dharma. Guru Rinpoche and Vajrapani were engaged in this activity, they took Garuda form and ingested the nagas—and transformed them. So typically when Garuda is depicted he has a naga in his beak and hands.

The ancient global myths of Thunder Lord battling serpents depicts the need to establish the conditions of cosmic and microcosmic balance, the movement from dark to light, gross to subtle, limited awareness to infinite awareness, Winter to Spring, death to life, illness to harmony. The serpents stand for what obstructs the light from shining through the earth and its life from flourishing. The name of the serpent in the battle which Indra fought was Vritra which means "covering" or "veil." Congealed energy is a necessary condition for life, but when it becomes impure by being cut off from wisdom, it obscures the light and there is decay and death. In our bodies, when the pure creative energy bestowed from heaven is obscured it creates endless mundane desires, which in the end must be disciplined like a wild serpent. We are free to allow them to get out of control, but they have to be reigned in again in the end. Pure congealed energy is the five phases of energy, like a rainbow of five electrical qualities which organizes into the universe (Rainbow Serpent). Impure congealed energy is energy which has been cut off from its wisdom-source and remains at a dark frequency manifesting causes of illness and death (malevolent serpent). This is the only real nemesis of the Thunder-beings, the causes of illness and unnatural death. They maintain balance between these forces so that creative energy can display itself freely, so that we can evolve our life-being into spirit.

Thunder-beings are the greatest warriors. They always fight for universal good as the Source of universal good. The war against injustice in the universe is waged and won by the Thunder Lords and their emanations. They battle untiringly to establish Truth on earth and equilibrium in all minds. Nothing can conquer their thunder-bolt. Their devotees are likewise great warriors on earth, they bear the Deity's heroic qualities and very often the Deity's outer marks as seen in visions. For example, Shiva devotees carry trident, damaru, conch and marks which symbolize victory over inner and outer obstacles, Tantric adepts use a vajra in ritual as a reminder of the awakened state of consciousness, its indestructible wisdom and skillful means, the weapon to destroy inner obstacles. The devotees become the extension of the Deity on earth to fight for the Truth to abolish suffering and guide people to the goal.

One of the most remarkable features of the visionary images of Thunder-beings is their fierceness. They usually appear as semi-wrathful or fierce. They are Lords of all fierce things in nature. They appear with two or four fangs, Thunder-birds might have rows of razor-sharp teeth, a fierce expression like a Horned Owl, wear a war-bonnet, carry a war staff, whip, dagger, sword, club or trident. Fierceness is not necessarily anger, but a manifestation of creative-destructive power, thunder-power. Their fierceness is their direct application of wisdom. The function of fierceness is to create balance by clearing out the causes of disease and suffering in the world. It is the clarity and will-power of the Deity to remove all obstructions (negativity) to the state of spontaneous growth, peace and joy in the microcosm and macrocosm. Because there are fiercely recalcitrant and wildly avaricious forms of negativity in the universe, there are much more potent and skillful means by which Thunder-beings subdue these negative forces. Certainly too, it seems there is something innately fierce about thunder, lightning, hail, twisters, hurricanes, blizzards and floods—because they cause destruction. People clinging desperately to their ego fear for their lives. They fear the unpredictable lest it should cause suffering or liberate their soul. Instead people should simply respect nature and act according to the Dharma of righteousness embodied in the activity of all Wisdom-beings. "The Fear of God is wisdom" means respecting everything created as the Lords symbolic Vision-body of Light. If we adhere to the Dharma or subtle law, especially aligning our heart with the Wisdom-beings, we won't have to fear being struck by lightning or having the house leveled by a twister. They will go around us and make a space for the Sunshine. Thunder-beings are super-mundane deities, their minds gone far beyond the ordinary dual state bound to emotions. They are the non-dual Wisdom which pri-

mordially embraces seemingly contrary states, such as gentle and fierce, joyous and angry, happy and sad. Fear or self-cherishing doesn't create the image or cause the Deity to appear fierce to you, as some scholars have thought. On the contrary, the Deity is fearless and self-less, perfectly serene and innately blissful. But, ones reaction upon seeing and feeling the Deity or upon encountering the thunder-method used by a perfected master may yield a sense of being scolded. The thunder-people and Deities are teaching people energetically to be more aware. They know precisely how to wake us up, both with unwavering penetrating directness and ego-melting antics, hot and cold. Their whip might appear to smart, but if we see it clearly, it actually causes our vision to expand, liberating us from suffering. Besides, if we are scolded or have our feelings hurt by such compassionate beings, which is sometimes the case, they are just expressing the mirror-like nature of nature. They mirror our mundane mind and our Transcendent Mind, so they might ignore us as we have ignored the universe of ourself and our world, and they might love us as we have loved and have the potential to love.

Because their minds are disciplined they have complete control over their actions, over the subtle and gross element energies. The inner and outer universe is their mandala, City, theater, play, their thunder echoes across the universe, their lightning is their sport. Thunder-beings appear fierce to denote their enormous indestructible power, its intensity and unpredictability, their outrageous contrary nature of peaceful creativity and violent destructiveness. Thunder-beings are the opposite or contrary to what we are accustomed to thinking about heavenly beings and nature. We think the terrific appearance is angry (with us) and is destructive, because we are self-cherishing. Actually they chose that form because there are incorrigible beings who think only of their self, because there are monstrously self-serving beings in the universe. Self-serving activity is contrary activity. Thunder Lords are contrary to all causes of suffering, so if they shock us, they shock us with the truth, they zap us so we'll see our wrong thinking and turn our heart to help others. Fear and desire are contrary to the natural state which is embodied by Thunder-beings. Their activity is contrary to any concretized ideas we have about God, angels and love, they are contrary to established hierarchy, mundane rules and ethics. They are luminous great perfection. They are fierce heavenly warriors, fighting with the all-conquering power of emptiness to establish Dharma by assisting people to actualize their own inherent goodness. Their power is like all of space, all-pervasive radiance, concentrated into one place and time. Through it they can achieve anything. Through them we can achieve anything within the broad scope of the subtle universal law.

Thunder-bird:
The Iconography of Sky-like Awareness

All Sublime Wisdom beings have the capacity to take the form of a man, woman or a Divine Bird. When Thunder Lords or spirits take this Divine Bird form amongst thunder and lightning they are called Thunder-birds, and can be entirely in the form of a giant Bird or as a half bird—half human. The Bird attributes are generally those of Eagle, but can also be hawk or owl. So what you see are the wings, face and feet of an eagle, human torso, head and arms—this is the case with Thunder-birds and Garudas—the Buddhas who take this form. As you will see with Lei Kung (Chief Thunder-bird) in Book III he has owl features, an owl face and wings and human torso and arms.

It is said that four primordial Thunder-birds protect the earth—they embody and are the origin of all Thunder-beings. It is said that they're in the four directions of space surrounding earth. It may also be true that Thunder-beings protect the earth with an energy field in the shape of a three-dimensional Star of David. This star is the perfect geometric image of divine wisdom. It designates the human heart which contains the star-drop of God. It designates the earth sphere which is the heart of God in our universe.

Thunder Lord's first revelation is the Thunder-bird. He is a Wisdom-being who is appearing with features of man and bird. He symbolizes purification. He comes at the end of an eon to purify the earth and can be supplicated to purify our mind and environment. Universally, Wisdom-beings have the capacity to become Thunder-bird or multiple Thunder-birds. Shiva, Indra, Vishnu and Brahma all have the capacity to become a Garuda (Great Eagle), which bears the attributes of man and bird. In the Tibetan Tantric tradition there are multiple Garudas, Lord Buddha was the first Garuda. He assumed this form in order to protect the nagas from invisible animals known as garudas who were harming the nagas. Lord Vajrapani also takes the form of Wisdom-Garudas. In fact all

Buddhas that I'm aware of take this form. In addition there are separate mandalas of Garudas, such as Padma Garuda, multicolored Garudas, 5 Garuda mandala. Thunder-beings from Siberia and Mongolia (Tengeri) to Africa and South America take Thunder-bird form. Usually Thunder Lord emanates Thunder-birds into the four directions of space, such as Tunka-shila and his four Wakinyan, Animig and his Animiki, Navajo Big Thunder and his four Thunder-birds, Yahveh and the four chayyoth (lightningbolts, which clothed, are the four archangels: Gabriel, Michael, Raphael and Uriel. Yahveh's Thunder-bird form is the Holy Spirit, the vehicle of God's revelation). Lei Kung of ancient China and his four emanations are Thunder-birds called Wu Fang Lei Kung or Lei Kung of the four directions, and so on. Every tradition has Thunder-birds. The Thunder Mind whether male or female can take the form of a man or Thunder-bird, woman or female Thunder-bird (one such example is Father Osiris and Mother Isis).

Their bird attributes symbolize movement through space. The ability to soar far beyond the mundane world of duality, the ability to ascend and to descend as lightning in the atmosphere and revelation in the mind. Their flight also symbolizes the flight of bliss of the liberated heart within inner space or tranquility. Their wings could be taken to mean inspiration, creative energy flow, compassionate motivation. On a more minute level their wings could be taken as white light and dark light, the two lights whose friction produces wind (both subtly in the heart and in the atmosphere) and whose wind develops into a sound, such as inspired thought (revelation) or thunder—the inspired utterance of divine thought. The flapping of Thunder-bird wings produces thunder, in which case the flashing of their eyes produces lightning. They are the joining of the powers of heaven and earth. They invisibly and visibly connect subtlest energy to grossest. Therefore they stand for our connection to the Subtle Mystery, and they stand for our melting into that Mystery. They symbolize revelation and inspiration, the creative power of the universe descending to fructify the earth and put creative ideas through the mind, to inspire growth in the earth and mind spheres.

Thunder-bird connects spheres through his thunder-bolt which is the actual transmission of his mind (coming through his eyes)—a living symbol of Wisdom-mind. He transmits it to the individual mind of his human messenger in a subtle form, and to the earth in a gross form. The lightningbolt transpierces the limitless sphere of being from which it arises out of Mind as Mind, and the sphere of existence to which it descends to awaken the minds of beings who had metaphorically fallen into the sleep of unknowing. It also hits the target and never ceases from achieving the pure motivation which is behind it, in fact it is pure motivation, what in Tibetan Buddhism is termed bodhicitta, "enlightened mind," heart and energy. It arises from subtlest Mind and manifests to touch the earth, awakening its life and sending out a signal that nourishment is on the way. To symbolize this, lightning comes from above the clouds, from the eyes, head or wings of Thunder-bird which are images of the Subtle Origin, of heaven or the subtle unseen beginning of things. Lightning connects the inner sphere of the Deity to the outer sphere of the Deity. Through his blessing-light he effects control over our development, as a vehicle for carrying their wisdom to the earth and hearts of all beings. His thunder echoes in the same way in our hearts and never passes away. Through his wisdom, which precedes light, sound or symbol, he effects control over the universe and all minds. His wisdom transmitted on the vehicle of lightning and thunder inspires the revelation of creative works, like paintings, books, masks, songs, images, ritual, antics, all of which penetrate with the power of thunder to the heart of the mind, awakening them and leading them back to the Origin.

The lightning is an axis mundi, akin to Thunder Mt. and Tree of Life. It can literally be used to ascend into the clouds (by trails that run along side it) and symbolically it is used to ascend into subtle states—that it, thunder-power, whose image is the bolt, is applied to raise ones consciousness by awakening gross energy into subtle states corresponding with divine frequency. Such a frequency is necessary for our entrance into the Cities of Lightning. (Though it should be known that the fuel and methods necessary to achieve the subtlest states of consciousness can come from any of the innumerable transmissions of Wisdom-beings, not only thunder-transmission.)

The Lightning-bolt becomes our connection, our plug into the Subtle Source of the universe. First it comes through the messenger so that through the messengers guidance people might attain the goal. Through thunder-dreams, the graceful heart-transmission of wisdom-thunder-power is sown in the mind (with the needle of the lightning) to form an electric blanket of light to be put amongst the people to serve to awaken them. The sparks of sound and light, Spirit

and energy, Mind and bliss become transmitters through which energy is gathered and radiated. This happens both in the clouds, in which case you have a storm which awakens the earth, and it happens in the mind of the master in which case you have some or no behavior and it awakens the minds of the people, (like when you are around someone who is overjoyed in love, that radiance rubs off on you and lightens your heart). Ones growth of wisdom is actualized through the Deities power which is symbolized by the trident and the horns of a Thunder-being (which adorn Shiva, Garudas, Osiris and Isis) and some thunder-masters like Moses.

Thunder-bird embodies wisdom, power, luminosity, authority, judgement, sovereignty, majesty, beauty, love, compassion, peace and spaciousness. They generally take on the attributes of predator birds, like eagle, hawk, owl and falcon. The human attributes symbolize evolution out of the human state into the divine symbolized by the bird attributes. The human form is the base (metal), the substance that will be transformed into sprit (gold): bird-form. Flight means the ability to leave the earth, rise into the sky, the ability of consciousness to expand into the limitless openness, the Undifferentiated or non-dual state—the Void. The wings which have grown out of the heart are actualizations of spiritual development, they are the sign of the expansive and radiating mind, the mind of wisdom and compassion, spirit and energy, consciousness and bliss. So this power represents our unbreakable link to the Truth. When lightning connects to the earth there is thunder. So it symbolizes our link to the heavenly powers, which produces a flow of luminosity (like lightning) and nourishment (like rain). Thunder-bird connects with the earth to nourish and restore it. Likewise through transmission he connects with the mind, to restore and nourish it. That nourishment shines in our pristine qualities. In Hindu myth Garuda flew to the highest heavens (or the moon) and brought back intoxicating nectar (soma) as a Thunder-porridge and initiated people with it during storms of vision. Thunder-birds (Tengeri) still do this in Siberia to initiate shamans. The Deity originated it and the yogi received it; it made him drunk and gave him power. The Deity's unseen grace exists as the intoxicating nectar, (often depicted in a skull-cup or vase), which, imbibed again and again produces the spiritualization of the mind-body. When the work is complete, what remains is a spirit, a bliss-body of consciousness, an emptiness-appearance, that is, something not subject to duality, like solid and space, big and small, etc. This new spirit, given birth to through the Thunder-beings, by their grace, is the baby Thunder-bird. Bird is a symbol of transmutation; we create something alchemically out of the base metal of our distorted energy, which rises by virtue of its increased vibrational frequency. It becomes subtle in frequency and thus becomes freed from the limitations of gross physical reality. So, as it flew here from the stars, it is capable of returning by flight. It can literally and figuratively fly. The mind becomes intoxicated in the desireless bliss of its subtle state, and flies free in the heart. Such is the meaning of inner flight—the flight of the Garuda.

Thunder-bird brings wisdom down to the people providing initiation and instruction, methods and fuel necessary to reach the same achievement as Thunder-bird. He is the completion of the alchemical process, the restoration of our original-mind, our convergence as spirit, our breakthrough into Infinity. They have already attained the state of complete awakenment and are going to assist us out of their boundless compassion. They are perfect models for our attainment. They draw us into their vast inner space, their City of Lightning as a subtle realm and a subtle resonance of our heart. The image symbolizes the configuration of wisdom, the enlightened qualities that the Wisdom-mind is going to awaken in us. It is a tool that directs the awakening and shift in consciousness. By aligning with the image and absorbing its qualities, it awakens the same qualities within us. And in fact the result is that we become of the same nature and reflect the same image as our god-parent or tutelary. It is like two people who live together all their life, who melt into one another and act and appear alike. In this case, because the Deity is immovable, it is we who melt into them and bear their image and nature. This must be the realization of being created in the image and similitude of Yahveh expressed in the Torah.

Thunder-bird creates wind and controls the clashing of fire and water. He is the inner wind or force of Thunder-mind—fully awakened mind. He is Thunder Lord's self-illumination. His rising is his infinite expansion or omniscient self-illumination. His descent is his concentration and revelation. He reveals himself through a dream to the mind, but this dream is real. And he reveals himself through the dream-fabric of reality, in the atmosphere. His image is bestowed out of that revelation. It is the heart of nature and God. It is earth, man-woman, bird, cloud, lightning, thunder, rain, sky, wind, space and Spirit. The deep nature of our mind corresponds with the nature of Thunder Mind, which allows us to align with him, know him, and merge with him based on our aspiration and his will.

Thunder either arises from his voice, wings, drums or whip. It is the sound of a connection being made, between powers or sparks. It is the sound of the spark of the Spirit. It is Wisdom and its utterance of divine will. It is the utterance of Eternity or Truth; what is said is truth through and through and always comes to pass because its Spirit knows past, present and future because its Spirit pervades past, present and future, unbroken. Thunder is a communication or transmission of visible speech (Mind and wind). It is Gods Thought. It is the first voice in the birth of the universe and on the earth—therefore it is the voice of all beginnings. It will also be the voice of all endings. The Thunder of the Spirit which initiated the universe is not produced by friction, but Mysterious Eternity. It carries the unspoken Truth across vast inner space and to the inner ear. It unfolds like a lotus as a self-expression of Wisdom through sound. Sound is the vehicle and the substance quality of the Wisdom, therefore when you hear thunder you hear Wisdom. It is the electric light of self-illumination in the vision of reality. When the Wisdom becomes electronic sound, it is thunder. When the sound becomes visible it is electric light. The light vision of thunder is lightning. When the lightning becomes solidified it is a thunder-stone, a living stone of Thunder Mind-wisdom. Similarly, with scriptural revelation, when the subtle wisdom becomes perceptual as sound it is self-illuminated as a bright idea in the space of the mind. When the revelation reaches paper it is solidified (in flux) and yet remains immutable living wisdom. When the revelation reaches the ear of the heart it echoes like thunder and produces awakening. Creative activity is eternal and never perishes—there is a memory whose impressions never fade. It arises for a time into this reality from that Reality, fulfills its purpose, then dissolves back into its originating field. Revelation is the disclosure of the divine, of the subtlest state of our mind, and comes like a streak of lightning in a clear blue sky. This is the very nature of our creative, spontaneous activity.

The Thunder of the Mystery is indestructible sound. Thunder-beings brought the first word to earth. It was electronic wind shaped into sound, it was living word so they could create or achieve what they wanted with it. We can reach this same achievement which is called "voice of thunder" or mantra-siddhi, by making our mind, the root of our voice, pure. The result is that what we say comes to pass, the Deity invoked appears immediately. It means we're cleaving to Eternal Reality and expressing its perfect Truth. Thunders awaken with their voice of thunder. They express the unfurling of wisdom within our life. Thunder is the symbol of wisdom or truth, the communication of what is beyond words. The voice of the spiritualized or enlightened mind communicates the inexhaustible wisdom and truth, therefore whatever is spoken has positive and far-reaching effects. Thunder is also the symbol of the spontaneous arising of form from the formless and its dissolution back into formlessness. To demonstrate this you'll hear a crack of thunder and simultaneously the Deity will appear, you'll hear another crack and he might change into another shape. Lightning is the spark of life that comes out of the Spirit, out of subtlest primordial energy-broth. It is visible thought or speech, a tongue of lightning in vast open sky. We are both this absence and this presence. What arises within us is likewise absence and presence, capacity and inspiration, emptiness and creative bliss, space that has been given shape.

Lightning is the outer and inner illumination, the clear light of Consciousness arising in vast inner space. It is the revelation of Consciousness in the atmosphere and the primal space of our awareness. It is related outwardly to stars and lightning and related inwardly to creative motivation and the light of awareness which is taking shape as thoughts. Thought is the expression of inner-light. Creative illumination is wisdom; it can appear as a lightning in the Deity-Mind-sphere, our vision of Reality. It travels through the eyes, or the primordial third eye of wisdom of Thunder-beings. Those are the eyes of heaven, the pure creative energy in the universe. Even in our body, the eyes are the only pure congealed energy (and the awareness-light that comes through the eyes is pure uncongealed energy). The eyes of Thunder-beings symbolize limitless vision or omniscience. They are the windows to omnipresent Mind. The Spirit is an eye. The Spirit reveals itself through the eyes.

Shiva, Durga, Kali, Lei Tzu and others emit lightning from a third-eye. Many Oriental Wisdom-beings are three-eyed, some emit lightning through it. The four-winged arch-angels and the Heavenly Ofanim (Wheels) of the Hebrew wisdom tradition, have eyes all over. Kalagni Rudra (Shiva) has a thousand eyes as does Thousand-armed Chenrezig. Indra took the form of a peacock with 100 eyes in its feathers. There is nowhere that the Spirit does not see, it uses our very own eyes. Eyes are conduits for awareness, the passage of consciousness in and out. When Thunder-bird opens his eyes, the universe suddenly becomes illuminated. The winged-power travels from the heart, through the eyes, the true windows of the soul. The illumination is pure love. He expresses the activity of depositing winged-power (wisdom and power) wherever lightning strikes. He puts it into the earth and the minds of his children who dream of him. His sight penetrates whatever it sees. What they see they become one with. Their penetrating vision sees all in the stainless mirror of itself, in such a way enlightening their children with luminous spirit. Their hearts are filled with undiminishing love. It follows a channel through the eyes (or another part of their body). They're looking upon us with their heart, with compassion. The awakened heart is winged. That heart is an eye.

In the sky the lightning follows a passage as well, that opens up between the heart of heaven at the nucleus of a thunder-cloud and the earth. In such a way are heaven and earth united. When the Mystery opens its eyes, the universe becomes awakened within its infinite being. This describes the emanation of the universe by Shiva and the activity of the light to awaken all minds. This opening is the revelation of the wisdom-mind, or our primordial awareness and is depicted by the third-eye. It is our inner opening called the mysterious pass or the eye of wisdom, it is our inner drop of wisdom and the gate to the City of Lightning. Awareness or awakening is the entrance to the City of Lightning. The method of entering or awakening is the purification or unveiling of our pure inner vision and is based on our alignment and the openness of our heart. If we open our heart and turn it toward the Dharma spheres, then the City of Wisdom will be reflected in the mirror of the mind, to allow Wisdom to work on us and through us.

Thunder-bird has the attributes of the eagle, but the two are not identicle. They are related, but the eagle is an animal, the Thunder-bird is not. Eagle, like Thunder-bird stands for illumination of the mind, creative power and fearlessness. Like their elders they have keen eyesight, are guardians and predators. They capture the weak and sick to help keep nature in balance, to prevent the spread of disease. Thunder-birds destroy the sources of illness in the macrocosm and the source of suffering in the microcosm. Those sources of illness are symbolized as serpents. Some eagles devour serpents like Thunder-birds. Further meaning of this activity will be elaborated in the interpretation of the three traditions given below.

Thunder-birds hatch eggs. In the macrocosm it is a symbol of fertility, new birth, the birth of lightning out of the earth at the beginning of time, in the spring and from the clouds each storm. The egg is potential existence, so it could stand for the space out of which solidity develops and the earth out of which life develops. The egg or sphere is the shape of the integral spirit in the universe. Clouds are the bodies of Thunder-beings; stars are likewise the bodies of natural deities. Our round head is an image of this energy, so is our complete energy-egg which surrounds and interpenetrates us. The seed, fruit, mountain, and circle are further representations of this unified Reality. The path of divine energy is circular, expressing itself through cycles. The egg is the capacity or creative potential out of which things develop, specifically the Thunder-egg or Garuda egg represents the human potential to become Thunder-bird. That sphere is the same womb that gives birth to universes as that which gives birth to enlightened minds. The egg or nest is what we build out of our life, the foundation of our present and future existence. Since the Thunder-bird nest is made from dried bones, or the Deities Palace sits atop a mountain of skulls, it symbolizes the indestructible foundation upon which we build our future life. The growth of the fetal Thunder-bird is symbolic of our real training, discipline, maturation and growth of natural wisdom that must take place in order to effect birth into the subtle realms as a divine being. Even if our aspiration isn't as high, if we want unbroken bliss and equanimity the mind-training must still be embraced. It just so happens that it results in immortality as the angelic state. It happens through the sphere of sacred light. We must undertake mind-training in order to mature into a spiritual being, which implies flight, both literal and metaphysical. The metaphysical meaning of flight is the goal of life and spiritual practice. Literal flight is merely a side-effect of practicing cultivation. Metaphysical flight is union with the Wisdom-being, the blissful expansion of the mind absorbed in the Undifferentiated. Such is the winged-heart. The essence of the training is mind-control, learning to tame the mind. All the spiritual practices have this discipline as their foundation. In the thunder-method, by concentrating on image and name, the mind is electrified, it becomes subtle by

being awakened and set free of its limitation, of negativity obstructing the mind. It is like a bird in a cage of its own illusions, and is going to be awakened to the fact that it is free from the beginning, that the mind is innately pure from the beginning. The thunder-bolt is unstoppable, so it clears out all obstruction to growth and happiness in the two spheres. The gross elements of the body dissolve into their light-source. What remains is an inherent foundation of empty space and light, which is our nest. The traditions abound in examples of those who, having reached the fruition of their practice, flew away, dissolved into subtle substance, rainbows or thunder-storms. Since the natural state of the mind, its capacity, does not degenerate, this achievement will be open to us. Accomplishment is the result of a natural life, spirituality appears extraordinary because what is ordinary (mundane) is unnatural.

Thunder-beings and Migratory Birds

There is another deep connection between birds and Thunder-birds, besides the spiritual one born out in iconography. Some birds signal thunder-storm activity, all birds are weather sensitive, and are able to respond to things before they occur. Many birds transmigrate North-South. Scientists cannot determine the real cause because it lies in the mind, the only instrument which measures this level of subtlety is the clear mind. Birds telepathically follow the fluctuations in the magnetic field that surrounds the earth. The shift in currents corresponds with the changing seasons. As its current shifts, the Thunder-birds move North or South, as instruments of seasonal transition. Migratory birds follow the same magnetic field. They have a crystal inside the front of their head which receives subtle impressions from the electro-magnetic current. The result is that the incidence of thunder-storms and the appearance of birds in a particular place are the same.

The magnetic field is being altered by human endeavors, by chaotic energy frequencies put out by T.V., radio, telephone, computers, cars, and a host of other electrical noise equipment. This directly affects the field and therefore affects seasonal transition which affects rainfall, which affects crops, which affects the earths inhabitants. A place that was once desert becomes a flood plain, a place that was once fertile becomes a desert. It is one factor which causes floods and droughts. Mother nature is a mirror, she is not indifferent, humans have become indifferent to the ways of nature. Nature simply responds to what people are creating. Children and sensitive people are also responsive to these frequencies, because their minds are like tender shoots. It causes the aggravation of our natural bodily fields, electricities and humors. It affects body and mind. It is a contributing factor to children becoming uncontrollable. It also affects the animals and birds that live in the sky. Such electrical chaos is very disruptive to life.

We receive our electricity from the atmosphere, so in a sense we get it from the Thunder-beings. It is from the fire (sun) and water. Manifold life explosion (nature) is woven out of these powers, but the organizational power precedes them as the wisdom-roots of the 5 element display. The gross element transformation of nature which we see and participate in is controlled by Primordial Divinity, by the spiritual-body of the Mystery. We receive subtle electricity from them, such as consciousness and internal energy for bodily and mental functioning, which sustains us on multiple levels. And we receive gross electricity from them which we harvest through generators' electric field, which appears to make our life simpler. Like fire, electricity was no doubt intended as a gift, and therefore must be respected. If we don't respect it, its not a matter of angering God, but the result is that we cause our own calamity. (The same is true of the body and mind, because people fail to respect bodily electricity through moderate activity they fall ill, because they fail to respect mind's gentle energy, by sexual misconduct and taking drugs, they cause mental problems. Guru Rinpoche says that drugs have an adverse effect on the mind's inner energy channels, flows, drops and chakras, which can manifest in our present or future lives. Therefore abstain from them). Electricity needs to be respected and should never be used destructively or unnecessarily. It should be used in moderation. Moderation is the expression of naturalness, and gives way to balance.

The Origin of Civilization in Oriental Traditions

People are a natural development of the universe and earth, of nature. By living close to nature we might develop an appreciation for life and respect for our temporary abode. The Oriental traditions (over the occidental Judeo-Christian-Muslim) emphasize an appreciation for nature and life. These systems present the highest or broadest view, which teaches the inherent perfection, and pristine beauty of all phenomena, which arise from a wisdom-Source, and never cease from shining as that inexhaustible and perfect Source.

We have arisen from Deity's vast-inner-space and are sustained by their all-pervasive light as extensions of their Infinite Vision. The spirits of living beings are from the living space, which is the Mystery's gossamer light-breath shaped into a super-mundane abode. Everything arises according to the pure energy of this Wisdom-Source. It arises as pure and undefiled; the Origin is the very description of our original nature. The two are never separate, we are as though immersed in the Spirit as a bead of dew in the sea.

The universe evolved the condition for stars, then planets. The earth likewise evolved the condition for life out of fire and water. Metaphorically, the stone head of the earth opened, exploding with thunder and lightning, its potential power from the Spirit. From thunder and lightning arose fire and water. So now when fire and water clash there is thunder and lightning. From fire and water arose the condition for manifold life. First out of lightning there was vegetation which created the conditions for harmonious animal life. Out of lightning arose harmonious animal life which created the condition for human life. And harmonious human life created the condition for angelic life. Harmonious angelic life creates the condition for melting into infinite inconceivable life.

People came through the doorway of the stars, the seven star crown of the Pleiades. The Primordial Wisdom-beings were the first people, we are their descendants. (They do not require space ships to travel. They do not look like E.T. They are not confined to a bodily existence on another planet somewhere. They do not abduct people. They respect our personal freedom.) We shouldn't make too much of the fact that we come from outer space. What is truly important is that we learn to become earth people first, to have respect for the earth, to learn to live amidst all its inhabitants in peace. We can gain wisdom from star-beings, our ancestors, but their wisdom simply instructs us in learning to live here on earth in a creative way. They do not teach us what is irrelevant, such as learning to live up there in space. The goal means cultivating openness like space and living like an angel, with golden heavenly qualities.

Thunder and lightning is the initiating vehicle for spiritual and earthly existence. Because nature has arisen from it, when it presents itself before us, there is joy and wonder, familiarity and astonishment. It is in the manifold heart of life. It is in the fire evolving us from within. It burns for God (subtle wisdom). Everything is on fire with God. It is the life of our life. It is the yearning which returns us to the beginning of the universe.

We have a natural relationship with all the beings of the universe, who share inherent nature. We can determine which Wisdom-sphere we are related to, which we resonate with and align with them. Their energy will be similar to our own, so they feel familiar. We are extensions of them on earth. They gave birth to civilization on earth. Originally people lived in harmony with the earth, we lived as our god-parents lived, whose ways we followed. Natural living meant wisdom was undiminishing, and virtuous behavior was its spontaneous expression. People were not primitive like apes and certainly didn't evolve out of apes. We've descended from Wisdom-beings. (Animals likewise have their own distinct spirits and nature, when Oriental masters speak of reincarnation in animal realms what they mean is the degenerate mind takes on the poor qualities and conditions attributed to animals; it is a skillful means to avert humans from animalistic behavior. However the individual classes of beings do re-incarnate, and the law of cause and effect does determine our future state. It is a shock tactic, which instills a sense of the preciousness of human life to teach that humans can incarnate as animals. It also causes people to have great compassion for animals which are thought to be inferior. Most Buddhist and Hindu teachers feel that this is truly possible, but the mahasiddhas taught this to shock people into virtuous behavior. This teaching suggests that as humans we have the greatest potential for attaining enlightenment of the 6 classes of beings. The activities ascribed to animals should not be embraced by people, or those ascribed to hell-beings, hungry ghosts, demi-gods or gods. These are pride, greed, laziness, lust, anger and impatience, we should only embrace Buddha activity which is patience, generosity, compassion, humility, by choosing these our state of mind becomes perfected, we become happy and at peace. We might see certain animal characteristics in people because they have accumulated this activity which is energy. The primordial state is not accumulated but is beneath and before all accumulation. To accumulate or gather light is actually the process of removing something, negative energy gathered by negative actions. Animals

have their own distinct souls and choose virtuous activity and to love just as we do. For this reason animals can and do achieve themselves as Wisdom-deity. They can appear to us in dreams and vision and give us their wisdom, which benefits us. So it is not just people who can attain the Primordial state. Several wise animals have come to me, particularly those associated with the Thunder-beings, such as horse, dog, butterfly, dragonfly, bear, dragon, whale, dolphin, owl, warbler, eagle. . . . The Primordial Thunder Lord, the Mystery has emanated the unique souls of all beings out of Wisdom. The Mystery has not emanated hell-beings and ghosts, those are people and animals and beings who lived horrible lives with no care of others, so they caused the reality they experience, it rises up to hurt them as they hurt others, it is their own mind being reflected in the perfect mirror of Primordial Wisdom. Sublime Beings see reality as a great blessing, a source of pure pleasure and inspiration, a magnificent display of wisdom. Nature supports them as they supported all beings.)

People have developed a taste for technology and a complex life-style, calling it evolved while it goes against nature, and as such creates unnecessary troubles. The Oriental traditions teach that the human mind, including the intellect was more advanced in previous civilization. Indications of this are the advanced medicine they had of performing brain and heart transplants, and the atomic weaponry developed and detonated in India. 50,000 years ago the previous civilization destroyed itself this way. Ultimately the previous civilizations degenerated and destroyed themselves or were destroyed by natural measures, like deluge, earthquakes, volcanoes or ice age brought forth by a shift in the poles. Civilizations arise and dissolve by grand seasons of the earth. Each civilization is separated by an ice-age, a winter that neutralizes all disharmonious life or a period of rest. These seasons are governed by the movement of the solar system around the Pole Star. Keep in mind the Thunder-beings control all seasonal transition, from the universal to the minute.

It is taught in the Tantric traditions that humans began as giants, spiritual and physical, then shrunk in size and wisdom. Then they expanded again to superhuman stature, with a tremendous life-span. This is most likely governed by the natural movement of the Solar system around the Pole Star. The Pole Star is the Dharmachakra or Heart Wheel of the universe, the spiritual government of the cosmos. As we move closer to it in our orbit, Dharma becomes stronger in the world, as we move further away, Dharma holds less sway in our lives. At a certain point Dharma becomes virtually non-existent, the world is completely degenerate, bereft of virtue; life-span decreases to 10 years and stature to smaller than a spider. It would be wise of us to make use of the Dharma and attain the state beyond the universe and its cycles, to become Lords of the Universe, Awakened Ones. In Vajrayana this state is called Mahamudra, one meaning of which is "great seal". This seal implies that all lower states of suffering are sealed off, that one is too pure to incarnate directly, but instead creates emanations and activity.

The Chinese tradition, whose origins are the divine immortals, speaks of 10 civilizations called Kis. Both Sanatan Dharma and Buddha Dharma speak of previous civilizations, spanning billions of years. In 30,000 B.C. the Indian subcontinent extended to Australia and Africa—this is referred to as Kumari Kandam or Lemuria. It is now submerged. In these traditions human life extends back billions of years; there are innumerable eons (kalpas: cosmic cycles), within which cycles of 4 or 5 world systems revolve. The basis of earthly development is cyclic, its arising is based on the cycles of the constellations around the Pole Star. The arising and falling away of humanity is based on the conditions of the universe and earth. Most traditional wisdom suggests that the origin of the present civilization is with the Wisdom-beings who descended at the end of the last ice-age before 12,000 B.C., gave birth to the first human beings, an act that they repeat successively, like the renewal of seasons, over at least 432 million years.

When civilizations become degenerate, when wars, death and immense suffering are the rule, nature mirrors that behavior. So previous civilization brought about their own demise. The earth has a natural way of neutralizing what is harmful. In winter, snow blankets the earth, burning up harmful bacteria and viruses. Likewise, the earth, during deluge neutralized what was harmful within its sphere, unleashing earthquakes, fires, winds and floods that wiped out previous civilizations. The deluge myth is universal; the Aztecs, Mayans, Hopi, Navajo, Australian aboriginals, Persians, Chinese, Hindu, Vajrayana and Judaic traditions all teach that previous civilizations existed and were destroyed through natural measure. Most often the Thunder-beings are thought to cause the deluge. But, in actuality, the Thunder-beings are serving their purpose as nature to destroy the causes of suffering in order to restore nature as a balance between forces. Their function is always to maintain harmony on earth. The ultimate cause is not necessarily the Thunder-beings, but with the nature of human activity. The universe is responsive like a mirror, so there is repayment for everything we do. The Thunder-beings preserve people who lead good lives, the universe protects them as they protected the universe. The wise activity of the Thunder-beings is unfathomable, until you become one yourself it cannot be understood fully. There is a story from India which tells how an entire village suffering from drought gathered at the temple of their Deity where they prayed for rain. The Spirit responded thus: "Whatever We do is for the betterment of our purpose. Ye have no right to interfere with our work . . ." (84 Khan). Nevertheless the people offered up their cries. The deity responded thus: "Your prayers, fastings, and sacrifices have induced Us to grant for this one year as much rain as ye desire." (84-85 Ibid). So the people prayed for rain and got what they asked for. An ideal crop arose, more than ever before. But all those who ate of the crop died. The survivors sought the deity in perplexity. He replied to their complaints thus: "It was our wrath but your folly for interfering with our work. We sometimes send a drought and at other times a flood so that a portion of you crops may be destroyed, but We have our reasons for so doing. For in this way all that is poisonous and undesirable in them is also destroyed, leaving only what is beneficial for the preservation of you life" (85 Ibid). The people prostrated saying, "We shall never again try to control the affairs of the universe. Thou art the Creator and Thou art the Controller. We are Thine innocent children, and Thou alone knowest what is best for us" (85 Ibid).

The Oriental traditions teach that wisdom had once governed the body. One indication of this is the duration of peoples lives which spanned 100's of years, another is the simplicity with which people lived. Our ancestors lived much longer because they practiced non-killing. Because we have taken life previously, our own life-span is vastly reduced. Yogis who live according to their spirit live the way people did millenia ago, and very often have the capacity to remain on the earth for a 120 year minimum. Yogis who purify all negative karma or energy in their body-mind attain immortality. Once the natural cycle of one life is over they usually disappear from ordinary reality, but continue to shine on the world and draw sentient beings to Dharma.

Our ancestor-deities were much larger in stature, which is a reflection of spiritual stature, wisdom-clear-light. The light is bigger so the container must be bigger. We have shrunk as a result of degenerate behavior, which has caused our light to diminish its field. Now when Wisdom-beings take a robe, like Melchisedek, Christ, Mahavatar Babaji, or Guru Rinpoche, it appears like our own, because it is suitable to our phenomenon. No-one would be able to relate to a giant on the earth, its hard enough relating to holy people's mind, we call them contraries and deem them crazy.

Our Deity ancestors were balanced male-female beings. Because of our attachment to the body our mind thinks it is actually conditioned by male-female, but wisdom-mind is untouched by this dualistic view. By aligning with Wisdom-deities our energy becomes balanced. One of the functions of worshiping a male form of Deity is to balance imbalance in female shakti. Likewise the function of worshiping female Deity form is to bring male shakti into balance. So you might say one of the reasons that Wisdom-deity manifests in a male or female form is to provide a tool for balancing these energies.

The early people did not require sleep, food or engagement in habitual acts which arise from bodily impulses. Because the Medulla Oblongata was larger and more developed, people were able to take nourishment directly from the sun through a chakra at the base of the neck. Our habits have created the condition in which we must ingest the sun in the form of plants and animals—this often requires the taking of life. The taking of life is responsible for decrease in our life-span.

Some yogis and yoginis have demonstrated the remarkable ability of deriving nourishment directly from the sun through a mantra-practice of ingesting the life-force through the chakra of the Medulla Oblongata and are able to successfully live without material food. These same individuals generally require little or no sleep as well. This is not to say that we should engage in the same, but we definitely need to follow the example of these accomplished ones by living according to the natural religion which sets us in harmony with all beings—the essence of which is truth, simplicity and love. Those who continue to practice natural religion live very simply as house-holders, yogis, shamans or earth-people, very close to

nature. Our ancestors were not ape-like cave-men, they were extemely wise, simple, beautiful people, who appreciated natural splendor and lived in blissful relationship with nature. Do not denegrate the saints who aspire to live this life today. They know that the Source of inner well-being is also the Source of nature. To connect with inner well-being is to connect with nature. Living in harmony with nature is a path to inner well-being.

Our ancestors never departed from their natural state, so did not require religion. When wisdom is the rule, there is no need to discuss it; such is the case in the subtle realms. So "Garden of Eden" might be an appropriate way of describing a state of mind and condition of early civilization.

Over thousands of years self-centered habitual behavior replaced spontaneous behavior. The body for many has come to govern the spirit as the impulses dictate. So the subtle system of inner channels and energy, the divine reflection in people has become obscured. We have become creatures of physical habit. Our bodies require nourishment based on habit. And our habits have turned wisdom-substance bodies into gross energy forms. Initially bodies didn't require such things as sleep, food, etc. Because the subtle body constitutes our natural state we can transform our gross vision bodies into subtle wisdom bodies supported by superluminal light. Celestial vitality is responsible for achievement of immortality. Because Wisdom Deity controls this light, we might say that it is not an attainment, but a gift bestowed upon us out of Deity's love. We invoke it and apply the light to refine what suffers, what changes into what is continuous, undying, free of suffering, beyond the universe. All three traditions believe in the attainment of immortality and realization.

We achieve this by changing our habits. Because poor mental habits are the root of our suffering and cyclic existence, we develop excellent mental habits, like mantra repetition. By doing so we develop the habit of ingesting wisdom (light), and dissolving ignorance, until the body of gross energy has dissolved completely into light. Once wisdom saturates the heart or mind, then it arises spontaneously or naturally, and expresses pure positive qualities as love. When all gross energy is dissolved into the Absolute or actual nature of nature, then what arises is not conditioned by the universe, but exists spontaneously as a light-projection of the Deity, which is free of the fetters of material existence, can come and go as it pleases, and has complete control over the elements which are light dancing in space. Such a person abides at the beginning of the universe and therefore has incredible control over the universe, by having complete control over mind and body.

When a particular civilization requires wisdom it is transmitted from the Wisdom-sphere to earthly messengers. Examples include the multiple transmissions of Taoist science to earthly immortals; the Tantras to mahasiddhas by Shiva, Buddha and Dakinis; Kabbalah transmisions to Enoch, Melchisedek, Moses etc. by Yahveh, and so on. Because spiritual reality is one unified continuum of Mind, we find immense parallels between the various religious symbols, they all have arisen from the same deep level of Consciousness. There is no dispute amongst the Deities of the subtlest spheres; where you read about such disaffiliation it is a symbol applicable to earthly existence, to human exile and the friction between dark and light forces and confused minds.

Scholars have speculated on the interconnectedness of human cultures by suggesting that all cultures were one, that the continents were one land mass. An educated guess, but incorrect. On the earthly planes, the universal spirit functions through its clear messengers to transmit spiritual reality and method. These people are called prophets or siddhas, perfected beings. In many instances they have traveled via clairportation or chariot to distant lands to transmit the dharma, which accounts for the same religious ideas in cultures vastly separate as India and South America. (From India ancient mahasiddhas traveled by chariot to South America). The Oriental traditions are closely linked in the same way. Mahasiddhas of the Shaiva Dharma traveled to China and manifested there as Immortals, and no doubt, Immortals from China traveled to India and did the same. One example concerns the great master of Mahavatar Shiva Babaji. The name of this mahasiddha was Boganathar. After teaching for perhaps a thousand years in India, he flew to China and took a body. While there he taught internal alchemy and was known as BoYang and referred to by the epithet Lao Tzu, the author of a principle text on Taoist teachings and the originator of a lineage of 12 profound sciences. There are other examples of such cross-cultural transmissions by beings that lived on earth for thousands of years. I think Mahavatar Shiva Babaji has been on earth for several thousand years. And who said the mahasiddhas ever left anyway? When we become inspired they are with us guiding our thoughts and causing good ideas to appear spontaneously. Such is another way in which embodied masters transmit ideas to vastly different cultures. The language they speak is eternal language of the Spirit, it transcends cultural distinctions. It goes out across the world as a subtle sound-wave, sometimes projected with seed-sound, sometimes enveloped in silence.

Internal Alchemy in Oriental Traditions

Our life being has been created through eons of spiritual development, through the generation of energy from the universe. We have created the present configuration and it stands to reason that we are creating our future life or destiny based on the mirror-like quality of the universe, of gross and subtle energy. Therefore we seek to live for the future, and not just the present life. Living beings magnetize and draw in natural energy from the field of existence, from stars, moon, storms, directional energies, the geography, such as oceans, mountains and the human environment. We can turn our mind-mirror upon the Dharmaspheres of Wisdom-beings, and receive nourishment of pristine qualities. This was how the first people lived and how the yogis live. If we choose to attune with the natural Wisdom-beings, through cultivating wisdom and kindness, then we become like those who achieved themselves before us. We have the potential for becoming an extension of the Wisdom-sphere in the universe.

There's a whole spectrum of energy in the universe from dark energy corresponding to the elements and cold energies of the directions to subtlest positive, creative energy which is the root of all form and corresponds with the subtle states of heavenly life or the Wisdom-beings. The universe is a mixture of both energies. In the microcosm the gross energies correspond with physical energy of the muscles and glandular secretions and is identified with the lower torso since most of this energy gathers below the navel. The subtle energies are primordial extensions of subtle spiritual beings and corresponds with the inner heart drop, mysterious pearl and crown drops, which are sparks of wisdom and blissful energy and might be referred to as our inner God or Light by virtue of the fact that it is our inheritance from the Wisdom-beings. In the Tantric traditions these drops are Deities or Dakinis.

Living beings have two capacities of transformation, one is receptive and absorbs energy, it is an open ear, the potential space of all minds in which anything and everything is possible, we call this magnetic. The other aspect is creative and radiates energy; it is the arising and display of appearances in the mind, it is the sunglobe, moon, cloud, lightning, thunder, rain, rainbows and the signs of life, inner and outer worlds effervescing in the space of the mind. We call this electric. Mind develops within an energy-egg in which energy is absorbed and radiated. Phenomena are reflected on the mind-mirror. To whatever sphere we turn our mind, toward whatever thought and activity, that is the sphere which the mind will reflect. The polarization of the two functions of energy creates the electro-magnetic body or egg within which beings have the potential to develop into spiritual existence, in which humans have the potential to develop into angelic winged-babies, and baby Thunder-birds. Because the multi-universe is growing, it typifies the nature of the wisdom-essence whose various attributes symbolize growth as being and the unfolding of wisdom as the way of the universe.

Our development happens through dissolution. If we have connected with wisdom there is a reduction, a transmutation, a cooking or firing, a constant death and re-mergence, a movement through fire from dark to light. Wisdom reduces the gross energy surrounding the heart to something extremely subtle and virtually indetectable, which can appear through creative energy however it chooses. We are reduced to our true nature which feels like the true nature of the Deity, like nothing, like tranquil open space. The root of all negativity is liberated or destroyed. That which obstructs the free-flow of the heart-of-unstained-purity is going to be eliminated, widdled down or refined into an ever more subtle and precious energetic substance. This whole process is referred to as alchemy in the three Oriental traditions and is reflected in the outer alchemy of transmuting base metals into gold. We refine our internal energy from something that is like mercury, into something like gold. Literally refined energy appears golden.

Mystically we die. We keep repeating this process in order to emerge continuously abiding in bliss, new and beautiful, adamantine and clear, an undecaying Immortal Wisdom-being. Once we connect with wisdom, the goal seems ineluctable; wisdom implies not returning to suffering. We keep recreating and destroying until nothing remains but the indestructible and immutable heart of the Wisdom-mind which we become through and through. From such a state the crystalline limitless Void radiates—one Supernal heart is radiating, and everything it does is out of love and produces liberation wherever it shines. The characteristics of all its natural emanations, which we are, are the free radiance from a limitless center and its ebullient responsiveness or mirror-like quality, its electro-magnetism together symbolized by sun and moon, fire and water, lightning-bolt and sky, heaven and earth, form and emptiness, male and female.

Together these poles produce existence. Through friction they create electrical stimulation in the universe, from lightning to our inner thought. The Infinite heart of these two aspects is the vajra. It is ultimate wisdom-mind unveiled and the power of the mind to assist others to unveil it: wisdom and compassion. It is concealed within the drop of the heart, as the lightning was inside the earth. (In Deity yoga we often visualize a vajra at the heart of the Deity). It came from heaven with us and can never be defiled. When conditions are right it arises. It is always arising either concealed or unconcealed, through our actions; those which are imperfect are the sign of a heart concealed in unawareness, those which are perfect are the symbol of the revealed heart. The breakthrough that the heart makes, the revelation of its wisdom through luminous compassion is symbolized by lightning and thunder. Sky symbolizes the capacity for enlightenment, thunder symbolizes the breakthrough, lightning the simultaneous revelation.

The achievement of highest spiritual evolution, our creation of spirit and arising into subtle space is the motivation of the Oriental traditions, while the human form is considered the most auspicious station from which to achieve this. This form is called the base, the place from which we begin our practice, what we have to work with. It includes the entire psycho-physical organism as a form of energy which is manipulable, which is non-dual as opposed to fixed. Non-dual first means that ones total being is a wisdom-extension of the Mysterious Source, there is nothing within it that is not inherently good, perfect and beautiful. Its contents are shining-deities, it is the palace or City of the Absolute, what we consider harmful and poisonous exists to establish harmonious existence, and needn't be regarded with fear, but with love, this love is bliss. Secondly non-dual implies something transformable, energetic, composed of space and light. If one falsely believes the mind to be dual, fixed, gross, solid, liquid . . . then one is less likely to think it can be liberated in the space of life. Perhaps this leaves one to rely on attaining enlightenment or God when one dies. But the mind must be controlled, stabilized and spiritualized in order to dwell in the midst of Supernal Light. The basis of spiritual practice is to restore the natural state of the mind, which in Tantra is achieved by establishing some connection or positive relationship to Wisdom-spheres. In this way at least we will become accustomed to the Light, and have the grace of the divine so that whatever future existence we move into will be positive. In this text we focus on the specific spheres where Wisdom-beings emanate lightning, thunder and Thunder-being imagery, and in the traditions presented herein the goal is achievement in one lifetime, this one! The Oriental traditions teach us how to connect with the highest positive energy of nature embodied in the Wisdom-beings who are its Source like a generator which provides electricity for an entire city, or the Sun which provides light and life for an entire planet and solar system.

Tantra is a way of plugging into the subtle current of the universe, the primordial energy socket of the Deity, to become liberated and to realize we're that very current. To realize this is to become a dharma-socket for others to plug into. In Tantric imagery and method the vajra has this significance. It is a reminder of who we are so that we can train to relax into that. Vajra is also the subtle electrical currents, the flames of transformation, the grace-waves of the Deity which are the Deity entering our mind to melt our afflictions. When the frozen brittle ice of mundane-mind is melted the true flexible fluid nature of Oceanic-mind is liberated. The roots of suffering previously generated by ignorant thought, speech and activity are barb-qued in the fires of wisdom. The nature of awareness changes, the mind and world actually have a tendency to appear brighter, fuller and deeper. The mind is lightened and set free and reality is perceived in the light of its heaven. We are re-created and re-assembled through that fire, arising like the golden phoenix bird, shining as a spark of primordial divine spirit surging in the Great Ultimate.

The mind recognizes its primordial nature by being purified in this way: Deity's vajra-grace electrifies the inner winds (energy) which obscure the pure drop of awareness. Impure winds manifest as thoughts and emotional afflictions. Purified winds allow the heart awareness to be clear. When it's clear it is responsive, soft and flexible, so it melts into sadness-bliss. It is reflecting, diamond-hard and imperturbable, so nothing can move or agitate it, it cannot become afflicted emotion.

If we develop a positive aspiration to practice spirituality and nurture some devotion through divine imagery then we will be blessed with that. It will cause us to embrace the work now, to gather together (in a sangha or kula, spiritual family), or pursue solitude. In either case the Wisdom-spheres will rain down their blessings, particularly when the chatter is complete and the practice begins. If we fail to pursue wisdom and continue generating poor quality energy through mundane activity, according to tradition, we can guarantee some future suffering. If we want to follow the way of yogis we must stop living for this life alone. Mind is without beginning or end, so we will inevitably experience the results of our actions. The way of yogis is to live for the future. We are creating our future now. Best to create an enlightened future by living compassionately and cultivating wisdom.

Karma cannot be escaped since we cannot escape ourselves, our actions remain with us. Negative traces of actions are actually annihilated, absorbed or awakened by the Light of positive traces. Therefore the way to purify oneself of previous misdeeds is through positive activity. Since the root of our activity is intention or energy, it is positive energy which must be cultivated. Because spiritual cultivation generates positive energy it is a positive act and a means to purification. Our aim is complete purification. Complete purification means ending rebirth. This becomes the basis, practice and goal of the Oriental traditions. The conception which spurs the change of heart, the realization which is tantamount to set the mind toward its goal is the understanding of the nature of cause and effect. With this in mind we develop a clear understanding of what kinds of activity propel us toward bliss and liberate suffering. The way to follow our bliss is always through virtue. Habitual tendencies generated from mundane activity recycle in the mind until the connection is broken by reconnecting with activity which brings about an unbroken state of bliss, equanimity and tranquility.

If a person dies the habitual tendencies become latent unless one recognizes the clear-light at death and merges with it, which still entails mind-training or purification. If this does not occur the habits become as seeds that magnetically draw the mind back to the world again and again, until through embracing the light, the cycle is broken. The Wisdom-light thoroughly awakens the condition of energy which draws one back into a body. This condition is attraction-repulsion, the veiled state of the heart. Its awakened state is pure electro-magnetic creative-receptive bliss-emptiness.

The grace of the Wisdom-beings which shines as an inexhaustible Sun in and as all things, is responsible for the turning of our heart. It takes the shape of a wisdom bolt, and is the power to awaken all hearts. This Sun produces the natural spiritual evolution and dance of all life, growth into spirit. Generally we call this Light by the name of the Absolute. It is the primordial condition of non-duality at the deep nature of the mind. In Vajrayana this state is known as Wheel of Supreme Bliss. In Shaiva Tantra it is Stellar-Wheel of Infinite Consciousness. In Taoism it is called Tao, Wheel of the Great Ultimate.

When the mind is connected to Wisdom, it expands and embodies higher and subtler frequencies of energy until it reaches its subtlest state, which is like a Star in space, which is denoted by the names Shiva, Buddha and Tao.

The physical realm is a transitional realm in which our purpose is to refine our energy into its subtlest state which will sustain a joyous existence wherever it happens to be, on earth or some other realm. We must not waste time, if the opportunity presents itself to learn dharma-paths from a qualified master to return to our true nature, then we are very blessed and hopefully will aspire to achieve our goal. And if we don't have such an opportunity, the initiation practices presented herein (like Shiva's mantra), if used properly and diligently, are excellent methods of connecting with wisdom. Often for Westerners such a simple introduction to the Deity is enough, and causes the Deity's response, which causes us to generate devotion and to seek the Deity in human form (guru). It is up to us to practice. The more we practice (methods of cultivation and compassion) the greater the flow of blessings, the quicker our enlightenment.

We have all come here to earth out of an enlightened choice We made, as Spirit. Our individual existence came about through Wisdom-deities motivation to benefit beings. We are the result of that motivation, we arose here to fulfill that motivation. Wisdom Deity chose to be in multiple places at once to benefit beings to help, so that is what we are. So we must adhere to this way, it is the supreme and sole reason for existence, the dream we lived before we were born. We are Light of the Unseen.

Another way that Deities choose to be on earth is in our temples, in the art, sculpture and so on. Originally Deities appeared spontaneously on the earth to benefit beings, in body's of light surrounded by a mandala or retinue of mind-born emanations. They took up seats in Mt. abodes, inside the mountains, or they descended with a temple in form or image. For example in ancient times beings requested Shiva to be present on earth, so a mandala descended in the center of which was an image or lingam—"symbol" of the Deity Undifferentiated. These objects continue to appear in various places. In recent times there are 12 spontaneously-arisen ones on the earth, called Jyotirlingam "light symbol." The Deity arose on earth and put a reminder on earth of the nature of who we are. Wisdom-beings continue to do this in modern times, images of Tara appear in stone, images of Guru Rinpoche appear in hidden treasures, images of Thunder-beings appear out of cloud and rainbow light, images of Wisdom-deities appear in bodies out of thin air, or lightning. When we invoke the Deity with mantra, the subtle image appears before us and within us. When we have images consecrated or "awakened" then Deity is actually there, alive before us. If your mind is clear you can see the image move, blink, dematerialize. If you're extraordinarily wise, then you can receive teaching through the image, anything is possible. So we are actually directing our devotion to the Deity through the image. When people gather in Deity's name he descends and blesses people. He often uses imagery to awaken our hearts. For example you could be looking at an image of Shiva with his beautiful white complection, moustache, black hair, cranial crescent, and all of a sudden are overwhelmed with love in your heart, this devotion invokes Deity to flood you with light. The light then awakens you, causes you to remember your unity with Deity, causes you to remember that's you, an image of your enlightenment.

The Alchemy of Clear-light Imagery

We have clear-light imagery to recollect our fully awake nature. The Thunder-beings provide us with their images, or revealed vision-bodies, which are efficacious in the visualization based practice of aligning ourselves with the all-pervasive Wisdom Mind, absorbing its qualities to awaken our fully awakened wisdom-nature, our complete potential. Their image, name and the method of their application can also be used with the altruistic purposes of healing, pacifying negativity, exorcising, redeeming souls and controlling weather.

Through an energy-body or cloak they project images of themselves, living image-bodies. These image bodies are light-vessels by which profound wisdom can enter the mind sphere of sentient beings. These image-bodies, appearing as the nucleus of a formless Spirit, are the dynamic, continuous forms of the Wisdom-beings. They are like a 3-dimensional film of dynamic-light, of movement through space, of dancing rainbow-light, of flying winged-power, of flashing self-appearing light. The Deity is not born, does not remain and is without end. His imagery is miraculously generated and is reflected in the mind and atmosphere for the benefit of all beings, based on the phenomena of sentient beings. They are a five-light garland appearing in Eternity as a concentration of grace, a focal point of spacious awareness and love. These images can be seen by the clear, natural minds of people. They are not remote from us as long as we are not remote from them. They are Wisdom-beings clothed in subtle garments of light-vision and music. We are extensions of the Wisdom-beings clothed in gross garments of light-vision and music. The very deep nature of our mind is simultaneous to the nature of the Wisdom-beings who are emanating us. When we see them in mystical vision we are seeing our ultimate nature, we are seeing who we are, and at the same time we are seeing a Mystery which is thoroughly beyond all human minds. This subtle divine nature, this consciousness is infinite, and houses within it the Wisdom-beings of the universe like drops or sparks. In the vast body of wisdom-space these drops are controlled to move, to transmigrate in the atmosphere, to arise and dissolve in distinct human minds. Therefore, through our minds, the Wisdom-beings can be perceived. The Wisdom-being can be discovered within as our true perfected nature. The Wisdom-imagery awakens our infinite Consciousness. The Wisdom-being shows us our perfected nature. The Deity can be conjured to arise, to bring his power, to bring a solution to the mind puzzle or a disease. We can awaken to his all-pervasive essence as it exists as our very own heart. He is a lamp and transmits his light of wisdom into our heart, so in the glow we see our true wakefulness. From his lamp he lights our lamp. And our nature is awakened like lightning. And his lineage chain of lightning is on the earth. We are primordially awake like the lightning. Deity is a lamp of the heart, he transmits his light of wisdom through our heart, so in the glow all beings will be liberated within our domain. Diverse natures are awakened when Thunder Deity sets up his chain of lightnings.

In all cultural forms the Thunder-method is characterized by instantaneous illumination. In Tantra it is thought of as minute flashes or pulses of illumination. Thunder and lightning expresses complete awakening

as the nature and function of Thunder Mind. The Thunder-bolt is the mind and vitality of the Deity. The power of the all-pervasive Mind is infinite; when it concentrates or converges it appears as a lightning. It is the immutable Clear-Light-Mind magically displaying itself through wisdom-elements, the subtle root of material elements. When the Thunder-being wishes to display a visionary form body, he gathers his Mind and energy and appears out of vast inner space. The motivation is always compassionate, directed toward liberating all beings from suffering. Most humans cannot perceive the subtle formless life of the Deity, so the Wisdom-beings create an image so we can generate the devotion necessary to connect with Wisdom. The Deity manifests an image-body to give us a reminder and a tool to awaken the mind, to cause divine accomplishment, so the Deity can establish an unbroken chain of blessings on earth. Deity manifests as image and name to put some of his wisdom on the earth. The image is the Face of the formless Reality; while it takes form, it remains formless. Mind is the screen upon which he-she projects a subtle play of light and sound.

By Cities of Lightning we are referring to the creative imagery and function of the Thunder-beings in the universe. The Thunder-beings are formless beings, yet take form for human benefit. They take form in storms, in the stars, in human bodies and the bodies of other classes of beings, they took form on the earth as giants in ancient times, they appear in our mind as selfless thoughts, and in our dreams as Deity imagery. Within the Tantra we utilize these sacred images to awaken our mind, to become Deity, to embody Deity's wisdom and compassion on earth to help beings.

We ascend the lightning, it brings us back to the Wisdom-Source. The image is given to us to use as a ladder, a golden key and doorway to formless reality: tranquility, wisdom and bliss. It is our Origin, our way and potential for divinity. Therefore we may have some recognition of the Deity upon seeing or feeling his Mind. That Mind is a mirror for our own divine face. Whatever we worship will leave its sign on our mind. Because the image is an embodiment of the Absolute's natural beauty, we generate devotion, sacrificing our ego and attuning ourselves with the pure energy of the universe, which puts us ever in the Presence of the Mystery. From their perspective they are recreating us in their Image.

The image is an ebullient, living symbol of the Deity. If you just take the image for the entirety of the Deity, then its like seeing the tip of an iceberg and mistaking it for its entirety. The image is Wisdoms' spontaneous expression, like the bloom of a flower. Because it floods the mind with Wisdom, when it reveals itself, and when it is concentrated on during practice with a clear one-pointed mind, the nature of the Deity can be perceived. The Deity is known through the image. The image leads us to the Reality in the activity of its light.

The visionary image is the medium between the Infinite Mind and its extensions in the universe. They are extending themselves to the minds of all beings through symbol. They are designed for our purification, to purify fear and doubt. The interpretation of these wisdom-symbols requires a pure-mind, one akin to theirs which is free of fear and doubt. They can be known through the heart or intuitive experience as creative energy and blissful tranquility. Intuitive transmission arises before thought as a pulse, a slight flash out of silence. This is the same state from which Thunder-beings arise into symbol out of the Void of formlessness. Their images cannot be interpreted properly by an impure or clouded mind, one filled with doubt—that was the kind of view which colored the initial interpretation of these images (such as with the Tibetan Buddhist Deities). Doubt and fear are a distortion of pure creative energy. They cause that people should attempt to create something other than the truthful expression of Ultimate Reality. What people manifest becomes destructible and broken because that is the nature of its originating energy. Only sincere creative activity dedicated to help all beings echos forever in every direction under Eternity, and only such activity therefore can sustain an unlimited existence in pure positive states. So the proper interpretation of these wisdom-symbols requires a heart which has dissolved into the Ocean of Wisdom from which they arise. These symbols are designed to bring us to that level which is the same as the Deity.

We use this imagery, we visualize or meditate on it, we create a vision of the Deity to align with the actual Deity. The Deity-mandala actually exists, we are aligning with it by visualizing it and calling the Deity's to come forth and electrify our created vision. By repeating the mantra the entire mandala enters us through the visualized imagery.

The icons are thus used as a device of concentration. One visualizes the image and hears or repeats the name. This causes a response from the Infinite Consciousness weaving our mind. The Infinite arises into ones mind through the light of the image and the sound of the name which are being reflected in it, and floods it with the radiant qualities of its enlightened nature. The Wisdom-being, the image and name and our mind are one thing, not two or three. When the practice is entirely internal the Deity arises through inner currents or lights, through the heart, throat, crown or any concentration-drop of our inherent wisdom-light (divine inheritance) to awaken our potential nature. When the practice is internal-external, when one chants the name aloud along with the image, the Deity is invoked to appear before you, by traveling on outer lights and energy currents known as blessing-lights or grace-waves. In such a way the Deity can be invoked to cause positive transformation in nature.

This kind of profound magic happens unconditionally and is controlled by the Deity. It is there whether you are aware of it or not. If you utter the name, the Deity is there, because name and Deity are not different. (Please be aware of this if you choose a mantra from this text. In the Hebrew tradition the most holy name of Yahveh was taken off the earth because it was "taken in vain"). The habit of listening solely to thoughts, emotions, gross-energy-expressions and external sound causes that we tend to close down to the subtler energy communication and the silence behind it. Most children can hear and communicate with subtle angelic beings, animals, and know the truth of any persons heart behind their words. With time our cultural and religious forms teach us to doubt our natural link to spiritual reality, to close down. Doubt forms a smokescreen; the divine message comes in but is readily dismissed. The subtle divine image appears when the name is intoned, but cannot usually be seen. The light arises but cannot fully penetrate the mind of doubt. Therefore in the beginning we must have some trust in spiritual reality, practice and the integrity of the human teacher behind its dissemination. The empowerment we gain from the Deity causes us to develop devotion and confidence, both of which are founded upon the experience of the Deity.

Spiritual method first works upon us by purifying doubt, fear and negativity, by opening us to inner knowledge, by awakening our inherent wisdom and truthfulness, by making the mind clear. The spiritual method of the Thunder-beings is like their method of awakening the earth—the cause and the effect are the same. What is bestowed out of the City of Lightning reflected in the awareness is the blessing-light necessary to renew our energy and sustain a life of unlimited positive qualities.

We have clear-light imagery to give us spiritual support, to give our minds eye a tangible focus on formless sublime Wisdom-Source. Because most beings cannot meditate directly on formless Wisdom-mind, the Deity's provide us with images. Through the image we contact he formless nature of the Deity and dissolve into it. We use clear-light imagery to direct our prayers, and Deity uses it as a vessel to receive our prayers and draw us to the Absolute. Because Deity enters consecrated images we have a means of actually worshiping Deity on earth. We use clear-light imagery to generate devotion; upon seeing the images of Sublime-beings our heart opens. Because our newly opened heart is a perfect vessel for the elixir of primordial wisdom, we use clear-light imagery for inspiration. Finally we have clear-light imagery as a visualization tool.

Imagery meditation is a way of becoming aware of our enlightened nature. We experience the enlightenment of the Deity's to recollect our own enlightenment. We use light, color and sound to awaken or brighten our awareness, so that its potential enlightened qualities will unfold.

The three traditions utilize imagery (light, color, and sound) to attain the same perfect blissful state as the Thunder-beings. There is real truth behind the use of colors to establish inner harmony.

The blessing-light of the Thunder-beings is the bolt of enlightenment. It appears white to symbolize its purity, blue to heal, vitalize and awaken our sky-like nature, yellow to establish righteousness, red to turn passion inside out, into bliss, or it might appear as a rainbow to awaken the complete wisdom of five qualities and to purify and dissolve the five gross elements into their light-sources.

In visualization based meditation we use not only colors, but enlightened form and sound to establish inner peace and unity. The fact is that what we're visualizing is quite real. Reality is infinite, so the images of innumerable Wisdom-beings exist with a single atom. So the Being we visualize does not exist "out there" in space, but exists within the space of our consciousness, the center of which is our heart, or wherever we focus our awareness. We call them forth, and by visualizing them, absorb their clear-light. When we call them forth, the actual light-form-colors appear within our mind. They are very subtle, but we feel them. If no-one experienced anything from this, there would not be any reason to engage in religion (that utilizes God or Enlightened Ones).

We visualize the Wisdom-beings as dazzling, present, dynamic, self-effulgent beings, yet realizing they are particleless emptiness of unobstructed wisdom and bliss dancing the shapes of luminous Vision.

We think of our body-mind in the same way, as insubstantial, light in space. We train in this view because it frees us from the suffering caused from viewing our body-mind as a gross collection of chemicals and elements. These are five lights dancing in space, or electricity like lightning, luminous, blissful, indestructible. If we have this view then we have faith that it can be transformed easily, whereas the view that mind-body is substantial causes doubts about its quick and easy transformation. So our training is in the view, in taking a right view, in having a truthful, totally honest vision of our life, which is free of fear and doubt and suffering. The view of substance is caused from the view of a concrete self, a self which is in need of protection, love etc. Therefore to hold the right view is to hold a precious jewel, the sublimity of which frees one from suffering. There is no concrete self, only shifting, pulsating dance of different colored lights which have different qualities. For example, the blue is fluidity, the red is heat, green allows motion, yellow is solidity. These are attributes of space.

We practice mind-control through concentration. If we concentrate on something positive, perhaps we're devising to help someone, our mind becomes light. By concentrating on a way of harming someone darkens the mind. By concentrating on pure positive wisdom-clear-light of Deity's form, the mind becomes that light. When we generate the image mind's light or subtle energy takes that form. At the same time we gather the actual light of the Deity, which is superluminal or celestial vitality. It dispels darkness in the mind by bestowing wisdom and bliss. It vitalizes the body, transforming it into itself—undecaying, immortal wisdom substance. Because our body is an extension of our subtlest mind through which Deity's light comes, the body can be totally transformed into immortal Deity. To demonstrate this accomplishment, Mahasiddhas appear as their tutelary Deity's.

Essentially the body is Deity form, inner energy is Deity speech, mind is Deity without form, activity is Deity activity. We practice this way to shift our view from limited illusion to unlimited Truth.

This is very real. An angelic spirit who does this practice takes the form of the Deity instantaneously, and when spirits see a person engaged in such practice they see the Deity form there and feel the Deity's wisdom-quality.

There is a story about my root master Haidhakan Babaji. In the 6th century he was in Tibet as a high lama. He would meditate all night. One night a student of his peeped through the door of his room and saw Babaji in the form of Shiva, effulgent sky-blue, with four arms . . . The student later sewed a shirt for him with four arm-holes and presented it as a gift. Shiva appeared to scold him for spying on the guru, but I think also accepted the gift chuckling warmly.

Eventually, through continuous abiding practice, our body, which is an energetic extension of mind, can take the form of the Deity. We know it is an extension of mind, because the mind can be so quickly read in the facial expressions, or dance, or speech. Deity and Guru practice yields that lineages of masters very often look similar to one another. And enlightenment yields the minor and major marks of a Buddha which all enlightened beings have, such as tapered fingers which express compassionate activity that rolled off them, a protrusion of the crown which expresses rising energy the birth of spirit there, counter-clockwise spiraling hair to express reversal to our origin, hair both tied up in top-knot denoting accumulation of wisdom and flowing to denote compassionate flowing activity, wheels on the palms, and so forth.

There is a story about a lady who by visualizing herself continuously as a tiger, appeared as one to her village. As a result everyone left the village. This only demonstrates the power of visualization in creating our appearance. Shamans can easily shape-shift into different forms, some can become invisible by visualizing themselves as not appearing to anyone. However this feat does not demonstrate the high achievement of enlightenment, where a master takes Wisdom-deity form. He achieved enlightenment through the wisdom-clear-light of his enlightened Deity—so he became that Deity, one of its many forms. He does not merely bare the image, but embodies the nature and enlightened qualities of the Deity. He is the luminous, fully omniscient Wisdom-Deity.

This is a much greater accomplishment than shape-shifting, because the inner contents are totally transformed into wisdom and bliss, and one realizes ones all-pervasive omniscience. The master represents outwardly what he is inwardly. He is Deity inwardly, so represents it in image and activity, body and speech outwardly. What is within is without—this is the meaning of living the truth, and of being created in the Deity's image and similitude. We practice truth, simplicity, love, awareness and self-control as means

of revealing our truth, our deepest omniscient nature, our inner wisdom-space and bliss. We bear Deity's implements to remind us of our enlightened qualities. We train to become what we've always been, to realize it. We shift our view to see that we are an extension of Wisdom-deity, one among innumerable forms.

Training in the imagery helps us to recollect our limitless blissful nature. Through it Deity awakens us. It is mind-light, so it awakens mind. The sun and lightning are material light, so awaken the body. The training with imagery entails that we get a sense of the nature of the Deity. The image we visualize and the enlightened wisdom and compassionate bliss are one. So when we focus on image and invoke Deity, we absorb the light of wisdom and compassion, and we become blissful. We continually taste this Wisdom, and we identify with it as our nature. We mix it with our mind until the two become one, until our gross energy becomes awakened and all that remains is the Wisdom-deity and his qualities.

* * *

The creation of images is a function and revelation of the spiritual reality. Although we say that nature is a reflection of Subtlest Reality, that Deity existed as Lightning since beginningless time, and appears in nature as a gross appearance according to our limited perception, occasionally, out of Deity's compassion spiritual reality, mystical iconography, is a reflection of nature as we see it.

Infinite Deity appears for us according to our phenomenon, for animals as animals, and so on. Deity's imagery is in a language we are capable of understanding, since we have the capacity for knowing the Deities. Deity appears as a man, woman or giant bird or animal, and his-her abode appears as a mountain, nest, tree, palace, cloud-house or cremation ground. The symbol is the creative Vision of the Wisdom-mind suited to the phenomena of individual classes of sentient beings. Its expression is the bridge between the formless emptiness and form, between Transcendent Mind and mundane mind. The image discloses an aspect of the Mysterious Source.

With devotion we magnetically draw the essence of the Deity's awareness to us, into our hearts. We can either connect with them through form or spaciousness, both are the same just different approaches. For all minds, the form is not meant to be a limitation of awareness, but a revelation of pure wisdom and energy. By choosing to direct awareness outward, away from the limitless mind, we have lost the original capacity to pervade all things naturally and display bodies as an unobstructed expression and function of Mind. We have forgotten that we're part of something profoundly deep and all-pervasive. Thunder-beings don't live confined to the forms they take, (and this includes, to a great extent, their incarnations). The image is the living dynamic reality of the Deity and universe. In many traditions it is taught that Deities emanate subtle fields around themselves where those who attained mergence with them go. That sphere is a field of emanations or transformation bodies. That sphere is the meaning of the City of Lightning, and represents the goal of enlightened awareness in the shape of an abode, an abode which can reveal itself in myriad worlds, in geography and our bodies. What various traditions define as heavens are the mandala-realms from which the wisdom of that tradition is transmitted. There are innumerable Pure Realms within the space of Infinity, therefore how can there be dispute among traditions since the root of those traditions is with the Wisdom-being of the Pure Realm?

The beauty of the actual clear-light imagery is inconceivable; artists, sculptors, poets have tried to depict it. Only the clear mind can reflect it—so that actually Deity makes his own images. A clear mind is Wisdom-deities temple. Because he makes the images, they're imbued with beauty and contain the likeness and semblance of the Deity. The shape you see is the shape of wisdom. It is not the image itself which is worshiped, it is the wisdom-essence of the consecrated image. It is the wisdom-essence that makes a person sacred Wisdom-deity, so that we might worship him, her or Self. It is our own wisdom-essence that we receive from Deity's grace which makes us worthy of practicing self-worshiping, body-mind. Imagery is the method Wisdom-deity's use to be on earth, to put light on earth, to draw beings to Pure Enjoyment Realm—to the blissful state.

So this is one purpose for having imagery, it corresponds with the need of beings to rely on an external support. The other purpose corresponds with the need of beings to have some internal support—a support which brings enlightenment very quickly.

The boundless intention of Deity is to awaken the inherent blissful state in all beings. So through sound this intention takes shape to appeal to beings faculty of hearing, and leads beings out of suffering by presenting enlightened sound in awareness spell (mantras), in thunder, in Deities voice, in teachings, in sublime music, in bird-song and numerous other sounds of nature. Through light this intention takes shape to appeal to the vision aspect of sentient beings, and leads beings out of suffering by presenting enlightened imagery, lightning, star-wheel, coloration, sacred geometry, rainbows, written language, and innumerable other beautiful forms of nature. The concentration of Deity's compassionate intention, his blessings on earth is the guru, who appeals to the sensory phenomena of sentient beings, leading them out of suffering by presenting the beauty and perfection of tangible experience.

The image is the visionary counterpart of the Deity, the name is the sound counterpart. Both are created freely out of the sound-light texture of reality. They are the sound and light body of the Deities, created as simply as we create images in our minds.. The image and name are like thunder and lightning because they awaken the mind, and in fact they might effloresce out of thunder and lightning since thunder is the speech of Thunder Lord and lightning is his Vision. So too, just as thunder and lightning are inseparable, the name and image are inseparable. Even though the name can be used without visualizing the image, the image still arises out of the name, and the name remains in the Deity image, inside its body and heart. Name and image are two aspects of one wisdom-energy: sound and light. The sound and light are utilized to merge with the Deity.

The Source of enlightenment is Wisdom Deity. The vehicle of enlightenment is the clear-light which rains blessings to awaken the stellar-seed of the heart. When we create or visualize the image and repeat the sound we absorb pure enlightened qualities of the all-pervasive Deity. By concentrating on imagery we're awakened by the actual Deity—the imagery is Deity's light—wisdom configuration. Our mind is subtly electrified, spiritualized at the cellular level, transformed into the Deity. If the Deities didn't exist this would not be possible, and we know it is possible since such masters have existed to show us by manifesting mundane miracle-powers bestowed by the Deity and the super-mundane accomplishment of becoming the Deity and revealing bodily form as the Deity.

Some scholars have suggested that the images of Thunder-beings are based on human thought association, but this cannot be applied to those Thunder Lords who originated out of visionary experience, like those in this text. They are alive and much more real than the limited-vision-reality—they are the root of Reality. The images are the universal-vision-reality, the symbol-body is the Thunder Lords Vision of Reality. To emphasize this Thunder-beings can descend in lightning, appear before your eyes as tangible-vision, shake whole mountains and crack rock under foot, they can take someone up and back down, inside a mountain by an entrance no-one sees, make thunder in a clear blue sky, bring storm inside an enclosed building, make it rain stones, create and destroy as they please. Those who have some doubt will have to begin having some trust to prove the miraculous existence of subtle life which is happening right around us.

Each Thunder-being is a unique living reality and yet arises from the same mode of subsistence of all Wisdom-beings which emanate according to function and activity. To us this is the level of highest realization. They all communicate this level of Truth, of Limitless Vision. It is so beautiful and profound. Because there are diverse natures, there are diverse Deity appearances. Because of the difference in their energy configurations, Wisdom-beings appear slightly different from one another, yet they all bear the same essential qualities. Because of this, some traditions say they're one being—one God, manifesting multiple forms. Yet those Minds exist distinctly; God is their nature in the sense that Wisdom is the singular substanceless substance which takes infinite forms, forms which dance within Infinite Light, Infinite Light dancing as all forms. We are as close to this Wisdom-light as our sight is to its eye. Because we cannot see this primordial awareness we feel it must not exist. In reality all our inner worlds and all outer worlds are its energy-expression. To prove its subtle existence, we must experience it energetically. Through subtle energy and bliss we can know the Spirit. That proof has arisen from the level of deep unmoving tranquility. The empty proof of the Mystery is like a blanket of space, and sets you in perfect peace. The electronic proof of the Mystery makes your hair stand on end and arouses your soul at the crown. The clear proof of the Mystery is an electric visionary form, a cosmic, superluminal person. The visual light form of the Mystery makes a loud crack in a clear-blue sky. The electronic sound-form of the Spirit zaps and makes a brilliant light.

If you say God is just formless and cannot be recognized through imagery, that neglects Gods activity to awaken us through form, and it denies the activity of the Light—it denies part of divine existence. It neglects a crucial part of nature and it denies God's compassion or skillful means. One does not need to use the images, although they are there as a life-preserver in the seething waters of the human predicament. Lord has uncountable images which the mystics of every tradition have become aware of. The creation and revelation of images is sacred divine activity. You have to be very pure to catch a glimpse. One reason why we might be instructed not to use them is if there is no longer a need to, when the seeds are sown you put the tools away, rest, and show others how to plant. Another reason might be the religious dogmatism. Perhaps some Western traditions are against imagery because originally there may have been a tendency to think that if the Deity has a form he must be limited like people, therefore masters skillfully taught people that the actual nature of God is formless and all-pervasive. But the Infinity of Wisdom Deity implies infinite activity, infinite ways of helping innumerable beings, so we cannot ever discount the existence and use of imagery.

The Thunder-beings are before sound and image, thought. They are Infinite Consciousness, Mind and energy, constituting one field or continuum. Their Mind aspect is immutable and controls the energy around their indestructible heart, to develop into a tangible frequency, a sound, light or electronic display. It develops into positive and negative polarity whose friction produces wind and then sound, such as when you hear thunder or think. The feeling quality of the free-radiating energy is bliss, so we say the nature of the Mind is emptiness and bliss. The Mind is an emptiness because it cannot be detected; through its energy it communicates itself—as bliss. In the atmosphere the Mind produces weather changes by friction of hot and cold directional-energies; in the heart, the Mind produces thought by the friction of positive white-light and negative dark-light. This Mind is our awareness from which thoughts arise.

When beings communicate there is a transmission of energy. Sound or movement (thought, thunder etc.) is a symbol of wisdom expressing itself through energy. The clear state of this energy is bliss. The actual wisdom-transmission is in the energy which precedes sound and can only be known by the heart of clear awareness. All knowledge begins in the heart and returns there to rest. The heart is both Word and Ear, pure creative energy and sky-like capacity. Since there is only one energy expressing infinite variety, there is only one deep language. It includes all symbols as its expression. The symbol is the vehicle to the Absolute. The Absolute is the symbol every-where you look. The symbol differs according to the multiple interpretation, according to our language.

Mantra as Voice of Thunder

The Thunder-beings are omniscient because they are omnipresent. They can hear our every call, we just need to know how to direct our call, we need to know the names, and to be empowered to use them by the Deity (who transmits his wisdom through the master or yogi). The core of most methods of accomplishment is the mantra and image, and their application or system of visualization.

Mantra is enlightened sound, invocation or awareness-spell, transmitted like thunder by enlightened minds. It is the voice, thought, name or sound resonance of the Deity. The Deity both has a name and doesn't have a name. He assigns a name to a particular energy-body, as our parents assign us a name at birth. The name carries the sound resonance of the Deity. As guru, Deity gives us his name because it connects us with the unfathomable, the nameless. It invokes his mind which arises with our heart and mind, effecting our entire life from within and without. The Thunder-beings guard these invocations which in some cases can be used for positive or negative. (Those presented in this text are unconditionally positive). They guard the song that creates reality, the creative-destructive power of the universe. Thunder-beings gave people the first language, electronic wind organized into sound. They awaken the earth with their voice of thunder. They provide a path by which their secret flame-language can be applied to awaken the mind. Mantra is essentially the key to entering their mind-reality, to merging with the Deity. With the mantra, one attunes with the mind behind nature and generates its natural powers. The mantra is a tuning fork by which our minds can be perfected, set in key with the Mind of nature.

The electric wind of their Mind booms across the earth as an energetic current of enlightened sound. It sets the world at peace by awakening the earth. It chases demons to the furthest corners and devours negativity in its path. Benevolent spirits come out to dance and kind animals and plant spirits come out to receive rain; meadows and forests buzz ecstatic. Good

people lift up their hearts in thanks and prayer, for it is a great blessing. Thunder-people dance and take refuge under the thunder-clouds. Thunders voice illuminates the earth. To illustrate this, Thunder-beings might appear with lightning issuing from their mouth as the visible thunder.

The thunder methods are a reflection of this enlightening activity. The method-sadhanas have this analogous effect upon the mind, of awakening it, devouring its negativity, of leaving it fresh, peaceful, vibrant, unobstructed. The empowerment transmits the spark of their Mind which is naturally attuned with their limitless qualities. Thunder-beings awaken through the sacrifice of themselves, their secret essence expressed through sound and light display. It vanquishes all negative states and provides the necessary light to recognize our true nature.

There is a subtle visible symbol or light display invoked with the awareness-spell. They go hand in hand. It is a display of wisdom-elements, or energetic qualities of solidity, heat, fluidity, motion and spaciousness. The image upon invocation arises from their formless body of Truth or Wisdom. Traveling on grace-waves or subtle energy currents, it enters through the heart, throat and crown, the electro-magnetic energy wheels in the body. If you call the deity with you mouth, he will arise in the sphere of existence, if you call him with your heart, he will arise in the sphere of mind. Based on your intention and purity, when he arises in nature, you will see the sign with your eyes, when he arises within you will feel the deity within your heart. It appears the image comes from somewhere, yet it arises from no-where in particular. It can make a light in the mind. It magically dispels clouds of confusion. It connects us to the deity, like a yolk or silk thread. Like lightning, it connects heaven and earth, subtle and gross, emptiness and form. The Deity calls its spark which falsely thought itself separate back into its sphere.

In Tantra there are various methods of utilizing mantra. Primarily we use them along with visualization and mudras. Through visualization we engage the mind to purify it. Through simultaneous recitation of mantra we engage the speech to purify it. Through mudras we engage the body to purify it. Although there are other variations this is the most complete form of practice. Some mantras are blessed so intensely that they can be used alone to attain the highest state, but they must be used clearly, with samadhi.

Samadhi refers to clear visualization or any concentration of awareness. In Tibetan Buddhism, the mantra of Chenrezig, Om Mani Peme Hung can be used as a method of attainment. Masters generally prescribe for practitioners of all levels to visualize the image at the crown with a descent of blessings while repeating the mantra silently or aloud. In Vajrayana you have three levels of repetition, one is totally internal, the next is just audible, and last is completely audible. In the Siddha lineages of Shaiva Tantra, masters prescribe the mantra Om Namah Shivaya. My own heart-guru taught everyone to use it no matter the religion, since Shiva is the state of all enlightened Wisdom-beings. He and many other siddhas taught that through silent repetition one can attain enlightenment. The power of the mantras has to do with the blessings that the Wisdom-deity put into it when he or she spoke it, the power of the accumulated blessings that people give to it over thousands of years, and the power of accumulated blessings that the individual puts into it—the power of ones own intention and faith. For example I have witnessed people with little faith or openess use Om Namah Shivaya and receive very little in return. I have witnessed the response of Shiva towards my own self-centered use of the mantra, and received little in return. I have witnessed a small group of Haidhakan devotees who used Om Namah Shivaya with great faith, and as a result caused the government of India to change. I have witnessed the response of Shiva towards my own altruistic use of Om Namah Shivaya, and as a result caused internal government to change.

Essentially what we're doing through mantra recitation is invoking a continuous stream of divine-energy or vibration, building up a powerful electric charge which harmonizes the subtle levels of the mind and heals the body. This electric charge transforms the mind into a Deity. This electric charge is like lightning happening in our nervous system which purifies all the subtle functioning at the root of mind and body. This electric charge leaves the mind clear and whole, tranquil and joyous.

This inner lightning-like pulsation mirrors the pulsation of lightning in the atmosphere—the cause and result are virtually the same. Eventually, if one's mantra-practice is excellent, imbued with faith and devotion, then the result of this accumulation is that one becomes a Thunder-deity with the capacity to help countless beings through the power generated from recitation.

Devotion: The Hearts Yearning for Sublime Wisdom

Faith and devotion need to be present to achieve the Deity. We can generate faith based on the inspiration we receive from hearing about the Deity and those who achieved high realization through the Deity. For example hearing about Moses and Yahveh through scripture inspires us to become intimate with this profound wisdom and to use "calling on the name of God" to align and reach the same state. Hearing about Shiva, his plays, and Tantra, causes us to seek him out. Hearing about Buddhas and their activity communicates their light to us, and this light we seek. It is the experience or taste of their mind that causes us to seek them. Even if we don't seek them immediately, their echo spans the three-times (past, present, future). Hearing about the fruit of practice, we seek it out. This is the turning of the heart, the awakening of faith. The seed of faith is the taste of Wisdom Unseen.

The degree of faith we have determines our degree of effort. So we should have more faith. When we hear about a Deity or Thunder-master and immediately feel inspired it is very often the case that we have previous life connection to them, and should cultivate this. Our connection which plants the seed of faith could be as simple as hearing a mantra or seeing a sacred image in a previous life.

Have faith that the practice is unconditional, because limitless Wisdom Mind is unconditional love. The Omniscient Ones over us live through unconditional love. Nurture devotion because that is the greatest invocation there is. Invoke Deity with mantra and he will arise. Have faith, because it is the openness which allows them into your mind. If you lack faith in the Deity or practice, they will not be able to come into your mind-body. If you lack faith in yourself, if you feel unworthy and overly sinful, they will not be able to come into your mind-body.

Devotion is the hearts invocation of the Deity, which causes them to arise therein, to effloresce. All Wisdom-beings are within us, so by having devotion they will rise to the surface of your mind like a lotus, they will enlighten your mind like a lightning-flash. By calling Deity's name we attract the Deity to ourself. By visualizing the image we create a perfect vessel to absorb the Deity's love. By having faith we create the openness which is necessary to receive this blessing. By having devotion we invite the Deity into our heart to saturate the mind and transform us. The Deity never disappears from the heart, but is only forgotten for a time. The imagery, the ritual, the implements of ritual, all these things are to help us recollect our unity with the Absolute. Devotion is the hearts yearning for Sublime Wisdom. Being present and aware in the heart is the method of conjuring and awakening this Wisdom. Devotion seeks to unify with the object of devotion. So our devotion will cause us to unify with our personal divinity. For this reason, devotion is the essence of Deity-yoga, of all religion that seeks unity with Wisdom-deities or God.

Devotion is love. Our devotion is our yearning to be the same as the object of our devotion. As thunder-people there's nothing we want more than to become a Thunder-deity. Perhaps it's because that's where we came from. Nevertheless, when the storms arise, we are not satisfied as a passive onlooker, so we participate by praying, supplicating for blessings, making offerings. There's wisdom up there so we pray to Thunder-deity and our prayers are answered. We pray to liberate all beings, to establish peace on earth, to stop wars, destructive storms, famines, harm-doers, obstructors, and so on. We are blessed by our altruism, and this blessing makes us like the Thunder-beings. It enlightens us. Mind becomes sky-like, body free of ailments. So when the corpse is left, the mind melts into infinite space, and is capable of manifesting the body of splendor in mystical deity-form, in thunder-clouds, and magical storm-display. The mind demonstrates its enlightenment in the body of storms and luminous clouds, in the speech of thunder, and pure vision of lightning.

When we love a Wisdom-being or guru, they arise in our heart as a light. They enlighten us. Devotion is the inspiration of bliss into the clear heart by the Deity. When we think with devotion, or a longing to be like our Lord, then they think of us with compassion. So there is a connection made. With Thunder Lord it's like being struck by lightning, only it liberates us from suffering without causing any additional suffering. Even when the power of enlightenment causes suffering, upset, turmoil, it means that purification is happening. If there was no suffering caused, then there would be no suffering experienced. So one who is pure cannot be harmed by anything, they're indestructible.

Because devotion is strong love, even if the guru to whom our devotion is directed is not enlightened, and we still have absolute certainty that he is, we will become enlightened and so will our guru. Perhaps a statue of a Deity becomes awakened by having devotion in the Deity towards whom we direct our awareness. (So that statue will be seen to talk, blink, drink milk, transform into something else.) This would indicate the blessings that come from devotion.

Devotion is the true invocation of the Deity, one can pronounce the name-invocation without devotion and the Deity will arise, but to actually experience the Deity within, it is necessary to have devotion.

True devotion means having some knowledge of the Deity, which suggests some experience or previous connection with the Deity which is rekindled in the moment that devotion arises. It is often a recollection, one hears the name or sees the image of the Deity, and snap, there's a feeling in ones heart of devotion. Devotion is the Deity's Wisdom Mind mixed with ones own mind. Because ones own mind has degrees of emotional energy, emotion is very often mixed with devotion. The less emotion, the more pure the devotion, the more clear one is able to see what happens in the heart, how it is moved, or awakened. Once some connection is formed with the Deity, through elaborate empowerment, dream or simply a sense of being comforted and protected by a particular Deity, then one can use that devotion, sense of gratitude and respect and love for the undefiled beautiful qualities of the Deity, to spring open, to burst into the bloom of enlightenment. Hearing the unsullied name is hearing the Sound of Deities Wisdom, seeing the unstained image in dream, painting or scripture is seeing the light of Deity's Wisdom, hearing about Deity's pristine qualities and pith instructions is knowing the Dharma of Deity's miraculous compassionate means. Within the instant that devotion arises the thought of the Deity causes the Deity to arise in the heart. If one looks into the heart to see and feel and live the Face of Deity's sublime miraculous reflection, ones own pristine heart qualities will awaken. Ones heart is tinged with Deity's luminescence, Mind is mixed with mind, like when lightning touches down and envelopes its target. In the same way, one is left feeling blissful, charged, purified, bright, open, fresh, like after a good lightning storm. By this experience we are inspired to go after the Deity, we are attracted to Wisdom and Love in its most unadulterated forms. We want from here on out to die to dissolve into the Deity, we want to be swallowed, subsumed in Light or consumed in lightning to become the Lightning. When the storms come there is exaltation, but also a sense of sadness and longing to be flying there, to be home, to be flashing out of intoxication, to be disrobed, naked again.

When devotion is free of emotion, it is Deity's wisdom-essence, inspiration or revelation and is depicted by the Dakini, female Awareness-being. By her dance of bliss and awareness, her inspiration awakens the heart. Deity's presence, breath, light of bliss is the Dakini. This perceptible presence is the Dakini. In Shaiva Tantra it is called Shakti. In Kabbalah this indwelling presence is called Shekinah. She is the fuel to awaken the state of Wisdom. When she flashes in the heart, that's inspiration.

Devotion is connected to our passion for enlightenment, so in the Tantra sexual union can be interpreted as the unified state of the mind, while sexual yearning is the fuel to attain this state. Instead of yearning for sexual union upon seeing the female or male form, we yearn for enlightenment upon seeing Deity's form. Instead of, or in addition to, nurturing devotion to a husband or wife, we nurture such passionate devotion for the Deity and his secret essence in our heart. We fall in love with Deity when we practice. So in Tantra, secret essence and heart are female vagina and orgasm. The bliss we receive from union with Deity, that pours out of every life experience, can only be compared to sexual bliss because in sex is the greatest enjoyment of mundane mind. Yet enlightened heart bliss is so far beyond sexual orgasm, it is upper body cellular orgasm, it rises like flames, instead of sinks like water. It comes out the heart as love, the throat like thunder, the crown like a lightning.

If we take Thunder-beings to be our gurus, our supreme unfailing teachers, our God, then, in order to show them reverence and to serve them lovingly we serve all beings and respect the earth. Thunder-beings represent nature by controlling it, by manifesting it, by embodying and embracing it, by protecting it, then we must also have deep reverence for nature. If we feel loving-devotion for Thunder-beings and want to serve them selflessly then we must respect nature and learn to live as Thunder-beings lived. Because we've gotten so far away from such excellent participation in nature, we need to take steps, such as training to be aware of nature, training in compassion for all living beings, including stone, water, fire and air. Because all beings contain the light of Thunder Lord we must act compassionately toward them. We should not be selective towards what is natural, and should not judge the activity of Thunder-beings or any master.

Thunder Specialists and Crazy Wisdom

If we're in need of wisdom, it is also efficacious that we rely upon one who recognizes the fact that he is an extension of Wisdom-deity who chose to come here out of pure compassionate intention. Innumerable suffering beings called out for help and innumerable wisdom-beings made aspirations to free those beings from suffering. They know the way out, they are the way out. They are with us as soon as we think of them, through their name. There is no more effective way of connecting with them, than through name and image. How else can we do so—we're so used to thinking, we need thought, sound and light, to reach what is beyond thought. Realization is recognizing all Wisdom-deities in ones own infinite mind. But for us realization can't come about on its own. We must work at it.

But the first thing we require is someone to show us precisely how to go about making this contact, we need someone who has already established an unbreakable connection to Wisdom Source, to connect our minds to it. This place is that of the guru. In this exposition the special kind of guru that we require is called Thunder-master or specialist.

Thunder-beings give us the power without which nothing could exist, which is born witness to in the fact that they can bring the dead to life, or heal dead tissue (or kill, since the same power at varying intensity causes life or its removal). They gave us the primordial spark of our consciousness, that which makes things visible and the electricity and conditions which cause life to exist and be constantly renewed. Thunder Lords light is diamond-light, thunder-power, so when it enters the mind it cuts and bar-b-ques the old and supports the growth of the new.

Those people whose minds are clear and controlled and are aligned with Thunder-beings, gain some of that wisdom occasionally to effect positive transformation on the earth, to effect the divine spiritual body. It is a catalyst to new birth. It causes the elements to rise up and dance; lightning is pure awareness-power. Lifeless elements can be struck by lightning and something living, sentient and sapient will arise (symbolized in the golem, the Frakinstein and the infusion of the breath of God into clay). All life arose out of the lightning long ago.

By connecting with Thunder-beings, some people have successfully transmuted their life-being, becoming children of Thunder-beings who in reality they always were. They are given wisdom and a method of accomplishment by the primordial Thunder-minds, which reconnect the mind to its Source through this natural power (symbolized by the three or five pronged electrical plug thunder-bolt). In a sense they mold the person through the application of their active light into themselves, they create us in their image, as extensions of them on earth. Out of this process we arise as divinity, with the powers of divinity to skillfully benefit all beings. So the thunder specialist gains the ability to change the weather freely, to subdue wild spirits, to heal, to bring the dead to life, to be in several places at once, to come in dreams, to vanish in rainbows. Essentially the Mystery has taken his image and he sets this pearl in the earthly galleries and draws all his forms back through it. All minds are potential symbolizations of Universal Consciousness.

The achieved practitioner, having connected with the subtle Mind and current of bliss through special training has the ability to take what is negative and make it positive. Like lightning the subtle energy absorbs the gross energy. He transmutes or recycles energy. He subdues malevolent spirits and turns them around to live by the dharma. He takes a clouded (negative) environment or situation and makes it positive. He functions from the center of the City of Lightning, so you are actually witnessing the Deity (not merely his signature). Such a one is an endless source of Dharma, skillful vision and radiance. Such personages are responsible for originating spiritual traditions and guiding many people into the Cities of Blissful Radiance. As an extension of divine energy the light penetrates magically; it is neither seen nor felt and its beginning is virtually indetectable. The divine energy guides in this way, functioning mostly unseen to people. So it has to manifest something, it has to appear so that we know it is there. When it appears in person as our guide, guru or lama, it is the focus of grace or creative energy of the deity-sphere.

Thunder-beings give birth to themselves on earth occasionally; this is who the thunder specialist is, a powerful child of Thunder-beings amongst the people. Listen, for the lightning follows its messenger. Watch, for the messenger follows the thunder. Thunder-beings give birth to children after their own heart, contraries, who take birth in the universe at some point then return through refinement to the subtle state. Through those messengers they transmit the subtle truth which is the basis of the Tantra and wisdom traditions, the foundation of Oriental thunder method.

Primarily, the thunder person is of the nature of his wise parents so he acts in tune with the subtle law and functions to awaken people. He appears to be crazy or contrary to the ways of mundane society, but in actuality he works for the Spirit and most of the people who view his outrageous nature are the real contraries. He knows what is right according to the subtle law which he feels as the power of the Thunder-beings ever-presently in his mind. He transcends the limited dualistic view of reality because he lives the view of Truth. The description of the thunder-master is the description of the Thunder-beings. He travels with the storms and awakens the people by controlling the bolt. He gets drunk on the very same wine and his stumbling forms a dance akin to the zig zag of his Father-mothers sky dance. He can scold you or raise you up, burn your ego or soak you in grace. There is a real sense of unpredictability—you never know for certain when the lightning's going to strike. The only thing that can be expected is positive transformation. The environment is benefitted greatly be such a one, both in the other realm and this one.

Thunder-master is liminal, usually living on the edge of society because his power is so great, its like having a lightning-bolt amongst the people. (Sometimes powerful masters practice what's called "insulation" to not stand out so much). With this kind of sacred clown anything is possible, the two powers of water and fire are together so there's bound to be a shock. The Truth is before you and nothing else, so one can always expect a rapid instantaneous revelation, a dissolution of ignorance. They flip reality over to complete our view. Sacred-lightning-clowns do and say things backwards. I heard about one who used to go around flattening things that were round with a hammer. He would just smash anything round. In Lakota lightning-tradition (heyoka) they have a story that demonstrates the contrary nature of these people. Two frogs sitting on their lily pads in center of the pond, it starts to rain, the one frog says to the other "we'd better get out of the rain else we get wet"—so they both jump into the water.

The thunder-master initiates according to divine law. He is the gate to Thunder Mt., his turning sword is the bolt. And his bolt integrates the mind. He is the medicine to cure ills. He shows us that we're the medicine, we're the bliss. Thunder Lord and master uses cutting techniques, or wrath. The power of thunder imbues the activity of the master, so he may intensely shock people with antics, with inexplicable behavior. The antics are outwardly humorous, so people laugh and this heals the mind. But the reverse or contrary behavior also prepares people for the Deity by opening the mind. Shock makes a space in the mind so the Thunder-being can be experienced, so the mind can be enlightened. Thunder-master is a shock therapist, when he shocks you, there is a space in the mind. When there is a space there is awareness, a whole mind.

There is a great story about a Tibetan Thunder-master which illustrates this activity. Dzogchen Thunder-master Dzong Dzung Rinpoche used to be seen carrying huge rocks all day from one side of a river to the other, then back again. Most people thought he was bonkers, but on one occasion an adept saw him and recognized him as a very high master. So he approached him and asked him to check his meditation. When the student took the posture, Rinpoche took up a large rock and brought it down on the students back. At the same time Rinpoche gave him an electric mind-transmission. So the shock opened him up to receive the non-dual energy of the masters accomplishment. The student received the transmission of the masters lineage at that moment, which to my knowledge is maintained to this day.

Thunder-master is ruthless and unpredictable, fire and water. At once severe and sublimely gentle, serious and yet a jokester. He is the crazy-wise, the mirror of the Mystery, yet has abolished the mirror to reveal the seat and empty center of the City of Lightning. You can never quite put your finger on the thunder-master because he is a symbol-body of Infinity. Anything is possible!

Crazy Wisdom in most traditions has its origin with Thunder-beings, examples include not only the yogis of Shiva, Chakrasamvara, Guru Rinpoche (Dorje Drollo: King of Crazy Wrath), but also the sacred clowns of Native American traditions, such as the heyokas of Lord Tunkashila.

Crazy wisdom has a tendency to give immature practitioners who newly hear about it license to act outrageously according to base self-cherishing energy. To get attention they act without regard for others feelings. Whereas the antics of thunder-master come from a strong motivation to benefit beings. The antics of thunder-master arise spontaneously, not thoughtlessly, from a heart that wishes all others welfare. The same goes for the lightning, thunder and rain. Living at a Tibetan Buddhist monastery I've had occasion to see immature practitioners justify foolish behavior with crazy wisdom antics, especially after hearing teachings by crazy wisdom lamas. Very often crazy wisdom antics are initiated by the sphere of Wisdom Deity. They might even instruct you to act this way. Most beginning practitioners need to practice nurturing good intentions and creativity. Creative work causes ecstasy, creatively we're destroying sufferings of others. Beginning practitioners should not engage in drinking, drugs and sex just because achieved masters do it. They underwent the process of mind-training, which most often includes living like a monk with lots of rules devised to train in self-control. Either the master practices crazy-wisdom to abolish the extreme of monk-hood to attain the middle or to shock peoples minds open. It loosens our rigid sense of duality to occasionally engage in these things. But the Spirit knows that 99.9% of the people are not prepared for this activity, so prescribes what is appropriate. Therefore I would not advocate this activity even though it is so close to my heart and is the way of my masters. The thunder-masters are this way because they have the realization of themselves as Deity and therefore nature as Deity's sphere. They know the contents of their mind-body are Deities and they experience the contents of the universe as Deities. Crazy-wisdom is the activity of Thunder-Deity sphere.

So what is the test of Thunder-master? In all traditions he is one who through his connection to Thunder-beings controls the clouds, rain, thunder and lightning. Some weather lamas and shamans have the ability to split the clouds, bring down lightning, ride the storms. They direct the bolt to remove suffering from beings. They can heal, avert danger and calamity, stop wars, anything is possible really. The surest sign of their authenticity is the sense of peace, clarity, bliss, love and crazy-wisdom. How you feel in their presence supercedes miraculous display.

Initiation and Thunder-dreams

Mystical experience of the Deities is possible for all people. There is wisdom running through the senses which electrically connects the mind to phenomenon. If we abuse this wisdom, we loose the wisdom and eventually loose the sense. If we nurture our wisdom and adhere to Dharma transmitted through the heart, then our wisdom-senses will remain as clear as they were when we were born. When we bring light into our mind, the senses become spiritualized, a saint can be recognized by the light which flows from the eyes, you might even see the light as a cloud in the eyes. Pure Wisdom eyes have the capacity to emit rays and lightnings, such as with Thunder-bird or Shiva Netra (3rd eye electric lamp). Through wisdom senses we perceive the Deities, our wisdom-light is naturally aligned with the light of Deities, so can be witnessed easily. Through wisdom we are able to realize our place in a universal mandala of Wisdom-Deities. Wisdom is dancing in us and all around us. So we can witness it through a clear mind. When we sleep our dreams will be dreams which tell of our alignment with Deities. The mind is clear and quiet when we sleep so whatever sphere we align with will present itself there.

Thunder-dreams, and all mystical Deity dreams, are both a basis for our awakening and the field within which the Thunder-deity transmits the method by which people can contact the Deity and achieve themselves through repeated empowerment (by bathing in the blessing-light of the Deity). Thunder-beings awaken the earth following winter with thunder, lightning and rain. Likewise they are going to restore the connection between oneself and the Wisdom-source of the universe within. Their electricity awakens the wisdom inherent in the universe, the part of all minds which is beginningless, pure consciousness. When phenomena separate from their Source, there is illness and death, the Thunder-beings have the power to reconnect life to its inexhaustible Source, which we call a Mystery because we cannot see it. The Deity's image and method becomes the sure-fire means whereby our form of psycho-physical being is connected to its phenomena Source of Unlimited Consciousness and life.

When Thunder-beings come in the Spirit you have either a vision or a dream depending if you're awake or asleep. You experience it with your entire being, especially if that lightning touches down on you. It is as real as atmospheric lightning because of its subtlety and power. In fact I don't think they are different except in intensity. It is thunder and lightning, the vitality and wisdom, mind and power of the Thunders. When struck there is a mind-transmission which occurs, one streak of lightning lights you up like an x-ray skeleton of shining emptiness. There are many kinds of thunder-dreams originated from the Deities own creativity. A soul-spark stays with the mind, like a thunder-stone left after a lightning stroke. By putting some of their wisdom in the mind, they're bringing

one through the entrance to their mandala. The thunder-dream is the City of Lightning because their sparks are their Mind. This dream is eternal or immutable because the Mind as such is immutable, therefore it stays with you above your head, and becomes a body of wisdom-light. By discussing this kind of pearl, or thinking about it, it is invoked. Those Wisdom Minds create us as their children. The total Mind then becomes City of Lightning. The dream-empowerment reminds us of an ancient connection we have with them. They are giving us the opportunity to connect with them on the deepest level and to refine with their light-essence. Because we're inherently the same, we can work to merge our lives with theirs. Their transmission or empowerment (grace) is a guide and method of awakening. Thunder-dream and instructional image are both revelations of primordially awakened Minds. You are seeing yourself in its highest evolution. Only those who arise from it will dissolve back into it. When you can see the image, you'll know if you have a connection or not, something will ring in your heart like a bell.

As the thunder-storm marks the transition between seasons and the awakening of the earth, the thunder-dream and empowerment or initiation by a thunder-master marks the transition in a persons mind from dark to light. The dream of earth and mind is the theater within which the Thunder Mind fulfills Eternity. Few people actually realize that what they see in nature is a glorious vision of splendor not different than Deity visitation in dreams. Pay attention during storms, be quiet and free of fear, listen, watch, all of nature opens up; feel the hair stand up from the lightning gel, pray, the essence of every Thunder-being, God and Goddess are there.

The Mind of Thunder-beings is joyous and tranquil, so when one receives transmission through dream and light through practice, one becomes joyous and tranquil. They set the earth and mind at peace, making things clear and luminous. To my knowledge there is no greater assistance than the thunder-dream. Through them Thunder-beings give transmission-fruit and they ask that you fulfill Eternity (some duty), that your tree bear fruit. Actually one becomes a conduit for their power and activity, for the lightningbolt. They plant the seed and the lightning-tree sprouts, and blooms during thunder-storms, and bears wisdom-fruits.

Their transmission and empowering-grace are forces of rapid awakening by virtue of the concentration of vitality. If you have such a transmission it means you're profoundly related to them, and if you don't you're still related to them and can recognize this in your auspicious heart. Everyone has some connection to the subtle realms and it just needs to be re-established. The broad pantheons give some indication of the breadth of the Origin emanating into subtle realms. To establish this channel to a particular Wisdom-sphere opens one to receive grace from there and protection and serves to assist ones re-birth into that sphere and deity.

The Deity initiates us into the sphere through the method. We journey to its center by gradual recognition of our mind as the center. The method is the bird mount which flies us to the top of the clouds to the Throne of Eternity in the City of Lightning. He initiates us into the means of achieving expansive awareness. Because this is the effect, the image of the deity-mind-abode is a circle, wheel, sphere, nest, egg expressing wholeness, a tree, mountain or cloud house expressing elevation of consciousness, ascent into Infinity. Many Thunder Lords live on mountain abodes in bodies of subtle vision, never entirely revoking their grace from the earth. To Shaivites, Mt. Kailash is the abode of Lord Shiva, Shakti and retinue; to Buddhist Tantrikas it is the abode of Chakrasamavara, Vajravarahi and retinue; to Bon po's it is the abode of a Lady of Lightnings and her consort. Vajrapani dwells on Mt. Chakpori which was once home to a Naga King. Lei Kung has been associated with Jade Mountain, Lei Tzu with Swallow Mountain. Examples from Occidental traditions include Yahveh who dwelt on Sinai, and many Native American Thunders.

To gain entrance into the mind-sphere of the Thunder-beings, an initiation is necessary. And in order to receive an initiation, to forge a powerful and auspicious connection with the Deities, one must be relatively virtuous, otherwise the universe will simply not be able to provide it. The initiation can come in visionary experience or from an accomplished thunder-specialist who might be a shaman, yogi, dakini, lama etc. who already has achieved mergence with the Deity. So in any case the deity is initiating you. The master is part of the body of the Deity. It is impossible to gain initiation without the grace of the Deity, so the master functions to introduce you to the deity and acts to guide you to the summit of awakenment.

The Thunder-beings closely guard their path; the prerequisites for receiving initiation are purity, uprightness, or a sincere aspiration to perfect oneself for others benefit. If these weren't met one could be burned or destroyed. One can go blind, insane, be killed by lightning or be severely tested or punished. In the Tantra there is a symbol to describe the preparation necessary to enter the sphere of Non-dual Tantra. A persons mind is like a vase or container; an unprepared, impure mind cannot enter the lightning path of the highest Tantra Deities without sufficient preparation, just as you cannot place the milk of the Snow Lion in a vase of base metal. This milk can only be held by a special vase. It is very strong and would just burn through anything else. Likewise thunder-power cannot enter an unprepared mind without possibly causing damage to ones energy. If there is a speck of darkness and one comes before the Power then it will burn. Such is another reason why the highest paths are secrets guarded from mundane minds.

There is a Native American story which illustrates this point. Once a foolish man decided to climb Thunder mountain (one of a few mountain abodes in which families of Thunder-beings used to live). There is a direct admonition against entering sacred space without the proper offerings and respect. Interest or curiosity alone won't cut it. This man, ignoring his own inner sense, and the wise words of his friends who refused the journey, hiked to the summit. It was shrouded in a dense white mist or cloud. From the cloud arose a crack of thunder out of which boomed the voice of Thunder Lord. He asked the man where his offerings were, and warned him about entering the cloud without a proper offering. The man wanted to see the Lord, so ignored the warning and stepped into the cloud. His last words were "I see them, I see them." He was immediately struck by lightning and thrown from the summit. No one can see the Face of God and live. Actually you must have already died to see that Face. What this means is that the stain of ego must be removed. In the Torah, only Moses was worthy to ascend Sinai where YHVH had alighted, the common people could not even touch the mountain let alone recieve the direct revelation. They were impure, the power would hurt them. Such precautions and protections are only for our safety. Therefore Tantric paths are called guhya, "secret." The path is protected by the Deity, the scriptures are protected by symbols. (Symbols which in some instances have been taken literally or misunderstood, such as with Kundalini Tantra and its interpretation as a system entirely of sexual arts). Please understand that the Wisdom-beings transmit practices for everyone, we certainly don't have to be

Moses or Shakyamuni Buddha to practice methods of accomplishment. Moses went up Sinai so God could give the people such essential practices, Buddhas transmit multiple vehicles for all different levels of minds. No-one is exempt from Dharma. In Tantra there are certain initiation practices which can be used to both prepare the mind for more intense and dynamic practices, and to introduce one to the Non-dual sphere. These practices are included herein, and should not be taken lightly, they are sufficient to take any singular person, at any level to the goal of a fully awakened heart.

I have to be quite honest about what I know. Most people at present have chosen a way which is contrary to the holy beauty-way of the Thunder-beings. It has caused us to retract before the Spirit, and in some ways it has caused the Spirit to retract based on our defilements. Many holy teachings have not been revealed of those which still exist. A small percentage are in our hands and some have been retracted.

The above story describes why the Thunders of the West left their earthly seats. Although in the Orient this is not entirely the case, Shiva and Chakrasamvara, and many other Deities maintain their primary seats (piths). I say, it is not entirely the case because it is possible for these geographic arisings of wisdom to fade and disappear according to the conditions of the people. The piths exist fully within our body, therefore the effect upon one part of the continuum ripples to the other parts.

Thunder rites are for those people who are chosen by Thunder-beings, who are pure vessels. But worship or alignment with Thunder-beings is for everyone. There are simple practices which anyone can use to attune with Thunder-beings. The nectar of God's name is the medicine to heal broken hearts and the ills of society. Therefore Cities of Lightning provides a few safe yet powerful methods, which can act as preliminaries to initiate anyone onto essential dharma paths. If you use them diligently and follow the subtle law dharma, then it is possible to receive initiatory dreams from the Wisdom-sphere. By using the names the Thunder-beings are made happy, especially when groups come together to send up one voice. The Thunder-beings advocate use of particular mantras which are sufficient to completely purify the mind and attain enlightenment. These invocations will be provided in the light of each tradition. The Thunders make their will overwhelmingly obvious when the time comes!

The Eastern Gate of Lightning

The entrance into the Cities of Lightning in Oriental transmission schools, is through the Eastern gate. The Gate to the City is liberation. The East is a symbol of the dimension of awakening, of wisdom, because it corresponds to spring, sunrise, birth, gentle clear luminosity, beauty, creation, initiation. When we wish to gather creative energy we face East, that is the reason for facing East to pray. Vajrayana mandalas have their main entrance in the East to symbolize initiation, movement into light. The Thunder-beings are in all directions, but when he or she comes out of the East, he embodies the qualities of the dimension which precedes the universe—the Unborn. When something is born it comes out of the creative-space and is nurtured by fresh life-force. The newly born reflect the dawn Sun. The Thunder-beings initiate our return to the dawn of the universe, they return us like lightning to our original nature which preceded our birth, which preceded our arising out of the Undifferentiated Primordial Wisdom Mind. They reconnect the mind to its Wisdom-Source (which is embodied in the Thunder-being). This Source is the root of our mind, the primordial state of all Minds.

Thunder path is a reversal because it returns us to the Origin. Their power is a reversal because it arises directly from the Unborn state and never disconnects from it, and because it returns things to that state by transformation, by awakening. They control the universe and mind by abiding at its beginning. They are the transformative power of nature to create, destroy and restore itself. The dawn is the time of initiation, of the opening of our eye of primordial awareness and its clear light. The dawn is also a symbol of the goal. It is the dharma-sun or Great Eastern Sun, the light of continued application and the culmination or fruition. Vajrayana is considered the fruition path or resultant path because we start from the goal, with the view that we're fully awakened to begin with, and we work to liberate our clear-awareness with the light of our wisdom-nature. So we seek enlightenment within ourselves, we never look for the Deity outside, the light shines as our consciousness. Since in Tantra we always start from the goal, from the abode of wisdom, Tantra is therefore a path of reversal, of returning of recognition, of recollection.

Thunder-powers reverse time, or the effects of time on earth. By invoking them we reverse time to get back to the nest of the highest, the state from which we were born. It is a movement from dark to light, from dissolution to growth. Essentially the Oriental traditions are born out of the Eastern abode as the dimension of awakening, because they present vehicles for awakening the mind with the light of the Primordial Thunder Mind. They were developed out of this clear wisdom light, out of perfect realization—the goal.

Each Thunder-being has its unique resonance and therefore its unique symbolic communication, just as from distinct flowers you receive unique fragrances. The image and feeling quality of their mind (which floods you) is the signature of the City of Lightning, any response you receive is the signature of that sphere. It is a great tuning fork; when it appears in inner space, it balances inner energies, the mind. When it appears in the sky and dances on the earth it balances the outer energies, the earth. The City of Lightning is the creative space within which the Deity arises; anything can happen within that space in order to awaken us. We might, after getting a taste of this divine nectar, opt to dwell there with them, to live according to the law of their heart. There you will find many things, like storm phenomena in a non-phenomena place. There is a possibility of being struck by subtle wisdom-bolt. The mind is illuminated in the flashing of lightning and the booming of thunder. You will be connected to the root of nature and will be made deeply aware of our earthly responsibility to live in truth, simplicity and love. You might appear to the mundane world as a contrary because you are painfully aware of what activity causes suffering and what

liberation. They teach us how to follow our bliss by living according to the subtle law. Your head becomes the clear-minded radio-transmitter. It might appear to make you more closely related to those above than to the mundane world. You are participating in their Mind which is reversing everything, like a film played backwards. If they didn't follow their bliss in such a way, the foundation of reality would fold like a dry skeleton. The lightning holds it up—that is, realized minds are invisibly active to provide subtle law, subtle guidance, subtle wisdom, subtle inspiration.

Entrance through the Eastern gate means initiation into the vision of lightning and Thunder-beings It means practicing to unite our awareness with the Awareness-being through the awareness-spell. It means settling or relaxing the heart into its silent creative potential. It means training to experience reality which is profoundly colored by the enlightened Wisdom of the Deity. Such a state is the effective means for experiencing Ultimate Reality, nature in its true state as luminous-vision and pure pleasure. The Deity literally becomes ones thoughts and perceptions. You might actually see the Deity everywhere reflecting his face in the great mirror of reality, and you definitely think of him all the time. If it is a Mother-being, you would experience reality as female, the Mother. So everything in reality is their nest. It begins through our awareness, once it is awakened, then every experience is awakened, blissful and everything perceived can shine with the crisp clear radiance of lightning.

Vajrayana: The Lightning-bolt Vehicle

Vajrayana is a Sanskrit term meaning Lightning-bolt vehicle. It is a wisdom-collection of the highest teachings transmitted by Lord Buddha in this eon, that took root in India, Tibet and Nepal, and has since spread throughout the world. Lord Buddha taught three main vehicles: Sutrayana, Mahayana and Vajrayana (Tantra); renunciation, transformation and intrinsic freedom. These are essentially different views and approaches which lead to the same goal. The Buddha transmitted these three vehicles to appeal to the varying capacities of students. He taught the first two vehicles and some Tantra while on earth.

All Buddhist vehicles or Dharma have their origin with Lord Shakyamuni Buddha. He was the teaching Buddha of this eon, responsible for bringing Buddha Dharma to sentient beings of this civilization. Although he was enlightened previously, he demonstrated the path of development and meditative training, of abandonment and realization. The essence of Buddha's path is the abandonment of harmful acts and habits, and the cultivation of luminous wisdom nature through the taming of the mind. This is the path which Buddha realized and transmitted for all sentient beings to attain the fully enlightened state, to attain the state beyond suffering.

When Lord Buddha set out on the path a great storm arose, and the Dharma-protector Muktalinda sheltered him. This storm represented his initiation onto the lightning path, which takes one to the goal as quickly as lightning, which awakens the mind in lightning flashes of realization, which invokes the lightning blessings of the Awakened Ones who attained enlightenment in previous eons. Lord Buddha's work was extraordinary. He had attained enlightenment in

previous lives, and according to the aspirations he made on the path, would be responsible for bringing the whole of Buddha Dharma to earth during this particular world system. He was born miraculously. Wise beyond words, he was able to talk and walk at birth. He was brought up a prince, yet left this lifestyle to pursue the goal. To signal his initiating movement from dark to light, Primordial Wisdom Mind arose as thunder-storm.

When Lord Buddha had completed his training this happened again, a thunder-storm arose overhead and remained for seven days, a time cycle which denotes highest spiritual achievement. This storm arose just before the Buddha was about to break through into the enlightened state, while he was meditating. This signaled his break-through, enlightenment, the dawning of clear-light in his mind. The Buddhas who preceded him were signaling his full realization or awakening.

To shield him from the storm Muktalinda came in the form of a seven-headed naga-serpent. (Some Naga-kings and queens are excellent Dharma-protectors; Muktalinda is especially wise, a Thunder-being, and was a central figure in Cambodian Tantra). With his seven hoods he covered Buddha's head. For seven days this storm raged, so for seven days he was shielded. This event is reminiscent of the story of Moses on Sinai, who received what we call Dharma-transmission in a thunder-storm over seven days.

The Buddha realized the perfectly enlightened state, so he became Wisdom-Deity on the earth, and very likely received Dharma transmission during storms. Muktalinda is a protector of specific teachings, so it is likely that the Buddha was receiving

74

transmission. Before Buddha there were countless Buddhas who attained enlightenment in previous eons, but Shakyamuni was responsible for introducing sentient beings of this eon to Buddha Dharma. He was the first of this world system to realize Buddhas enlightened body, speech, mind and wisdom within his own body, speech, mind. (He is the fifth Buddha of this Bhadra Kalpa, "fortunate eon". This is considered a fortunate eon because 1000 Buddhas will appear. While in other previous and future kalpas few or no Buddhas appear. More will be said on this later).

For the Sources of Dharma, the Buddhas, Dharma is the clear expression of realization. Dharma is realization, it is the wisdom-clear-light of the Buddhas. For us Dharma is the means to develop and maintain realization. We invoke the light of Dharma when we invoke and pray to Buddhas. The perfected mind receives continuous instruction or Dharma from the heart, from wind, sky, trees, spirits, clouds, Deity's, thunder, lightning, animals. Everything is Dharma, the Source of enlightenment. Teachings appear instantly according to wish. When the mind is clear, unagitated, soft, free of fear and doubt, Deity's clear light reflects itself perfectly in a flash. This is the symbolic meaning of the storm: Shakyamuni's breakthrough into the vast expanse of Wisdom Mind. If we have this dream where we're the Buddha and a thunder-storm is over us, then it represents our experience of enlightenment. Even when we experience the minds of other enlightened Buddhas, they are introducing us, reminding us of the experience of our own beginningless enlightenment. We practice Deity yoga in order to fully recollect or awaken this experience of enlightened Mind within. The storm means that Thunder-beings are enlightening us—giving us wisdom, mind-transmission. Mind-transmission is an integral part of Buddhas vehicle. Without the grace of the Buddhas, enlightenment is impossible, so they give us their wisdom-clear-light—the taste of enlightenment—in mind-transmission. They literally mix their mind with ours. It is by invoking their enlightened mind and qualities that we receive the grace (of mind-transmission) which is necessary to attain enlightenment. Only Vajrayana or Tantra has this special feature—thus only through traversing this path can one attain enlightenment in one lifetime. The reason for this can be looked at in different ways. Through negative activity of body, speech and mind over countless lives we have caused our Buddha nature to be obscured. Therefore we need a means of purifying our body, speech and mind. We do this through

Tantric practice called Deity Yoga, which means mixing the Enlightened Mind of Buddhas with our own obscured mind. In this way we are enlightened or purified. In Vajrayana it is taught that our enlightenment comes about by the grace of the Wisdom-deity's; it is bestowed upon us by our personal tutelary Deity.

I feel that the above story concerning Shakyamuni's enlightenment symbolizes outwardly the bestowal of supermundane-siddhi (enlightenment) by the Buddhas who preceded him (in previous eons, such as Chakrasamvara, Amitabha, etc.), and inwardly it symbolizes his breakthrough into the fully enlightened state. Because this state is non-dual (beyond inner-outer, self-other), what happens without is what happens within—so the thunder-storm was his own Enlightened Mind, his awareness merging with and dancing in space. The lightning is Buddha's union of awareness and bodhicitta (compassion).

This story demonstrates the true meaning of the Vajrayana, or Lightningbolt vehicle, which is that our enlightenment is based on the blessing-light of the Buddhas who went before us. All Buddhas attained enlightenment through the grace of those who went before them—the Tathagatas—those who have crossed over to the other shore of the sea of suffering and transmigration. It is their vessel which is responsible for guiding us and transforming us, for bringing us to the other shore—to realization, to the state beyond suffering. In the iconography depicting the Buddha sheltered by Muktalinda, the Buddha sits in meditative posture symbolizing that the essence of Buddha Dharma is the practice of meditation, that enlightenment comes about through meditation.

Once enlightened certain Deities like Brahma and Shiva urged the Buddha to teach the means to attain this precious state. He did this in the Three Turnings of the Wheel. It was Lord Buddha's duty to establish the precious vehicles of Buddha Dharma on the earth in this eon. He taught 84,000 collections of teachings geared for beings at different levels of spiritual development. He taught three main vehicles when he walked the earth. These are Sutrayana (Lesser Vehicle), Mahayana (Greater Vehicle), and Vajrayana. The first two vehicles are said to take many lives to reach the goal, but with Vajrayana it can be achieved in one life. Because not all beings are prepared for this vehicle there are lesser vehicles. Lesser implies not less great, but that it is geared for beings of lesser capacity. It is concerned with renunciation, giving up bad habits, creating discipline. Its aspirants seek enlightenment for their own sake. This path will take them to Mahayana. In the Greater Vehicle one seeks to attain enlightenment so one can benefit all beings, one literally strives to attain enlightenment for the welfare of oneself and all beings. In Mahayana one is seeking to include all beings in ones aspiration for attainment. This is the path of transformation or purification. One seeks to purify the results of bad habits and to create new good habits. In Vajrayana, the outward discipline of Sutrayana and the expansive view of Mahayana is included, but the approach and the methods of attaining realization differ. They are geared for attaining enlightenment very quickly, they deal with rapidly enlightening the mind, with liberating negative states into wisdom. In Vajrayana, the Buddhas or Wisdom-deities are used to achieve ones aim. This division into three vehicles is used by Kagyu and Gelugpa lineages. The Vajrayana is then divided into three higher vehicles: Father Tantra, Mother Tantra and Non-Dual or Highest Yoga Tantra. The fruition in Highest Yoga Tantra is called Mahamudra-siddhi, or the "Great Seal." One reason it is called a "seal" is because once one attains it, lower afflictive realms are sealed off, transmigration ends. This great "seal" or "gesture" also refers to the nature of the mind, the gesture of enlightened realization.

Originally little Vajrayana existed in this realm, but was in the Pure Realm known as Akinishta amongst the Dakinis (female Buddhas). Akinishta represents the state of realization of which there is none higher, the Dakinis represent stainless wisdom. The Dakinis and yidams (Buddhas) transmitted these teachings through Shakyamuni. It is said that the Buddha took the form of the Yidam and gave the Tantra of the yidam, the profound teachings and sadhana. The Buddha taught some Vajrayana while on earth, such as Kalachakra and Guhyasamaja Tantras, but primarily gave secret Vajrayana transmission through visions and dreams. He gave the Kalachakra Tantra to the King of Shambhala who requested it and took it back to his kingdom. The other Highest Yoga Tantras, like Guhyasamaja, Chakrasamvara, Hevajra, and so on, he gave to the 84 Mahasiddhas, like Saraha (who is now incarnated as the present Karmapa, head of the Kagyu lineage), Goraknath, Minapa, Krishnacharya, Tilopa, and so forth. Guru Rinpoche received these precious teachings in India and brought them to Tibet were they have existed ever since.

All Buddha Dharma stems from Shakyamuni Buddha, it is because of his compassion, the aspira-

tions which he made in previous lives, that we have Buddha Dharma today. The fact that we have encountered Buddha Dharma indicates that we have made aspirations in our previous lives to do so, and it indicates that our karma is good. Dharma practice is the sole antidote to suffering in our life and the world. To symbolize this in iconography the Buddha has the medicinal plant myrobalan in his begging bowl; this plant is a universal cure among plants so symbolizes that the sublime Dharma is a universal cure for the afflictions that plague sentient beings. Through Dharma practice we can fully eliminate suffering— permanently. So we are very fortunate. Of the one billion realms (triliocosm) there are some realms where the beings are not able to hear Dharma, where it is a dark age and there is no Dharma or even peace. We are fortunate that we have come to earth during a time when Dharma exists and is quite fluent. According to some oral teachings (Kagyu) we are in a golden age, not a dark age. We are fortunate for living in this culture where we are free to practice if we choose. We are very fortunate to have this human body which makes it possible for us to practice it. Only through the human body can we fully comprehend the meaning of Dharma, and practice this meaning. Only through the human body can we practice the union of compassion and wisdom (Dharma). Other beings like animals can practice virtue, self-control, generosity, love, but it is very rare to encounter other beings, like animals that practice the cultivation of wisdom (although some do).

Even though Buddhas take the forms of animals and other beings, these beings do not possess the awareness or leisure to practice their instructions. For this reason we should pray that all beings in less fortunate states receive the blessings to attain a human body to encounter the Dharma, to attain the state beyond suffering.

The light of Dharma, the compassionate expression of the Buddhas extends virtually everywhere, to all realms, but there are beings in lower realms, such as hungry ghosts and hell-beings whose minds are so obscured by negative karma (wind) that it is impossible for them to receive this grace. Everything they encounter appears tortuous according to their obscured view. What to us is a flower, to them is a painful thorn, and to the Buddhas is a brilliant jewel. All the beauty we perceive through our mind is the result of the Buddhas light of Dharma in our mind. If our minds are clear then it fills our mind and we perceive beauty.

If our minds are clouded by fear, doubt, desire, hatred, then this light is clouded, so we perceive things through our obscured vision, as less beautiful or ugly. If we invoke the Buddhas, inviting them into our minds, then our mind and reality will be transformed into a beautiful vision, a dance of light and sound. In Vajrayana we must seek to purify that which obscures us from seeing our mind as it is, and reality as it is. These are called the two obscurations, they are the result of negative activity, activity we engaged in that was harmful to others. In Tantra we seek to purify these two obscurations through Dharma practice.

Tantra is a collection of the most sacred methods of accomplishment which are designed by the Buddhas for taking a prepared or initiated practitioner to the goal in one life-time. These teachings were transmitted from the Buddha's boundless heart of compassion for the liberation of all sentient beings from suffering. Buddhist Tantra is the enlightened speech of the Buddhas arisen from their Omniscient Mind. These teachings arise spontaneously because of the aspiration made by Buddhas when they were training. They are methods of alignment with the Buddhas, by which a devoted practitioner can gather the wisdom-light of the fully Awakened Ones and apply it toward the purification of the two obscurations. These are the methods by which our Wisdom-parents draw us to their level of highest accomplishment. Most Buddhas have gone through the human realm and have achieved themselves while on earth, and are extending themselves, their grace, their sail, vessel and wind, unconditionally to see all beings on earth reach the same state of enlightenment, of omniscient wisdom and unstained bliss.

It may appear that many Deities are responsible for originating the special Buddhist Tantras, however, it is taught that all Buddha Dharma originates with Buddha Shakyamuni. In order to transmit a particular Tantra he would take the form of the Deity of that Tantra, then give the transmission. So all the various Deities can be thought of as Buddha. But they can also be thought of as distinct minds, which exist in perfect unity, which exist simultaneously as opposed to spacially. (They interpenetrate one another). We're so used to viewing reality as being one way or another, that we fail to understand how all beings and phenomena are a unity—that the space of all minds is unified space, that we all share the same spacious deep nature, which is only distinct on the surface. This deep nature is the deep blue Vajradhara, the form Buddha has taken to transmit the Tantras. This form is the very image of our spacious oceanic nature—the unchanging state free of elaborations. Vajradhara is the same for every being—it is our Buddha-nature, who we are, our perfect potential for omniscience. Vajradhara is like the ocean of all the Buddhas.

Buddha is our mind free of limitation. Because we falsely believe it to have limitation, because of our unclear awareness of our true limitless nature, this mind took on limitation, it takes on bodies. In essence it is still free, it is unceasing and unlimited. So we need to have faith in our masters, in the view, in the fact that our nature is unlimited. With this kind of faith we'll actually be able to realize our unlimited wisdom-mind—blissful, free as a bird in the sky, unstained. Wisdom Deities are those who have attained this limitless state, they embody it perfectly, they are totally free of fear, desire, hatred, they are free of suffering. For this reason it is efficacious to worship them. They are responsible for guiding our every virtuous and wise action, they are responsible for setting us on the path, their light is responsible for our bliss and wisdom, for our pure motivation, for our perfection and refinement. They awaken us, make our mind clear so we might see the limitless state and experience its unbroken bliss.

Buddha is our complete potential, it is the state from which we arose into the universe and the state to which we will return. Buddha, or Buddha's Wisdom Mind is the primordially pure and perfect state of our consciousness. Vajrayana is the vehicle for attaining this state, for unfolding or awakening our complete potential for wisdom and compassionate bliss. The general image of this state in Buddha Dharma is that of Buddha sitting in meditation. The special image in Buddhist Tantra of this state is Vajradhara, the "Thunder-bolt Bearer." Vajradhara is the form the Buddha took to give the first Tantric transmissions. Vajradhara is the omniscient state which we arose from, which Buddha Shakyamuni realized, and which all beings who attain Buddhahood realize. Vajradhara is our indestructible nature of perfect equilibrium and peace, the imperturbable or immovable state of our mind. He appears midnight blue to symbolize the oceanic state, he has long black hair half of which is pulled up into a knot, the other half flows freely. He wears gold ornaments and holds vajra and bell to symbolize that the enlightened state is a union of wisdom and compassion, or emptiness and bliss. The lamas do not take him to be a person, but rather a representation of the primordially awakened state of all minds. Because this state is wisdom or clear vision, each distinct mind, each Vajradhara, through its enlightened realization, through its all-pervasive omniscience, realizes the interdependence of all things, the unity of all minds. By existing in perfect unity with every mind, every mind is known perfectly. Perceiving the suffering of innumerable beings, love is spontaneously generated. Out of this love arises the limitless skillful means necessary to assist the innumerable suffering beings to the goal of Vajradhara, the state free of suffering.

When the teachings relate that the supreme mahasiddhas or perfected ones, (like Tilopa, the origin of the Kagyu lineage) received teachings or Tantra from Vajradhara directly, what is meant is that their accomplishment was that of Buddhahood, the state of Vajradhara, and from this state arose the natural insight crystallized into Tantric transmission. Every moment Tantra arose in the form of profound insight suitable to the hearers of the doctrine. In this way the Tantra remains fresh. Each master realizes the meaning of Tantra or Buddha Dharma in their heart, then transmits that realization spontaneously from Vajradhara, the enlightened heart—Buddha. Because each master has realized the same state as Buddha he is able to transmit the complete stream of blessings that arose with Shakyamuni and all the realized masters of his doctrine. Because masters continue to attain realization, the power and blessings of Buddha Dharma do not diminish. Therefore the vehicle that we enter into today is just as powerful a means to liberate us as that of the vehicle the Buddha presented to the mahasiddhas. Iconography depicts the stream of Buddhas' blessings as the vajra, while the Omniscient (open) mind, the perfect vessel to receive those blessings is the bell.

Another way the vessel of our mind can be depicted is as a vase. If we take good care of our mind, practicing openness and compassion, then our mind becomes a worthy container for receiving Tantra. A mind which is full of doubt and fear, which lacks faith in the doctrine, master and Buddhas is not a worthy vessel for receiving Tantra. It cannot hold the precious nectar of teachings or the blessings of the Buddhas. The view of Buddha Dharma is Truth, it is openness, so the mind-vase must be open. The view of the Dharma is unstained Truth, so the mind-vase must be unstained and pure. The Dharma-light of the Buddhas' blessings is totally pure clear-light, so the mind-vase must be pure and clear to contain this light. The initial

practices we engage in is to purify our mind-vessel so that the nectar of Buddhas wisdom and bliss can be held. The minds of the mahasiddhas were totally refined and purified, so they could transmit the wisdom and bliss of Vajradhara. In Dzogchen this mind of enlightenment is called Youthful Vase Body.

The root texts recording the advanced teachings and practices of Vajrayana are called Tantras. The Tantras are simply the mind or heart transmission of the Buddhas, and can be referred to as a revelation or distillation of Buddhas Wisdom-nature. For this reason Vajrayana is called Tantrayana. The Tantras contain the methods of accomplishment of the Wisdom-beings, which are the methods by which the Wisdom-beings emanate image and sound as a device to liberate minds into Buddhahood. Because Buddhas are too pure to take a body, they create emanations and activity. Their first emanations are clear-light images. They exist continuously in Pure Realms or mandalas. The mandala is the situation in which the five certainties are manifested: teacher, teaching, audience, time and place. There are mandalas in many realms, such as Pure Realms, god realms, humans realms, naga realms, and so on. In all realms the teacher is a Buddha (in god, human, or animal realms the teacher emanates in a form suitable to the phenomena of the hearers). In all realms the teaching is Dharma. The audience in Pure Realms are Bodhisattvas, highly achieved ones. In other realms it is those with vary good karma, such as ourselves. The place and time is continuous in Pure Realms, where things are woven from unchanging wisdom-light. In other realms the place and time depend on where and when the Buddha emanates. All mandalas are organized around a unifying center. At the highest level ones clear mind can be thought of as a mandala, ones cells, the universe. It is the family unit of Deity and disciples.

A master who has realized Buddha's teachings may enter the mandala of a Wisdom-deity, meet the Deity at its center, and be given a transmission. The transmission is the Tantra, the practice and its teachings for attaining unity with the Wisdom-deity of the mandala. The master will accomplish the practice and transmit it to prepared students to do the same. Accomplishment means visualizing the imagery as the Buddha transmitted it, and using the respective mantra(s) in order to receive the Deity's blessings. There is actually more to it than this, but that will come later. It is sufficient to understand that such practice invokes the Buddhas wisdom clear light to awaken our own wisdom-mind, characterized by joy, equanimity, loving-kindness and compassion.

The Tantras are developed by beings who have attained the highest level of realization of Buddha's Wisdom Mind—perfection, intrinsic freedom. The Buddhas and their sadhanas might be thought of as extensions of this Primordial Wisdom Mind—which is the deepest nature of all minds and highest level of realization. Each Wisdom-being and method (Yidam: Deity) is a symbolization of the Buddha's Wisdom Mind, expressing itself through an enlightened heart, enlightened will-power, and enlightened activity—compassion. Each Deity emphasizes a unique aspect of the Buddha's wisdom, power and compassion. These are the three outstanding qualities of all Buddhas. Every Buddha embodies all three, but manifests or emphasizes them differently, so the images appear different from one another. They do this to help beings who need to emphasize one quality over another. We need to awaken all three, but beings who suffer primarily from stupidity need to awaken wisdom first, beings who suffer from hatred need to awaken their clear will-power, beings who suffer from passion (desire for self) need to awaken their com-passion. In the Vajrayana pantheons there are innumerable Yidams and their emanations which are utilized as tools to awaken the aspect of Wisdom Mind within us that is embodied in the Yidam. All these innumerable beings might be called the forms of Buddha or Vajradhara. It is taught that there are one hundred Buddha families. These can be condensed into five, the five into three and the three into one—this is Vajradhara. All beings arise from this tranquil state into existence, and all return to it. Because most people are not able to realize it through formless meditation, because people are not able to stabilize their awareness in samadhi (sameness), the Buddhas teach us to use Tantra: mudra, mantra, and samadhi.

Through harmful activity of body, speech and mind, such as stealing, killing (body), lying (speech), and generating negative thoughts and emotions (mind), engaged in over countless lives, we have obscured our awareness from realizing its true nature. These obscurations are the cause of mental and physical suffering, and they cause us to continue practicing non-virtue. For this reason we must purify our body, speech and mind. Virtue alone will not achieve this—because virtue mostly purifies the body. At best, through excellent virtue alone, one can be born as a form-deity, and this is difficult because without prac-

ticing wisdom, our virtue is imperfect. In order to perfect our kindness, to develop a true sense of compassion we must practice wisdom and the generation of bodhicitta "enlightened mind," this increases our capacity to help, and it perfects our actions, so our virtue will be imbued with true love. The light of wisdom that we invoke and awaken through the practice of Tantra is also love. Because we cannot fully purify our mind with virtue we also practice wisdom. This implies visualization (samadhi), mantra, and mudra. By concentrating on awareness light (imagery), and by invoking it (mantra and mudra), the body, speech, mind become purified and luminous.

The Buddhas are not just tools or representations of our nature, as is mistakenly taught, they are true, living, omniscient beings. True, the image of Vajradhara (Samantabhadra) are symbols used by the Buddhas—to depict the formless unchanging state, the Buddhas DO continue to exist. Their minds are like space, they are a union of awareness and inner space. And they're also present, blissful, loving awareness. Buddhas can protect us and bring us to the enlightened state because they have four special attributes; they are free from all fear and suffering, they have skill in liberating all beings, they have great compassion for all living beings, and they are without partiality.

They are omnipresent consciousness so they exist in our minds, not outside in space, the stars or the sky. We know them through our mind. The fact that we can know them through our mind tells us that they are not something different, not another substance than our mind. It tells us that we can attain the omniscient state, because we are extensions of omniscient Mind. It tells us that we are much closer to the Buddhas and more like the Buddhas than we think. It tells us that realization happens here, that the domain of Wisdom Deities is here, it is wherever you happen to be and think of them. It shows us that realization happens now, since we are Buddha now.

It is taught that the Buddhas (including our mind) are never born, never cease, and never remain, they only appear in the modes of space and time according to our needs. All sentient beings have Buddha nature; the body a being takes is based on the meeting of karma (previous activity) and conditions. A beings condition can be imprisonment within suffering or liberation from suffering based upon ones karma or activity. Therefore the first point of Dharma and the most important thing one must understand is karmic law, cause and effect.

In Buddha Dharma, we begin by having some understanding of karmic law—the infallible link between causes and results. Essentially whatever activity we choose, positive or negative, will inevitably bear results in an indeterminate future. We seek to abandon misdeeds or harmful acts because the result is suffering. Beings imprison themselves in a cycle of rebirths through their activity. Through harmful activity to others, they cause a future rebirth of tremendous suffering. Through compassionate activity they cause future rebirth of great bliss and awareness. Harmful activity causes the mind to be darkened or obscured. This confused, obscured mind is blown by the winds of its karma into rebirth in realms which are full of suffering and pain. Compassionate activity enlightens the mind, makes it clear, unobscured, harmonious. This clear mind, is free of confusion and is free to choose where it wishes to go, it is motivated, moved by the force of its loving compassionate intentions to benefit others. It is free to take a body as an animal, human, god or in another world (realm) in order to benefit beings by teaching Dharma. Essentially the animal realms including naga realms, the human realm and the god-realms make up one realm. There are one billion realms in Vajrayana—together these are called the Triliocosm. Our aim in Buddhist practice is to embrace positive compassionate activity, to practice the six paramitas. This enlightens us and of coarse it frees others from suffering.

The life of our mind-continuum is beginningless and endless. During innumerable previous lives all beings have been our mothers, so we ought to view them as we view our own mother, and seek to free them from suffering, by giving everything of ourselves. All beings want what we want, to be free of suffering. If we find it difficult to practice compassion, if we feel helpless, or just lack heart-felt love for others, then we should practice wisdom, because wisdom is the capacity for kindness. A wise person is compassionate. Compassion is wisdom—they go hand in hand—just as Vajradhara (and all Buddha imagery) demonstrates. But Vajradhara also demonstrates that wisdom and compassion need to be practiced together, just as bell goes with dorje. If we practice meditation and mantra, then the wisdom-deity's will awaken our heart of compassion if we start by dedicating ourself and our activity to helping all beings.

The axel of the wheel of existence, of rebirth is our hearts intention. If we nurture good intentions for others and ourself, treating our body and others as

Wisdom-deities or Buddhas and Dakinis, then we will be blessed by the light of this intention. It is called bodhicitta or enlightened mind. Our intention gathers the all-pervasive light of the Buddhas, out of the ocean of Buddhas Wisdom-Mind. If our intention is limited to freeing one being from suffering, the light that arises will be somewhat limited, if our intention is vast and unlimited—to liberate all sentient beings from suffering—then the light gathered will be vast and unlimited. When we pray for one being, one person, we also include all others. That way, the being we pray for, ourself and all sentient beings will be fully benefitted. Eventually, depending on the force of our intentions, what we wish for will come true. What the Buddhas want is to free all beings from suffering, so if we also want that and pray for this in their name, then this intention will come true, and we will become a part of their chain of enlightened intention, a part of their work to achieve this object, a lamp of their infinite light.

It is because of our intentions or aspirations to free beings from suffering that Buddhahood is attained. The result of the intention to help beings brings immediate joy. The greater, more vast and profound our intention, the greater our joy. If we can include all sentient beings in our heart, the light gathered from such an intention awakens the heart to realize its natural luminous perfection—wisdom and bliss. Our heart just keeps opening to include more and more beings into our compassionate vision, until we're like 1000 armed Chenrezig, with 1000 eyes in each hand. This boundless all-seeing love is the goal of all wisdom traditions—it is the essence of Buddha Dharma, without it nothing can be achieved. It is the light of love which causes our realization or Buddhahood. All forms of Buddha Dharma are just different methods for opening the heart, cultivating compassion and wisdom.

By cultivating bodhicitta the wheel of cyclic existence is broken. The hub of the wheel is our ignorance or lack of awareness of our true nature. This causes us to fear, desire and hate. It causes all mental and physical afflictions. It is through the compassionate blessings, the intense bodhicitta of the Buddhas that preceded us that this ignorance is destroyed, that omniscient awareness is awakened. It is through our invocation of Deity's blessings or bodhicitta that we're able to achieve enlightenment. Specifically the lightning bodhicitta destroys ignorance at a glance. One moment we were feeling afraid or desirous, generating negative energy—a future state of suffering, then we think of the Deity and instantaneously our negative emotion disappeared, and we're left feeling quite alive and vibrant, uplifted and fresh, like after a storm. This is the secret meaning of Vajrayana—Lightning vehicle—that bodhicitta awakens mind like lightning. This is how close Thunder-Buddhas are to us, this is how quickly their blessings work. Like a diamond their wisdom cuts through the most fierce obscurations we have. There is nothing, no inner negative state that stands before their lightning-bodhicitta. This is the meaning of Thunder-beings subduing demons, that they remove our ignorance, lack of clarity, confusion, mental affliction, all the causes of suffering in the universe, the causes of cyclic existence or rebirth.

Through our activity of body, speech and mind we give birth to ourselves in six realms of existence: as hell beings with intense suffering, as hungry ghosts, as animals, as people, as demi-gods and as gods. There are many unique characteristics to these six states, but mainly they're all typified by suffering. Through six predominant emotions we give birth to ourselves into these states. Beings with intense hatred become born in hell realms. As an emotion anger is the worst poison because it creates so much harm and destruction to beings. Hell-beings suffer from violent heat and cold. Miserliness causes one to be born a hungry ghost, they suffer from insatiable hunger and thirst. Ignorance causes one to be born an animal. Animals suffer primarily from ignorance or stupidity, they spend their lives unaware of how to perfect their lives. Humans are born because of desire. We suffer because the objects of desire fail to cause true happiness, because we're unaware that true happiness is not based on external conditions. Demi-gods are born out of jealousy, they are engaged in constant struggle against the gods. Gods are born out of pride. Gods have the greatest ease in their life, but might feel little reason to practice dharma. When they're about to die, they experience great suffering because they have visions of their next life—they see what they're about to lose. So it is taught that of these six classes, only as humans do we have the greatest potential for Buddhahood. The reasons for this can be explained on various levels. Mainly we can purify the two obscurations (above) and we can complete the two accumulations, of compassion and wisdom. We can practice compassion, generosity, kindness, patience, joy and wisdom. Everywhere we look there are suffering beings, so our accumulation of merit is potentially limitless. If we don't know what to

do about them, how to liberate them, simply by practicing Dharma we will come to radiate luminosity which benefits them spontaneously, and we will perfect our ability to truly help beings. Dharma benefits the immediate beings around us and all beings. We can't necessarily see this light, some people and spirits can, but mostly we feel it. People who are simply genuine, virtuous feel still and are uplifting to be around. Those who practice wisdom-cultivation and perfect virtue are such a great blessing. Just by encountering them, ones mental and physical afflictions disappear. This comes about as a result of their boundless intentions to liberate beings which they've made over countless lives. We can practice wisdom with this body, we can meditate, practice mantra, worship, pray, etc. We have a body with which we can practice what we learn, and a mind to realize what we learn. It is said that through this human body alone can we complete the two accumulations, of wisdom and compassion. By practicing in this way the two obscurations are removed. These are our unclear view of our mind, and our unclear view of reality.

The human body is our most precious possession, so we can offer it to release beings from suffering, and seeing that we have given up what is most precious Wisdom Deity puts his lamp on the earth. He sees that what he gives us we are going to share with the world. To sacrifice means to make sacred. By sacrificing this body-mind we become sacred—Buddha. On a deeper level the human body is necessary because it is composed of the six elements—bone, marrow, semen, flesh, skin and blood. In Vajrayana practice these elements are dissolved into wisdom (their wisdom sources—the five female Buddhas or wisdom-dakinis).

All Buddhas who attained complete realization attained the self-perfected state through making an aspiration to do so for the benefit of all sentient beings, their wisdom impelled them to think, "I will not cease working to liberate all sentient beings, until every one is free of suffering", this is called bodhicitta of aspiration. Like a human, a tiger or fox chooses to better his state by being patient, choosing not to kill, choosing to love. Some animals have hearts of gold, like horses and puppies. The reason for this is that they chose not to kill or harm. Horses, dogs, dolphins and numerous birds are actually very loving animals. They can become exceptionally wise, and visit us in dreams, giving us the wisdom they were given from Deities. Some animals are full of avarice and some are full of fear, they make things hard on themselves, the same as people. And like people, all sentient beings of the six realms have the potential for Buddhahood. But it so happens that the conditions of human existence are better suited for it than the conditions of the other realms.

Because the Wisdom-deities are all-pervasive awareness, they live with the sufferings of all sentient-beings. They not only see this suffering, but are quite intimate with it. From this state they spontaneously develop boundless compassion to free these beings from suffering. They had developed the intention to free all sentient beings from suffering and they developed the natural perfected wisdom to be able to do this. One feature of it is the ability to see the causes and know the results of our actions, and the ability to know the solutions to all problems. They trained to develop limitless compassion and their mind-training gave them the clarity and insight to truly help beings by freeing them from suffering with their light or bodhicitta, and by providing a means that all beings could use to liberate themselves from suffering. Love is the singular antidote to suffering, what all beings need is love. What all beings want is happiness, but most beings don't really know how to get it, they don't know that they have to go to the Source to get it. It's like a bird thinking that it can quench its thirst by drinking the clouds, instead of going to the source of the clouds, which is the earth's waters. We have to go through Love to be happy. Love means creative self-less activity, wanting to make others happy, and it implies the Wisdom-Source, the Buddha's. To have love, one must love, one must give. The more one gives, the more one is given, until ones love becomes inexhaustible. Even when we worship Deity's they help us realize that our practice is so that the Deity and our mind can love, can truly liberate suffering beings.

Through positive aspirations we gather light through our crown. It is the light of all wisdom deities. It is the grace they give us to give to others. They light our lamp from their flame—so their flame enlightens us to enlighten all beings. This light which appears as a massive ocean or sun, is what they gathered and gathered and gave and gave. It is endless, inexhaustible. The more we give, the more it gathers. We just keep offering it (mind and bliss) to liberate beings, and our mind-body becomes more and more luminous and blissful as a result. The way to liberate ourselves from suffering is the work of liberating others from suffering. This blissful clear-light pervades space—inner

space. The two are inseparable. We call it Chakra-samvara—"Wheel of Bliss," and depict it as a Father-mother in union. Blissful Love is the only revelation of spacious wisdom mind. All beings it is said arise from this Wheel of space into clear-light and then into bodies. This Wisdom wheel is the primordial unchanging nature of all beings from beginingless time. In the clear-spacious hearts of all beings arise a dance of blissful light. In the clear mind it appears as the light of Dharma, the insight and compassionate means to liberate beings from suffering. This light is the virtue of all beings—loving compassion, joy, kindness, generosity and so on. This light or enlightened intention is responsible for all beauty inner and outer. Because we have inner beauty—love, we are able to experience outer beauty. Hell-beings may live in the same place as us, but because they are without love they experience intense suffering from those things which bring us joy. Buddhas of coarse who are saturated with bodhicitta, experience unquenchable bliss, samarasa, "one taste" of pure enjoyment in this realm where we experience a residue or mixture of positive and negative states. Buddhas are the light of the world. All harmonious flourishing, existing and passing away is the result of their love. In order to attain true well-being we seek to dissolve into this light, we gather this light with the intention to liberate all beings. The greater the scope of our intention the greater the light that is gathered and the greater the benefit to all beings. We are this wisdom clear-light, so we invoke it to clear away what obscures our recognition of it within.

This wisdom clear-light manifests innumerable forms to inspire our lives, to draw us to the state of highest realization. The imagery gives us an understanding of formless wisdom-mind, of our nature and the nature of all things. Because we're in the habit of conceptualizing, of fixating on beautiful forms, of getting attached to forms, the Buddhas have developed a skillful way to end all fixation, to bring us to the state free of fixation or attachment, the state of Buddhahood. They have developed imagery whereby we might fixate or attach our minds to beautiful forms which are pure wisdom-clear-light. This light awakens our mind to its natural non-fixated state, its limitless, free, blissful state of Buddhahood. They have given us a form of fixation to end all fixation. Our mind craves the beautiful forms of the world, so when they pass away we're grief stricken. Our mind fears things which we believe cause us suffering, so when we're unable to protect ourselves from an enemy then we experience intense suffering. The imagery destroys our fear, desire, hatred, sadness, all negative states, by enlightening us, by awakening us to our self-less state. By invoking Deity's blessing through imagery and mantra all our barriers are dissolved, our sense of self-cherishing is destroyed. To concentrate or think of Deity's smiling, peaceful form, like Guru Rinpoche when we're sad, brings instant joy and peace. For someone full of fear (of an enemy) to think of Lion-faced Dakini instantly liberates fear. For someone full of desire to concentrate for an instant on Chakra-samvara liberates desire, the cause of rebirth and suffering, so we experience bliss. For someone who is extremely impatient, to concentrate on Vajrapani, causes anger to be liberated into a force of great compassion.

The light of bodhicitta spontaneously arises from the vast sky of our mind like lightning. It makes a light in our heart of inspiration, it is our pure intention to help beings and the actual force that liberates them. It awakens our awareness to see the suffering of others, it dissolves the obstructions to our all-pervasiveness. When these obstructions are removed we naturally feel compassion for all beings. Our compassion and wisdom flashes in our heart like lightning, directed to remove the sufferings of all sentient beings. Wherever it is directed beings are enlightened, just as the lightning in the atmosphere which is directed by achieved beings to benefit nature. The speech of the Buddhas, the voice of dharma is like thunder, whatever beings hear it are spontaneously liberated. Because Dharma is the sound of pure intention, whatever beings hear it, though they may not understand the form of the language, still they are awakened by the light of this sound. Because it is one language of pure intention, no matter what beings encounter it, animals, spirits, people or gods, though they may not understand the form of the language they are still enlightened, just as all beings who encounter the thunder are awakened. Essentially Dharma teachings are the language of all hearts, so all calm minds can receive them directly. Confused or unclear minds, minds full of thoughts and strong emotions, need the medium of language. Some beings do not respond to this language, so require more intense wrathful transmission—such as thunder, howls, cackles, 12-tone laughter, snorts, squeels, neighing, roaring, growling. We will encounter some of these methods in this text; for example Lion-faced dakini roars, Vajra-varahi's sow-head snorts, Vajra-pani's horse head (hayagriva) neighs. These sounds subdue various fierce forms of self-cherishing. Through such skillful means all beings can receive and understand Dharma. It is said that when Buddha taught, all the beings gathered who spoke vastly different languages understood. A Buddha speaks in the language of the heart, this enlightened speech, like thunder goes directly to the source to awaken it.

The language of imagery is understood in the same way (as that of sound). The imagery is received through the hearts clear capacity (to reflect). We see or visualize the face of wisdom, if we're clear and calm, we understand its meaning perfectly, and we will realize that our nature is the same (as Deity). If we're not clear it will awaken our clarity. The vajra-master who originates the transmission receives it in perfect clarity. For most chatter-box minds, we require mind-training, visualization, calm-abiding , Deity's blessing, purification practice, in order to realize the Deity. Our mirrors need some cleaning before the Face of Wisdom can reflect in it perfectly. When it can, one becomes a Source of Dharma, all Buddhas emerge in our mind as wisdom and blissful compassion, they teach through us spontaneously. One can take the form of any Buddha simply upon intention to teach beings who need that Buddhas practice. Examples of this include Shakyamuni, and Guru Rinpoche (the second Buddha) who would take the form of a particular Buddha to give the empowerment or Tantra of that Buddha. The clear mirror of the heart becomes the perfect temple of all Wisdom Deities, so they reflect their light in our mirror-mind, which we can turn onto the world to enlighten beings. Its like holding a mirror up to the sun, then turning it to illuminate something.

This exposition is based on my devotion for the Thunder-beings presented herein, and my alignment with them through practice. Their Face simply reflects itself in my mind. If the mind is clear then the Dharma reflection will resound clearly. If something appears clouded or unclear, then certainly it is because my mind is unclear, so unfortunately you will not understand perfectly what the Deity is like.

The elaborate empowerment given by the vajra-master works like this as well. The Deity empowerment is a way that we're profoundly introduced to the blessing power of the Buddhas. The guru's concentration connects the electric cables of the Wisdom Deity to our heart. This inspiration causes devotion to arise within us, and through our devotion we can continually invoke the Deity in our heart. When the Deity arises there then we're enlightened. When we pray to the Deity in our heart then our prayers come true. Having received empowerment we have continuous access to Deity's unconditional grace—love. We come under the Buddhas protection and guidance. No matter what Buddha we take as our personal Deity we have a means of fully attaining enlightenment. A gate is opened for us to enter that Deity's Inner and Outer Pure Realm. A path of Rainbow light is connected to our minds. If we use the practice with faith and devotion it can completely transform our life by purifying the mind, dissolving our obstructions to omniscience. The guru sows the seed in our fertile heart; through our practice of invocation, the Deity comes, and his grace works upon us like thunder, lightning, rain and sun upon the earth—the ground of our mind is fructified, purified, the seed is nourished and electrified, so that it grows into a Tree which houses all Buddhas, a tree under which beings can take refuge and come to the Dharma, a tree heavy with jeweled fruits, a tree of immense blessings to the world. This tree is the result of the path. We tapped the Deity's blessing power or bodhicitta and realization. Through their attractive love they draw us to their level of realization. Their light works upon mind, awakening awareness and love.

The activity and forms of the Buddhas depends mostly upon the aspirations they made during their training. Because they made vast, heart-felt aspirations, then they attained Buddhahood. If they made a specific aspiration to liberate the most recalcitrant monsters, to bind them by samaya as protectors, to use thunder-power to awaken all beings, then such aspirations give rise to the actual ability to fulfill these aspirations. Whatever we desire strongly will come true. It is reflected in the universe and the universe will find some way of giving you what you want. Either Wisdom-deities will give you enlightenment (if you were virtuous), or dark forces will give you calamity (if you were extremely unvirtous). Vajrayana is the lightning path because through bodhicitta we generate vast and boundless aspirations to enlighten all beings, and this aspiration enlightens us when we transmit it through our prayers to Wisdom-deities who've made aspirations to liberate all sentient beings. Boundless intentions gather boundless light. This light awakens our mind, our ability to fulfill our heart, to insightfully and skillfully liberate beings from suffering. This light is the clear-light of all Buddhas. They want to light your lamp so their wisdom-light can be on the earth, so their aspirations can be fulfilled. They want to fulfill

their loving intention to liberate all beings. So they liberate us and reflect their Wisdom in us to liberate beings . . . and so on. When we radio our aspirations through wisdom-deity they gather intense power to come true. For this reason Vajrayana is both quick and dangerous. If one prays ignorantly for harm to others, then that prayer is augmented for others and oneself. But if one prays to liberate all beings from suffering, then that prayer is augmented a million fold because it is what Deity wants. So they enlighten us, and cause our aspirations to come true. Without their blessing power the path to liberation would be impossible. It would not even exist. If they could simply disappear into some everlasting samadhi-heaven, then there would be no path and no attainment. It is because of the aspirations of all previous Buddhas that attainment is possible. Specifically it is through the aspirations of the Primordial Buddha that realization is possible. He-she is the Source of Tantra and the Source of all Bodhicitta. We call him-her Chakrasamvara. It brings me such joy to be able to say the littlest thing about him. Chakrasamvara is the womb of all Buddhas—the state from which all arose, the state that pervades our countless lives, and the state to which we will return. He is the first Buddha, and all Buddhas. He is our pure potential mind of enlightenment. Enlightenment would not be so if it were not for the Buddhas and Bodhisattvas. Specifically if it were not for Chakra-samvara there would not be Dharma, since he represents its origin. He is the enlightened heart of all the Buddhas.

Our achievement is based much more than we think on the Wisdom Deity's. Even practitioners who do not rely on Deity's support, are still graced by them. We're immersed in this ocean of blue light (Chakra-samvara)—it is responsible for the enlightenment of all Buddhas—it is the ocean of compassion which helped them achieve enlightenment and which will assist us in the same way. It takes the form of countless Buddhas and Bodhisattavas, of our own personal Deity (yidam). Whichever way we connected with it in the past is the way it will present itself to us in the present. Whatever way we connect with it now is the way we will connect with it in future. Ultimately we will realize it within. It becomes our supreme vehicle to enlightenment. Through our personal Deity's grace and our devotion we will attain enlightenment. It is taught that the yidam bestows the two siddhis—ordinary and extraordinary. The first is miraculous display (miracles) the second is full realization or omniscience. The first siddhi implies the power to control inner winds—inner elements, and therefore outer elements. The second means complete control of the mind.

Because of change or impermanence there is suffering. We mistakenly feel that we and all objects have a tangible permanent reality. We feel this because we are unaware of our mind, because we have developed the habit of living through our senses, of not paying attention within. If we remained attentive of our mind from the start, we would not experience suffering—because our true nature is free of suffering, peaceful, unagitated, blissful, perfect. So all Dharma practice has to do with paying attention within, either through form or formless meditation. Such is why most Buddhas are figured seated in meditation. Because we are in the habit of paying attention through our senses, our mind becomes obscured to us. So we forget that we are limitless, fearless, indestructible, blissful, tranquil—Buddhas. We think that what we are is the limited body, and a limited brain contains the mind—so all of our activity is based on protecting this self, cherishing it, living for it. Because we hold this view of our self, then our view of the world becomes equally limited—phenomena seem quite permanent to us, yet in truth their nature is totally impermanent. We try to hold onto them thinking they will provide happiness, but they just slip away and we feel grief-stricken by this. Because we fear for ourself, we develop the habit of self-cherishing. This habit is totally responsible for our suffering. All Dharma, view and practice is aimed at destroying our sense of self-cherishing. It awakens our awareness, so we can see that there's no self to cherish. To realize this takes us out of our heads, so we can devote ourselves to cherishing others. So at first we seek to shift our view of self and reality. Dharma is Truth, true view of things. The Buddha realized this view. If we view our nature as without self, limitless, this will cause omniscience, tranquility and equilibrium to dawn. When you feel the peace of a master you feel the self-less state. This view will also cause us to stop living for ourselves alone, it will cause our hearts to open to others. If we view all external phenomenon as impermanent, then we will not hang on to anything, we will not grasp at things rigidly (because its just going to pass away), but will offer it up generously to benefit others, to make them happy. In truth we derive happiness from making others happy.

This view of phenomenon includes our body. It is an impermanent vessel for the wisdom-deity to come here to benefit suffering beings, and can pass away at any time, so there's no use hanging on to it, and spending so much energy and time cherishing it. It is said that Yama, Lord of Death strikes like a lightning flash. So at any moment, this life might end, and then we're simply left with whatever cultivation we did in our life. If we lived a rotten life, we'll unquestionably be blown into embodied existence of suffering. There's no telling when such an existence or cycle of rebirths will end. Such a life is too distracted by suffering to practice Dharma. If we lived virtuously we'll either return here or we'll be taken to a Pure Realm to learn Dharma in the body of a form Buddha—like an angel. Our positive energy (karma) will support us, our subtlest energy and mind will continue until it realizes its all-pervasiveness. Generally the path of the form Buddha is known as the Bodhisattva path, or path of the "enlightened warrior." Our perfected nature (represented by Vajradhara or our personal Buddha) is unchanging tranquil nature. It is indestructible like diamond, luminous like lightning, unshakable and vast like space. It has been called Vajradhatu—vajra-sphere or space). It is our unwavering state of perfect awareness. It is blissful emptiness.

This oceanic Wisdom Mind focuses its wisdom clear-light for us by creating images. We have developed the habit of ordinary conceptualization (thoughts) and ordinary appearances. We view our mind and phenomena in a limited, fixed and ordinary way. Our view causes us great suffering. Our unclear view causes us to think the body is permanent reality and reality is permanent, solid and fixed. But in truth reality is impermanent, a dance of illusion. We developed this habit over countless lives. It obscures limitless wisdom-mind. This view actually causes us to take bodies which seemingly limit mind spacialy and temporally. The truth is that mind and phenomena are a union of emptiness, insubstantial like space, and bliss. If we hold this view we will have no reason to grasp strongly at a definable ego, since none exists. No definable, limited self can be located if we make a concerted effort to look into the mind. It is an illusion which causes all of our suffering to think of ourselves as a definable self, which needs protecting and cherishing. To be free of this attachment or fixation on a limited self, permanent body and phenomenon, then we will give freely of ourselves. We must train to loosen our grasp on self by giving freely of ourself. If we loosen our grasp on what we hold most dear, we will be free of the causes of grief, desire, hatred, jealousy, pride and fear. So we train to give freely of ourself, and all that we possess. Our greatest possessions are the body-mind. So the greatest offering we can make is that of body and mind. In the stories of Buddhas' previous lives it is related that on several occasions he sacrificed his body to free others from suffering. We may not be in the position to actually do this, so we make the offering in our heart while visualizing it. This method gathers boundless merit and does help countless beings.

Because the body is a precious vehicle for attainment of Buddhahood, we offer it, body, speech and mind to liberate all beings. Our body, speech and mind are then purified, spiritualized. If we visualize ourselves as totally pure—a Buddha, and offer what we are, then the benefit of such an offering will be even greater. This practice is the essence of Chod (which will be elucidated later).

Great achievement comes with great sacrifice. If we sacrifice our sleep every night to meditate we gain a clear tranquil mind and receive creative inspiration through light. If we sacrifice our sense of self-cherishing, we give up the cause of suffering and attain true well-being. If we sacrifice all our time and energy by offering it to liberate others through whatever practice we're doing, then we gain enlightenment. If we sacrifice our body-speech-mind it becomes sacred, the body-speech-mind of all Buddhas. And finally if we sacrifice our enlightened wisdom-mind and blissful compassion, everything we gain from practicing Dharma, then we attain the highest fruition—Buddhahood, and all sentient beings will truly be able to attain enlightenment. The meaning of being human from the very start is sharing oneself. Through our previous positive aspirations we have this precious human body. Therefore we must share this body, offer it as our most precious possession. We must offer it to Wisdom Deity until it no longer exists, until only space and bliss exist—until we're Infinity. Our body appears solid because we cherish it, because we want to hold onto things, because we view them as solid and permanent. It becomes emptiness-light when we sacrifice it, when we give it away. It becomes Deity's light-display. It becomes a lamp to guide sentient beings to enlightenment. It becomes a vessel of intoxicating nectar which is freely distributed to intoxicate beings. When this vessel, called Youthful Vase Body, breaks, when one's mind leaves the earth—there are miracles, weather changes, storms, rainbows, beautiful sights, sounds and smells, wisdom disperses like the scent when a rose-perfume pot is broken. To those who experience this, their minds are liberated, intoxicated upon encountering it.

Vajrayana means that the Buddhas inexhaustible blessings returns us to the empty, spacious, limitless state as quickly as lightning returns form to emptiness. When lightning strikes something the shock is usually so great that it turns to a tiny heap of ashes, the essence of the form returns to the emptiness from which it arose. For this reason Vajrayana is called the Lightning path. By rapidly illuminating our mind, we return to our empty luminous blissful state. Lightning is mostly a metaphor in this case. It is not that all Buddhas strike us with lightning when we practice. It means that the force to enlightenment is like that of lightning. It does not mean that all Vajrayana people are out invoking lightning in storms, praying that it strike all beings, so they become liberated. This misunderstanding, however amusing, is quite absurd.

We have arisen out of light into form. Mind is subtle wisdom-clear-light, body is gross wisdom-clear-light. Out of limitless wisdom we have arisen into form through light. Through light we practice to dissolve back into limitless wisdom. Through practice with the Source of enlightenment we are illuminated. This Source appears as lightning to rapidly illuminate us. Lightning in all spheres rapidly returns form to emptiness. So when we receive the grace of a Buddha appearing with lightning, our mind is being enlightened, returned to space instantly. When we hear thunder and see lightning our mind is shocked—it stops elaborating, so our naked state becomes apparent and its compassionate-bliss shines through. When you visualize Thunder-Buddha or Dakini Lighting, the mind is awakened. It is a unique characteristic of some Buddhas to use thunder and lightning amongst clear-light imagery. By visualizing it, and by invoking the blessings of these Buddhas, the mind is rapidly illuminated. Enlightening grace-waves can be manifest by Buddhas in infinite ways according to the needs of sentient beings. Because certain minds are in need of rapid crystal-clear enlightningment—Buddhas manifest thunder and lightning imagery. And of coarse these same Buddhas develop methods whereby we can invoke them to arise in the atmosphere to bring rain, pacify, subdue demons, protect Dharma, cause miracles, etc. Because nature is in periodic need of rapid illumination to purify the earth, these Thunder-beings manifest tangibly in storms.

* * *

Vajrayana is called Lightning vehicle and Diamond vehicle. It is called Lightning vehicle for two reasons. First for its speed and power; it is able to bring the sincere practitioner to the goal in one life-time, whereas other paths are reputed to take life-times or eons. The other reason is by virtue of its ultimate derivation with Thunder-beings, or Wisdom-beings who use subtle thunder and lightning as a method of awakening minds. The Vajrayana is an immeasurably vast and sacred vehicle, many Buddhas and Dakinis are responsible for its origination and do not function through the wisdom-configuration of lightning. However the Primordial Wisdom Mind behind all transmission vehicles is a Thunder-being. The Buddha's Wisdom Mind (Chakrasamvara) has appeared to me as a Thunder-being, whose imagery will be elucidated herein. Their vehicle is one of unstoppable power and speed, and the lightning-bolt represents the wisdom and force to achieve the goal.

Vajrayana is the enlightened heart vehicle. The vajra signifies the fully enlightened heart, its adamantine immutable nature. The vajra or thunder-bolt symbolizes Buddha Mind, the primordially perfect state of the mind, its immutable awareness and clear light. The enlightened Mind reveals itself through wisdom-light as a Lightning-bolt. In doing so it reveals its fully awake nature (wisdom), and its spontaneous activity of enlightening minds (skillful means). The vajra stands for this indivisible union of insight (into reality and the mind) and the skillful or compassionate means to guide and assist all beings to the enlightened state.

The Tibetan "insiders" chose to translate vajra as dorje "lord of stones," while their word for lightning-bolt is sky iron. Lightning-bolts were generally thought to be iron, meteoric iron flashing in the atmosphere, and appearing as metallic stones where they touch down. The dorje's held by numerous Vajrayana Deities are metoeric iron bolts of five or nine tines. It does not necessarily imply that they are Thunder-beings, that they live and are going to appear amongst thunder and lightning. The vajra symbol suggests the nature of the Buddha's Wisdom Mind which is LIKE a thunder-bolt, and the vital-force or indestructible wind and self-arisen light of the fully awakened Mind. The nature of subtlest Mind (wisdom) and its radiance (bliss) is vajra. So the two sides of the vajra symbolize wisdom and bliss. To symbolize this most Buddhas appear with a vajra, in their hand, their hair, on their bell, staff, at their heart. . . . Like a thunder-bolt, our absolute wisdom-nature (represented by all Buddhas)

is immutable, unbreakable and all-conquoring, there is nothing which can destroy it or defeat it. It is the indivisible union of wisdom and compassionate method or emptiness and bliss. It is the awake-nature of our consciousness which remains immutable through innumerable lives, and through innumerable inner transformations. Our minds are fully awake like a lightning-bolt from beginningless time. The Primordial Buddha bears the vajra emblem and flashes lightning to symbolize the radiant, wise nature of our minds.

Wisdom Mind rides an unobstructed energy current (figured as a windhorse, or Garuda), displayed as a lightning-bolt. It is the spontaneously arisen Deity of awareness and clear-light. The thunder-bolt is Mind, its concentration, revelation or pure display. Just as the imagery or iconography can provide immense insight into our true-nature, so the thunder-bolt or dorje can provide insight into our true-nature, by representing it. Perhaps you might have thought the images of Thunder-beings were about some other beings, but in truth these images are about who we are. Perhaps now you might think they stand for the part of who we are which is beyond us, but if the method is embraced then the Deity will reflect us to show us that we are the same—one continuum, "Tantra."

The thunder-bolt is ungraspable, in a like manner the mind cannot be pin-pointed, it abodes both everywhere and no-where. It is in the brain, heart, channels, chakras, drops, body and yet is beyond them. The thunder-bolt is luminous pure energy in union with mind, it is the concentration and only reference to that Mind. Likewise the mind appears as a radiance, whose vision produces a display of thoughts, images and feelings. The thunder-bolt penetrates anything unobstructedly, so does the minds nature of awareness, of knowing, which penetrates by its subtlety and all-pervasiveness. To know something we burn into it with our awareness (light), until we're one with it and can experience it in this way. The thunder-bolt also arises spontaneously wherever you see it, our mind and nature, our awareness can also be characterized by spontaneous arising, (as in thinking or imagining). The thunder-bolt of the Deity is the Deity, it is pure awareness. The Vajrayana Deities are called Awareness-beings. The Thunder-bolt Deity, the Vajra-being (Vajradhara or Vajrasattva: Enlightened-being), can take the form of a stone as a potential power. This was the shamanic experience of the vajra. Legend has it that the first dorje fell at a place in Darjeeling—dorje ling, meaning "where the dorje fell." And is has been the experience of some yogis while doing the Vajrapani, "Vajra in Hand" sadhana to be rained on by stones from thunder-clouds. So the Thunder-deity can manifest this way. Our mind has potential power like this kind of thunder-stone, to become Buddha and to appear as a lightning-bolt or stone or innumerable subtle emanations and earthly incarnations. But we need to train to recognize this potential. Just as the thunder-stone appears to an ordinary mind as stone, so the ordinary mind sees itself just as an ordinary mind, as a mind we're conditioned to think is limited and dual—one way or another. The reality of the thunder-stone is that it is really alive, radiant-wisdom, a piece of Thunder Lord which can dance and flash and move in your hand. So also the reality of each person is infinite, we are unlimited Vision, this seems to be best demonstrated in the fact that we're always learning and growing, always expanding, and that our hearts never stop thinking, which demonstrates inexhaustible radiance.

Now, whether we can see our true nature clearly or not is based on our degree of awareness and mental clarity. Tantra has the aim of purifying the mental obscurations which veil our clear awareness, our clear-light mind, so that we can realize the Truth of our nature and reality. Our obscurations prevent us from seeing our present omniscient state. Our view of our mind and reality is limited because we developed the habit of not paying attention within. Our mind-training can be formless meditation to develop the positive liberating habit of paying attention within, and it can be form meditation for enhancing or enlightening our awareness so that it sees its true limitless nature, and knows the nature of reality.

The vajra is our potential for unlimited consciousness, inexhaustible radiance and bliss, and boundless unconditional love. The vajra also denotes the strength of awareness of concentration. In some cases the Deity shoots a lightning-bolt of Illumination from his third eye, which is a symbol of primordial awareness, and this lightning-bolt usually destroys a being which symbolizes confusion or obstacles. So the vajra is the power of our concentration. The lightning-bolt is literally the concentration of all-pervasive awareness-light of the Thunder-being. The vajra and lightning-bolt is Infinite Vision, the non-dual state of our Mind which sees the two truths—of Ultimate Reality (reality as it is) and reality as it appears to relative mind.

The Wisdom or sub-atomic continuum at the root of the elements (Phenomena Source) is one Mind, one deep Wisdom. It represents the beginning of our mind, the beginning of a display of illusion, the universe, insubstantial like space, yet containing immense potential power. When the power comes out, you have something near an explosion, you have light and sound. There is one wisdom-light branched into five wisdom-lights of the colors of the rainbow, and these are the element qualities. The singular Consciousness Light-Source, which exists through all minds, dwells at the beginning of things, and for this reason has control over reality and mind. This state, denoted by the vajra, represents the mode of subsistence of all Buddhas, and is referred to as dharmakaya. It is depicted as the deep blue Adi-Buddha, Samantabhadra in union with his consort Samantabhadri, Vajradhara and Chakrasamvara. It has two aspects, wisdom truth body, which is immutable and nature truth body or awareness, which is impermanent. Wisdom truth body is characterized by diamond hard stabilization and emptiness. Its cognitive aspect is wisdom and it precedes light. Nature truth body is characterized by awareness, energy and bliss through which the Deity arises as light, sound, activity and imagery.

The accomplishment of the Buddhas is formlessness, which is also complete selflessness and is expressed in kindness. It is like space, devoid of any inherent self-existence, and is referred to as Void. The path to this omniscient state, to Buddha-hood is through selflessness and compassion. Because it is difficult to reach this state by relying on our own limited energy, we tap into the unlimited power Source of the Buddha's Wisdom Mind, and this helps us to accomplish our goal. Because it is difficult or even impossible to connect with the Buddha's all-pervasive emptiness, we must connect with him or her through light and sound, through Deity's image and mantra. Because only other Buddhas can perceive the subtle formless aspect of the Deity, he emanates into pure light form, called sambhogakaya or body of complete enjoyment. He projects these into Pure Realms and functions through them. He lives there in this body as a concentration like a drop of dew in an ocean, or the point of a diamond. He draws devoted practitioners there when they die. Accomplished practitioners can travel there freely while they live. These complete enjoyment bodies—or visionary forms are said to be continuous; they're not totally unchanging and yet they're not impermanent either. They possess what are called the five certainties: certainty of teaching, place, retinue. . . . So they teach Buddha Dharma in Pure Realms to Bodhisattvas . . . and so on.

So the formless body of the Buddha is aligned with through form. When we connect with the Buddha Minds, we align with this deep or empty body and its energy. This image-body exists as a true and dynamic living presence, it is woven and projected out of pure wisdom and light. In Vajrayana there are innumerable Buddhas and Wisdom-dakinis existing in innumerable Pure Realms or Realms of Pure Enjoyment, in a possibly infinite subtle space. The Buddhas manifest these Buddha-fields with their Minds, within them devotees come together like chemical light compounds. These Pure Realms (mandalas) and their Buddhas exist fully within our psycho-physical organism. They exist simultaneously, not necessarily spacially. Invoking them calls them into our field of direct awareness out of the emptiness or all-pervasive depth of the mind.

Vajra applies to Buddha Mind before it manifests, in which case it is called vajra-mind and vajra-wisdom. And it applies to Buddha Mind as it manifests through light in which case it is called vajra-body and vajra-speech.

The vajra is the nuclear energy or radiating life force in union with awareness and bliss. It is the refined mind, or the refined winds which support the mind. These winds are electrified by the power of the Awareness-deity into pure light currents. Some exceptional siddhas achieved themselves through the thunder-powers, through the Thunder-bolt of Wisdom and Illumination of those who went before them, and layed the foundation for the path. Vajrapani for example, and Guru Rinpoche achieved themselves eons ago and are going to assist prepared practitioners to the same accomplishment. Certain practitioners may be awakened through the configuration of the Deity's Lightning-bolt, which is extended to those whom the Deity wishes to have it. This revelation is the force of the Buddha's attainment, the flow of his grace and shape of his blessing-lights. He or she simply presents it that way. We are witnessing the Unborn, Uncreate Wisdom Mind, the enlightened heart and its enlightened activity of bestowing wisdom. By giving of itself, it helps all sentient beings to attain enlightenment.

In early Buddhist iconography the Buddha was figured with a vajra at his heart. The vajra stood for the pure power, luminosity and wisdom of the Tantric deities. They reveal themselves to yogis as Lightning-bolts—amongst thunder and lightning as visionary phenomena. The vajra is the emblem of the Thunder-beings, the Unborn wisdom and primordial power of the universe. The Buddhas control the mind, they control the power of awakening minds, so their path is called Vajrayana. The origination of the Vajra vehicle is with the Thunder-beings, the Buddhas who manifest amongst thunder and lightning as visionary phenomena, who use this power to awaken the mind and release beings from suffering. These Buddhas are Vajradhara "Thunder-bolt Bearer", the Father of the Vajra family and the Buddha in charge of transmitting Tantras, and his primary wrathful Vajra emanations: Vajrapani and Chakrasamvara and his consort Vajrayogini. Their iconographies and place in the Tantra will be discussed below. Because the origination of all Buddhas and Wisdom-dakinis is the Primordial Undifferentiated Adi Buddha Vajradhara, it is fair to say that the power and configuration, the vajra goes back to him.

The Lightning-bolt is the Deity's awareness-symbol or mudra. Because it signifies the awakened state of the Mind it might be termed the Mahamudra, the "Great Seal" or "Great Symbol"—the omniscient state. The vajra is a sign which signifies the Mind (wisdom), the unimpeded power of the Mind (will-power), and the unimpeded activity of the Mind (compassion). These are the three qualities of all Buddhas. Certainly our minds are not appearing as lightning-bolts presently. If you look for the mind, all that can be found are its attributes, and its thoughts and signs. But the mind is actually very much like space, or radiant space, and is without signs, so is deemed emptiness. It is without self-existence or something which can be pin-pointed as "I," it is invisible and limitless like space. The primordial state is the empty nature of the cosmos, Mind merged with space. It is the Truth Body of Ultimate spaciousness, the Absolute from which all Buddhas arise to display themselves, incarnate then remerge with space. We have arisen out of formlessness as emanations of the Buddhas Wisdom Mind. We are inseparable from it. We are light dancing in space.

The Buddhas, with the exception of the two Primordial Buddhas, attained enlightenment in previous kalpas (eons) and, because of their capacity for wisdom, know the precise solution to the restoration of all minds. They know the past, present and future of all minds perfectly. They know the practices suitable to the diverse dispositions of people, which will carry them to Buddha-hood. So the Buddhas develop methods which resonate with each individual and methods which can be used to fine tune all aspects of ones being. For example, if a person is in need of healing, the Azure Radiance Tathagata can be supplicated, if one needs to liberate anger, then according to the master, the Vajrapani sadhana might be prescribed, if one needs to liberate passion, the Chakrasamvara practice might be prescribed. So the sadhanas could be used in this specific way as medicines to heal and awaken the enlightened aspects of Buddha Mind.

It also happens that certain Buddhas—the Thunder-beings, develop thunder rites, methods whereby thunder-power is gathered through the Yidam and directed for altruistic purposes of healing, weather-making, performing exorcisms, etc. Examples of such sadhanas include, Vajrapani, Vajra-varahi and Trolma Nak mo, whose images are presented herein. Any Wisdom-being might be supplicated to act in this function, especially Vajra family deities, performing such feats to them is a simple gesture (mudra).

The prerequisite for siddhi (feats of controlling the elements) is realization, not the Buddha's family affiliation. Take for example Guru Rinpoche, he was able to control lightning as a siddhi, but is a Lotus family Buddha. We refer primarily to Vajra family Cities of Lightning because these Buddhas tend to appear mystically as Thunder-beings, and their sadhanas tend to be the ones used to control weather. The wisdom of any Buddha, I feel, can take the form of lightning to awaken minds. It is viewed as a skillful way of appealing to and awakening beings in need of this unique transmission.

Because most humans are in need of some assistance in restoring Buddha-nature, the Buddhas shed the light of their nature freely, in fact this iridescence is the nature of Ultimate Reality. It acts to guide and awaken us based on our openness to the light. It guides everyone whether we realize it or not. The grace of this light, the method of gathering the light, and its rapid illumination are the Vajrayana. Although it is there as the nature of things, in order to affect spiritual transformation, it is necessary to embrace the mind-training and it is efficacious to invoke the blessing-lights of the Buddhas which will directly awaken us. The blessing-lights magically destroy ignorance and afflictive emotions, all hindrances to the omniscient and blissful state. It is the power which purifies the mind. It dissolves the gross energy which limits our inner vision and causes us to see the mind and reality as fixed and dual and a cause of suffering. If we see ourself as a fixed limited entity, an "I" which is separate and destructible, then we feel we must need protecting. The adamantine-light, the grace-waves of the Buddhas, destroys this erroneous view, it gives us insight and removes ignorance simultaneously. This light expands our mind from within, like a lotus unfolding.

The Deity mixes his Wisdom or Mind with our mind, and awakens us in this way.

Because their Mind is an absence (immutable emptiness), it has the power to remove obstacles, to create a space or absence in our mind. Because their Mind is a presence (awareness), it has the power to bestow insight, and to make us present. The absence is Wisdom Truth-body, the presence is Nature Truth-body. When the Deity reflects his nature in ours, we are able to see by its illumination, by its presence, and what we see is that we lack inherent existence, that we are truly absent. This absence (space) is wisdom and tranquility, this presence (light) is awareness and bliss.

All images of Buddhas and Wisdom-dakinis are various pure symbolizations of Vajradhara, they are its wisdom, power and expression. Chakrasamvara is the union of all enlightened minds. It is one City of Lightning; like a wheel it displays multiple deity-methods like lightningbolts emanating as spokes into the four directions. Each Buddha expresses a unique coloration or fragrance of the Wisdom Mind (the center), and each Buddha can be taken as a totally individual presence, like a drop of color dissolving into a sea of light. The directional emanations express the unique functions or activity of the central Buddha through its five wisdoms. The vajra has five tines or rays which emanate from a central spark and then come back together at a point. The tines symbolize these five wisdoms, and the five Buddha families. The countless Buddhas in the universe are grouped into five families, each family corresponding to an aspect of the Buddhas Wisdom Mind. These families and their fathers, from East to West to center, are: Vajra—Akshobya; Jewel—Ratnasmbhava; Lotus—Amitabha; Action—Amoghasiddhi; and Buddha—Vairochana.

Originally all humans are Buddhas, pure aspects of Adi Buddha and his Wisdom-dakini. The mind-stream is beginningless and endless. Individual existence was said to last 80,000 years and there was no material existence, so no bodily habits like eating and sleeping, and no disease because there was nothing to obstruct the mind. The mind was nourished upon undiminishing energy, infinite bliss and pristine wisdom. This is the state we're seeking to return to. Buddhas at some point in the development of the universe began taking bodies on earth. First we appeared as giants, then according to the thickness of our mental obscuration, began shrinking and living shorter lives. In the golden age (1st yuga of this eon) beings radiated light from their bodies, they could move miraculously through space, live without food, sleep or material supports. (The universe has been said to be a vast ground in which for Buddhas to practice skillful means, for this reason, Vairochana created this universe, which is the 13th in an uncountable number. It is known as "Universe of Enduring"). The Vajrayana delineates the process of incarnation into eons, each consisting of five world systems. At the beginning of each eon, Buddhas descended from a Heaven of Clear Light to initiate the Five Worlds. Vairochana, the "One Who Make Things Visible", initiates the first world through mind-emanation. He also incarnated as the teaching Buddha of that world. Each world follows the cyclical nature of the universe, of birth, growth, decay and death. At a certain point it becomes necessary for wisdom to be restored through spirituality, so during each world, a Buddha descends to restore Dharma by presenting a suitable form of Vajrayana. Each yuga ends in a purification. The Garuda descends to usher in this purification, which consists greatly of storms. He signals the transition between a season of ignorance and decay and a new one of light. He functions this way in nature and in the mind-sphere. The first world and each succeeding one is dissolved through winds, fires and floods. In the coarse of the first world, many attained Buddhahood and some did not, so a new world was initiated by Akshobya through the activity of Vajrapani. During this world people belonged to the Vajra family and reflected it in their mind and activity, which might imply inherent power, most likely the abuse of which created the necessity for a new world. The teaching Buddha then was called Dipankara. Though many attain completion, still there are many who failed to. The third world system is initiated by Ratnasambhava. The teaching Buddha then was called Kashyapa. People were giants then, their life-span was 1000's of years. Everything was in proportion. So I've heard about grains that still exist from 2 million years ago that are huge. The fourth is the present. It was initiated by Amitabha, Buddha of Boundless Light through Chenrezig, Buddha of Compassion and Mercy. This makes us children of the Lotus family. Certainly our fathers have had a strong place in the past 2000 years. The Buddha Shakyamuni and Guru Rinpoche are both Buddha emanations of Chenrezig-Amitabha and are responsible for transmission of Vajrayana. The emanations Karmapa and Dalai Lama are both emanations of Chenrezig and are responsible for sustaining Vajrayana in pure form.

This degenerate age is characterized by the five degenerations—shortening of life-span, degeneration of environment, of views, decline of faculties, increase of negative emotions. This includes increase in disease. The Buddha prophesied that 5,000 years after his coming, the Dharma would die out (until Maitreya comes in the next world system). We are presently at the 2500 year mark. It is said that the Dharma will decline until the end of this world. This world system will be destroyed by winds, fires and floods. Many have and will continue to attain Buddhahood, although it seems many will fail. The fifth and last world of this eon will be initiated by Amoghasiddhi, the All-accomplishing One, created out of dark-green light. We might anticipate energetic activity in the pursuit of Buddhahood. It is taught that only Vajrayana will be practiced in this age, because it will be too difficult to practice formless meditation. Its teaching Buddha will be Maitreya. Maitreya will attain enlightenment millions of years from now. Life-span will have increased to 20,000 years. When this occurs life-span will increase to 80,000 years. In the oral teachings of the Kagyu it is said that the present Karmapa will be the teaching Buddha to follow Maitreya. His name will be "Lion's Roar." The entire eon follows a cyclical movement which sees humans returned to their original state.

The Buddhas and Dakinis which serve the function of Thunder-beings in the unverse tend to be Vajra family mandalas. (Although I know of Deities of other families, like Amitabha's who manifest as Thunder-beings as well). It is the Eastern family who bear the power of awakening and the wisdom of initiation and continuous expansion, which can take the configuration of lightning or remain symbolized in the vajra emblem. (There are also groups of other Thunder-beings such as dragons like the Turquoise Blue Thunder-dragon, and Naga Kings, but these are separate classes of natural deities and are not pertinent to this exposition). It is taught that the Wisdom-Garuda ushers in the purification at the end of the eon. He might be equated with the Thunder-bird of other traditions. He will be discussed in relation to Vajrapani below.

All Buddhas have the same essential qualities, but each is totally unique. What makes them unique is the arrangement of Buddha qualities or the five wisdoms. Each family emphasizes a particular aspect of the totality—Buddha's Wisdom Mind, the purpose of which is to guide humans of diverse dispositions to Buddhahood. The five Buddhas stand for all-pervasive forces in the universe at the level of vast inner space (Mind), and the Five Wisdom-Dakinis, the consorts of the five Buddhas, stand for all-pervasive forces in the sphere of the universe. The five Buddhas and their wisdoms are as follows: Akshobya—form, Ratnasambhava—feeling, Amitabha—ideation, Amoghasiddhi—action, and Vairochana—consciousness.

The five elemental forces are as follows: solidity, fluidity, motion, heat and spaciousness. When obscured these wisdoms act as emotional afflictions in the mind, when liberated they manifest as wisdom. When obscured these elemental forces act as limiting factors, when seen through pure inner vision they are five Wisdom-dakinis—lights. The enlightened qualities of a persons mind are a rainbow. An Enlightened one emanates rainbows and can dissolve into rainbows. This means the Source of the elements (emotions, mind) is totally purified. (I want to also mention that the five Buddhas govern the five realms from hell up. All realms are actually pure realms governed by a particular Buddha family. For example the hell realms are governed by Akshobya. When the mirror-like wisdom is clouded as hatred, it is experienced as hell. So out of hatred the beings experience this realm as great suffering. Our realm is Amitabha's realm, we experience it as the "realm of desire" because through the habit of desiring we perceive things this way. In reality this realm is the "realm of pure enjoyment." Each of the six realms together are actually one out of one billion realms. The six realms are realms of experience which are conditioned by our habitual activity. Poor habits of hatred, greed, ignorance, desire, jealousy and pride are what cause beings to experience hell, hungry ghost, animal, human, demi-god and god. Whereas excellent wise habits such as patience, generosity, awareness, compassion, loving-kindness, humility, cause beings to experience Pure Realms governed by Buddhas. Out of compassion to try to liberate beings embroiled in these realms the Buddhas incarnate in all of them. In the lower realms the conditions for understanding and practicing Dharma are not good, so it is very difficult to be extricated from them. In the upper of the 6 realms, such as our own, it is much easier to understand and practice Dharma).

Tradition delineates three root delusions which are the causes of all mental and physical illness, these are: ignorance, desire and hatred. Jealousy and pride are developed out of these three. The root of the five is ignorance, or the erroneous view of our nature and reality. The clouded delusions are the same energy as wisdom, only differing according to frequency or our degree of awareness. With this in mind we might see how much more easily we can change the mind, Tantra presents the mind as energy which we are able to manipulate and work with, as opposed to a fixed neuro-chemical reality. Tantra utilizes the process by which these deluded energies are liberated to reveal their original expansive state.

When the wisdoms become obscured (by turning the lamp of awareness onto the objects of sense to seek fulfillment, and by becoming fixated on those objects) the wisdoms appear as delusions. So the process of Vajrayana is to reverse this process through the application of Buddhas subtle light of wisdom, and through concentration on imagery. Visualization uses color, light and sound to awaken the mind. Through these methods, the delusions give way to wisdom and egocenteredness to compassion. The imagery and mantras enhance the minds clear awareness, purify the inner wind-energies and clear blockages in the inner channels so the energy can flow freely. There are certain aspects of the images and mantras (and mudras) which actually are designed by the Buddhas to untie the knots of negative energy in our system, to awaken specific deluded energies to give rise to wisdom. For example Buddhas of the Vajra family can in many instances be used to awaken anger and hatred, and these Buddhas design their imagery with this in mind: they very often present fierce or wrathful features, and are blue. Even though this is the case, it is still possible to utilize any one Buddha to accomplish the goal, their fully enlightened nature of five wisdoms is inherent in the imagery—the body is made up of five-colored light, the five colors liberate the five negative states, the vajra emblem of five tines, the crown of five skulls, the howl of HUM. (Since the letter HUM has five points or parts which correspond to the wisdoms).

Practically speaking what we're seeking to do is dissolve the root of fear—or self-cherishing. All spiritual methods are designed to achieve fearlessness, because when all fear is liberated, the Absolute presents itself as Reality. This is the true state of the mind as inherently good or perfect, peaceful and blissful. This state of mind reflects reality in its true and perfect state as well. Therefore all experience, all clear perception is imbued with pure pleasure. This state of wisdom-mind is the level of realization of all perfected beings. Poison is only harmful if you're afraid of it. If you decide not to fear that which appears harmful, then it becomes medicine. This seems to take unshakable faith or certainty in the indestructible nature of the mind. With this confidence (vajra-faith or knowledge) we need not fear for ourselves, without this fear our true nature can shine, can perceive reality clearly, as beautiful, as a pure realm filled with Buddhas. Parasites, bacteria, volcanoes, twisters, fierce animals and people—all are inherently beautiful in the light of ones Buddha nature. All things are wisdom-display, only a limited view causes us tó see these things in the cloud of fear. When a Buddha sees water, what is seen is a Dakini, a god sees precious amrita, a person sees nourishment, an animal sees an abode, a hell-being sees molten metal. When the self-perfected state is able to radiate, the Absolute becomes ever-present, the mind becomes an endless stream of pure pleasure and literally shines with wisdom-light.

Dakinis: Sky Dancers of the Great Secret

The term dakini has very broad meaning, for example, from the perspective of the Buddhas, the overt elements are dakinis. Dakini stands for the feminine energy in the threads of the universe, which manifest as five lights which dance together to form phenomenon. Dakini also means wisdom, the female Buddhas represent wisdom. Basically dakini means female Buddhas.

There are mundane dakinis, who are women who do not practice Dharma or possess realization, but are potentially dakini. And there are supermundane dakinis who do possess realization. Dakini permeates a woman's being, it is the beginningless enlightenment of a woman. Tantric scripture distinguishes four types of dakini: (1) Transcendent dakinis of their own right; (2) Dakinis born from karmic predisposition; (3) Dakinis from a Pure Land that have manifested in a human body; (4) Dakinis born from mantra. There are countless dakinis figured in mandalas, but essentially they're all born or emanated from Vajra-yogini or Samantabhadri—the Mother. They have the common trait of being able to change their form and appearance at will. They have the ability to lead practitioners to the Pure Land of Dakinis. What they all share in common is the dance of awareness and bliss. Blissful intoxication is what makes them dance. Their dance is an expression of radiance, like the universe itself; the dance of white clouds and snow, the dance of lightning and rain, the dance of plant spirits and sprouting vegetables, the dance of creative-destructive thoughts, the dance of natural beauty, the dance of universes, the dance of all minds.

As an internal reality, she is everyones female-nature or energy. Each person and being contains female and male energies. Originally these where balanced like Father-Mother union. But now we need to bring them into balance. More will be said on this later. There are practices shared by Ngakpang's and sadhus for balancing these energies. Some of these practices are action mudra (sexual), some not. Men can align with the Dakini or Mother to cultivate and balance his energies. He might use a secret consort thought of as dakini to cause this. He has more male shaktis or pieces than female (In Shaiva Tantra its 7 to 5 ratio). The woman, by viewing herself as male deity or holding a secret consort (daka), will cause a similar balance. By viewing reality and oneself as the Wisdom-dakini, one becomes the Mother and realizes the ultimate nature of reality as the Mother, as female. In all three traditions of Tantra the purpose in taking a consort is to generate energy of transmutation to awaken ones openness and compassion. For a man, it awakens the dakini in him—so he will be complete. For a woman it awakens the daka in her so she will be complete.

In the earlier Shaiva Tantra, dakinis were accomplished female Tantrikas, called yoginis. They were attendants of the wrathful forms of Shiva and Durga, known as Mahakala and Mahakali or Bhairav-shakti (Undifferentiated Reality). The yogi would ask Kali to cut out his heart (ego) to unite with him, so his consciousness would be charged with her power. The imagery associated with this practice is Kali sitting astride the corpse of Shiva. She is the gate (keeper) to Shiva Mahakala's mandala, and functioned to dissolve the ego and initiate and usher the Tantrika inside. The Tibetan Dakini is sometimes supplicated in the same way (as in Chod—below), with a similar end—absorption in the undifferentiated.

She is part of the trinity of yidam, dakini, and guru. The yidam is the tutelary deity, who bestows siddhis, the dakini is the energy of the path, of transmutation and inspiration. The guru is the bestower of blessings, who makes entrance, progression and completion possible. Just as it is possible to work with a yidam without dakini, it is also possible to take a dakini to be your personal Deity. But it is not possible to dispense with the guru, he or she is an extension of Deity or Dakini on earth.

Dakinis are guardians of the Tantra. Their Mother, the womb of all Buddhas, Vajra-varahi, is the protector of Vajrayana, She is also its origin. Dakinis are bestowers of mystic doctrine, such as Tantras and Termas (hidden treasures), and the bringer of divine offerings. Dakinis appear in visionary form to bestow intiation, transmission and instruction. They also come to realized practitioners to aid their practice by providing protection, clearing obstacles, bringing food, and so on. As a main practice the dakini provides siddhis, bliss, realization, and so on. They guide practitioners through their mandalas. They introduce the mind to non-dual reality, the emptiness of phenomenon. As related in this text there are certain dakinis who can be supplicated to cause weather-changes, exorcisms, healing, and so on. The dakinis have the ability to cause weather-changes, thunder, lightning, rain, and a host of other feats. Those that appear later in this text are Vajra-family dakinis. Their mystical lightning revelation is a method of awakening minds.

Dakini means "sky-goer," "ether-goer," "sky-dancer." In Tibetan dakini translates as "kha' 'gro 'ma which means "she who flies" or "moves through space." This applies to mundane and super-mundane siddhi. Dakinis are able to fly as a personal power or siddhi, they appear in visionary form or in the sky flying and dancing. Their flight means they can control their mind, their dance means they're blissful. The dancing-flight of the dakini also signifies their realization, the union of emptiness (space, sky) and bliss. Dakini is the state that they dwell in, and the state of all enlightened hearts dwell in. Dakini is the heart of all mahasiddhas, dancing in space. Kha means inner space (shunyata), ultimate truth, and gro signifies the mind absorbed in this inner space. So they stand for the free blissful state of realized beings. All dakinis possess the nature of a Buddha and perform Buddha activity. Her nature is emptiness (shunyata), awareness (jnana), primal space (dhatu) and pure pleasure (mahasukha). The activity she performs is pacifying, enriching, controlling and destroying.

Dakini is the symbol and embodiment of the Universal Mother, Divine Wisdom as Feminine Ground (Samantabhadri). She is the ultimate nature of woman, and the relative human reality, woman as perfection of wisdom. Dakini is a woman who attains Buddhahood. Dakini is the union of awareness and bliss, space and awareness for men or women. Her sky-dance is the cosmic dance of illusion, the element-display of phenomena, the display of enlightened nature. She is the ultimate or true nature of form and emptiness. She is the nature of receptivity, all enveloping openness, symbolized by the yoni, or secret center and the cave. So when she appears with a male form, in union (Father-Mother) she represents this wisdom. When she appears alone as a yidam—like Lion-faced Dakini or Vajra-varahi (below), she is both wisdom and compassion.

Vajra Imagery and Deity Yoga

In the vast skillful means of the Wisdom Deities they have represented themselves to show that the enlightened heart is a union of wisdom and compassion. By visualizing this imagery and invoking wisdom and love of the deity, our own nature will awaken, our wisdom and compassion. The imagery continually reminds us of our natural state, of wisdom and love. The image is a vessel of wisdom and luminous compassion—it is wisdom-clear-light through and through. The image is Deity's wisdom activity through the light of love.

Our goal, what we seek to achieve for ourselves (through wisdom) is the limitless oceanic state known as dharmakaya or Truth Body, depicted by Vajradhara. It is the immutable or unwavering samadhi of deep luminous tranquility. And what we seek to achieve for others (through compassion) is the ability to emanate, to be in many places at once to help beings. The Buddhas, once they attained themselves, set out to liberate all sentient beings. They accomplish this through their limitless skillful means, or insightful compassion. Through cultivating loving-compassion one literally attains the ability to manifest in multiple forms, places and times to benefit as many beings as possible. The actual ability to do this is only possible by cultivating wisdom. So we simultaneously generate the aspiration to see all beings that fill space free of suffering, and we cultivate wisdom by meditating. Buddhas path is totally centered around meditation, without it no realization can be achieved. Tantric teachings tell us that we're inherently awake, but in order to recognize this we must train with the energy and wisdom of enlightenment. This wisdom-light is the essence of the imagery. Meditation on this wisdom-light dissolves the root of our negative states into emptiness, so that our mind will manifest as bliss, its natural state.

In order to take rupakaya, Buddhas arise out of the all-pervasive space, the womb of Tathagatas, through light. The light bodies are perceptible to clear minds.

These are called "Complete Enjoyment Bodies," and have a continuous existence in subtle inner space, in Pure Realms. They can appear to us in dreams, and are the actual images we visualize to contact Buddhas, and are the actual light we use to dissolve mind into dharmakaya. We use the Deity, in the form of light-imagery to focus on, to clear our mind, and awaken love through devotion, gratitude and service. Through practice with Deity's clear-light imagery the two accumulations can be completed. The light we absorb is wisdom and love, it awakens our wisdom and love, it liberates us into the pure state of the Deity.

All Buddhas or means have the ability to awaken the complete Buddha-Mind, of wisdom, power and compassion, because these are the qualities of all enlightened minds. It is through the imagery that this is achieved. The practice of visualization intensifies clarity of awareness, so we might realize our enlightened nature.

Because everyone has a certain previous life connection to wisdom-beings we choose those that we resonant with the most. If we do not know the guru will tell us, or the Deity will when we're ready present him or herself. Another reason for having so many methods of attainment is because the path is graded, we have to move upward step by step. Yab-yum and mandala practice might not be suited to someone who doesn't have any clue as to what they're about, so more easily understood practices are suitable. The path is suited to all levels of practitioners. More advanced practitioner are ready to do mandala visualization and dynamic multi-deity practices where there's many things happening around you. The dynamic technology of Highest Yoga Tantra practices may be the quickest methods of accomplishment, but they're certainly not for everyone, so there are numerous simple practices for attaining full enlightenment.

Any one Buddha can be utilized to bestow the enlightenment typified by all Buddhas, (all Buddhas lead to the same goal) therefore accomplishment of one Yidam practice means accomplishment of them all. Each Buddha symbolizes the fully awakened state of all Buddhas, therefore it seems that each Buddha can be taken as the Father-Mother of all other Buddhas. This depends on ones singular devotion. For example Nyingma lineage yogis take Guru Rinpoche as their main tutelary deity, the one through whose grace they will attain the goal, so they view all Buddhas as emanations of him and all Wisdom-dakinis (female Buddhas) as emanations of his consort, Yeshe Tsogyal. In the Kagyu lineage Vajradhara is taken as

Buddhas Wisdom Mind, so he has a strong place in the tradition, and is often viewed as the goal, his active aspect, known as Chakrasamvara is the primary tutelary deity of the Kagyu and is the symbol of the Absolute. Therefore all Buddhas could be said to be his emanations and all Dakinis, the emanations of his consort Vajra-yogini.

Each Buddha symbolizes the goal and path, method or skillful means to attain this goal. Through any Buddha this goal can be achieved. To symbolize this many Yidams appear as male and female and are termed Yab-Yum, meaning "Father-Mother"; the male symbolizes compassionate method, while the female symbolizes wisdom. The union of the male and female, such as you will encounter with Chakrasamvara, symbolizes the inseparable union of wisdom and compassion, or emptiness and bliss. Vajrayana is the means whereby the goal of spiritual awakening can be reached through the union of wisdom and compassion, emptiness and bliss.

Because the dharmakaya can be perceived only by other Buddhas, the Deity takes Visionary form, he manifests light and imagery. Because not everyone has purified vision to see this body, the Deity takes physical form, (Tulku) to give instruction, grace and guidance. The guru in Vajrayana is considered indispensible because this person is going to introduce us to the Wisdom-spheres, and provide us with the methods to achieve the enlightened state.

Though empty of self, the Deity is very much alive, the living embodiment of the enlightened energy that pervades the entire universe, that flows through the interwoven threads of reality. The Deity arises from the same sphere from which all things arise and dissolve, all beings and thoughts. There is nothing before this state which can be discovered, and it feels like nothing, so is called shunyata or void. What has arisen from this state is not different than it, thoughts and phenomena are just shaped emptiness, emptiness arising through energy or light. Thoughts arise and fall away like all phenomena, and yet there is a thread of awareness, a mind-stream which is always perceiving this dance of phenomena. It doesn't feel like anything, it feels like nothing. Substanceless phenomena is the nature of our being.

The first emanation is intangible appearance, equated with an energy-body of subtle vision. It is created by wisdom through subtle winds (lung). At this level of subtlety energy is subtanceless, before light or electricity, which are substance energy. This display of emptiness is the sambhogakaya. It is the seed state of the universe, the emanation body of the Buddhas. They are designed to benefit sentient beings. Through them the Deity gives blessings, instruction and transmission, by appearing in subtle vision. And through them (through visualization) we gather and absorb the Deity's wisdom qualities. Buddhas likewise manifest as form bodies on earth, known as rupakaya or tulku. Tulku is the energy-body coalescing as form. Everyone is tulku or Buddha, but because we may fail to recognize ourselves as energy bodies arising from vast emptiness, we prevent ourselves from having this realization.

The three bodies exist as one singular field, the Vajrakaya or "Indestructible Body." The three states exist simultaneously as the undivided quality of the enlightened nature, they might also be referred to as emptiness, clarity and compassion, they exist fully within us. Whatever arises in this state is said to be an ornament of the enlightened state. In order to actualize this state, we need to unify emptiness and form through entering the sphere of energy, the current of grace of the Deity. It is accomplished through the joint practice of compassion which results in the form body, and wisdom which leads to the formless Truth Body and the Thunder-bolt Body. This process can be seen as merging the mind with the Buddha's form body, then proceeding to merge with the formless body. This is the purpose of Vajrayana, and is referred to as completing the two accumulations—of merit and wisdom. Completing the accumulation of merit through compassionate activity is sufficient to give birth to oneself as a form deity (an angelic being whose mind maintains a subtle form and exists in a Pure Realm). Completing the accumulation of wisdom through spiritual cultivation is necessary to give birth to oneself into the incomprehensible as a formless Buddha with the capacity to manifest rupakaya or Tulkus. Vajrayana presents a complete path for the attainment of Buddhahood because it presents tested and proven methods of completing the two accumulations.

The spontaneous arising of the Deity is a teaching method. It arises out of the impulse toward liberation (bodhicitta). Its function is to liberate people into the inherent condition of the Deity which is the nature of all Buddhas.

The image always points back to the non-dual reality. The image connects form to emptiness and transmits the non-dual quality of Ultimate Reality, its primal purity and blissful radiance. One has to be open to receive the transmission. Being open suggests emptiness, absence of conceptual thoughts and presence of awareness. This might be referred to as a calm openness, a calm-abiding, which is often a sought out state (of meditation) before engaging in Deity Yoga, the practice of union with the Deity.

Buddhas achieved the enlightened state through the grace of those who preceded them. For example, Guru Rinpoche achieved himself through Amitabha long before he appeared on earth out of a lotus and lightningbolt. (Therefore he is often considered an emanation of Amitabha). We receive immeasurable grace from the Wisdom-spheres. Guru Yoga or Deity Yoga is the best practice for attaining enlightenment. All Buddhas became enlightened through faith and devotion to the guru-Deity. "The eighty-four Mahasiddhas in India and Guru Rinpoche's twenty-five main disciples in Tibet, the treasure finders, awareness holders and accomplished enlightened sublime beings, all became enlightened through the mind-transmission of their Gurus. The unbroken lineage has been passed from the Primordial Buddha, Samantabhadra, to our own root lam who is the essence of all buddhas of the ten directions and the three times . . ." (Lame Tharchin p. 38. A Commentary on the Dudjom Tersar Ngondro: The Preliminary Practice of the New Treasure of Dudjom.)

Deity Yoga is the central practice of Tantra; all the distinctive practices of Tantra are based on this technique as a lightning path to the goal. Deity Yoga is practiced wherever Wisdom-beings are used as methods of accomplishment. To my knowledge all four main lineages use Deity Yoga—Nyingmapa, Gelugpa, Kagyu, and Sakya. The degree to which the mind is dissolved into the Deity (which determines the attainment of Buddhahood) is determined in the division of Tantra classes.

Deity Yoga involves alignment and visualization as the process of connecting with positive beneficial states of consciousness, which pervade the universe in the form of enlightened beings. It involves turning the mind-mirror toward the Dharma-sphere, to reflect the Buddhas wisdom-lights. Deity Yoga involves creative visualization of a fully enlightened Buddha in order to achieve this state.

Tantric scriptures are instructions on training in two stages, the creation stage, the way of perceiving mind and phenomena as pure and perfect, and the perfection stage, the training in the method of attaining primordial wisdom, union of emptiness and bliss. The development phase of generation or creation stage is divided into two phases—"approaching" and "accomplishing" the Deity. Approaching means familiarizing oneself with the Deity by visualizing the Deity and reciting its mantra. Accomplishing means becoming one with the Deities wisdom-nature—that is—refining the frequency of ones energy until it is the same as the Deity.

Generally there are three levels of visualization in Creation stage, (which somewhat correspond with the classification of Tantras). The first level is approach, which entails visualization in front. One visualizes Deity above ones crown, usually 7x's larger than oneself, and while reciting the mantra, doing mudras and liturgy, one visualizes a descent of blessing-lights from the Deity into oneself. In one practice with Guru Rinpoche for example, lights comes from his body, speech, mind centers to purify our own body, speech, mind and wisdom. Because this level of visualization might prevent one from realizing oneself as Deity, we move to the next level, sometimes called near-accomplishment.

At this stage one visualizes the Deity (and mandala or palace) in front, and one visualizes oneself in the form of the Deity. This is very important because it causes two things. First it helps us to recollect our nature as same as the Deity. Secondly, it helps facilitate the descent of blessing-lights into the body. Normally our solid gross body is impure, but if we visualize it as a Deity, then it becomes a pure vessel, a stainless vase for containing the Deity's amrita. It is said that good clear visualization can be seen by other beings. Evil spirits will see you as the Deity and leave you alone. Deity's will see you as one of their own, and rain blessings on you. The "accomplishment" level entails visualizing oneself from the start as a Deity. Because people are not prepared to view themselves as an inexhaustible Source of blessings for the world, we practice the first level. Gradually we move to the point at which we are the Deity, the Source of blessings, radiating light to all beings.

The accomplishment of the practice is the ability to perceive all forms as the forms of the Deity, all sounds as the voice or mantra of the Deity, all thoughts as the mind of the Deity. This is the inward sign of accomplishment. The outward sign is radiance, joy, equilibrium, unconditional love, and so.

The Deity is our potential for enlightenment, a symbol for the subtle state we're seeking. Practice requires emptiness and clarity in order to generate oneself as the Deity and have a sense of what it feels like to be the Deity, to be flooded by him. That experience is introduced during initiation, and once it is introduced it is accessed in the mind each time one practices generating the Deity. In the process of practice the Deity gives empowerment in the form of blessing-lights or grace-waves—his mandala or energy sphere becomes manifest, rises to the surface of the mind to effloresce through its own light. The visualized form of the enlightened being evokes a response at a very subtle level of mind and causes transformation through gathering and absorbing the living qualities of the Buddha. The ordinary vision of the mind is purified. Visualizing Buddhas helps us to realize the pure state which already exists within us, because the image is the great Symbol or state of all enlightened minds. The image connects us to pure awareness and helps us to realize the thread of our own pure awareness. The Buddha, its symbol, (image and mantra) and our own mind are one continuum, one great Symbol, Seal, Mind.

One visualizes oneself as a Buddha with a clear appearance and feeling of oneself as the Deity (vajra-pride). Our training with imagery necessitates that we truly believe our appearance to be the Deity's. There was a Tibetan Buddhist monk I heard about who practiced Yamantaka, the bull-headed Destroyer of Death (who appears much like the bull-headed Blue-star Katchina of the Hopi's). Because he believed he was Yamantaka he would actually bow his head when he went through doorways to account for the horns on his head. One who develops Deity Yoga has the ability to view appearances as the display of the Deity and one thinks of oneself as performing the activities of the Deity for the benefit of others. This is not merely an imagined state, because the Deity's wisdom-energy is there.

Because all images are Deity's five-colored wisdom light, the five negative states can be transformed or liberated into the five wisdoms, and the five overt elements can be dissolved into the five wisdom-dakinis. One becomes a Tulku or form body of the Deity. This is called "training in the result," the view that one is a Buddha is the base or truth from which we begin practice, it is the reality we're training to awaken ourself to, it is the path or thread of enlightened energy which awakens the mind, and it is the stabilized realization of ones nature as Buddha.

The method-sadhana is composed of mantras and prayers (enlightened or vajra-speech—the union of sound and emptiness), mudras and images, together representing the enlightened aspects of the Buddha. The method describes the iconography and qualities associated with the Deity. In the process of emanating or projecting the mandala and Deity, the practitioner praises the Deity, asks for blessings, envisions the mandala or palace, seat and Deity, and views oneself as the Deity possessing all its qualities which are absorbed. Once initiation is given one enters the mandala freely and trains in the fact that one is in the center and seat. The Deity must be seen as alive, pulsating radiance, yet a display of subtle elements, like a rainbow—transparent, luminous and empty of concrete self-existence. The Deity is present as awareness and rainbow-light, and yet absent of any inherent existence. One must also see oneself as such. The mind which is clear, self-luminous and energetic can be transformed. The mind is supported by subtle winds. When they're purified by the elixir of the Deity's light, the goal is attained. Imagery and wisdom is made internal as a way of dissolving our limited dual vision and awakening our naturally inherent luminous vision. Imagining oneself as the Deity does not imply that one is going to appear at first as the Deity, but the continuously applied concentration and the force of the Deity invoked in the mantra transforms the subtle winds into the Deity. The mind reflects the Deity through and through, so one becomes a Deity.

The Deities have designed their sadhanas in such a way as to mirror the process of giving birth into a Pure Realm as a Deity and dissolving that body into Infinite Space. One arises out of emptiness and bodhicitta as a Deity, which establishes the mind, through repeated practice, in the state of an omniscient Deity abiding in a boundless Pure Realm. In a peal of thunder and flash of lightning we arrive here as a Deity to perform enlightened activity of body, speech, mind in order to skillfully bring all beings to the self-liberated state.

This stage of the practice transforms the mind, which has given birth to itself countless times out of ignorance, desire, hatred, pride, and jealousy into realms of suffering, into a mind which is able to give birth to itself out of wisdom and compassion into realms which are thoroughly beyond suffering.

In a flash and peal of thunder we dissolve Deity's play of wisdom and form into Infinite Space. This stage of the practice transforms the mind into emptiness and wisdom. The effect of performing these two stages of practice is that one abides simultaneously as an all-pervasive Deity manifest in countless places at once.

The actual attainment of Buddhahood happens through the completion stage meditations, which are very dynamic alchemical practices by which the body is transformed into an illusory or subtle body, capable of transcending the universe. These practices are sometimes called rasayana. The Shaivite mahasiddhas (Siddha Siddhanta) practiced rasayana transmitted by Lord Shiva long before Buddha. In some instances they lived thousands of years, some disappeared, some remain on earth. The later tradition of 84 mahasiddhas transmitted rasayana practices for the highest achievement, from Shiva, and the Buddhas like Chakrasamvara. The achievement was called mahamudra-siddhi and usually culminates in the siddha's achievement of an illusory body which eventually takes off for the Dakini's Paradise. The Mahamudra transmissions have survived until today both in the Kagyu and Gelugpa lineages.

More will be said on completion stage and rasayana in the exposition of Chakrasamvara and his Highest Yoga Tantra, for now it is sufficient to simply have a basic understanding of the two stages. In the first the heart projects the image, mandala etc., of the Deity, and the mind takes the form of the Deity and its Wisdom. In completion stage everything is going to dissolve into the heart and the heart, as a diamond-point of light will dissolve into space. Through these two stages we dissolve into the form and formless bodies of the Deity

Prior to engaging in Deity yoga it is necessary to have instructions and guidance from a qualified vajra-master, a lama or yogi. In order to practice Deity Yoga which forms the basis of Tantric practice, the enlightened transmission of instruction and insight is necessary. This initiation is given by an enlightened vajra-master, who is a Buddha and realizes the spontaneous arising of his Non-dual energy. He transmits methods out of his visionary experience of the Deity. The transmission originates with the Buddhas; the vajra-imagery and vajra-sound are symbols of the non-dual energy sphere, and are passed down to the present day through unbroken lineages of accomplished masters.

Elaborate Empowerment into the Vajra Vehicle

In Tantric tradition the gates of lightning or enlightenment must be opened before we can practice and traverse the path. We can also learn only so much about the tradition since 99% consists of secret oral instructions on Deities and sadhanas and fruition practices.

In Vajrayana we speak of a blessing empowerment which comes from the Deity we're practicing with at the moment. Anyone can receive this empowerment who uses a mantra with clarity and devotion. We also speak of an elaborate empowerment which is an initiation given by the guru embodying the Deity, which allows us to practice the sadhana of the Deity. It is necessary to receive this kind of empowerment in order to practice secret mantra Vajrayana. Extraordinary beings receive it directly from Deity's, this is how it comes to earth from Dharma-space. There are generally four parts to the elaborate empowerment, these purify the four bodies consecutively. The Vase Empowerment purifies our body so we can meditate upon the form of Deity, and attain the nirmanakaya—the Body of a Buddha. Next is the Secret empowerment which purifies speech, empowering us to practice meditation of channels, winds, drops and chakras (since these appertain to communication, movement of energy). This empowers us to attain sambhogakaya, (Light-display and Speech of a Buddha). Next is the Wisdom-awareness empowerment, this purifies our mind to attain the dharmakaya Mind of a Buddha, to realize bliss-emptiness. Finally, the Precious Word Empowerment is given which allows one to attain the Vajrakaya, the integration of all aspects of enlightenment.

Practice requires that we are introduced to our Buddha-nature in the form of energy and symbols. Symbols arise out of the emptiness which we are going to dissolve ourselves into. The Buddha uses the imagery as a vehicle to surface out of emptiness into form, and he gives us that vehicle so we can dissolve into emptiness out of form. Out of the emptiness of the space of our mind we are going to arise as the Deity.

In order to practice with Deities wisdom we must be introduced to it through an initiation empowerment. We're being introduced to the stream of Deity's blessings. We're being introduced to the taste of enlightenment. To arrive at this point we need to have chosen to adhere to and practice this tested, proven path under the pure lineage of masters who are embodied in ones present guru. The vajra-master must be qualified, he must be able to introduce pure Tantra, he must be capable of communicating Deity's undefiled qualities and he must have the ability to invoke and concentrate this quality of enlightenment in the heart of the aspirants. The vajra-master concentrates the Deity's wisdom mandala into the nada or indestruc-

tible heart drop. It is from here that we will invoke the Deity through devotion, it is through devotion that we will realize love for all beings in our hearts. Through love of our Deity-guru we will love all beings who are our Deity-guru. We will realize all beings and things as our personal Deity. Through this love we recognize the interrelatedness of all things. It is in our heart that we will remember the Deity and generate the visualization of the deity. It is here that we will invoke the Deity through his mantra, and it is through our heart that Deity will cause realization, that we will dissolve into wisdom and bliss. Through the heart Deity's light-essence will arise and circulate throughout the body's subtle channels, to purify the energy or winds that reside in these channels.

In our hearts we awaken wisdom and love—these are not two separate things. To depict this the vajra or dorje has two sides joined in the center. This is a picture of the heart. So generally in our sadhana we visualize it in our heart. It is a way of training in the result. The whole path is a way of training in the result. This is the unique characteristic of Vajrayana and the excellent skillful means of the Buddhas. So Vajrayana is called resultant vehicle. It is actually a part of all Tantric paths, such as Shaiva and Taoist. Because wisdom and compassion are not different we cultivate them together. When they're cultivated separately—realization or Buddhahood is not possible. It is said that the cultivation of compassion gives birth to oneself as a form Deity. The cultivation of wisdom can stabilize ones tranquil state, but in order for it to be luminous, fully awake, full of love, compassion must be cultivated. So in Vajrayana, before you embark on any wisdom practice, form or formless meditation—you develop what is called the "mind of bodhicitta," the intention that what you're doing is for the liberation of all sentient beings. Throughout your practice you keep referring to this aspiration. And in this way your practice becomes luminous and blissful. This luminosity comes from the Deities (of the practice) who are everywhere and are happy with this kind of dedication. Then when we finish whatever we're doing, we dedicate everything, all the merit we've gained. It goes out to fulfill our intention to liberate beings, to create beauty in the world, and then by virtue of our dedication the Buddhas shower us with manifold blessings which makes our body and climate truly beautiful. We do not lose anything by giving up our self and what we have been given, instead we gain unimaginable blessings and our merit is increased a thousandfold, everything we need is provided for, all present and future suffering is removed. This is a reality known by those who practice it. At the outset we must simply trust what we are taught, we must have faith in our masters realization. If you have faith in nothing else by reading this book, have faith in these reflections on precious bodhicitta. It is something that every single being in the universe should be aware of.

Initiation establishes a deep connection between the disciples mind and the Deity; he is introduced to the sphere and energy of the Deity, and given permission to practice the method of accomplishment by the Buddha (embodied in the master). The adept is given permission to use the Deity's mantra, which embodies in sound the same enlightened qualities that Deity's image embodies in form and color (wisdom-lights). This is so because when the mantra is repeated Deity's subtle image arises in the space before you in grace-waves.

Guru Rinpoche, The Precious Guru "Lightningbolt of Compassion"

Deity yoga can also be referred to as Guru Yoga, because any Deity we take as our personal yidam we take as our guru. If we view our earthly guru as a Buddha (even though he may not possess this full realization) then we can attain enlightenment through our devotion for him. In essence he is Buddha, and so are we. Our loving devotion will cause us to awaken fully, and if our guru is not fully awake, it will cause him to awaken as well. In Guru Yoga we view our root guru as Wisdom-deity. Our devotion is our yearning to be like him, our love of him which awakens the realization of our unity within. We supplicate the four bodies (Vajrakaya) embodied fully in our earthly guru. He represents the focused blessings of all-pervasive wisdom Deity on earth. It is through his blessings that we will attain enlightenment. It is through deepening our relationship with him, becoming truly intimate that we will attain full realization. He mixes his mind with ours, which awakens our omniscient awareness. Every thought imbued with devotion brings the guru closer to us; he arises in our mind.

Although any of the Buddhas can be taken as ones guru, there is a special relationship between Vajrayana practitioners and Guru Rinpoche. He is the master who initiates masters. He is yidam—Thunder-deity (in view of this text), and personal guru. He brought Buddhism to Tibet, so is the special guru to Tibetans.

He is behind the unobstructed spread of Vajrayana across the world, so is the special guru to all Tantric Buddhists. He is considered the second Buddha and the Tantric Buddha of this world system. Even though Buddha Shakyamuni gave all the Tantras originally, his work was mainly in laying the foundation of Buddha Dharma, which is Sutrayana and Mahayana. While Guru Rinpoche is known almost solely for transmitting the Tantric Vajrayana teachings. Guru Rinpoche, the Precious Vajra Guru can be taken as ones personal guru and yidam simultaneously. Through his practice alone one can attain the highest realization.

In Vajrayana, Guru Rinpoche is known as the second Buddha. Shakyamuni Buddha prophesied that he would appear within a hundred years of his parinirvana. He walked the earth for 1400 years, from 420 B.C. to the mid 8th century. He is responsible for the spread of Buddhism throughout India, Sri Lanka, Tibet, Nepal, Bhutan and Sikkim. Wherever he went became a sanctified place, the earth and this realm have been made sacred by his presence. (Secret sacred lands, such as Pema Kod, arose as the result of his special blessings). He is responsible for the precious fruition path known as Dzogchen, the "Great Perfection", and the Terma or "hidden treasure" tradition. The Great Perfection vehicle is the most profound lightning path, which takes you to the goal in one life. In the Nyingma lineage Guru Rinpoche is taken as the Buddha's Wisdom Mind, the Absolute. All the practices of the tradition take the aspirant to the indestructible state embodied by Guru Rinpoche.

There are three different ways of looking at his birth. It is the most widely accepted belief that he was born from a giant lotus in Lake Danakosha in Orgyen, which is now present day Afghanistan. Others believe that he was born from human parents—as son of a king—like Shakyamuni. And finally, he might be taken to have been born from a lightningbolt on the Mt. of Meteoric Iron (namchak) in South India. This form is known as Sampa Lhundrupma, and is the main focus here. The image associated with this revelation refers to Guru Rinpoche as the "Lightningbolt of Compassion". He represents the compassionate splendor of the Victors. Surrounded by a wisdom-flame aureole and lightning, he displays magical Buddha activity in stance and dance. He is white skinned, symbolizing his stainless purity. He possesses all the major and minor marks of a Buddha. His stare is unblinking and fierce. He wears four vestments of white, blue, red and brocade which stand for the four vehicles, his complete attainment. He wears a red and blue hat on top of which protrudes a half-vajra. He has long black knotted hair denoting his ascetic practice in secluded charnel grounds. He holds the katvanga (trident) and vajra in his right hand and the skull-cup of amrita in his left, which symbolize the inseparability of wisdom and means. Guru Rinpoche used these weapons to subdue local gods and demons. He raises his trident aloft, signaling victory over the three poisons, over the root of all suffering.

Sampa Lhundrupma is a Thunder-being. His lightning is the luminous compassion which liberates negative states at a glance. He arose through the lightning out of the infinite womb of origination (Amitabha). He is the concentration of the blessings of all the Buddhas. He arose on earth out of a lightningbolt on the Mountain of Meteoric Iron, in South India. Meteoric Iron (namchak) is the substance of the symbolic vajra of the Tantric Deities, the tangible wisdom and means of the Thunder Deity. This namchak is not made by humans, it is made by celestial beings, such as Vishvakarma, whose activity is related in both Shaivite and Buddhist scriptures. This namchak does exist on earth in the form of ritual daggers and phurbas found hidden by Guru Rinpoche in Termas. I mention this phenomenon because it is universal to all cultures, most traditions have some notion of bolts of lightning that can be found after storms which are known to be made of no substance known to humans, a substance which is alive, which has incredible healing properties.

Because Guru Rinpoche arose from a lightning-bolt we can say that he came to enlighten all sentient beings, to remove their obstructions, to dispel the darkness of ignorance, to subdue malevolent beings, to spread the Dharma like thunder echoing across the land. In short all the functions of lightning are symbolically Guru Rinpoche's functions. His compassionate activity is the rapid illumination of all minds. He lived as a supreme Thunder-specialist, as Thunder-deity on the earth. He continues to live on earth, and in other realms. He lives within our heart of devotion.

His dharmakaya (Amitabha) is the vast open sky Mind within which arose the cloud of wisdom and clear-lightning display, his sambhogakaya (Chenrezig), out of which stepped his unimpeded activity, the nirmanakaya (the Vajra Guru). These exist together as the indivisible experience of enlightenment or Vajra-kaya; Sampa Lhundrupma is all of these together. These are the Mind, Speech (thunder) and Body of all Buddhas, as well as the Buddha (Sky-Mind), Dharma (thunder) and Sangha (body).

In the Deity/Guru Yoga, our own limitless nature is the sky-simile, our luminous compassion is the spontaneous lightning-display, our body and activity is the expression and activity of enlightenment. Guru Rinpoche is an emanation of Amitabha-Chenrezig, like Shakyamuni Buddha. He and Amitabha-Chenrezig are one being—the yidam aspect is Chenrezig, the guru aspect is Guru Rinpoche. Guru Rinpoche achieved enlightenment in a previous life through Amitabha.

It is taught that Guru Rinpoche demonstrated the path of abandonment and realization like the Buddha before him. He received Dharma transmission in India and perfectly realized the four vehicles within his lifetime, for example, first he learned and realized Sutrayana, then Paramitayana, and so on. He attained immortality and complete enlightenment. He lived on earth for hundreds of years. He is an example of the perfect practitioner and vajra-master. He has a very close relationship with the Tibetan people; his compassion was responsible for Buddhism in Tibet. And because we practice Tibetan Buddhism, you might say his compassion is responsible for the presence of Vajrayana in this country and throughout the world. Just as it is held that Guru Rinpoche never left the earth, one might say that his activity of spreading Dharma has not ceased.

Tibet was a land of demons and recalcitrant-minded people, so the kings supplicated Guru Rinpoche to come and he subdued and bound the malevolent forces by commitment to the Dharma. These beings became protectors, and obstacles to practice became less. (To say Guru Rinpoche's name alone leaves spirits in trepidation. It isn't by word of mouth or telephone they know about his activity. When you say the name with devotion, faith and reverence, Guru Rinpoche comes—he arises. And if you've received the empowerment to practice his method of accomplishment, then the spirits will actually see you as Guru Rinpoche and feel his presence.) His work was so profound that once Dharma spread throughout Tibet, it was transformed into a Pure Realm on earth in which it is said that all men were Chenrezig, (or Guru Rinpoche) and all women, Mother Tara (or Yeshe Tsogyal).

I will relate two stories which demonstrate his activity as Thunder-specialist, as Thunder-being on earth. In the first a king was building a monastery, and he seemed to have difficulties attaining lumber. A malevolent Naga (serpent) came to him and basically tempted him; he told him that he would provide the lumber for him quickly. So the king struck a bargain with him. The Naga king was afraid of Guru Rinpoche so he told the king to rendezvous with Rinpoche in a certain cave—(where the king would unknowingly disturb Rinpoche as he did practice to pacify the Naga). He went there and found Guru Rinpoche in the form of a Garuda devouring the serpent. When the king arrived there, it is said that he interrupted Guru Rinpoche's concentration so the tail of the serpent remained unsubdued. This story demonstrates the most common theme among Thunder-beings—that of taking Thunder-bird form to subdue troublesome serpents.

In the next story the spread of Dharma was again being obstructed. Heretical scholars were bothering the monks at Nalanda monastery. Buddhist scholars were unable to refute them. The Buddhists all received the same dream. In it, Dakini Zhiwa Chog (Supreme Peace) prophesied as follows: "You will not be able to defeat the heretics. If you do not invite here my elder brother Dorje Thothreng Tsal (Vajra Skull-Garland Power, Guru Rinpoche) who lives at the Dark Cemetary, the Dharma will be destroyed" (169 Thondup). The scholars asked how they could invite him when it is so difficult to go there. The Dakini told them to "Set up a great offering on the roof of the monastery, with music and incense, and with one voice recite the vajra prayer" (169-170 Ibid). She gave them the prayer and Guru Rinpoche mantra. When they recited it, Guru Rinpoche came instantly from the sky. He presided over the Buddhists at Nalanda and defeated the heretical scholars. When they threatened him with magical powers, he opened a casket given to him by the lion-faced Dakini, in which he found a secret mantra of "fourteen-letters". By reciting it he eliminated the evil ones among them with a rain of lightning-bolts, and converted the rest.

The mantra which the monks were transmitted to invite Guru Rinpoche, distilled from the vajra 7-line prayer, is as follows: in Sanskrit: Om Ah Hung Benza Guru Pema Siddhi Hung. His mantra can be translated in several ways. In truth it is his sound-counterpart, his enlightened speech (vajra-speech, voice of thunder). Because the sounds are him, he arises in the space before us and the space of the mind. Each word denotes an aspect of his body, speech, mind and wisdom, or his light and its activity. Om Ah Hung stand for the enlightened body, enlightened speech, and enlightened mind of all Buddhas. Benza stands for the indestructible nature of all enlightened minds, the indivisible union of wisdom and compassion. Guru Pema is Guru Rinpoche, and signifies the full blossoming of our Buddha-nature (Padma—lotus) as a movement from dark to light (Guru). Siddhi means divine accomplishment. And Hung stands for the Wisdom Mind. The mantra also has a distinct linear meaning, which asks Guru Rinpoche to bestow divine accomplishments and realization.

When his mantra is recited, Guru Rinpoche arises in subtle light, and in the light can be distinguished images of himself. He sits in a majestic position on a moon mat atop a sun-disc on a lotus. He appears as white-complexioned to symbolize his stainless purity, his face is joyous and his eyes are unblinking and clear. He radiates five-colored light from his pores. He has long black locks to symbolize the powers he developed by practicing a life of austerity. His locks spiral counter-clockwise (which is one of the marks of a Buddha); each strand is a dakini. He wears four garments of light: white, blue, brocade and red, symbolizing his perfection of spiritual disciplines, of the 4 vehicles. He wears a red hat, from the top of which protrudes a half-vajra, on the top of which is fastened a vulture feather, which symbolizes that his view is the highest and broadest, just as a vulture flies the highest among birds and thus has the broadest view. Adorning his hat is a small crescent and sun, denoting wisdom and means. In his right hand he holds a vajra to symbolize his indestructible power and skill, in his left he holds a skull-cup of nectar symbolizing the union of emptiness and bliss. In the crook of his left arm is a trident with three heads on it. It symbolizes his consort or wisdom. The three points symbolize the three natures of all Buddhas, emptiness, clarity and compassion, which destroy the three root delusions of ignorance, desire and hatred. The three heads: skeletal, old and fresh symbolize the three Buddha bodies—Wisdom, Complete Enjoyment and Form, or formless, visionary, and incarnate. Beneath the heads there is a half-double-dorje which symbolizes that half of his activity can be witnessed, half is mysterious and unseen. Below this is a vase. Also, tied to the katvanga are silks and a damaru.

When you recite his mantra visualize him above and in front of you. Visualize rays of rainbow light radiating from his body. Visualize a ray of white light shooting from his forehead into your own. This purifies your body. Visualize a ray of red light shooting from his throat into your own. This purifies speech. Visualize a ray of blue light shooting from his heart into your own. This purifies the mind. Then visualize them together entering your three places. Do this for 1000, 10,000 or more mantras. In this way one receives the four empowerments, which sow the seeds for enlightened body, speech, mind. Then dedicate the merit to benefit all beings.

Guru Rinpoche's pours are filled with the mandalas of all Buddhas—so he is deemed the Embodiment of all Buddhas. His secret aspect is the red Amitayus, Buddha of Limitless Life, in which he taught dakinis. He is the supreme essence of all enlightened minds. He is the emanation body of Samantabhadra. Through him, one attains Buddha's Wisdom Mind.

Like most Thunder-beings, Guru Rinpoche dwells in a mountain abode. Accounts relate that Guru Rinpoche took off for this realm riding the sun-rays on a blue horse through the sky surrounded by rainbow light. Just as Guru Rinpoche lived in this world for awhile to help us, presently he lives in the land of the maras (demons) to help them, and to protect us, because it is said that they were planning on destroying us. So he protects people from the maras. Guru Rinpoche's wisdom-abode is in the West, it is called Padma Od, "Lotus-light." Within this realm is an island called Chamaradvipa. On the island is a mountain called Paldo Zanghri, "Glorious Copper Colored Mountain." On the summit is Guru Rinpoche's palace. It has three levels, on the top is five wisdom-Buddhas, center is the Guru Rinpoche (image) below. The lower level is the fierce mandala he has taken to subdue rakshasas (vampire-like beings). It is said that he will remain there until the end of this universe.

Accounts suggest that he never actually left the earth. People tell stories of meeting him—in human bodily form. Really he is wherever someone thinks of him with devotion. Masters tell us that receiving blessings, visitation or visions from him is relatively easy.

Guru Rinpoche can take the form of any Buddha to visit you. He is the embodiment of all Buddhas, all Buddha mandalas might be seen within his body, all Deities are within him. Therefore to attain his state is to attain that of all Wisdom Deities. Guru Rinpoche is likewise the embodiment of the Three Jewels, the Buddha, Dharma and Sangha, which correspond to his Mind, Speech and Body respectively. He exists in all minds potentially, and is revealed in all enlightened

minds. We can understand him to have been a Thunder master having walked the earth and established the Dharma in many lands and many minds and then in one body took off to Copper Mountain to establish beings of that realm, another body remains on earth, and through taking numerous forms of the six classes of beings, teaches Dharma. He is wherever he is invoked, and can be felt and seen. He has taken a vow to be wherever someone does his practice or else he will go to vajra-hell.

Primarily we embrace his practice to tame or pacify our minds. He is deemed that which tames the hard to tame. If you're having troubles, feeling depressed, grief-stricken or sad think of his peaceful smiling image, repeat his mantra and have faith, anticipate that he will liberate these feelings. Recalling Guru Rinpoche's peaceful and blissful image brings joy to the heart. Recalling Guru Rinpoche's presence can open up your heart revealing your nature and his as inseparable. Guru Rinpoche said that by reciting 100,000 mantras 100 times you will reach the same level of realization as him. (This achievement would require clear recitation, which means clear-visualization, and perhaps initiation from a master or Guru Rinpoche. If we have devotion and no empowerment, using his mantra can attract his blessings and empowerment).

Anyone who resonates with the Vajrayana tradition, with the Buddhas and Dharma, can align with the Dharma-spheres through Guru Rinpoche, through the joint practice of repetition of the mantra and visualization of the image. His mantra is addressed to all his forms, including Sampa Lhundrupma, and to all Buddhas and Bodhisattvas which he embodies. His image might be visualized before you as the mantra is repeated. With any visualization the Deity's body is one of subtle crystalline light-particles, it is real, yet illusory like a rainbow. It does not appear ghostly or phantom-like, so should not be visualized this way. The mantra can be repeated aloud or silently. It has the beneficial effect of strengthening the mind, purifying it, awakening its pure nature of wisdom. Through the mantra and image we absorb the positive enlightened qualities of the Buddha, pure awareness, clarity and compassion. Guru Rinpoche mixes his light with our own energy to purify, body, speech, mind and its wisdom-ground.

Yeshe Tsogyal says that mantra alone is not sufficient to attain enlightenment. If that's all you do is recite the mantra aloud, the most it will do is purify speech. To purify wisdom, mind, speech, body, it is necessary to engage in his sadhana with devotion and faith. The sadhana means the form-meditation, and the dissolution of that form into emptiness at the completion of the practice. We use the Complete Enjoyment Body described above to dissolve into the Buddha's Wisdom Mind or Truth Body—the form takes us to the formless. Our form meditation is like a thunder-storm, the wisdom-light awakens us just as the lightning awakens the earth, the wisdom-light leaves the mind fresh and calm, just as the lightning leaves the earth fresh and calm.

If we practice Guru Rinpoche sadhana, then while we visualize ourself as him and utter his mantra, we might think "I am Guru Rinpoche, like lightning I've chosen to come here to bring light to the minds of all beings, to dispel the darkness of their ignorance . . . my body is rainbow light and contains all Buddhas, my speech is wisdom sound of all Buddhas and contains all Dharma". . . and so on.

Guru Rinpoche's practice is a tested and proven method to attain enlightenment. Those of his disciples that have attained fruition through it, demonstrate miraculous signs at death, such as weather changes or rainbow body (in which the body dissolves into rainbow light and sparks. Fruition of Guru Rinpoche practice means becoming an emanation of him, and is often characterized by the Rainbow Body, the ability to dissolve ones bodily form into rainbow-light. This is the result of the training: the five elements are dissolved into their Wisdom-sources which are the five Wisdom-dakinis; the five emotional states are dissolved into their root which is Guru Rinpoche as five Wisdom Buddhas—Dorje Tothreng Tsal, Karma Tothreng Tsal, Pema Tothreng Tsal, and so on.

In Vajrayana it is said that as times become more degenerate, Guru Rinpoche's practice will become stronger. The antidote will become stronger as the degeneration becomes stronger. So people will have an equal chance to attain liberation.

Guru Rinpoche's special transmission is called Dzogchen, Great Perfection. It is the name of the fruition vehicle of the Nyingma, or "old translation school." Dzogchen or Maha-ati is the path of intrinsic freedom. In Dzogchen the nature of the mind is pure, total Presence, Samantabhadra. The point of view of Samantabhadra has no center or periphery—like vast open space. In Dzogchen one seeks to experience this directly by relaxing into ones natural unagitated uncontrived state. One seeks to realize the self-perfected,

primordially pure state—as the union of wisdom and means. If you know your true nature you know the majestic nature within everything—and will be at perfect peace, imperturbable no matter the situation. This is the deep meaning of the dorje. If you were to place Guru Rinpoche in a volcano he would not be moved (by negative emotion), his only motivation is compassion—pure Presence—Bodhicitta. He is our true nature—its image. We use him on the path to awaken this imperturbable, immovable state, union of awareness space and bodhicitta. This union is the Great Perfection.

There is a division within Dzogchen into three classes: "mind class, "space class" and "class of pith instructions." The first class is for people concerned with the workings of the mind, the second is for people whose minds are like the sky, the third is for those stars in the dawn sky who transcend all effort. I want to mention the Dzogchen view for three reasons: 1. Because it has been compared to Shiva's Non-dual School of Tantra which is espoused in Book II of this exposition; 2. Because it is the view transmitted by Thunder-beings such as Vajrapani, and 3. Because it is the culmination of the Tantric vehicles. The base of Dzogchen's "mind class" is that all phenomena are a play of mind-as-such, of self-existing wisdom. The base of the "space class" is that wisdom and all phenomena, arisen from its continuum, never separate from Samanatabhadri, thus remaining pure and liberated. The base of the "class of pith instructions" is that there are no obstructions to be rid of and no enlightenment to be acquired. To realize this allows a lightning arising of self-existing wisdom.

The goal of Dzogchen is to maintain recognition of the ultimate nature of mind as primordially pure, unstained and perfect. The natural mind rests in its own wisdom and reflects all phenomena as perfect, a display of wisdom. The fruit of the distinct practices, like Trekcho ("cutting through concreteness" to reveal primordial purity), and Thogal ("direct leap" to spontaneous presence), is that one dwells on the level of Samantabhadra "Ever-perfect" and realizes the face of wisdom unobscured.

Many Dzogchen teachings and practices come from Terma or Dharma treasures, which Guru Rinpoche developed and secretly hid. These treasures are an integral part of Guru Rinpoche's tradition. Out of his compassion for beings which he saw would be suffering in the future, he hid teachings, practices and images to be found in the future. He saw that these teachings would be suitable in the future time and place of their discovery. He hid these treasures in rocks, sky, water, and mind. He determined that future generations would benefit immensely from such treasures, so he arranged it so that a particular disciple of his, a treasure finder (Terton) would discover the treasure at a certain time in the future. The termas are often written in secret language called dakini-cypher, a symbolic language developed and transmitted by the dakinis to protect the Tantra. Only the treasure discoverers can decypher this language. The terma is generally in scroll form written on saffron parchment and hidden in a casket. He entrusted them to certain dakinis and Dharmapalas to protect.

One of the main terma and practices in connection with the Thunder-beings of the Great Secret is the Barchey Kunsel. There are five Thunder-beings associated with this practice which is aimed at dispelling obstacles through the unstoppable power of the Victorious Ones. This power is embodied in the Deities of the Barchey Kunsel. These Deities are: Sampa Lhundrupma (above), his wrathful emenations Guru Drakpo and Dorje Drollo (below), Vajrapani-Hayagriva-Garuda (below), and the Lion-faced Dakini—Sengedrolma (below).

It is well known that Crazy wisdom has its origin with the Thunder-beings, I addressed this in an above chapter. The main Vajrayana Deity associated with Crazy Wisdom is the wrathful form of Guru Rinpoche known as Dorje Drollo. In the Barchey Kunsel he is referred to as "King of Crazy Wrath," and "Crazy King of Wrath." He appears amidst black cloud banks of wisdom, himself swollen like a thunder-cloud. Purple brown in color, he rides a pregnant tigress which is Yeshe Tsogyal, here representing passionate space. (Other Thunder-beings have tiger mount as well). He is surrounded by flames of radiant wisdom. From his eyes he shoots lightningbolts. He holds a 9-pronged vajra and a phurpa (ritual dagger) to rapidly liberate the three poisons. Like most wrathful Thunder-deities he roars HUNG dispelling all obstacles. Like most Thunder-beings overhead soars Garuda.

Not only is Dorje Drollo the main yidam associated with Crazy Wisdom, the unique universal expression of Thunder-deities' counter-clockwise wisdom, but he is also associated with certain thunder-rites such as exorcism. Dorje Drollo is one of Guru Rinpoche's Eight Great Manifestations. There are eight dances associated with these forms of Guru Rinpoche. The eight forms are associated with his activities to

subdue, tame, pacify and subjugate malevolent forces as he dwelt in the eight cremation grounds. So Guru Rinpoche would take a particular form, and that form would dance and perform the rite associated with the dance. He gave these dances as a transmission to perform the same feats he did. Presently there are yogis who engage in these dances to embody the eight forms of Guru Rinpoche for performing his eight activities.

There are thunder dances of the Thunder-deities and rites in most traditions. In Taoist Tantra, there is the step of yu; In Shaiva Tantra, the 108 mudras of the Tandava; there are rain-dances in most shamanic traditions. These serve the function of bringing Thunder-beings to earth. They reflect and embody enlightened activity in the universe. Thunder specialist repeats or mimics Thunder-deity's dance in order to bring his wisdom, power and activity to earth.

(There are certain similarities in iconography between Guru Rinpoche and Shiva. Parallels in imagery will be presented later in the section on Shiva. The two images are very close, their wisdom-quality is somewhat similar. Both Rudra-Shiva and Guru Rinpoche have eight main forms. It is said that when Guru Rinpoche left the earth, he was riding a horse through the sky. I once saw Shiva riding a giant horse amongst thunder and lightning. They are different Sublime Beings, but the resemblance in imagery is unmistakable. The images of them which appear within a storm theophany are usually standing and active. Both Shiva and Guru Rinpoche are Lords of the cremation grounds. They act to subdue malevolent beings, spread Dharma, and pacify suffering through rapid illumination.)

The Lion-Faced Dakini

Another Thunder-being of the Barchey Kunsel mandala is the Lion-faced Dakini. The practice and 14-lettered mantra which Guru Rinpoche received in the treasure-casket to clear the obstructions to the spread of Dharma was that of the glorious vajra-dakini known as Simhamukha dakini (Sengedrolma): Lion-faced Dakini. Guru Rinpoche did this practice for seven days and was able to destroy the sorcerers with lightning to clear the path for the spread of Dharma in Tibet. Do not be alarmed by this activity, if you look closely you'll find instances in virtually every tradition where sorcerers, very evil people who cause immense suffering in the world, are destroyed by Thunder-beings—often through lightningbolts. It is out of great compassion for those who suffer and cry out for help that the evil-minded are destroyed. For obvious reasons I will not provide her mantra. Know that her practice is very beautiful, there is nothing dark or unrighteous about it.

Her lineage is called "Lineage of the Lightning Meteor." She is a supreme protectress and destroyer of obstacles. She is the emanation of Vajra-yogini, Mother of all Buddhas, Source of Vajrayana. Her origin, as recounted in the Terma was in ancient times. There were female demonic beings known as mamos who were afflicting beings with mental disease. Vajra-yogini, out of boundless compassion emanated as the Lion-faced dakini to subdue these female demons. Like many demon subduers she uses thunder-power, wisdom as thunder and lightning to achieve her aim.

In more modern times, her practice stems from the treasure discoverer Barway Dorje Lotsawa, who received it in dreams in which he was walking through a City (mandala) and encountered her as a bodiless dakini. I have been fortunate to receive the lineage transmission which comes down from this origin. The imagery presented below comes out of this Terma lineage, that of the ". . . Lightning Meteor," which I am a part of.

Her mandala has seven dakini emanations in it. Her central form is dark blue, symbolizing the oceanic nature. In her right hand she holds a raised crescent-moon flaying knife with a half-dorje handle which symbolizes her skillful ways to cut off the root of all afflictions. In her left hand she holds a skull-cup of blood. The blood symbolizes bliss and love. The cup symbolizes emptiness. She has a wrathful white lion-face, symbolizing absolute fearlessness in the face of all obstructors. She bares her teeth and roars dissolving all obstructions. She displays three blood-shot eyes. She has a skull-head-dress and mala of human-heads. Her head-dress symbolizes the outstanding Buddha qualities. Her mala symbolizes her ceaseless activity to liberate sentient beings from suffering. In the crook of her left arm she has a mystical staff adorned with a crossed dorje, tiny damarus, silks and three heads. As her body symbolizes wisdom, her staff denotes her skillful means. She wears a tiger-skin skirt, symbolizing fearlessness, an elephant hide symbolizing victory over great obstacles and ego, and a black silk robe. She dances on the corpses of ignorant view and is surrounded by an aureole of flames which are the power to burn up all negativity. Even though she is supremely wrathful in appearance, this is merely a mask, a skillful way to subdue or win over truly wrathful, hateful beings. In truth she is totally blissful, tranquil and loving. Her wisdom displays intense power to destroy all obstacles, and this power is both invisible- mysterious, and visible—electric—present—as image and sound. Fiercely recalcitrant beings don't respond to peaceful imagery or methods to draw beings to Dharma. So Wisdom-beings manifest wrathful forms to conquer them.

Primarily what most people can learn from her image is fearlessness. It is not a symbol of divine rage or human rage. It is non-dual wrath, compassionate wisdom-energy that conquers all obstructions. Traditionally all obstructions and obstructors have their root in our mind. They come about because of fear. If we do not fear, then we will not believe that evil spirits or sorcerers can harm us. Fear allows obstructions to occur, it allows dark-energy into our mind. Obstructions dissolve naturally if we choose not to fear, but instead care for all others first. Love is the real protectress. Lion-faced dakini, more than anything symbolizes the wisdom and love that protects us. In order to actually realize this view we need to realize that our nature—wisdom—is indestructible, and can never be damaged. Our mind is indestructible. This is the meaning of the vajra (thunderbolt) symbol held by most Vajrayana deities, and it is the meaning of Lion-faced dakini—she is the indestructible fearless wisdom which stops at nothing to free beings that do fear from negative forces. She awakens her own fearless wisdom and love in our hearts through her practice. And She always protects us in the face of danger whether we're afraid for ourself or not. She is there for good people who think of her. If you could see into her eyes you would see the supreme joy and the love. It is love which is able to face without fear the greatest enemies in our life and to win them over, by skillfully representing Dharma. When great yogis and saints came up against thieves they would offer them everything, they would love them and win them over. Thunder-beings tame the most hard to tame monsters with the force of love. This force takes wrathful forms through clear-light(ning) and subdues the demons. How beautiful this mystery is.

(Thunder-beings of other traditions also appear with lion-head, these include the male Simhamukha forms of Shiva and Vishnu and the female Sun goddess of the Egyptian pantheon—Sekhmet. The underlying quality in these forms is always fearless protection. Simhamukha Bhairava is a bodiless being above the entrance to Shiva's mandala [recall story above]. The bodiless Dakini of Simhamukha that Barway Lotsawa encountered in her City [of Lightning] was just a head. I've heard of such beings existing in others realms such as Dewachen where they're offering goddesses. They're heads which manifest appendages as needed.)

Vajrapani-Hayagriva-Wisdom Garuda

If you study the sutras you will discover that Vajrapani was one of Buddhas main attendents, and protected him from harm with the miraculous powers he developed. In Vajrayana he has a much greater place. Of the three qualities of all Buddhas, compassion, wisdom and power, Vajrapani stands for the enlightened will-power. Of the three roots, body, speech and mind, he is the mind of all Buddhas. His symbol is the vajra, he is the indestructible wisdom-mind of all the Buddhas.

Tantric teachings were transmitted on earth through Vajrapani and the 84 Mahasiddhas. The teachings originate with Chakrasamvara or the state of Vajradhara, and are guarded by Vajrapani, and taught in the 6 realms by him, Manjushri, and Chenrezig which represent the three outstanding qualities, and mind, speech, body (respectively) of all Buddhas.

The Buddha prophesied that after 28 years the higher Vajrayana teachings would appear in the East (abode of wisdom whose Lord is Vajrapani). There were five holy sages who were in samadhi, a god, yaksha, rakshasa, naga and human. They arose simultaneously out of their samadhi and gathered at the Mount Malaya (which I think is the same Mt. Malaya as the Mt. of Meteoritic Iron where Guru Rinpoche appeared out of a lightningbolt). The 5 sages prayed "who would dispel the world's blindness. . . ?" Vajrapani appeared and taught them various Tantric texts. The rakshasa wrote these Tantras with ink made of powdered lapis lazuli on gold paper. Then he hid the books in the sky. The same year 18 volumes of Tantra and a statue of Vajrapani fell from the sky like rain onto king Ja, a disciple of Vajrapani. Later he received from Vajrapani the Tantric teachings which he transmitted to Guru Rinpoche and then passed down in unbroken lineage to the present.

Vajrapani is King of the Vajra deities, mantras and lineage. Buddha Shakyamuni entrusted him to protect all the Tantric teachings. He is known as Guhyapati, Lord of the Secret, which refers to his protection of the truth, Buddha Dharma, A.K.A. the guhya mantra Vajrayana, or Secret Mantra Vajrayana or Tantrayana. It is through Vajrapani that Buddhist Tantras are disseminated in the human realm. Vajrapani protects mantras, the awareness-speech of the Deities, the key to their power and our clear awareness. Because there are people who would, without connection to a lineage or qualified transmission, proper training and guidance, attempt to gather immense power, thus damaging their energy, there is a great protector to prevent people from harming themselves. Vajrapani controls the activity of the descent or availability of knowledge of the Absolute, which is the power to awaken the adept to higher consciousness.

The pure enlightened will-power of all Buddhas is embodied in the Vajra family, and specifically in its Lord-Vajrapani. The father of the Vajra family is known as Akshobya, the Imperturbable, or Vajradhara the Bearer of the Vajra. As Shakyamuni he gave the lesser vehicle Sutrayana, Paramitayana, and greater vehicle Mahayana, as Vajradhara he gave the Secret Mantra vehicle—Tantrayana or Vajrayana. In this case Vajradhara-Akshobya took the form of the other Tantric Wisdom-beings to transmit the Tantra of their mandalas, such as Vajrapani, Chakrasamvara, Hevajra, Kalachakra, Guhyasamaja, Vajrabhairava, and their Wisdom-dakini consorts, who are regarded as inseparable from the Buddhas.

Akshobya is the father of the Vajra family which suggests that his power is with these Buddhas. Akshobya's quality is the adamantine wisdom that penetrates reality, to see the Ultimate Reality. His empowerment or extension of blessing lights through the practice of sadhana causes the penetration of the infinite (his Mind) into the finite, like lightning descending from the sky to penetrate the earth. To symbolize this Akshobya touches the earth. The energy of ignorance is liberated to become expansive radiating energy, like space. To designate this his color is blue and his attribute is the vajra. His vajra is the instantaneous penetration of vitality and wisdom from limitless nondual inner space. His self-appearing light doesn't come from any outer space locale. Akshobya or Vajradhara represents the Absolute. Like rays of the dawn sun he enters into the heart to awaken the mind of enlightenment, the vajra-wisdom.

Akshobya's wrathful form is known as Vajrapani. Vajrapani bears Akshobya's vajra. Vajrapani is considered Lord of the Vajra family. His name means Vajra in Hand, so his primary attribute is the vajra. His primary function is as a supreme protector of teachings and practitioners. Vajrapani had incarnated during the time of Shakyamuni and acted then as his protector, in one instance he used his power (siddhi) to destroy a boulder that had been hurled maliciously at the Buddha. The Buddha put him in charge of gathering, protecting and disseminating Buddha Dharma, the advanced teachings and practices of Tantra.

The power of all Wisdom-beings is embodied in Vajrapani. He is the Monarch of all Wrathful Deities and protectors. He is the total wisdom energy of the five Buddha families. He is a Thunder Lord, a fully enlightened being who had attained the great perfection eons ago. His vajra stands for the power of wisdom, its indestructible and unstoppable nature as well as its natural counterpart, the power of thunder. He is known as a rain-god and has been supplicated in this activity, to bring beneficial rains and avert harmful storms like hail. We know he is a Thunder Lord however not by his common feats but by his visionary revelation and by the activity of his Wisdom-Mind. His Vajra family mandala is called "the mandala of Victory over the Threefold World"; his family power is restoration and his magical power is destruction. Such are the capacities of all Thunder Lords. The Vajra family emphasizes wisdom and power, they're called Knowledge Bearers. Their self-arisen wisdom-light is the pure, clear, unstained light of dawning, known as rig pa or "ground luminosity" in the mind. It takes a subtle ebullient lightning revelation. It is in the eyes and lightning which are both associated with the Vajra family. They represent penetrating vision, knowledge or wisdom.

The Vajra family Buddhas and Dakinis work through this indestructible power, which is the subtle pure light currents which coarse through their bodies of vision, as vajra-body, vajra-speech, vajra-mind and vajra-wisdom. To demonstrate this power they take a mystical lightning revelation. Because this light is not different than our mind we experience it, we live its reality. Through this lightning the Buddha transmits his Mind, mixes it with ours, empowers and awakens us, purifies our body, speech, mind and wisdom. He awakens his qualities in us. He restores the mind and destroys our obstructions to the omniscient state of Buddhahood.

Vajrapani comes out of the East, he is the combined powers of the dawn, spring, awakening and the vajra of penetrating wisdom. The subtle white light of the dawn is like the subtle clear light of consciousness, which has the effect of awakening the mind as the light of dawn has the effect of awakening the body. But the ground luminosity is the nature of the mind, its radiance arising spontaneously. Vajrapani is waking us with his subtle living rays of wisdom after the sleep of consciousness. He awakens our primordially pure wisdom-nature, our nature of unobstructed awareness and bliss. This form of initiation and dawning which Vajrapani stands for is not something which happens once and that's it, it is an on-going process by which the pure mind is liberated (from its erroneous view of itself and reality), by which internal energy is transmuted and refined until it has returned to its originally open and clear state. Vajrapani controls the power of thunder and lightning which is the rapid, instantaneous method or application of his power of awakening. Since this is his enlightened vitality or bodhicitta, then his method is represented by the vajra. The power arises from the eye of primordial wisdom, the crown, signifying vajra-body, a body of enlightened power, it arises from the throat signifying vajra-speech, his enlightened activity or skillful means, and from the heart signifying vajra-mind and wisdom, his enlightened nature. In one image, at these three centers appear Garudas. These three Garudas symbolize enlightened body, speech and mind, and Vajrapani's power to pacify all obstructions of body, speech and mind.

The initiating grace which he gives is very much the goal. He assists us toward the goal by removing obstructions to the awakened state. Obstruction refers to obscured energy within the subtle wind passages of the mind, which are the causes of mental and physical illness; it refers to lack of awareness which gives rise to ego clinging or mental fixation which gives rise to desires and habitual tendencies.

Vajrapani's power is the activating power, the power of the beginning and ending phases of creation, of thought. The beginning corresponds with form and thought arising from emptiness, the potential or creative space. The ending phase corresponds with the dissolution of form and thought into the emptiness it arose from. This dissolution is actually the realization that emptiness and form are the same, that form is the appearance or display of wisdom, of the enlightened mind. This realization is possible when the mind is clear and open, the clear and open mind can see its thoughts as its self-radiance. Vajrapani's force of restoration-destruction makes a space in the mind. His power stills the mind. Within the space, opened up between thoughts, the nature of the mind can be realized or self-illuminated. This can be called inspiration because it is the activity of Vajrapani's enlightened wind or bodhicitta. Bodhcitta means enlightened mind and implies the energy or wind of pure motivation to liberate all minds—love. The result of his loving activity is awakening. Something has been removed which obstructed realization of the Unoriginated Mind, and something new is going to shine in its place, wisdom. Because the wisdom or empty nature of the mind was there all along we say the mind was restored. The form of destruction associated with Vajrapani and all Thunder-beings is a form of positive transformation, because it removes suffering, because it yields the clear light of inherent purity.

One way Vajrapani appears to the mind and in the atmosphere is with thunder, lightning, cloud, rain and wind. He has been supplicated to cause weather changes, positive transformation in the sphere of the earth. In the same way he can be supplicated to cause positive transformation in the sphere of Mind, which is not ultimately two different spheres. Both arise from the same ultimate ground of emptiness, so the wisdom-force has the same attributes and manifestation in both spheres and its function is the same. One is a subtle vision seen with a refined eye of awareness, the other is a gross vision experienced through the sensory doors. But it is one consciousness, it experiences subtle vision directly and experiences gross vision indirectly. Primarily we're speaking here of the arising and application of subtle wisdom in the mind. Since this subtle wisdom is the root of reality, it is necessary to achieve the ability to control the same vajra-power in the atmosphere (as a siddhi).

Vajrapani destroys what is old and out of balance, literally like the lightning, his power absorbs and dissolves gross energy, it liberates it in order to allow the free-radiant flow of new growth. If the creative space is obstructed it cannot radiate pure energy or bliss, so instead what arises is suffering and illness. The space that opens up and the clear light that shines as bliss in that space is the measure of creative capacity, insight. This capacity for insight, to have the ability to find solutions to the multiplicity of problems in our lives, is wisdom. The light which arises from this wisdom is the motivation to liberate all suffering beings, it is bliss, its application is skillful means or compassionate method. This is the full meaning of the vajra.

The lightning mandala of Vajrapani, his City of Lightning is called Vajrapani, Hayagriva, and Wisdom Garuda. Vajrapani, Hayagriva, Garuda comes out of the East, he stands on a sun disc supported by a lotus throne. He stands poised, watchful and active, which symbolizes his protective activity for the benefit of all sentient beings, his vajra-activity of removing obstructions, inner and outer demons. As Thunder Lord it would stand for his ability to restore the earth, to awaken beings, particularly since he might be figured trampling snakes which symbolize rain and fertlity. In his lightning revelation he would be seen amongst the thunder-clouds. His body swells blue-black like a thunder-cloud. His blue-skin symbolizes both sky-like awareness and the wisdom-element water. His giant body and belly are a stove of pure unquenchable energy, vajra-heat. He wears a tiger-skin to symbolize fearlessness. He is adorned with nagas, which tells us that he's a protector of this class of beings (as Nagapani), and that he is the power and means to transmute gross energies into enlightened energy since he subdues all malevolent beings (symbolized by nagas). Our awakened energy becomes a creative electrical force—vitality, so the controlled nagas can represent our radiating energy and the lightningbolts of the Thunder-beings, their own fully awakened energy. He wears a garland of skulls around his neck wich symbolize his ceaseless activity for the benefit of all sentient beings. He wears a diadem of five skulls to symbolize that the five wisdoms are inherent, he is their embodiment. His hair stands on end, an effect of his radiant energy. He has a wrathful expression, exposing four fangs. This indicates that a great amount of power has arisen to clear a path to omniscience, and that he will stop at nothing to pacify suffering and tame the mind. He is a supermundane Deity, which means that he is beyond bondage to emotion. His vajra-wrath demonstrates his fierce directness and power, transmuted heat. When anger arises it is inner heat, energy, whose true nature is blissful will-power. Anger happens because our will-power is obstructed, our frustration is the obscuration of bliss. We wanted something that would bring us or another person bliss. When our act is obstructed, our bliss gets cut off, and our heat rises under pressure. If we swallow it, we transmute it, if we vent it, others get burned. Vajrapani teaches us to swallow all negative states. In mythology his body turned blue from swallowing the poison generated from malevolent beings. He is also known to devour nagas, which are called snakes of anger. So his wrath and nagas represent the power to face and digest negative states, to liberate wrath. If anger is released from feeding anger and redirected toward a positive end, the mind becomes clear and concentrated—adamantine. An increase in ones level of awareness results in the liberation of the inner energies. The taming of the mind is the essence and goal of Vajrayana practice. So when anger is turned inside out, it reveals itself as enlightened will-power, which in the inner and outer Deity mandala can appear as thunder and lightning. It expresses the energy of instantaneous or rapid awakening in which the mind sees directly the empty nature of itself and reality. It is one manifestation of the Mind as pure primal iridescence and awareness. The lightning revelation is the Mind of the Awareness-deity sporting in ones own mind. To symbolize his complete awakenment, Vajrapani has a third-eye electric lamp. Typically the third-eye is the conduit for the pure power to bridge emptiness and form, by issuing a lightningbolt, which, striking, lights up the mind. Vajrapani's three eyes represent the ability to see the three times clearly.

There is nothing violent about the Deity's inner nature, they're peaceful and joyous. In Vajrayana there are nine qualities embodied in the wrathful Deity as they are associated with vajra-body, vajra-speech and vajra-mind. They are: of body—haughty, heroic, fearful; of speech—laughing, threatening and fierce; of mind—compassionate, powerful and peaceful. Their body is captivating to lead beings with desire out of suffering through light. Their body is heroic to lead beings with hatred out of suffering through light. Their body is fierce to lead beings with ignorance out of suffering through light. So the wrathful body leads all beings out of suffering who see it or visualize it. The Deity utters attractive laughing sounds to lead beings with desire out of samsara through sound. They utter harsh, threatening sounds like HUM to lead beings with hatred out of samsara through sound. They utter thunderous sounds to lead beings with ignorance out of samsara through sound. So the wrathful speech leads all beings out of suffering who hear it, think of it or repeat it. The Deities Mind of compassion leads beings with desire out of samsara, their mind of power leads beings with hatred out of samsara, their mind of tranquility leads beings with ignorance out of samsara. So the wrathful Deities Mind lead all beings who suffer out of samsara. Anyone who thinks of their mind or qualities is freed of suffering.

It may seem exceptionally contradictory of a pure being to manifest in such a violent guise, but Vajrapani is pointing the way beyond bondage to emotional bewilderment. His expression of wrath is a contrary teaching device to show us that the way to bliss is through the energy of wrath. Unenlightened energy is merely a distortion of enlightened energy. Vajra-wrath is non-dual energy, clear, penetrating power with neither subject nor object. If the limited vision or sense of self-cherishing is destroyed then the radiant-space of ones mind extends itself compassionately, spontaneously and unconditionally, without subject or object. Vajrapani applies his wisdom-fire (inner heat) to benefitting beings, it is the meaning of his vajra. It is his ability to achieve anything. He is unstoppable.

Vajrapani is surrounded by an aureole of flames which issue from his pores. The flames are the fire-aspect of wisdom, the radiance of the Mind and its ability to fly upwards (sometimes within these flames are Garudas). It is the power to burn up all neurotic states, to transmute and awaken the energy of the mind, to turn the ego into a pile of ashes. As a primordial wisdom-element, fire stands for ascent, heat. These arise from his deep blue body which denotes the primordial wisdom-element water, together they are his power to destroy obstacles. We could say these qualities connect him to vast inner space, the sky, rain and lightning, since the clashing of water and fire produce lightning, which has the qualities of ascending heat (fire) and descending and flowing (water). These are the aspects of his wisdom, its luminosity, and ability to gather and flow. In the atmosphere Vajrapani gathers the hot and cold energies together, the red rays of the sun and the blue vapors of water. He brings them together like electrical cables. With his right hand holding the gold vajra aloft, Vajrapani subdues planetary spirits. With his left hand at his heart, Vajrapani makes the gesture of destroying hindrances (vajra-fist), single handedly driving off demons. With this hand he subdues all nagas below. This gesture is also called "the horns" (horns of the garuda) and is the universal mudra for warding off negativity. The weather lama uses it to drive away harmful storms. Vajrapani tramples all harm-doers, destroys all obstructions and obstructors, dispels all obstacles, burns up all hindrances, and overwhelms all recalcitrant spirits.

His vajra symbolizes the indestructible wisdom-nature and enlightened power of compassion, his power of lightning-illumination and inherent bliss. His vajra is said to be like a boomerang; after it hits the target (achieves its purpose) it returns to its source-void.

Like other Thunder-beings, Vajrapani utters the battle cry or vajra-shout—HUM, which echoes across the universe. It is the vajra-speech or activity which carries his power into the universe and mind to destroy negativity. It is the victory shout over all negative forces that bind the mind, it is the vajra-sound of penetrating wisdom in the universe. The visible counterpart of the Hum is the vajra, as the visible counterpart to thunder is lightning. The Hum letter has five points which correspond to the five wisdoms. The Hum stands for the vajra-mind and vajra-wisdom of all Buddhas. The Hum is the sound counterpart to Vajrapani, his seed syllable. His vajra-hum penetrates invisibly, magically dissolving all hindrances to enlightenment. It initially precedes sound and light, when it develops into sound it becomes Hum, when it develops into light it is white light or lightning.

Vajrapani manifesting amongst thunder and lightning is crowned by a horse-head (Hayagriva) whose neighing goes out across the universe dispelling negativity. Above him is the Garuda devouring a serpent. Hayagriva is an actual Wisdom-deity, the wrathful form of Amitabha. The Wisdom-Garuda is an emanation of Vajrapani. This mandala combines the essences of these three Deities. The Hayagriva, "horse-neck," in the previous traditions was related to the sun, appearing with other deities like Brahma and Vishnu. In the Hindu tradition it is said to hold and give away secret knowledge. Shiva cut it off when Brahma was jealous of his brilliance, as an act symbolic of destroying jealousy. Vajrapani's horse-head crown represents the transmutation of jealousy, its awakened state (which is all-accomplishing wisdom). This image of Vajrapani is also a giver of revelation, the practice is called "the union of Vajrapani-Hayagriva and Garuda." Vajrapani is also responsible for transmitting secret knowledge, such as Tantra and Dzogchen teachings. So I don't think the earlier interpretation of the symbol can be entirely overlooked.

Hayagriva is also a Thunder-deity. He is a subduer of nagas, a great protector. His sadhana works with the transmutation of desire and jealousy, and the clearing of fierce obstacles. I've heard it related (in Terma) that he arose as a thunder-storm to clear obstructing influences to the Dharma in Tibet. The sign of accomplishment of Hayagriva is that a neighing horse-head actually protrudes from ones crown. The horse symbol is related to Thunder-beings in other traditions as well, such as ancient China, and the Lakota pantheon. These are horses-snorting-lightning, messengers bearing revelation from the Thunder-beings. Earthly horses were also created by Thunder-beings, so they bear some of their attributes, like strength, speed and courage.

Vajrapani has taken the form of the Wisdom Garuda who flies above his head. Thunder Lord takes the form of Thunder-bird, he can appear as Deity, a bird or a Thunder-bird, a fusion of Lord and giant Bird. Thunder-birds usually have the attributes of eagle and man. Garuda means "Great Eagle," and "Brilliant Luster." Wisdom Garuda isn't a bird, he's the true human, the Buddha. Garuda is the ancient Indian Thunder-bird and Sun-bird, the inner and outer aspects of the universe, the purusha and prakriti, Mind and Energy. Shiva took the Garuda-form, as well as Vishnu and Brahma. Garuda is the luminous power of the universe, the celestial light and the super-luminal light of consciousness. Garuda designated the cosmic and microcosmic body and its circulating forces, such as the rays of the sun or rays of lightning—"winged power," such as the rays of the heart or rays of bliss-consciousness. Garuda's head is the heavens, the subtle formless state, the sphere of the deity. His eyes are the sun and moon, male and female, hot and cold energies which give rise to lightning in the atmosphere, and enlightenment when retracted up the central channel in the spinal column. His upper body and wings are the vastness and power of the sky. His wings are the movement of the wind and storm clouds, and the activating movement of internal winds (energy). His body can appear as clouds, his wings as lightning issuing rain. Garuda's belly is the pit of the earth, full of fire, liquid seething lava, surrounded by stone, ores etc., and it is the belly of the microcosm, full of inner heat, vaporized generative fluids and electricity. Garuda is the mergence of the individual mind and space—the universal cosmic body. Garuda is the omniscient state, so in Vajrayana he symbolizes Buddha-nature. He is very simply the mind freed of all limitations. He is the self-luminous heart, its emptiness and bliss. He appears flying in the space above the Buddhas, and symbolizes their activity to pacify negative forces. Most Buddhas take the form of the Garuda. It is said that the first Garuda appearance was that of Shakyamuni. Evil nagas were causing harm, so the Buddhas asked Shakyamuni to do something and he took Garuda form. Garuda appears in innumerable mandalas demonstrating this ability to pacify negativity. All Garudas and Thunder-birds serve the same function in the universe—so embody the activity of pacifying, controlling and devouring nagas.

He stands for the power of the Deity to fly in the space of the universe, and the power of the heart to fly, to radiate bliss freely in the space of Universal Mind. He is the "winged-power," or secret inner wind of the mind called in Tantra—lung. Our refinement can be symbolized by the birth of Garuda, his ascent and flight into space. It suggests the mergence of the mind and space, the complete revelation of wisdom in the mind. Garuda is a revelation bird; he stands for the Deity's revelation, the mixing of his mind with ours, and the revelation of our own inherent nature. The Wisdom-beings use Garuda as a vehicle to descend, that is to extend themselves, their bodhicitta to all beings in need. So when the Garuda is a mount it can symbolize the enlightened lung of the Deity (which has also been figured as a horse called lungta—windhorse). In one particular image Vajrapani rides the Garudas back through the skies, hurling down phurpu missiles at his enemies, inner and outer negativity. When Thunder Lord descends from heaven, from his cloud house to earth, he travelled in the lightning trail which is the Thunder-bird. He emitted the lightning through his eyes. It came from his heart, as enlightened energy traveling in two channels to the eyes. Garuda is the revelation of the Deity in the sky and mind. He stands for inspiration, bliss, and wisdom-transmission. He stands for the movement of the heart, its pure motivation. Garuda is the skillful means of the Buddhas, he descends from the summit of enlightenment with divine nectar, with thunder-porridge to enlighten the mind. He is the blessing-lights or grace-waves of the Deity, the creative force of inspiration, of purification, of pacification. He is the creative space spontaneously giving birth to energy which appears as light, lightning, a bird with man features and man with bird features. He has arisen from emptiness into form through energy, either as subtle light saturating the mind, flashing in the mind deep insight into reality, or as gross light flashing in the sky, insight into the nature of nature. Garuda is a symbolization of the dharmakaya, our greatest potential. The completely awakened state. If he takes a body on earth as tulku, then he has the recognition of being the body of the Buddha (Vajrakaya) and will evolve into the primordial shape after fulfilling his heart (Dharma), and return to space. The Garuda is actually a form which an achieved practitioner can take. Often it is used for pacification, as with Guru Rinpoche, but it might be assumed for departing from earth. Mahasiddhas of the three Tantric traditions, Shaivite, Buddhist and Taoist (and shamanic traditions) have often been witnessed in man-bird-form, one example is Guru Rinpoche, another is Kukkuripa. Since we are potentially tulku, potential Buddhas, the Garuda is the vajra-vehicle by which we ascend to the height of the world mountain (Meru)—the height of achievement. Garuda has giant wings to symbolize the union of wisdom and compassion, or emptiness and bliss. They express high achievement by their great wing-span. They symbolize the completion of the two accumulations which allows us to take off from the nest of earth. The wings are the spontaneous motivation to return to assist others, they have radiated from the heart of pure bodhicitta, unconditional love. Garuda has a man's torso and arms, and the legs and feet of an eagle. He has the beak of an eagle, and the head and hair of a man. These combined attributes stand for the transmuted body into its subtlest spiritual state. Garuda has an enormous belly of energy, the cauldron where the process of alchemical refinement of all elements of ones being are going to be transmuted into gold, or subtle inner heat (tum mo). Garuda can appear blue, white, yellow, red, green in the five directions and black and multicolored. He has horns which are antenae, symbols of omniscient wisdom. He devours a naga, who is his mortal enemy. The nagas stand for negativity. Garuda is Vajrapani's power to pacify all negativity. He devours outer demons and subdues them, and enlightens our inner demons.

The Deity descends to earth by riding the Garuda, or by becoming the Garuda. Garuda is the wisdom which transforms the mind, and pacifies suffering. Garuda is destroying obstacles to the omniscient state by devouring nagas. Of coarse he is teaching us to face and swallow our inner negative states to gain mastery over them, and he is the blessing-power to achieve this. So he is the fuel of the path, the vehicle and the goal. He is the Thunder-bird of the Tantric Wisdom traditions, he stands for the wisdom and powers of the universe and mind. He stands for transmutation. Buddhas have the ability to fly, subdue, pacify, heal, control weather, kill (to destroy causes of suffering), expand into infinite space, contract to make themselves available in many places at once by manifesting numerous transformations or rupakaya.

As the lotus born Deities arise fully grown from their lotus, the egg-born Garudas arise fully grown from their egg. The reason being that they were awake inside the egg the whole time, our ultimate nature can never be defiled. This suggests the singular thread or ground of all states of mind and matter, shunyata, the mode of subsistence of all Buddhas, the deepest nature of our mind. And yet there is still a real transmutation to be affected before we are liberated to fly and merge with space. We are inside the egg which is our limited energy-mind, our limited vision or sense of duality. The egg represents the phase of the body inherited from our parents. The arising of the egg is our first birth. We are either lost in the dream displayed on the inside of the egg, or are tired of bondage and pecking to get out, training our mind to open by refining our energy. The Garudas (Buddhas) are like mother birds. They will be our second parents, the real parents of the awakened mind inside the egg. They give us the assistance we need to make the transition from limited to unlimited vision. The arising from the egg is our second birth and actually entails a symbolic death in which the limited energy of the body dissolves into the subtle energy of the deity (wisdom-Source), in which a body of purified vision arises. When the egg cracks open, Garuda soars directly into outer space as the fully awakened mind. According to Chogyam Trungpa Rinpoche, the Garuda represents the "dignity of outrageousness"—the mind gone far beyond the limited ordinary vision of reality. Garuda is the mind which apprehends emptiness, the conceptionless or non-fixated state which perceives the singular thread of dual-experience, the one taste of pleasure and pain, positive and negative, space and solid, hot and cold, happy and sad. Garuda is the unstained mirror of the mind which reflects the Ultimate Reality, the Awareness-deity reflecting himself, the empty field of phenomena and the empty phenomena of the feild. Garuda embodies fearlessness, strength and limitless vision, unobstructed awareness and light.

He controls the thunder-power in the atmosphere and applies it toward positive transformation. He controls the mind through the subtle substanceless energy. So we can say his work is magical or mystical, because we don't necessarily see or feel it. It precedes energy like electricity, yet evolves into it by changing frequency. You can feel that energy at a certain point as an inner freedom and bliss remarkably tinged with the quality of enlightenment. At a certain point you can see the light, like a mist or cloud, a living radiance or flashing, yet it is still not recognizable force. When it becomes force, it is like the feeling you get under charged storm clouds, and makes your hair stand on

end. Since the entire spectrum of energy is immutable, the power, the light and the silent empty field which precedes it are one. Therefore we say the power was concealed, then revealed itself.

When Garuda appears above Vajrapani he has a naga in his mouth, meaning he devours negative states. His descent tells us he's already been to the summit of the mountain of awakenment and that he's bringing back his realization to assist all sentient beings. He tells us therefore that tireless compassion is essential to the attainment of Buddhahood. His compassionate activity of pacifying negativity, the root of all suffering is denoted by his devouring nagas. He tells us that we must be strong and come face to face with negativity, as a warrior. He battles ceaselessly against negativity. Thunder-birds, since the earth was young have been coming down to protect people and animals by subduing the causes of suffering. Garuda transmutes the serpents into gold, his own body. Thunder-bird often strikes them with lightning. Once devoured in this way they serve the subtle law of the universe—the Dharma body.

Nagas are one of six classes of beings, inhabiting lower water realms, earth and sometimes sky (in vaporized water). Nagas have some control over earthly nourishment. The avaricious ones can poison waters, they are negative directional energies. They can cause disease and mental problems, because they are inner energetic poison. Thunder-beings are their enemies. They are in charge of subduing these negative forces, to cause balance between negative and positive forces. Thunder-beings subdued the giant mother snakes on earth, then went up and subdued their spirits, destroying and pacifying them with lightning, making them into Dharma-protectors. Some examples are the Naga Kings, like Muktalinda, who coiled the Buddha, protecting him during his passage into complete awakenment, and who continues to protect teachings and give assistance to people through thunder-dreams.

The Naga kings can generally make storms. Nagas can be controlled by lamas to make storms; there is a Gelugpa sadhana for rain which controls nagas. They are the lightning tools of Thunder Lords, like Vajrapani and Shiva. Vajrapani is known as their protector. His mountain abode was once home to a Naga.

I think our pure positive vitality, the electrified inner winds, can be referred to as Garuda. The devoured and digested nagas of negativity become part of our new spiritual body of unobstructed wind and vision. Nagas in this case would symbolize the knots which obstruct the free flow of inner winds and the energy around the heart which prevents it from radiating clearly. The inner naga is struck by the bolt of Deity illumination, and thus becomes that illumination. The Garuda's flight pertains to the movement of "winged-power" within the inner and outer mandala, the mind and universe. Garuda's flight pertains to the movement of purified wind upwards within the pure body, to its union with clear light mind.

The ordinary mind must be transmuted into its original state as clear light mind, Transcendent Mind or Buddha's Wisdom Mind. This is achieved by refining the coarse winds which support the mind. The wind is the support for awareness which is ever-undefiled. The frequency of the wind is karmic-generated, its quality depends on the actions we've chosen. By planting seeds of negative thought and action we sow brambles of negative thought and action. By planting seeds of positive thought and action we sow dharma-flowers of clear thought and action.

The spirit or crystallization of refined energy, is given birth to at the crown in the form of a Garuda. Or the mahasiddha is actually able to take the form of Garuda, or whatever form he or she pleases, to pacify monsters, leave the earth, to disappear in rainbows, appear out of a lightning-bolt, soar through space as a mount for ones fully enlightened Mind. The symbolic position above Vajrapani-Hayagriva represents both emanation or symbol-vehicle of the Buddha, and, the birth of the spiritual body of light above the crown, or our birth as Buddhas. The Garuda is the ability of the Buddha to be both forms at once. The position of Garuda above Vajrapani further denotes the Thunderbird who is projected by Thunder Lord during storms, who flies out before Thunder Lords as "shield bird." The two are one powerful being. (Thunder-bird further projects messengers out in front of him, who incarnate as such, bringing thunder-power and crazy-wise law among the people. Together they are Vajrakaya). The shield bird is a strong protector and warrior, he battles all negative forces, rapidly and vigorously transmutes all negative situations in all spheres. He is in the position to descend in lightnings, to fine tune electrical imbalance, and to fine tune our hearts according to the key-note of the Dharma. He is positioned in the five directions to protect all sentient beings by maintaining harmony between forces. He cleanses all spheres polluted by monsters. His lightning electrocutes demons that happen to fall in its path, and his thunder drives the remaining hordes out to the far corners. This is Thun-

der Lords direct method of dealing with the causes of suffering, the energies which prey on the hearts of gold.

Vajrapani-Hayagriva-Garuda is a supreme warrior, a Bodhisattva warrior—meaning he fights fearlessly to assist sentient beings until samsara (the cycle of becoming, of the continuous rebirth and suffering of beings) is empty.

Vajrapani's method of accomplishment consists in gathering the subtlest radiant energy in its pure positive form to bring about rapid spiritual enlightenment. By generating the image of Vajrapani-Hayagriva-Garuda, symbolizing enlightened power and wisdom, focusing creatively on it with single pointed concentration, we stimulate the awakening of our own enlightened power and wisdom. The purpose of visualization is to absorb the qualities demonstrated by the image, and the purpose of the image is to convey those qualities to us in a communicable way. The Tantric sadhana is to be utilized to come under the wings of the Deity. They give us protection from the start. Eventually we shine with their light, and identify with them at the deepest level, and our mind takes on the aspect of its object, our limited sense of self dissolves, and the practice of vajra-pride coupled with a perfect vision of ourself as the Deity becomes a fact. We are dissolving into the fact that the Deity pervades the heart of consciousness. We are opening to the graceful arising, to the self-arisen existence of the Deity within our mind-stream. This means the Deity is already there and we're awakening to its luminous existence. We feel like the Deity and appear like him simultaneously. We take on the three outstanding qualities of all Buddhas: universal compassion, wisdom and power.

Vajrapani's magical vision awakens all less subtle energy of the mind, in such a way the mind is tamed. His vision might imply something near an explosion, the ecstatic breakthrough to omniscience. He represents the release of nuclear energy, of wound-up energy, of tightness. There is a gathering, a build up of energy, then a discharge, a breakthrough, like the birth of lightning from a swollen thunder-cloud. The accumulation of awareness-mantra is like the accumulation of a thunder-cloud, with its billowing head and high-voltage luminosity. We're awakened through this accumulation. We ingest the luminosity of this accumulation. We recite the mantra to accumulate the cloud of wisdom, we visualize the image to become a pure vessel to receive it. We further visualize the descent of blessing-lights into the vessel to enlighten and purify body, speech and mind. Once fully purified, at the accomplishment level of the practice, one becomes the Thunder-deity, radiating emptiness and bliss like a thunder-cloud emitting lightning.

The power of Vajrapani-Hayagriva-Garuda to awaken the mind, works on the mind the way the lightning works on the earth. It removes what is obstructing the upwards movement of energy within the microcosm. In this way Vajrapani removes inner obstacles, one moment there was fear and doubt, the next the clear light of awareness is able to shine. The vajra goes right to the source and awakens it. It doesn't imply a shock, but the power has the same result, it makes a space in the mind, so that its peace, clarity, wisdom, love can arise spontaneously. As lightning achieves its goal quickly and without hindrance, Vajrapani awakens the mind. As Thunder-beings leave the earth peaceful, fresh, vibrant, so these sacred practices, the grace of the Deities, leave the mind fresh, vibrant, and expansive. Vajrapani brings us back before an erroneous dual vision of our mind (as self-existent) to the root or beginning of our mind, its primordially perfect awake state, called in Dzogchen "Youthful Vase Body."

Vajrapani provides a path of transmutation, symbolized by the vajra and lightning trail. Through vajra-grace he provides the fuel of our enlightenment. His light(ning) is a living wisdom—it destroys and recreates at a glance. Through the entrance to his City of Lightning he reveals his nature in our nature, our nature in his nature, the inseparability of Mind and self-appearing light. Garuda descends as Mind and Light in the transmission waves. His grace-waves and those of the innumerable interpenetrating Buddha Minds are responsible for all righteousness in the world, for Dharma, which is why Garuda stands for inspiration—creative energy flows through us in the moment of spacious clarity. The smallest acts of kindness come from the same potential space, awakened ideas as well as the power of miracles. Thunder, lightning and rain are equally bodhisattva activity, they purify, awaken and nourish the earth. All the seen and unseen grace we receive in our lives, comes come from a heart which is immeasurably loving and tender, that has been pricked by its own sad-bliss into raining down tears. Thunder-beings are happy crying gods. They are the healers of hearts, minds, bodies. There is no illness that stands incurable before them, there is no problem for which they do not have the wisdom to correct.

Vajrapani-Hayagriva-Garuda rapidly illuminates reality like lightning. His condensed mantra is Om Benzapani-Hayagriva-Garuda Hung Phet. He has other mandalas, practices and mantras, but this mantra is the essence of them all, it is his heart essence; it invokes the wisdom-mind of all the Buddhas; it bears the power of all enlightened beings. (I do not recommend using it without the empowerment, because it can be harmful).

Vajrapani stands for the greatest force in the universe. It has been said that whatever mountain Garuda lands on becomes flat. His thunder-power is not destructive without being creative. He establishes the radiant-wisdom of his mind on earth. It restores the state of things to spontaneous perfection through the illusory dance of lightning in the one earth-mind dream.

Vajrapani is said to be the greatest protector. He is our void nature. If there is no self, then there is nothing which can be hurt, so no affliction can touch us. Supplicating and taking refuge in Vajrapani or any Wisdom-being means taking refuge in our void self-less nature. Vajrapani also embodies compassion. Our compassion also protects us. It is an attitude of not caring for oneself, but of putting all others first. The luminous clarity gained from this attitude acts like a shield. Void and Compassion—these are the two wings of the Garuda which shield us, they are the wings of our heart, they are the two sides of the vajra which stands in our heart. Void and love is what protects us from external obstacles and acts as a weapon for destroying internal obstacles.

Because Garuda ushers in the purification necessary to dissolve a degenerate civilization so a new one can arise, Lord Vajrapani will be an important wisdom-being to align with. I feel he will have an important role in the purification, in protecting good practitioners. Within this very lifetime I recommend that Buddhist practitioners seek out this empowerment and work diligently with the practice—the future is uncertain.

(It is worthy to note that there is some strong iconographic similarity between the images of Vajrapani and other Thunder-beings which has caused some scholars to label these beings identicle without actually becoming acquainted with the deity-essence. The mistake is made in considering Vajrapani the same as Indra. Though their iconography is similar and Indra was deemed Vajrapani, the two are not the same. In the Vajrayana pantheon, which has been developed from the profound mystical experiences of perfected masters [mahasiddhas], Indra is considered a lokapala [sphere-protector] and lord of the gods of the heaven of the 33, and is not Vajrapani. There is also some similarity between the images of Vajrapani and the 64 Bhairavas [terrific forms of Shiva]. So too, the story often told at the Vajrapani empowerment by the lama explaining how Vajrapani turned blue from swallowing the poison of the churning of the amrita was initially a myth attributed to Shiva to explain his blue throat. Nevertheless, Shiva and Vajrapani have distinct places in the Tibetan pantheon. I think we can trust the omniscient vision of the siddhas who are intensely familiar with the Deity's essence, above the scholars who are only familiar with the symbol of the Deity. The iconographic similarity may be viewed in the light of the fact that the nature and function of the Thunder-beings in the universe is similar. They are similar methods utilized to achieve the same goal.)

Chakrasamvara: The Lord of the Wheel of Supreme Bliss

Chakrasamvara (Korlo Demchog) is a Thunder-being of the Vajra family. Actually I cannot tell you how important Chakrasamvara is in Vajrayana and Thunder transmission. He is the source of the tradition and the origin of the chain of lightning, the power and wisdom which Buddhas manifest. He is Buddhas Wisdom Mind, the Emptiness from which all beings have arisen. He initiates our birth into subtle space and our return to emptiness-bliss. 100 Buddha families can be condensed into five (Wisdom Buddhas), the five into three (Body, Speech, Mind), the three into one (Mind). This Mind of all Buddhas is Chakrasamvara.

His name clearly communicates his nature, which is the nature of all enlightened minds; chakra means wheel, it symbolizes wisdom, samvara means supreme bliss, thus Chakrasamvara is the union of wisdom and bliss, a pure symbolization of the enlightened state. Because the wheel is a circle it denotes wholeness, harmony, the integration of energies within the mind. Because the wheel emanates spokes of radiance, it symbolizes the enlightened heart which naturally radiates bliss and love. The spokes can be taken as the Deity's emanation-bodies, his rupakaya going out into the directions, his methods of extending himself, his compassionate means or grace-waves flowing out to enlighten all beings, the emergence of bliss from emptiness. When the Deity is a Thunder Lord we might think of the spokes as lightnings, since this is the configuration of their grace, the manifest blessings of the Unmanifest.

He is commonly referred to as Heruka, which is the name-essence of his mantra, and the name for all fierce male Deities, especially those of his assemblage. The etymology of the word is as follows: He means supermundane bliss, ru means superluminal light, ka means supreme love. So Heruka denotes the revelation of Wisdom Mind. His practitioners take him to be the Absolute, a powerful symbol of Ultimate Reality, the union of emptiness and bliss. Indeed by aligning with him he rapidly returns the mind to the spacious state where bliss and love can shine freely. His power works as quickly as a thunder-storm, and as mysterious as void. He is a yab-yum or Father-Mother, the male form embodies the bliss of all the Buddhas, his consort Vajra-yogini embodies the wisdom of all the Buddhas. The two are one inseparable Reality, the unified state of the enlightened Mind. To demonstrate this they are in active union (karma-mudra).

In Dzogchen he is said to be the fierce emanation of Samantabhadra. In Mahamudra he would be considered the direct emanation of the noble Vajradhara (who is Samantabhadra). Chakrasamvara is the active sambhogakaya form of Samantabhadra, while Vajradhara is the peaceful form. This Deity is the origin of the Buddhist Tantra. Vajradhara is deep blue, two armed, and holds bell and dorje crossed at his heart. He is adorned in gold ornaments and sits in vajra posture, sometimes with consort. The two armed form of Heruka is the active form of Vajradhara, in this case he is deep blue, one-faced, standing in union with his consort Vajra-yogini, holding bell and dorje crossed to embrace her. He is the tutelary Deity or patron of the Karma Kagyu lineage, representing the crown jewel of the path—mahamudra. Many early Mahasiddhas achieved enlightenment through his Tantra. His Tantra was one of the first Vajrayana Tantras transmitted. The origin of the Kagyu tradition, the omniscient Tilopa, was Chakrasamvara. In the Kagyu refuge tree, his peaceful form Vajradhara takes the center, a few spaces above him is Samantabhadra, and just below him is Chakrasamvara. Essentially these three are the same.

The first mahasiddhas to receive the Chakrasamvara Tantra were emanations of Shiva, such as my own master Gorakhnath. Gorakhnath and the other Nath siddhas who received the Tantras attained immortal bliss body through Shaiva Tantra rasayana, and had been living on earth for several hundred or thousand years when they received the Chakrasamvara Tantra. Chakrasamvara, like Shiva, has his geographic seat on Mt. Kailash with his 64 deity retinue. One of Lord Shiva's 1008 names used in ancient times was Samvara, which is also used for Chakrasamvara. In terms of iconography he is nearly identicle to Shiva Gajasurasamhara who dwells on Kailash. In terms of the Tantra of profound instructions there are similarities in view and practice. For example the Kundalini practices are extant in both traditions, the generation of inner heat, the use of mantras, mudras and visualization, and so on. However, the method known as Chakrasamvara is unmistakably resonant with the Wisdom-spheres of Buddhas, and his Tantra is 100% Buddha Dharma. Chakrasamvara and Shiva, and all other Wisdom-beings represent the same state of attainment, they are the same ultimate Wisdom functioning through unique avenues in the inner universe, one Vajrayana, another Sanatan Dharma. So there is a level at which they differ and one in which they're the same. They're distinct yet share the same level of profound subsistence.

Chakrasamvara has five main forms of his mandala, from two-armed, to twelve-armed, to many-armed many-headed. I have also seen Garuda imagery in his iconography. His twelve-armed form is the central form in his Heruka mandala, the one we're concerned with, the one associated with a lightning revelation, and the one which resides on Mt. Kailash. He is known as Demchog Heruka. He stands in active union with his consort Vajra-yogini, "Thunder-bolt Mistress of Spiritual Union." Both have fiercely passionate expressions. Heruka's wrath awakens the wisdom of the union of emptiness and bliss. The wrathful form is a powerful method for taming intensely negative forces.

The union of Heruka and Vajra-yogini symbolizes the enlightened transformation of sensual desire into desireless bliss through the union of wisdom and compassion. His name Heruka has a secret meaning alluding to drinking blood from a skull-cup which suggests the liberation of passion into exaltation. Their passionate expressions seem to allude to this as well, for she is sipping nectar from Heruka's lips. They are enjoying one another. This transformation occurs through the completion of the two accumulations (wisdom and merit), through cultivating wisdom and unconditional love. Their union really means that

from practicing the union of wisdom and compassion comes the greatest bliss, which is akin to, but much greater than sexual bliss. Their union also means that by practicing compassion, wisdom is awakened (penetrated), and vice versa.

He has four faces, each three-eyed, symbolizing the four doors of liberation: the view that all phenomena, causes, actions and results are empty of inherent existence. His body is blue symbolizing emptiness or our sky-like nature. He wears a tiger-skin symbolizing fearlessness, a garland of freshly cut heads symbolizing his activity to liberate sentient beings. He wears bone ornaments symbolizing the six perfections, wisdom, patience, giving, etc.. He embraces his wisdom holding vajra and bell to symbolize the union of bliss and emptiness. He holds up an elephant skin symbolizing the power to conquer ignorance. He plays a two-half skull damaru to enhance the bliss of enlightened minds. He wields a dagger and curved knife to cut off the three poisons (ignorance, desire, hatred), and a trident to pierce the delusions of the three realms of existence. He holds a staff to symbolize bodhicitta, his insight into the nature of things, and a skull-cup of blood to symbolize blissful wisdom as his nature. He holds a noose to signify that he binds people to bliss beyond suffering, and a severed head of a mundane deity which tells us he is a super-mundane Deity, free of delusions. He is surrounded by a flaming aura of radiant wisdom. He laughs outrageously in 12-tones.

Chakrasamvara is the 12-spoked wheel of Dharma that breaks the 12-spoked wheel of samsara (dependent origination). His 12 arms represent the wisdom and means to end suffering and rebirth. The causes of suffering and rebirth (samsara) are known as the wheel of dependent origination. The Glorious Heruka is the Wheel of Dharma, the practice of wisdom and compassion which destroys the causes of rebirth and suffering. His 12 weapons represent this wisdom and ability to break each of the 12 spokes of dependent origination that cause suffering and rebirth. The 12 weapons of Demchog represent the unfolding of enlightened qualities within the mind-stream, they represent the liberation of negative states into wisdom and bliss. They represent the power to awaken these qualities in our mind, to awaken our full potential. Our potential is here depicted as Demchog. His grace is the means to attain it.

He flashes white lightning as a tool to awaken the mind. His method unfolds the heart in bliss. He personifies the bliss aspect of Buddha-consciousness. He is the delight in the reflection of forms in the mirror of the Mind. His wheel is the unstained mind-mirror, the indestructible heart-drop, the dharmachakra (heart-chakra), the clear awareness-seat, the fully enlightened heart. He is called the "Net of Dakinis." He is the space-womb of all phenomenon. He is the Mandala of Dharmadhatu. He is the Dance of Primordial Luminosity in Space. He is the Wisdom (emptiness) and its blissful display (form, dakini); Mind and Reality. He is also deemed "The Comprehending and Enclosing Cycle of Space-time." He is the symbolization and method of attaining the state of Consciousness which comprehends the ultimate nature of all things by enclosing or transcending duality. The mandala of the Dharmadhatu refers to the perfect awareness merged with space, and it refers to the circle which contains all Wisdom-deities in its retinue. So Demchog is at its center. As its center he is the origin of all Dharma and the womb of all beings.

Vajra-yogini stands for his Wisdom. She also denotes love. Her red is love as a heart is red. She embraces him. She is a distinct being, yet is inseparable from her blissful Method. To symbolize this, when figured alone she bears a trident which stands for Demchog. She is Mother of Primordial Luminosity. She is a sixteen year old girl with skin the color of rubies. She holds a skull cup of nectar (bliss in emptiness) and a hooked knife of compassion. She sports as sweet crimson lightning. She wears a mala of skulls each symbolizing the letters of the Sanskrit alphabet, which are the sounds of the purified inner winds, which makes her mala a symbol of the purified mind. Her seed syllable is a pink Bam (which is also Durga's). Her three-om mantra purifies body-speech and mind. Occasionally she manifests with a sow's head protruding from her crown, so is called Vajra-varahi, "Thunder-bolt Sow." The pig's head rumbles, overwhelming the three realms. It symbolizes the liberation of ignorance, or the awakening of consciousness by virtue of the fact that it arises from the top point of the central channel—which symbolizes consciousness. To Vajra-varahi is ascribed a weather-making practice, the mantra of which is Om Vajra-varahikrotikaliharinisa om char ya chur ya.bhaya stambhayanan. Whatever name you call her, she is the embodiment of the Wisdom of all the Buddhas, and is the emanation of the Mother, Samantabhadri. Energetically she is similar to Durga and Isis, each of whom use pink and red rays or lightnings, and rainbow lights. In Nepal there is an emanation of Vajra-yogini

known as Sarva Buddha Dakini who has the same iconography as Chinnamastaka, the "Severed-Headed," one of the 10 mahavidyas or primary aspects of the Mother Durga. Devotees of each tradition worshiped along side one another at one time.

Another parallel concerns the shakti piths or geographic seats of the Mother. The shaktas initially took these locations as Durga's shaktis, (places where her body fell). Buddhist practitioners later took these sites as aspects of Vajra-yogini's wisdom.

Vajra-yogini is the capacity or openness, the womb of the Buddhas known as guhyagharbha which means "secret essence" or essence of the vagina and refers to the essence or wisdom of the enlightened heart. Therefore Tantra will veil the meaning by speaking of the vagina and blood whereas what is meant is the heart and its fluid-bliss, its awakened passion. In Sanskrit the word for essence also means circle. Circle is a profound universal symbol of wisdom. All of these are identified with the heart, and the word for heart "hrdaya" can also mean essence, circle and wisdom. So the words guhya, hydaya, chakra, mandala are in deep meaning related.

The essence of the heart or awareness is the realm and condition of bliss. So the net or realm of wisdom-dakini is the heart. Demchog is awareness united with space whose friction produces the luminosity of bliss. The Mother is the capacity and power to give birth. In Buddhism phenomena arise spontaneously, any creative activity is spontaneous. When the heart (awareness-space) spontaneously arises, space takes the mode of subtle sound through luminous wisdom, and transmits the Absolute. What arises is wisdom and bliss. We seek to merge the essence of awareness (the heart) with space, which is enlightenment. We connect with our primordially unstained nature which pervades space. It is symbolized by Chakrasamvara. Whatever arises from this clear state is limitless and free and quite beautiful. It is therefore compared to nectar, jewels, gold etc. Since awareness is indestructible, so is what arises from it. These are the two sides of the vajra, one being wisdom or vajra-essence, the other compassion. Like a diamond this awareness cannot be cut or damaged, so there is no need to have any fear, there is no need to close to the open and tranquil state. Like a lightning this insight can penetrate anything. It is perfect insight by being naturally one with all space, with all minds.

Vajra-yogini (or Vajra-varahi) is the main wisdom Dakini. She is the protectress of Vajrayana. Her luminosity is flaming bliss energy, which might appear as crimson lightning. The Thunder-bolt Sow could represent the union of dark and light, luminous awareness shining in space. She is the mirror and its first reflection or thought before fixation, before attraction-revulsion. She has a hooked knife raised to strike, the hook is her compassion, her magnetism or love that draws beings out of samsara (transmigration) by incisively cutting off our wrong views and self-cherishing which cause transmigration. She will stop at nothing to help beings, even if the shock is painful at first. In her left hand she holds a skull-cup brimming with menstrual blood or white amrita. The cup is the heart (the capacity, the vagina), the blood is the essence, the power of the dakini known as red bodhicitta. Her katvanga or 3-pronged magical staff symbolizes her blissful energy (Demchog), her ability to liberate the 3 poisons of ignorance, desire and anger. Impaled on the staff are three heads symbolizing the three kayas. Because it symbolizes her "hidden consort" it stands for the integration of male energies. Her hair is black like most Deities symbolizing unchanging nature, unable to be stained. Like most Buddhas, half is pulled up on top and half flows freely, symbolizing wisdom and compassion.

Vajra-yogini is a trickster, a true-to-the-bones thunder-lady, a crazy-wise contrary, what in Tantra is called a Wisdom-dakini, what in shamanic language is called sacred clown. She appears as an old hag, whereas in truth she is infinitely youthful and beautiful. She is telling us that she's deathless, that she is the path and fuel to the deathless, pristine state—beauty. She's a shock therapist and breaks our duality. She is sharp yet totally gentle. She forces us to be open, in fact she doesn't leave us much choice at times. She is always helping us to move beyond the limitation of self-cherishing. The shock opens the mind to its inherent state. She helps us to open to all of life, not to be afraid or doubtful of any aspect. To do this She might offer you what is seemingly impure, since what a Buddha or one who is totally open sees of the rotten is purity and beauty. There is great hilarity in the horrific and rotten, in the cremation ground can be found haunting beauty and bliss. Negativity is generated from attraction to what is seemingly good, revulsion for what is seemingly bad, this thinking forms the habits of fearing, clinging at half of life and denying it and craving for the other half. When She breaks ones self-cherishing, attraction-revulsion is transformed, one becomes clear and open and able to

accept everything, nature, and to laugh and see humor and delight in the seemingly dark, left hand side of life, which upright society with all its rules denies and suffers with and tries to throw away and keep good enough distance from. She is a playful sacred clown, she definitely loves you, but she doesn't play any games, she's peaceful and fierce, happy and sad. She shakes things up and makes spirituality exciting and vibrant. She tends to offer the opportunity for purity by offering the impure. In one instance when I met her, she drew me in with her love (bodhicitta), then transformed in my arms into an ugly hag, fitting the descriptions given by Naropa and others. She offered me a substance (often found in her skull cup) which I considered impure, and refused. I deemed her impure, while it was my mind which was impure, since the mind creates reality. I probably refused the opportunity for purification and unquenchable bliss. This is what she is.

This has been the experience of other yogis. In one story she offered a siddha rotten food, but he rejected it. The idea behind contrary behavior, besides making you laugh and cry, is to annihilate the ego, the limited view of reality, like good-bad, pure-impure, holy-unholy. Our dualistic conceptions must be annihilated to free us from suffering, since the dualistic view creates our suffering. The yogis teach us that reality is the wisdom-display of the Deity.

Chakrasamvara dances with his consort on the bodies of two worldly deities, Bhairava and his consort Kalarati, who symbolize ignorance and desire. The story is related in the Chakrasamvara Tantra how various classes of malevolent beings were making blood sacrifices to Bhairava (Shiva) lingams. The Buddhas were not happy with this, so Vajradhara manifested as Demchog and subdued these malicious beings (along with Bhairava and Kalarati). Chakrasamvara's mandala was superimposed over Bhairava's. Therefore these two Deities came to symbolize ignorance and greed. Other stories relate how Mahadeva and Rudra (Shiva) were also subdued and turned into Dharma-protectors. These stories are entirely symbolic and cannot be taken literally. Religious opposition does not exist in the Pure Realms amongst these Wisdom-beings. One can only recognize this by becoming familiar with these Deities. These stories tell how Deities like Shiva function through the Vajrayana pantheon. If one studies the Tantra of both traditions one will discover immense parallels between Dermchog and Shiva, deep parallels. Shiva is likewise symbolized by a wheel, a wheel of 12 shaktis. In this case Shiva denotes wisdom and the spokes of light are the mother(s). Shiva is the symbolization of the Non-dual Reality and the fully awakened state, the very definition of Buddha's Wisdom Mind—Chakrasamvara. I have experienced Shiva, Samantabhadra and Chakrasamvara in visions and they represent the same state of perfection. Shiva is Eternal, his name and forms have been on earth since previous eons. It is degenerate-minded people who have thought to sacrifice animals and offer blood. And it is Shiva or Buddha who put a stop to it, by turning their view back to true Dharma.

There is one Dharma (and one Ultimate Reality) which takes different forms according to time and culture. (To show this unity Sambasadashiva manifested with three faces, of Buddha, Haidhakan Shiva and Christ). The Tantra, which tells stories about subduing beings like Shiva, is written in deep symbolic language, which might be called twilight language. The symbolic meaning of the stories is that Heruka stands for our natural luminosity which subdues our ego (Rudra). The use of symbolic language is to protect the Secret from unprepared minds.

Chakrasamvara is the embodiment of the Wisdom-Mind of all Buddhas. Wisdom is the ability to see clearly and perfectly. The Wisdom-deity has eyes which are everywhere. Because this is so he suffers with all beings, lives fully with all beings. To be a Buddha is to be fully with all beings, to suffer with them (compassion). Because all Buddhas are fully within the light of our heart, they have immense compassion for us. Another aspect of wisdom is the limitless capacity to help all sentient beings. So in order to become a Buddha we train in openness, we cultivate wisdom or omniscience and compassion. If we realize the nature of our mind, insight pours from the mind continuously as skillful means of liberating sentient beings from suffering.

We cultivate with Wisdom-deities because they shine in our hearts. Chakrasamvara shines as wisdom and bliss, emptiness and compassion. Chakrasamvara awakens our enlightened luminous mind of compassion. Chakrasamvara shines as our enlightened intention, so if we practice with him to become him then we become inexhaustible wisdom and unquenchable bliss. Through him all Buddhas have attained enlightenment, through the union of compassion and wisdom. He is the enlightened activity of all the Buddhas, the energy which is responsible for bringing all Bud-

dhas to the goal. To demonstrate this unity, Chakrasamvara is in union with Vajra-yogini. There's nothing especially sexual about this, it just demonstrates that the union of wisdom and compassion brings the greatest bliss. Heruka again means perfect love, perfect light, perfect bliss. Chakrasamvara means Chakra—wisdom, samvara—bliss. To cultivate love is to awaken wisdom and bliss.

Demchog and Vajra-yogini are in sexual union to denote that the union of wisdom and compassion is the greatest bliss. Their union also could signify that we practice wisdom and compassion together to attain enlightenment. Their union indicates that cultivating wisdom awakens compassion, and cultivating compassion awakens wisdom. By focusing on Deity imagery, wisdom-love light awakens our heart of wisdom and love. By acting compassionately we gather love-light from all-pervasive Wisdom-mind, which awakens our heart of wisdom and love.

It is taught that in this degenerate age the blessing of other Deity's are harder to receive because our level of wisdom has decreased. However, such is not the case with Chakrasamvara. When Vajradhara emanated the mandalas in which he transmitted Tantra, generally he would reabsorb it. But with Heruka he did not reabsorb the mandala, but left them in tact. They still exist in various places in the world—such as the 24 holy places (which were originally Shiva piths). Because of this fact, we have a special relationship to Heruka and can quickly receive their blessings. You can view all men and women as Heroes and Heroines in the retinue of Chakrasamvara.

Chakrasamvara's method figures prominently in the transmissions of the 84 mahasiddhas, many of whom attained completion through this method, spent hundreds of years on earth and ascended bodily into the Dakini's paradise. According to the Gelugpa and Kagyu lineages, among the four classes of Tantra (Action, Performance, Yoga and Highest Yoga), the Chakrasamvara Tantra is Highest Yoga Tantra (Anuttara Tantra). This means it is a dynamic system of internal alchemy, much like what the earlier mahasiddha (siddha siddhanta) tradition developed under Shiva's tutelage.

The practitioner of Highest Yoga Tantra creates an illusory body, a deity-form, which merely appears in the universe without being governed by it. It is a transcendent body of wisdom, a body of Light and Vision. It is the body of the Wisdom-deity on earth, the establishment of the Deity mandala on earth, in which case the vajrakaya is extended indivisibly from formless emptiness into a pure form which walks the earth and teaches as guru, and realizes the primordial wisdom-nature as inherent and the Deity mandala as the body and nature, in which case all people are recognized as Deities, all activity as Deity's wise activity, all sounds as Deity's wisdom-speech, all phenomena as Deity's wisdom-display.

In the generation stage practice with Demchog one begins by cultivating the conventional mind of enlightenment by cultivating the five perfections and aspiring to lead all sentient beings to attainment. Next comes the cultivation of the ultimate mind of enlightenment, which is to see all phenomena as pure by nature. One visualizes oneself as Heruka. In the two-armed visualization which I'm aware of, above his top-knot is a wish-fulfilling jewel, on top of this is a vajra, to the left of this a crescent moon. At their three centers are white Om, red Ah. At Demchog's heart is a blue Hum, at hers a pink Bam. From each syllable radiates light inviting the wisdom-beings of the five families. They arrive and bestow grace, filling ones body (of Demchog) with wisdom-nectar, purifying all defilements. Overflowing, the nectar becomes Akshobya above ones head and Vairochana above Vajra-yogini. The Buddhas then dissolve into you. To receive blessings one visualizes various Deities at the five centers, then one recites the mantras of essence and inner essence of Demchog and Vajra-yogini. Heruka's essence mantra is Om shri benza he he ru ru kam hung hung phat dakini zwala samvaram svaha. His inner essence is Om hrih ha ha hung hung phat. (These mantras should not be used unless one has the elaborate empowerment. If one feels devotion for Samvara, uttering his name and using the mantra of Guru Rinpoche (above) is sufficient. Guru Rinpoche's mantra invokes all the Buddhas who are within him).

Do not be confused by such an image. It is simply a meditation on emptiness and bliss, a way of attaining Mahamudra siddhi. It is one particularly potent method developed by the Wisdom deity. If we use it properly to benefit others it is immensely sacred.

Chakrasamvara awakens our awareness to its primordially unified state of awareness and great emptiness. We call this merging with space, or unifying awareness and space. Chakrasamvara told Karma Pakshi that he is the mandala of the Dharmadhatu, awareness and emptiness. Vajra-yogini is the light, and love arising from this space. So the visualization awakens the union of love and wisdom, which causes bliss. Chakrasamvara awakens our clarity in which all appearances are reflected perfectly as they are, in which absolute and relative truth is realized. Chakrasamvara awakens the adamantine clarity of indestructible space—and might bestow our complete awakening through lightning.

In the completion stage meditations of Highest Yoga Tantra, the transmutation of the psycho-physical organism is completed by thoroughly purifying the mind aggregates and internal winds. When the 10 vital winds enter the central channel (avadhuti) this produces realization of ones pristine wisdom nature—mahamudra-siddhi. Generally the impure winds (which obscure our minds clarity) are gathered into the central channel by concentrating on the central channel. Visualized as Chakrasamvara one receives blessing-lights which electrify or enlighten our inner channels, winds and drops making them pure, so they will dissolve into the central channel. Visualization (of central channel) may also aid this process.

Our body composed of the six elements is not our actual unceasing body. Our true body is called very subtle body and very subtle mind—these are what transmigrate. When we become a Buddha—the very subtle wind that forms our very subtle body transforms into a Buddhas form body—a clear-light body—with which to benefit many beings. Our very subtle mind becomes the omniscient mind of a Buddha. The very subtle wind (body) and mind are indestructible, unchanging. Our gross mind of delusions is temporary. Through practice it will be purified.

When semen and menses, which are potential bliss, are purified they become subtle wind energy. When lymph is purified it becomes seed-essence, or the feeling quality of awareness as pure pleasure. What this means is that coarse energies are made subtle. This awareness and pure pleasure forms a dimension of consciousness known as thig le. Thig le is often described as essence-drops or subtle concentrations of mind and wind within the subtle channels of the body. They are a union of awareness and bliss.

When semen flows out, the thig le become depleted, or temporarily damaged, their pleasure flows out, thus, the tradition emphasizes that such flow be ceased, because that energy will be purified into bodhicitta (blissful energy, love). Once purified, it collects in the heart, manifesting as human kindness. It is energy of pure motivation.

Because the frequency of the wind is increased (through sadhana) to vibrate at a higher or faster rate, it rises to the heart and expresses itself as bodhicitta, compassionate motivation. Likewise the channels in which the wind moves are cleared of blockages which cause afflictions of body and mind. This transformation is affected through the Deity sadhana.

Chakrasamvara clears out obstructions to the free bliss radiance of the mind by clearing the channels. He clears them by blessing them. When left and right channels are cleared, desire and hatred become transmuted into bliss and clarity. When the wind of the central channel is purified ignorance is transmuted into wisdom or awareness. His light increases the frequency of the winds, the mind. In such a way the mind is liberated and inspired, transmuted into its natural state of pristine wisdom and bliss.

The subtle body's vibratory energies are moved by the power of the mind from their central channel chakras. There, the winds distill into essence drops (thig le). The accumulation of drops produces a purified subtle body of awareness and bliss, the foundation upon which the clear-light mind (rig pa: awareness, "ground luminosity") reflects the empty nature of reality. Clear-light mind is the awareness of the ultimate nature of things, it is the mind-stream which threads all perceptions, the awareness whose radiance produces thoughts. Immutable life wind is the basis of the purified subtle body for blissfully attaining the state of Buddhahood. Buddhahood is the primordial union of clear-light and immutable wind, mind and energy, wisdom and bliss, and is symbolized here as Demchog in union with Vajra-yogini.

The body of purified wind electrifies an increasingly more aware and luminous consciousness. The material body (gross energy) dissolves into subtler energy which is awakened through the blessing-lights of the Deity which flood the body-mind. Chakrasamvara awakens his own unique qualities which exist within ones energy, as the bliss and wisdom of all the Buddhas. The body is recreated or refined first into an "empty body," then further refinement produces subtler "pure bodies" which are purified states of awareness by virtue of the fact that the purified wind is the mount for the mind. The final stages of refinement give rise to an indestructible and radiant "vajra body." This represents the necessary state for merging with the Buddha's Wisdom Mind. The process itself mimics death in the sense that at death the gross elements dissolve. But we don't die the normal sense of the word. The gross body gradually dissolves into light and forms a new body of five wisdom-lights, which can appear as a subtle body in the image of the Deity, or as in Dzogchen as a rainbow body. The gross body actually dissolves into rainbow-lights because it has become the root of the five elements which are five-colored light. The gross elements dissolve into their wisdom-sources—the five wisdom-dakinis.

Because the gross body dissolves, suffering ends, since the gross body (vision) was the condition for experiencing a gross limited vision of reality. When the mind aggregates are purified—the relative is experienced as the absolute non-dual Reality—the mind is revealed in its true empty nature (mahamudra) and thus all appearances are experienced as empty—light. Thus all forms, sounds, tastes are Deities. Wherever one focuses at this point Deities and their pure realms appear.

This subtle body arises from the indestructible heart drop and can travel anywhere like the dream body. In the Highest Yoga Tantra it is called an "illusory body"—it is a Buddha's appearance, Demchog's appearance. It lacks inherent existence. Its nature is purified unobstructed wind and mind. Its substance is insubstantial like a rainbow. It is white in color and radiates light. Its shape is that of the yidam through whose light it was created, since the yidam bestows this attainment as the greatest siddhi (mahamudra). It is immortal or indestructible. It is a rainbow-body, meaning it is capable of disappearing in rainbows, sparks and lights. This body is an infinite "spiritual body" manifesting as light. It is primordial wisdom and pure luminous awareness (dharmakaya's two aspects). "The purified wind takes the form of an indestructible body of light and serves as the necessary vehicle for the enlightened mind" (Gold 81).

An integral part of practice in Tantra, and especially with Chakrasamvara concerns sexual practices. These are fluent in all three Oriental traditions, and have been the most misunderstood, right up there with Deities peaceful wrath. There are two main ways sexual yoga can be applied. First of all Tantra teaches naturalness so there is no denying what is natural. Tantrics hold an attitude of openness to what is natural, moderation in what is natural enhances ones bliss. The clear mind is free of fixation, so you can dress up like a king for a day and leave it, get drunk and leave it without any sadness or desire. This is the difference between mundane people and Tantric masters. Since anything conceived and acted upon by a vajra-master is Dharma, has wisdom at its root and involves pure intention, whether its drinking, eating meat or having sex, it is supremely good, causes bliss and liberates beings. What truly brings bliss is the barometer of right activity. Bliss arises where there is no fixation. If drugs, sex, meat, wine, swearing, clowning, cause one problems and pain because of limited view then they must be abandoned until there is no longer any limitation. This is Sutra path and Sanyasin path, which is fine. There is good reason for having such rules and vows, they lead one very close to the clear limitless state. But in Tantra it is suggested that to truly enter mahamudra siddhi one must take a secret consort and perform ganachakra, and rites where there is wine, meat, sex. They help us move beyond duality. To a Deity they are pure enjoyments, so its part of Deity training. If one does not have access to a dakini consort, the Highest Yoga Tantra visualization has one in union with an imagined consort. If you are Chakra-samvara, you are in union with Vajra-yogini. And instead of creating desire, desire is liberated by the Deity practice. Chakrasamvara in this way awakens bliss. His lightning has this effect, simply thinking of him has this effect! Of coarse this practice cannot be done by everyone, very few practitioners will receive this practice because one has to complete the system of preliminaries at least once, sometimes it is required that one be in a traditional retreat to do this practice. It is dangerous, so I know the essence and inner essence mantras of Chakrasamvara-Vajra-yogini but I'm responsible for what I teach, and these practices can only be embraced by those empowered by the vajra-master.

So the first reason why someone embraces sexual yoga is to transform passion into desireless bliss, to invoke light, to open up awareness by purifying channels. It is a means of using dirt to clean dirt, injecting water into the ear to remove water from it. This can be achieved with a visualized consort.

We generate profane sexual visions of ourselves in union with worldly dakinis and sometimes bring this to fruition which cause not enlightening bliss, but obscuring desire and ignorance and binds us to the wheel of samsara. In Tantra we create a dynamic sacred sexual vision in which we're Buddha in union with Wisdom-dakini. We imbue our vision with passionate motivation to free suffering beings through the liberation we gain from sacred vision. Such a vision makes us a worthy vessel for receiving blessing light which liberates our passion into bliss and love. We create this vision from the start as a means of sacrificing our source of negativity and our source of wisdom. This sacrifice makes all beings happy and we become

sacred. Our passion creates both varieties of vision. We bring the second to fruition and the result is our liberation from samsara—our enlightenment. The cause of being born is desire, this is the realm of desire, our parents desire brings their white and red together to bring us here, and our desire causes us to be attracted to our parents to come here. So passion is the primary cause of being human. This realm is called desire realm; we seal rebirth here through liberating our passion into compassion. Our compassion is the primary cause of becoming Buddha. Our compassion causes us to generate a vision which quickly liberates our mind into an inexhaustible ocean of compassion. The vision of Chakrasamvara liberates our passionate suffering into compassionate bliss.

The second reason for taking a consort, and the one which is really relevant to our culture has to do with the quality of human society. The quality of our society is directly related to the quality of sex and sexual partners. Two people who practice spiritual cultivation, or at least who are virtuous, have high energy, positive energy, so when they have sex, light is generated through friction and bliss, love arises in the heart, bliss at the crown. When the white drop of life force meets the red drop of blood, there's a spark in the spirit realm and that spark is the combined resonance of the male and female, daka and dakini. It attracts a spirit of a like resonance or frequency, and that spirit enters the womb from there and develops into a fetus.

Since the energy of the man and woman was high, pure, clear, good, the child will be of a like nature. Some practitioners, out of compassion for sentient beings will do a particular practice before and during sex to bring a saint to this realm. When two people come together who are not virtuous, let alone spiritual practitioners, their combined spark attracts a lower frequency, less evolved spirit, and the child they give birth to may be wild and recalcitrant and cause suffering in the world. It will be like the parents or worse. So the quality of society can be greatly attributed to the quality of sexual relations. The degeneration of society is caused by perpetuation of poor sexual relations. Many people come together like animals, or, drunk, they have unwanted pregnancies, they wind up with unmanageable children who might have mental problems, who have a good chance of winding up in jail, or perpetuating the problem by ignorantly having children. It is because of this that religion teaches that people should not have sex without being married and without the intention to have children (for the sake of glorifying God or being a benefit to the world). When two people are married in the eyes of the Wisdom-beings, there is a certain energy which exists like a third amongst them. In Kabbalah this is called the Shekinah. We might call it Shakti. It really does exist there at least for two descent people, and it unites them and causes joy. For this reason marriage (union of daka and dakini) is sacred, it is Wisdom-beings that make it so.

In the Chakrasamvara lineage of mahasiddhas, there are many amazing stories which elucidate the high achievement of actualizing Buddhahood through Demchog's sadhana. One story in particular tells of the mahasiddha Ghantapa as having attained the "illusory body." Ghantapa was an accomplished yogi who practiced in a jungle. He became emaciated from his asceticism and discheveled from his freedom from dualistic appearances. When the local king saw him he encouraged him to come to the city for clothes, shelter and food. Ghantapa infuriated the king when he replied, "just as a great elephant cannot be led out of the jungle on a thread, I, a monk cannot be tempted from this forest even by the immense wealth of a king" (136 Landaw, Weber). The king took revenge by offering a reward to any woman who could seduce the monk into breaking his vows. One woman, a wine seller who was actually a dakini, said she could do it. She went to Ghantapa who initiated her into Tantra. Years elapsed and Ghantapa conceived the thought to awaken people to the dharma. He told his consort to go to the king and relate that she was successful in seducing him and their consummation had given birth to two children. The king then brought Ghantapa to the city on an appointed day, on which he was going to attempt to humiliate this master. Ghantapa staggered into the city drunk on wisdom-nectar, with his consort, son and daughter. Women poured wine into his bowl. The people insulted him, they felt he wasn't a good example of a Buddhist monk.

Ghantapa pretended to get angry and cast his bowl upon the ground. It split the earth open and water began pouring out in a flood. Ghantapa's son and daughter transformed into the vajra and bell (bliss and wisdom) and his consort transformed into Vajra-yogini. Ghantapa transformed into Chakrasamvara, took up his vajra and bell and embraced his wisdom dakini and flew away. The people and king prayed to Ghantapa to save them from the ensuing flood. Ghantapa instructed the people to pray to Chenrezig. When they did, Chenrezig came and placed his foot on the fissure, stopping the flood. This play had the effect of instilling faith in the closed hearted people to practice Dharma.

Kalike: The Vajra Lady and the Chod "Rite of Severance"

In the Vajrayana tadition, Kalike (Trolma Nak mo), the Wrathful Black Lady, serves the particular functions of a Thunder-being. She is a principle Vajra Dakini and is used in thunder-rites by lamas, that is—in exorcisms and weather-making. She can be considered an emanation of Vajra-varahi, (Or, as in the Nyingma school, an emanation of Yeshe Tsogyal, Guru Rinpoche's dakini consort or Wisdom.) It is taught that Vajra-varahi is a leader of Dakinis of the great secret (maha-guhya-dakini). She manifested in a bluish black body and brought all Dakinis under her power. She resides in the dakini-realm, Active in Space (Khechari).

In the Chod tradition Kalike is considered an emanation of the Primordial Mother Yum Chenmo who represents the essence of reality (dharmadata), the pure expanse of emptiness, the matrix from which arises all Buddhas. Another tradition suggests she's an emanation of Mother Tara. These are just different names and images for the same Ultimate Reality.

In the Shaiva Tantra, Kali also known as Kalike, is a Lightning Mother, an emanation of Durga, Universal Mother. She was emanated from Durga's third-eye as a great warrior. Durga is also known as Varahi and takes some forms similar in appearance to Vajra-yogini (who becomes the Vajra Lady: Kalike). Durga-kali's imagery will be presented below in the section on Shiva.

In Vajrayana, Kalike's practice is generally aimed at rapidly severing the ego. Like lightning her mind liberates our sense of self-cherishing, like thunder her mind awakens inner and outer demons. She utilizes vajra-thought and imagery which appears vastly contradictory but is actually alluding to the destruction of the limited dualistic view of reality. Her name means black and time, and yet she is the flip side of these. She is creative-effulgence, not destructive, so she reverses time or destroys it. She is black yet shines. Her color relates to space, vast inner space, the creative potential. Her color denotes wisdom, the cosmic mirror. She is fierce, yet compassionate. Her vajra-wrath is the indestructible power to transform anything. Like a thunder-bolt it cuts through our most recalcitrant confusion and awakens kindness. Vajra-wrath is her compassionate expression. She has flaming hair, a copper flaying knife in her right hand, a skull bowl in her left, her eyes roll, her tongue flickers lightning. She has a snorting pigs head emerging from her hair. She tramples the corpses of egos, wears human-bone cemetery ornaments and a tiger skin skirt. She has a trident in the crook of her left arm ornamented with a skull, rotten head and a freshly severed head.

Often a warrior might take something of her defeated enemy to reveal her power and victoriousness so that others will be encouraged to take sides. Thunders take the serpents they defeat, and subdue monsters to work for the Truth. Trolma symbolizes the means whereby self-cherishing (the pig's head) is destroyed and compassion manifested. Her snorting pig's head means she conquors ignorance, it symbolizes the awakening of ignorance. Her wrath indicates that she awakens aversion, her triumph over hatred and form. Her cemetary ornaments symbolize impermanence. Her copper flaying knife cuts off delusions at their root, severs the ego; it symbolizes compassionate method. Her skull cup catches the sacrificial blood, the life-essence, the awareness. It symbolizes blissful wisdom. The sacrifice of awareness brings bliss. Her trident symbolizes her consort—compassionate method. On it are three heads which correspond to Om Ah Hung, symbolizing enlightened Body, Speech and Mind which correspond to the three chakras of crown, throat and heart. So the trident with heads symbolizes Trolma's compassionate motivation (bodhicitta), compassionate speech and compassionate activity.

Kalike's tongue flickers lightning. Some Thunder-beings breath lightning, dragons have tongues of lightning. Their life-breath is lightning, enlightened awareness and pure power. It symbolizes voice of thunder or Truth, it symbolizes vajra-speech, speech which accomplishes its aim, speech which fulfills Eternity. Thunder-bird devours his children, then gives birth to them as his thundering voices. This word is pure enlightened power. It symbolizes spontaneous activity, the spontaneous arising of enlightened speech and activity. This kind of speech is an activity which awakens the mind (hence the lightning). So Thunder-bird is enlightening his children. Kalike Trolma is enlightening her children as well. Her lightning-tongue is vajra-speech and vajra-activity thundering forth from her body of vajra-essence.

Kalike's secret sadhana is called "Laughter of the Dakinis upon Cutting Asunder". This cutting or severance means that the ego, our sense of self-cherishing, the root of all afflictions is going to be severed. Just as

when a plant is severed at its root and never grows back, so also, with Chod practice the root of all afflictions is cut and never grows back. Kalike is responsible for having disseminated specific teachings and practices in Tibet, known as Chod rites or "rites of severance". She incarnated as Machig Labdron to collect and disperse these practices, which, although they appear in many ways similar to shamanic rites (Bon po), clearly have a Perfection of Wisdom (Buddhist) base.

According to the three lineages of Chod—Sutra, Mantra and Sutra-Mantra—the origin is the Buddhas, such as Manjushri, Samantabhadra and Samantabhadri who transmit it to the living dakini Machig Labdron. It is likely that the Buddhas who originated it, considering the cultural context in which they would give it, made it suitable to the people by reflecting some aspects of shamanistic tradition. There is also much similarity between Chod and ancient Shaiva Tantra. Machig was a Nepalese yogini, and Shaivism was the first and main religion in Nepal. But Machig attained enlightenment through the Buddhas, under the Indian siddha Padampa Sangye (who was an emanation of Guru Rinpoche). Machig went to Tibet and there received the transmission from the Buddhas of the Chod rites. Chod is the first Tantric practice originated in Tibet, the others from India, were planted in Tibet.

During the secret empowerment we are told that Machig Labdron is outwardly Arya Tara, inwardly Yum Chenmo, secretly Vajra-varahi, and most secretly Trolma Nakmo. She is also said to be the last of Yeshe Tsogyal's four rebirths.

The Chod is known as the rite of severance because it cuts the ego off at its root in order to attain realization of Buddhahood. By cutting the ego off at its root, one unites consciousness and space (shunyata). One achieves this by giving oneself away, through self-sacrifice.

In the Chod Deity-yoga meditation, the adept visualizes him or herself as an aspect of Vajra-varahi or Trolma Nak mo, and at the same time, savors the feeling of being her. The yogi practices the perfection of generosity and the renunciation of attachment to form by presenting his body as a food offering (in one of four great feasts—white, red, multicolored and black). The mortal remains of the body is transformed into wisdom nectars and a hundred marvelous substances which assemblies of goddesses present to the lineage lamas, the deities of the four classes of Tantras, the dakas and Dakinis, the guardians and protectors of the teaching, and to all sentient beings of the triple world. One creates a giant skull-cup, places oneself in it after being cut up by Kalike. One is transformed into amrita, then presented as feast to the four guests to benefit all sentient beings. Hollow tubes of light shoot out from the mouths of the yidams and they ingest the substance.

The purpose in making such a sacrifice is to complete accumulations of merit, purify obscurations, and repay karmic debts, which are requisites for attaining Buddhahood. There is nothing unwholesome about making such sacrifices of oneself, the visualization actually arises out of an instructional vision of the Deities, and is very sacred, and reflects the natural act of compassion exemplified by Buddhas and Dakinis.

We sacrifice ourself to the Deity through devotion in order to become the Deity through and through. We know what his state feels like, so we go after it this way until we become it. Mind takes the form of what we think, and embodies the light inherent in the form. If we think of harming others, mind takes this form and itself is harmed. If our body takes the form of the mind to act out such a thought, then the body will be hurt. Body is extension of the mind. If you think of Deity continuously with devotion and reverence then mind takes this form of light and is enlightened by it. Our body takes the form of our mind which has become Wisdom-deity, so eventually we are Deity through and through.

Spirituality is always about giving what we are, about accruing light by having less obscuring negativity. Everything we have is energy. It doesn't belong to us really. It comes to us for a time and then disappears. It will not sustain our joy as we might think. The cause of joy is giving what we're given. If we're given objects of beauty we give them away to make others happy. If we're given a body we give this away through service to make beings happy. If we're given wisdom and bliss we give these away to make beings supremely happy. We even offer the universe and all its contents (as a mandala offering) in order to make beings happy. The more we give the more we have to give and the more happiness we spread through our spontaneous natural giving, and the happier we become. We gather more and more light, by the law of karma. The mass of light of our Wisdom-mind becomes a measureless ocean of light. When we experience Buddhas, the immensity we come before is this bodhicitta, this inexhaustible source of Dharma, of love. This is the body of joy that the Deity accrued by

giving, through self-sacrifice. To sacrifice means to make sacred. Spiritual practice or Dharma is about giving all that you are, offering to benefit all beings, until there's nothing but infinite space—dharmadhatu shining everywhere. If one serves others, uses the light to give and help, one gathers light of the higher realms and is drawn there automatically.

The Dancing Skeletons

The dancing skeletons appear in the Chod or "severance" rites as emanations of Chakrasamvara. They appear in his assemblage as symbols of his wisdom and bliss. In the shamanic traditions the skeletons are images of the souls of people and can often make rain. They are universally emanations of Thunder-beings. They are the contrary imagery of the Thunder deity, they are his play and antics. They show us the Reality or Absolute Truth which is very often the opposite of the mundane view. They are alive but appear dead, they tell us there's no such thing as death. The mind-stream is beginningless and endless. The skeletons represent this dance of illusion. They sing contrary songs and dance amongst the lightning. They clown around, fearlessly expressing their view toward death. They remind us of life's impermanence, the need to work to restore the mind, to strip our mind to its luminous foundation (skeleton), its wisdom which supports a limitless future existence. They teach us that each mind-moment is of the utmost importance, so should be used wisely. Tantrikas use every moment as an opportunity to awaken the mind, to relax between thoughts or use emotional energy as a tool to awaken the mind (which is called "removing water from the ear by injecting water into the ear"). They develop a crisp, keen sense of the efficacy of the non-dual view (the four doors) and the impermanence of life. So each moment is utilized for practice. I don't think a good practitioner stops practicing methods of self-discipline and he or she certainly never stops practicing compassion, giving and generosity. Even once the perfected state is attained then ones practice can be used entirely as a way of focusing the rays of the Dharma-sphere to liberate sentient beings.

The skeletons appear in the mind-emanated cremation ground, they're not different than Chakrasamvara; they stand for the Wisdom Mind, the immutable vajra-essence, and its bliss. They dance as awareness and pure-pleasure. Their bones are luminous and radiant like lightningbolts. Their bones are symbols of the enlightened mind-stream, the only thing which remains after the dissolution of the body. They have space for eye-sockets to symbolize the emptiness or spaciousness of Buddha Mind, mind merged with space. They are reality stripped to the bone, awareness abiding in shunyata, partaking of the one taste (samarasa) which threads all experiences.

As Lady and Lord of the Cemetery, they stand for Wisdom and compassion respectively. They signal the ending phases of creation, the passage of form, life, thought into the emptiness from which it arose. So they stand for the culmination of the path, the result, our fully awakened mind which threads all transformations. They are the blissful nature of the Transcendent Mind. To the relative mind they are a dance of illusion. They represent the path or skillful means to attain this state of ultimate bliss, so they symbolize the ultimate generosity. They have given everything, flesh, blood, sinew and marrow. Since nothing is left, they give us their bones (what remains is mind-stream); they sing and dance to bring delight to the mind.

The Thunder-beings give of themselves to make the whole earth happy, they sing (thunder) and dance (lightning). Every thunder-storm is a sacrifice for the welfare of the earth. All life is a sacrifice. The Mother sacrificing herself for herself. Compassionate activity is natural for sentient beings, but still must be cultivated. Shabkar says that it doesn't necessarily arise on its own out of wisdom but must be cultivated. Other masters suggest that it arises spontaneously from wisdom. The dancing skeleton and the Buddhas, the achieved ones tell us that the development of awareness and compassion brings the ultimate delight which naturally constitutes the goal.

The skeletons symbolize the dissolution of the gross material body into a body of pure Consciousness (citipati). The subtle body itself appears white and is full of blissful radiance. It is a projection like a film of subtle Vision arising as wisdom-light. So the skeletons tell us that we must die in order to live, that the gross energy must be completely dissolved into the phenomena-Source, the five Wisdom-dakini-lights. The material body inherited from our parents from the universe is not really who we are. Who we are comes from subtle space. The gross body is subject to the universe of change. Because there is change there is suffering. The skeleton represents who we are, our immutable essence (heart)

Because our vajra-essence (skeleton) transcends the universe, it transcends change and suffering. Therefore to actualize this empty state symbolized by the skeleton, liberates us from suffering. The skeleton represents our second birth, our death-birth, our emergence as Buddhas, fully awakened and blissful beings. Out of the Mothers womb of space we are born as Mind, nurtured on her milk of human kindness and her light of secret mantra Tantra.

The Cremation Ground as Wisdom Abode

Often the Vajra Yidams, Skeletons and Dakinis appear in a mind-emanated cremation ground, (of which there are eight, reflecting eight actual charnel grounds in India), in a palace atop a pile of skulls surrounded by lightningbolts. This is the kind of sacred imagery associated with hauntingly beautiful Chod rites. The symbol is a reflection of reality. The mind-created lightning symbol, utilized by the Vajra Yidams and Dakinis stands for the place where the mind is going to be awakened. The cremation ground stands for the place where the ego is going to be annihilated, burned up like a corpse. It cannot stand before the Deity. "No-one can see the Face of God and live !" So the Wisdom-beings appear trampling or dancing on corpses which are symbols of ignorance and greed. The charnel ground is a contrary symbol, like the Deity, because it is the domain of awakening, dawning, the City of Lightning in which spiritual birth is going to take place, in which one is really going to begin living. Yogis and yoginis for centuries have spent time living in cremation grounds practicing sadhana. Many of the 84 mahasiddhas lived in Cremation grounds, there are eight central ones. Guru Rinpoche practiced in the eight. There's nothing gruesome about it, they were directed there by the guru's pith instruction, or in visions by the Deities like Shiva and Kali, Demchog and Vajra-yogini, Guru Rinpoche, and so on. The purpose is not really twisted; it instills a blatant inescapable sense of impermanence. If everywhere you look and smell reminds you of the impermanent nature of life you might appreciate the precious opportunity of having a human existence, and make the most of every mind-moment before the body is lost to the universe. Certainly too the cemetery causes you to confront fear head on, to destroy it or be subsumed by it. It causes you to transcend duality, like dirty and clean, poison and medicine, good and bad. It has also been a playground in which to subdue spirits and practice mundane and super-mundane feats. Yogis since ancient times practiced in secluded places like cremation grounds. In ancient times the main charnel ground was in Kashi. Lord Shiva actually had an invisible space-abode there. His lineage of Vama (left-hand) Tantriks practiced rites very similar to Buddhist Chod. They would ask Kali, Shiva's consort to cut their heart out. By eating her children, they entered the body of Bhairav-shakti, they became a part of that body or City.

Essentially the cremation ground is the City of Lightning; the place of symbolic death and cremation is the place of liberation. We offer ourselves into the sacrificial wisdom-pyre of our Yidam, who turns us into space. It is the place where the gross body is literally going to dissolve into its subtle Wisdom-source—the Deity, where our coarse winds are going to dissolve into their subtle roots (Wisdom-dakinis), where our dualistic vision is going to dissolve into non-dual vision, where our indestructible heart-drop will melt into the City of Lighting of our Awareness-being, where we will merge with him.

The mandalas of the Deities are awakened within our sky-like receptive nature, within the body, mind and its heart. The Cities of Lightning are awakened in the deepest wisdom of the mind, through our minds they present themselves. If our minds were of another substance than wisdom this revelation would not be possible. Because each City of Lightning is unique, it awakens a unique Vision of seeing the inner subtle workings of the psycho-physical organism. Some might say that the distinction among various systems, of seeing the subtle channels, drops etc. lies in the fact that it is being created with the mind, maybe even superimposed. But I feel that the unique mandala being awakened in the mind-body has the vision within itself, like a film.

Our mind is the open circle, at least first we must make it open or clear and pure. It is the cremation ground where the ego will be severed by the lightning-bolt of rapid illumination of the Yidam or Dakini, where the mind will pass through fire to come out shining, itself a lightning-bolt. Keep in mind the vajra-master is the one who initiates us in the beginning and middle, directs the bolt and instructs us in the view and practices and guides us to completion.

The City of Lightning is Deity's method of extending himself and liberating us. It is what he looks and feels like when he floods us and awakens in our heart. He-she is our method of ascending or dissolving our mind into its true state of bliss, which is the Deity's state of bliss.

In his City of Lightning he dances to extend his wisdom and blessings, and we dance to dissolve our sense of self-cherishing; he emanates pure wisdom-light and imagery as a vehicle to assist us and we absorb pure wisdom, light and imagery to dissolve our self-cherishing. He extends infinite Vision to dissolve our limited vision. This infinite Vision is in the lightning which awakens us. It replaces ignorance and negativity with awareness and bliss. The bolt is sharp, it severs the root of delusion in a flash; it lops off the ego of erroneous views in a glance. It awakens the heart to fly and dance in space.

The City of Lightning is the enlightened state of space and compassionate bliss, luminous emptiness, like lightning of compassion flashing in space. The City of Lightning is the mind merged with space, so the flight of the heart symbolized by Dakini and Garuda is the experience of pure pleasure within empty space. The City of Lightning is the Wheel of Thunder-beings' Mind, it is their Father-Mother Dance of emptiness and bliss. The City of Lightning is the reality of wisdom reflected in the mirror of the mind, the heart-drop, the Thunder-beings innermost circle and essence. The City of Lightning is the limitless awareness of Omniscient Mind. It is the Mind which knows everything simultaneously, so is perfect insight, a perfect mirror reflecting Reality. And it is the Mind in which compassion is fully awakened. The City of Lightning is our natural state of full enlightenment.

BOOK TWO

Shiva: The Primordial Thunder Lord of Infinite Consciousness

Shiva is the Source of the ancient Indian tradition we call Sanatan Dharma "Eternal Religion, Unchanging Truth." Sanatan Dharma (Shaivism) was the original religion on earth, all later religions, such as Judaism, Christianity, Sufism, Buddhism, Jainism are born from it. Shiva is the God of all religion. Sanatan Dharma is the oldest tradition, it spans billions of years, while all others can be traced to an origin in time. Sanatan Dharma are the teachings of Shiva and his retinue, present since beginningless time. Shiva originated the tradition by passing it down orally, and he maintains the tradition even in degenerate times like our own, by providing specific Tantra which is suitable to peoples nature.

Shiva walked the earth as a giant at different times over hundreds of millions of years, teaching his consorts (Shaktis) and siddhas his vast systems of instruction. Shiva spoke the scriptures to devas, rishis (seers), sages, and siddhas. These are divided into two systems of instruction: Veda and Agama. Veda are the general scriptures, and imply a dualistic approach to Shiva. Hinduism is the science of Veda. The Tantras are the special scriptures. They are the means of attaining Shiva-state in this life. They are specially suited to people in this particular era. Agama or Tantra implies Non-duality, that the siddha realized his Deity "continuum" and received transmission as a process of self-reflection. Tantra is the means of becoming Shiva through the descent of his grace into the body-mind.

Originally Shiva gave 164 Tantras at the beginning of the mahayuga, 4,320,000 years ago. These were spoken by Shiva's five faces, Ishana, Vamadeva, Sadyojata, Tatpurusha, and Aghora. The Tantra has flourished and died out several times within this cycle. Numerous civilizations have existed within this time frame, the previous one destroyed itself through atomic weaponry. Others were swept away by deluge. Sanatan Dharma literally extends back billions of years, kalpas. One kalpa is 432 million years, we are in the 23rd kalpa. The 164 Tantras were divided into three cycles: Shiva, Rudra and Bhairava. (These are different manifestations of Shiva: peaceful, fierce and wrathful, and they are different approaches to Shiva. These are presented in this text.) The original oral teachings died out in the Kali yuga and Shiva incarnated and gave Tantra suitable to this age. Shiva again gave instructions through his five faces. The crystalline-hued fifth-face, Ishana, gave 28 core Tantras which to this day exist. Shiva transmitted the present Tantras to Shakti, from shakti they were given to Sadashiva, Maheshvara, Rudra, Vishnu and Brahma. Then the Tantras were given to 66 siddhas, nine of which are primary. The nine primal Tantras were revealed in Sanskrit and Tamil simultaneously by Shiva, for North and South Indian people. The first nine siddhas who received these instructions were commanded by Shiva to go in the four directions to disperse the teachings. These teachings were transmitted orally for thousands of years, then between 4,000-3,000 B.C. were written down in Sanskrit and known in eighteen other languages.

The Tantras are countless in number; the siddha Thirumulanath speaks of "One billion-million twenty-eight." They include vast teachings on philosophy, deities, universe, time, lokas, creation, yogic science, modes of worship, sadhanas, mythology and ancient history, astrology and astronomy, chemistry, alchemy, kaya kalpa, medicine, rasayana, spells, magic, and so on. In addition Shiva is the origin of the sciences of music and dance, language and poetry, and sacred architecture. He is the origin of secret and revealed sciences of Tantra, and its crown jewel—the science of Immortality.

Tradition reckons the celestial Deity's and rishis were on the earth at different times, one of which is between 75 and 20,000 years ago, as the ice and snow receded after the previous ice age. Tradition recounts their exploits and activity in symbology and fact as it was seen or known. (Veda: Vid: to see and know), and their teachings as they were directly transmitted (Tantra). Lord Haidhakan Shiva tells us, that at this time Shiva walked the earth and dwelt first at Mt. Kailash in Haidhakan India. (This is the first of five Mt. Kailash). Other Deities like Vishnu, Hanuman and Hayagriva also spent time there. It was named after Hayagriva, Haidhakan is a contraction of two words meaning the place of Hayagriva. Another etymology gives it the meaning: "sanctified place." The area to the North (Tibet) was all snow and ice, according to Shiva. Shiva moved North to the second Kailash in Tibet, and there initiated human civilization—the first man and woman, Manu and Shatarupa. In the Shiva Puranas (scriptures), they arose from the splitting of Brahma's body in two through Shiva's will (This is symbolic for initiation, they took miraculous birth. Many of the first beings to populate the universe were Shiva's mind-born emanations). These two were exceptionally wise and learned people. They initiate each manvantara cycle of four yugas: cycle of civilization, giving birth to the first wise people through intercourse. I suggest this was before 14,000 years ago. It was at Kailash that devas, siddhas and people were taught the Sanatan Dharma tradition which they practiced in the form of fire ceremony (Dhuni). Since the essence of the Sanatan Dharma (of Veda and Agama) is the mantra Om Namah Shivaya, the practice of japa or mantra yoga began with the first people who worshiped Shiva as their supreme master, primordial guru, and as Lord of the universe. But this mantra existed in previous eons as well.

Within the past 12,000 years Sanatan Dharma spread throughout India, Nepal, Tibet, Siberia, China, South East Asia, Kumari Kandan (Lemuria), South America, Egypt, Atlantis, Judea. Shiva manifested as Deities (like Sadashiva, Rudra, Maheshvara, Vishnu, Brahma, Hanuman, Durga, Yahveh-Elohim) to transmit Sanatan Dharma throughout the prehistoric world, and he manifested as rishis or siddhas to receive these profound instructions. Shiva manifested as perfected immortal masters to maintain Sanatan Dharma in ancient history. He continues to manifest free of ignorance as siddhas and yoginis in the present times; these people are called mahavatars or lilas (divine-play of appearance). It has been through such beings that Lord Shiva has initiated four great paths to liberation; these are the naths, shaivas, pashupatas and kapalikas.

Originally there were nine siddhas (Nava Nath lineage) who were rishis that lived and received instruction directly from Shiva. These Naths and many others were mahavatars—they did not have human parents. These Nath siddhas moved around the world through clairportation and flying chariot or airplane. (There is even a Tantra for chariot making.) Once at the appointed destination they practiced intense Yogas through sun, rain, hail, thunder and lightning, and attained celestial status. The names of some of these ancient siddhas are as follows: Agastyar, Boganathar, Nandi Devar, Sundaranath (Thirumular), Matsyendranath, Goraknath and their disciples like Mahavatar Babaji Nagaraj making a total of 18 Naths. All the early Nath siddhas in this lineage were emanations of Shiva's various internal organs and bones and are said to still exist in forests and mountain abodes in India. They also exist in other realms, such as Siddhaloka and Shivaloka. Rishi Sundaranath went to the South at Shiva's instruction and took the body of a dead cowherd, leaving his own body, (which Shiva stole). He is responsible for the Tantra(s) known as Thirumandiram, "Holy Garland of Mantras," which is an exposition on 9 Tantras (of the 28 Tantra system above). Boganathar flew to South and Meso-america to found Dharma there. Aztecs, Mayans and Incas have accounts of their founding teachers who arrived by chariot: bearded, robed, tall, who demonstrated miracles of rain and fire. They instituted Shiva worship there, and went to South East Asia, to Thailand, Cambodia, Malaysia, and instituted Shiva worship. They also went to Atlantis and Egypt; there are many similarities in worship between the traditions there and Shaivism. Boganathar flew to China to teach yogic sciences as Lao Tzu (Bo Yang) in the 1st millenium B.C. He compiled the Chinese system of yogas known as Taoism.

These siddhas were the founders of the ancient Siddha Siddhanta school of South India. They received the original transmission of the kriya yogic sciences from Shiva, which they (Agastyar and Boganath) passed to Babaji Nagaraj who attained immortality at Badrinath and retains a body there to this date. He is known as the Eternal Himalayan Yogi Kriya Babaji. He is responsible for sustaining these sciences in this yuga. He passed them to masters like Lahiri Mahasay, Haidhakan Babaji, the yogini Bhairavi, and so on.

The famous Nath lineage of Kapalikas, Kapalia's, Kamphatas, (Gorakh's religion) originated in the North with Shiva—Adi-nath, the 1st Nath, in the following transmission: Matsyendranath, the "fish-siddha" took the form of a fish and swam to the bottom of this river where Shiva (Adi-nath) was giving Tantric instructions to his consort, Parvathi. Parvathi fell asleep, but the fish-siddha was near by and received all the instructions. When Shiva asked if his consort got all of it, the fish-siddha disguised his voice (as hers) and chimed in that he had. This became the origin of the well-known Nath Tantra, which was transmitted to Goraknath. Goraknath's name is also in the bible. He manifested miraculously in Judea as Melchizedek to teach the essence of Judaism to Hebrew masters. He taught Adam and Eve, Moses and so on. The Kabbalah of profound mystical Judaism is incredibly similar to the Shaiva view.

Goraknath lived 9000 years ago. He attained the immortal bliss-body and remains on earth to this day as Haidhakan Babaji—my master. He was also an important teacher of Vajrayana Buddhism, the first to be given the transmission of the Chakrasamvara Tantra from Buddha-Vajradhara, which he transmitted to Nagarjuna. He initiated Krishna and Christ (at different times) at Madhuban India. Although the tree of the Shaiva tradition has been lost and dogmatized in most cultures where it was transplanted, the masters who originated it keep it alive in its native soil and in the hearts of excellent practitioners around the globe.

In the light of Shiva's infinite vision, he is the origin of all transmission vehicles (religion), which together are deemed Sanatan Dharma. This is so because Shiva is the "auspicious" or inherently perfect state of all minds. Shiva is the light within all beings, our pure spirit. Shiva is the jeweled lamp in the hearts of all beings, whose flame requires no fuel. Shiva is the omniscient state of our Being. Our body in Shaiva view is a temple of Shiva, whom we must enshrine in our hearts to attain perfect liberation. To demonstrate this, Indian temple art reflects the bodily temple. The outer images are merely reflections of the inner divine. Countless Deity images represent aspects or attributes of Shiva within and beyond us. The outer temple is designed to remind us of our inherent Deity-nature.

Shiva is the City of Lightning of Vast Stellar Wheel (Tarak Chakra) and Vast Heart Wheel. Liberation is the "City's Gate"; the City is the unstained heart. He is the quintessence of all natural religions, he is our inherent wisdom seeking to return itself to its self-illuminated, blissful state. Shiva is the state of intrinsic freedom (absence) and its bliss (presence)—this state is called samadhi. Shiva is pure Presence which is without end, timeless. Because there is Presence we call Shiva "Self." Because there is absence we call Shiva "Void." Because Shiva has no boundaries we consider Shiva self-less and timeless. Because Shiva is unchanging nature we call him "Eternity." Shiva preceded the universe, and is said to have created this one and many others. He weaves them like a dream, where all its contents are His-Self. Shiva is totally inexpressible and mostly incomprehensible, but tradition uses language and symbol to communicate this deep experience of our natural state.

Sanatan Dharma is the unspoken Truth of spiritual or Absolute Reality. Any transmission of the Truth is Sanatan Dharma, it is the path which unfolds from the omniscient state (Shiva) to lead all beings back to their Origin. Sanatan Dharma is ancient guidance of Sublime Beings as they walked the earth, as Shiva, Rudra(s), Bhairava(s), Indra, Vishnu, Hanuman, Durga, rishis, siddhas, yoginis, etc. It is the wisdom of the subtlest spheres which continues to inform the human heart, it is the insight or brilliant knowledge that arises spontaneously within the space of the heart.

Occasionally Shiva teaches in secret languages, although the Tantras are transmitted primarily in Sanskrit, a language of pure sounds arisen through intuition. It is said to be the language of the gods. The Mother wears a mala garland of letters denoting this experience of language, and suggesting the Source of the universe is sound (nada). Ordinary words cannot express the direct complete experience of Shiva, but act as symbols to denote this spontaneous experience, which is like a flash of lightning and is very subtle. Extraordinary words can express Shiva, words which were spoken by Shiva. The experience corresponds with our deepest nature—there is Shiva, and out of this tranquil space arises knowledge as subtle sound. This sound is experienced in the heart and is the foundation of Tantra. Because the sound is an expression of Shiva's wisdom it can precisely reflect the experience of aspects of Lord Shiva. When it conveys the experience, it invokes the experience, it invokes Shiva, it invokes the samadhi experience. So we use it to attain samadhi—through mantra.

Sanskrit is considered one of Shiva's sacred languages and expresses with great precision and subtlety, the sciences of spirituality which have arisen through direct intuitive experience of Shiva. The sounds and letters are woven out of Shiva and exist within us as the strata of pure soundless energy (light) and sound. (The etymology of the word Tantra is "warp and woof," a weavers instrument). Sanskrit is used both to communicate spiritual ideas, by communicating the pure energy-language of the Spirit behind the ideas, and to invoke the Spirit to communicate its enlightening experience to the mind. Devotion is key. When we speak of Shiva's pure qualities and activities with devotion light arises through our minds, it enlightens us and those with whom we speak. Dharma arises from our heart and mouth as light and awakens those with whom we speak. Therefore always speak with devotion of your Shiva or tutelary Deity and he-she will be present.

Lord Shiva is both without attributes, form or Qualities (Nirguna) and with attributes, form and Qualities (Saguna). We worship the Nirguna Shiva as Sambasadashiva which is Eternal Shiva and mother. We worship Saguna Shiva as the 1008 forms of Shiva, our guru, our own body and the body of the universe which is Shiva's natural manifestation. The universe is Lord Shiva and Lord Shiva is beyond it. He creates space and time and destroys it—as a play of His Transcendent Mind.

Shiva is attributeless, so throughout innumerable kalpas (one kalpa is 432 million years) creates Deity-emanations. He has five main faces: Ishana, Sadyojata, Vamadeva, Tatpurusha, Aghora (presented below), from these he spoke the Tantras, emanated Deities to control the universe, and created the multi-universe. From his limbs he brought forth Vishnu and Brahma, from his heart Lord Rudra. He also becomes Sadashiva and Maheshvara. These five deities are aspects of Shiva, and yet Shiva is beyond them. Shiva controls the universe through these Deities. Through Brahma he creates, through Vishnu he sustains, through Rudra he destroys, through Maheshvara he conceals, through Sadashiva he reveals.

Shiva is the formless aspect of all Deities and beings. From his heart he emanated as Rudra. Rudra takes eight main forms, corresponding to Consciousness, bliss, knowledge, and the five elements. Shiva created 350 million Rudras identicle to himself which filled 14 realms. From his Shiva Netra (3rd eye) he brought forth Bhairavas—wrathful forms. Shiva emanated 64 Bhairavas. He arose as all the gods, space, star and Thunder-beings. He emanated Rishis from his bones and organs. He gave birth to all beings, sentient and insentient. In traditional philosophy these can be divided by three qualities, six classes, and seven realms from earth to Shiva-loka (7th heaven). In Tantric philosophy Shiva arose through shakti or energy into subtle sound (nada). Then nada became a flash, drop, concentration of light (bindu). The Bindu then arises into Deities—energy-bodies. By stepping energy-sound-light down in frequency Shiva creates the universe, all realms and beings. The energy, the sound and light from which Shiva brings forth the universe is Shiva. So in truth, the body is Shiva, the five subtle elements, gross elements and organs of sense, internal energies, winds, chakras, subtle nerves, are all Shiva. This is enumerated in Tantric philosophy as the 36 Tattvas or principles of existence. Everything is being emanated by Shiva Tattva, who is pure Eternal bliss-Consciousness, so we seek to return our entire being to Shiva, to rest in the state of Shiva.

In the outer theater Shiva arises as the universe and sets the law of cause and effect in motion. Our spirit is inherited from Shiva, while our human body is inherited from our parents going all the way back to Manu and Shatarupa who were exceptionally wise beings, who did not have human parents. We have human parents because our ways have degenerated.

Shiva's pure subtle mind-born emanations are the Deities of the universe. They are his vast assemblage or mandala, who shine as his spiritual body. He is like the sun-globe; if you stand back you see a great wheel of radiance, and if you look at it another way it is defined by its individual rays, and if you look into these rays you might see they're composed of particles of consciousness, minute flashes of light. These emanated rays function as the universe, as 350 million star-beings, as 118 worlds. Shiva is the universe and all beings. Shaiva Tantra speaks fluently of 118 outer worlds which are emanated, maintained, and dissolved by Shiva. The stars are his chakras (jyotis-chakra) which rotate in orbit by wind-energies (vata), which are like spokes.

We too arise from Shiva as sparks or rays of Infinite Consciousness. Shiva is our natural Infinity, our essence or soul, our profound limitlessness. Shiva is fully embodied in each unique consciousness. We are his unique aspects.

All beings share the same qualities of Consciousness: love, knowledge, bliss, being, truth, and all beings have the same five powers of Consciousness: to preserve and dissolve, to will, know and act; and all beings have the same five capacities of Shiva: to create, preserve, destroy, conceal and reveal. Shiva shines as a full spectrum of ambrosial qualities through our consciousness—these qualities are called the 16 Kalas. These denote both the 16 digits of the moon and our inherent qualities which shine forth during meditation. Some of these are patience, gentleness, emotionlessness, dispassion, one-pointedness and so on. When all 16 qualities shine clearly, then Shiva shines like the moon when full.

Even though we take Shiva as one or all Deity's, a great Yogi, a dweller in cremation grounds, a rider upon the clouds, a star-deity, a creator of worlds, a destroyer of demons, we don't necessarily take him to be one person, a distinct being existing "out there" in space and time. Really Shiva is the ocean of all minds, the profound, deep and tranquil space of each person. Shiva is the unified or Non-dual state of all beings, the unity beyond difference. Shiva is the space and light from which the universe of 118 worlds arose, Shiva is its creator, sustainer and destroyer. Shiva is the all-pervasive, infinite Source which effloresces into the perceptible universe of forms. He projects it as an illusion. He is the unchanging nature of all beings, and the blissful dance of all beings and phenomena. The timeless Source displays manifestation like a dance. This dance is creation, maintenance and dissolution, or birth, growth, decay and death, the cycle of seasons, of an individual, the earth, a world or universe, everything.

Shiva is beyond form and name. To worship and attain this state, Shiva arises as images, (and as a pillar of light, which contracts into a lingam for human worship. It is not a penis, but a symbol of the meeting of the formless and form. It can be worshiped externally in crystal, stone, metal images, or it can be worshiped in the heart). All images of Shiva signify that the infinite light is ones own heart. When Shiva takes embodied forms and names for worship, he also creates systems of worshiping and meditating on them to achieve the highest aim. By meditating on the image or mantra we are meditating on Shiva. These practices are recounted in Tantric scriptures.

The essential view of Tantric tradition which originates from the ocean of Blue-Gold Light known as Shiva is that all beings are one Self, one Consciousness. Beings only differ on the surface. They are one Consciousness with different looks, faces, hair, sizes, etc. It is the practice of this view (religion) to realize this Consciousness. In Tantric tradition we call it "recognition," in yogic tradition it is called "Self-realization" or "God-realization." We are seeking to recognize or realize that we're Shiva, that we have always been Shiva and always will be Shiva. Shiva is this Self, Consciousness, Spirit, Light—that we are. Shiva is the creator of thoughts and the witness to them.

We generally think that we have a mind and body which experiences, does and remembers everything. But the fact is that our mind and body is a congealed form of Spirit, infinite Consciousness. Infinite implies everywhere, which includes the body. The Spirit (Shiva) experiences the universe through the body. The Spirit lives and acts in the universe as the body. The fact that through our body we might experience enjoyment, beauty, nature, all things, suggests that Shiva—Consciousness is in the body. The bliss-enjoyment that we receive from mundane acts comes from Shiva's beatitude in our body. Health and harmony of mind, body, vital energies and so on, come from Shiva within the body. Does it not follow that we should worship Shiva to enhance our bliss, well-being and inner peace? It is through this body that we seek to recognize what or who it is that experiences and acts in the universe. The body is a precious vehicle for attainment, without it we could not attain the deathless and effulgent state of Shiva, transcending the universe and rebirth.

This recognition destroys or ends suffering, because what we recognize is that our Self, our heart-nature, our Shiva does not suffer, that, on the contrary, it is pure bliss, it is what all beings desire. Haidhakan Babaji says "The Lord is beyond name and form. No one is able to pretend to have reached this stage of realization. Worship remains an essential part of preparation and purification of the heart." However he does say that the state of tranquility and bliss can be achieved during ones life, and he recommends for people in this dark age to use the practice of internal mantra recitation (Om Namah Shivaya) and self-less service.

The backbone of this tradition is veneration of Lord Shiva. Even the 330 million mahadevas, such as Brahma, Vishnu, and Indra, worship Lord Shiva in order to realize their Shiva-nature and thus attain his realm called Shivaloka or Shivapara, "City of Shiva"—which is the omnicient heart totally beyond change and suffering, time and space. Lord Shiva can be worshiped directly and as multiple deities. The multiple deities of the pantheon and all beings are energy-bodies, rays of Shiva, deriving their existence, sovereignty and power from him. As emanations of Shiva, their nature is Shiva. Shiva is reflected in their hearts. Shiva is the name of the Father-Mother Consciousness of the Thunder-beings, of all beings and things. He assigns his countless emanations forms and names, through which we might worship them.

Shiva is the Source of all things which are congealed light. Shiva is the origin from which we've arisen and the changeless tranquil space to which we will return: Unborn and Immortal. The essential aim of the teachings is re-mergence with Shiva who creates, sustains and dissolves universal existence. This is represented in mythology in the longing of Shiva's consorts, like Parvathi to attain union with him. This recurring mythology both represents the longing of our heart to attain union with the state of Shiva, and it can be taken literally—that Shiva had many dakini-consorts. One reason iconography depicts Shiva in union with Shakti is to tell us that we're inseparable from our true nature, our Lord within.

Shiva is in our hearts as wisdom-light, and from here creates thoughts and inspires us to practice Dharma because it brings the greatest joy. Our heart nature is tranquil, joyous, wise and radiant. This is depicted in mythology as the Lord of Yogis (sometimes seated next to Nandi the bull, symbol of Dharma and bliss, and his consort, symbol of shakti or divine energy).

Shiva is creating our thoughts, inner worlds in our heart. Thunder-beings are just as much in the inner world flashing and dancing as in the outer world. Everywhere they're awakening us to our blissful, tranquil nature. When we allow God to control our mind or when we pray, it always causes us to help others, and in this way it brings supreme bliss. If we're always helping others then supreme bliss will be our heavenly inheritance. Shiva at our crown and within our hearts yearns to help others. Whether we're aware of this or not, it is true. The light that shines over us and within us is the light of love. When it enters our heart it is the wish to liberate beings from suffering. The wish that caused us to come to earth originally, to appear in a body, remains with us. When we act continually from this wish then we have attained the goal of human life—Wisdom or Dharma, and we break the wheel of rebirth. When we act from desires for the world, this desire brings us back into the world. When we follow

the light internally by acting upon our inherent goodness, then we return naturally to Shiva. We return to our internal state of perfection, of bliss, tranquility, and when we leave this body we melt instantly into wisdom and infinite light (laya: dissolution). If Shiva controls us through our heart, if We control the body in other words, then the outcome is always totally positive. We never loose our sense of uniqueness and individuality. Have you ever known a yogi who appeared like the ordinary faceless masses? A good practitioner stands out amongst all beings by virtue of his or her brilliance, bliss, love, humor, and wisdom. Every ray or spark of Shiva is totally unique, yet We're all the same in essence.

The meaning of being human from the very start is to live as Shiva on the earth. At least this is the means of dissolving into Shiva, of recognizing our self-nature. This implies taking the view that we are not an individual self, which needs protecting, which needs to have in order to experience true happiness. Shiva is limitless tranquil space of our mind and the thoughts, feelings and body (of light) which arises in this space. Shiva is always awake like a fish. Shiva is indestructible like a lightningbolt, so is called durjaya-linga and vajra-linga, "sign of the indestructible." Shiva is always directed to help others, to share and give of his infinite Self or ocean of love-light. True happiness and well-being comes from giving and sharing what we have and what we are. We are a body and mind and it brings the greatest joy to give of these things. To live this way is the meaning of the word Dharma, truth, religion, naturalness, righteousness. That is why Nandi ("joy"), Shiva's bull form symbolizes Dharma.

If our motivation does not adhere to our primordial nature (Shiva) which is always for others, but if instead we choose to live for our individual body, then we create the condition for having to return until we change our view and activity. A self-centered view causes us to act unvirtuously to harm others, and this in turn draws us back into the body to experience the results of our actions. It clouds the mind by generating unclear or dark energy (karma) which prevents our recognition of the original state (Shiva). In essence because we fail to recognize others as ourself we cause them harm, creating the condition of our future rebirth. Because there are innumerable beings who suffer from this ignorance, who are in need of a means of purifying the mind and destroying the cause and results of suffering, Shiva has created a way, religion or method of returning to our natural or primordial awareness, returning to the state were the Spirit or heart controls the body. Shiva is our self-less all-pervasive inner space and the ideas arising in this space. These ideas define who we are and they create our body as a means of helping beings. The Spirit projects the appearance of a body out of wisdom-light. The body is a configuration of the Infinite Conscious-ness, it is the signature of the Spirit. Every body reflects the body of Shiva. The image or energy-body of Shiva is every jiva of every being. They not only reflect Shiva, they are contracted forms of Shiva. It is the view of this tradition that out of intrinsic freedom, to undergo the cycle of the universe, of birth, growth, decay and death, each being closed, went to sleep. Shiva contracted in order to undergo expansion. Shiva concealed him Self in order to reveal him Self. Shiva went to sleep, dreaming the universe, in order to awaken him Self. It seems mysterious, unreasonable, but it is simply natural. Shiva makes all jivas sleep then awakens them. This sleep is depicted by Vishnu sleep-ing in a couch of the serpent Infinity and Brahma sleeping in a lotus issuing from the navel of Vishnu. They represent the phases of concealment. The phase of revelation is represented by Lord Rudra and Bhairava destroying the universe, awakening beings with thunder and lightning. Shiva is the means of returning to Infinity through illumination.

Shiva is a means of living on the earth which will return us to Infinity. Identifying with matter we have arisen into finite material form. Identifying with Infi-nite Shiva, we can arise into Shiva state. All yogic systems come from Shiva and are aimed at achieving this state. Shiva is the soul (jiva) at our crown and its Lord. Acting as Shiva means giving up the view of an individual separate self, and always considering oth-ers first. If we fail to recognize that others and who we are, are one unchanging Consciousness, then we will fail to treat others as we wish to be treated—as pre-cious. If we can have some respect for God and wish to serve God, then, because this God is everything, we might view all sentient beings with respect and love. If we hold the view that all beings are Shiva, manifesta-tions of one continuum of pure primordial wisdom or Spirit then surely we will want to cherish them and see them free of suffering. This is the view of Shiva. We are not other than Shiva, so this is how our soul that is over us sees things. If we rest our minds we will be able to hold Shiva's vision, we are this all-pervasive wis-dom. We are this wisdom that experiences the suffer-ings of all beings by being in all beings. We simply

have to shift our view from limited material existence to unlimited spiritual existence. From limited ability to help others to unlimited capacity to help beings. Shiva is our unlimited nature of pure Presence and space. Our aim is to seize hold of this Presence, to live from love and bliss, and to relax our awareness in its space, to meditate. The means to achieve this aim is yoga. There are many yogas which Shiva has devel-oped, such as siddha yoga, kriya yoga, Tantra yoga, kundalini yoga, nada yoga, hatha yoga, mantra yoga, mansa yoga, bhakti yoga, karma yoga, and so on. All of them utilize various means of unifying the indi-vidual spark (Shiva) with its Father-Mother flame (Shiva), or you might say of dissolving the limitations which prevent our recognition of natural unity (Shiva) within.

Boganathar held a conference of siddhas at the beginning of the Kali yuga (3102 B.C.) to determine which yogic means would be best for people in the coming degenerate times: they decided upon Bhakti yoga as the best means. Shiva is love, the greatest way to realize Shiva is through loving him. All other yogic practices should have as their essence—devotion.

To think and work compassionately for others, and to think of God (Om Namah Shivaya) is a method for unveiling the love of our heart. Since love is none other than Shiva, we will be able to unify with Shiva through it. Whenever we love others we're practicing yoga, union of Shiva with Shiva, consort with Shiva. All positive activity, such as compassion, generosity, meditation are yogas or methods of returning to the unified state. Meditation quiets the mind, so we can become aware of its tranquil nature. Compassion brings light into the mind so we can become aware of its luminous presence. There is a very commonly told story which depicts Shiva's compassion for the world. There is in some Tantras a six-faced form of Shiva, in which case the sixth-face looks down with compas-sion upon the world. It is blue or blue-necked (Nilak-natha).

At one time mischievous beings (gods and de-mons) wished to procure the elixir of life from this great milky ocean. So they started churning it to get the nectar of immortality. But the stick they were using, the intention, was a harmful serpent that injected poison into the ocean. This poison filled the atmo-sphere and threatened to kill all beings. In order to protect them Shiva drank this poison and saved them. It turned his throat blue. So when he appears with white body and blue throat, we refer to him as a great physician who can heal us by drinking or dissolving our inner poison, our suffering. He drinks the cause to liberate us. Though we do not know it, he protects us from much suffering. We are immersed in his ocean. When we invoke him our suffering disappears instantly. An inner interpretation of this myth, which is one of Shiva's "eight great deeds," is that we must swallow our internal negative states in order to be unified with God. Our impure energy will be liberated to fly upwards, to radiate bliss and love to help others. So, from an outer perspective we use Parashiva to dissolve our afflictions to realize Shiva is within. When we realize this, then we use Shiva within to control the mind through yoga. There is also a secret Tantric way of interpreting this myth, but it isn't pertinent now.

Shiva's initial intention as beings was to come into being to express boundless burning love for his own Self and to experience the bliss of that love. The siddha Thirumulanath describes this activity as the sun beating down on the ocean, which, evaporating, leaves behind forms of salt. Shiva's love produced the manifestation of all things out of his homogenous Ocean of Consciousness.

All things of the five elements are Shiva, very much cognitive and alive. So we should treat the earth, stones, plants, water, air and all beings as precious—as Shiva. Shiva arose out of mind and light as the elements, He steps down or changes frequency. Because all beings have perfect freedom (to choose) they can choose to express their hearts while on earth, to adhere to their Shiva-nature, or they can choose to cause suffering for themselves through unvirtuous actions. Shiva is the only one acting in the world. Wise actions mean we have some compassion, our sense of relatedness to all beings is strong, we live others suffering and joy, our heart is open so we experience it as our own. Being here as Shiva we must always consider others first, they are what we are, even if we can't feel their suffering as our own. Because we have suffered we can still understand what it must be like and seek to alleviate it. We always know when we've acted right, when Dharma has shined through our heart, because it brings us immediate joy. This is called "following your bliss." Nandi is bliss.

To practice Dharma, Nandi's Path, we must first identify with Shiva, viewing our nature as an unlimited Source of Dharma, of wisdom, beauty, truth, love, and skillful ways of alleviating all suffering beings. We don't merely say, "If Shiva were here he would do

such and such. . . ." We say, "Shiva is here," and we make Shiva utterly present by repeating his name internally, then spontaneously in our heart will arise wisdom and love. Or we might visualize ourself as Shiva. And aloud or silently repeat his mantra to make him utterly present to us, to cause us to recognize that we are Shiva. Shiva's image is peaceful, blissful, effulgent brilliant blue in color, two-armed, one-faced, crescent-moon crowned, adorned with rosary's, nagas and gold bars on his forehead. He has long matted hair, half of which is coiled on top his head, half of which hangs down his back. He holds the trident on his right. He walks in the thunder-clouds over the wisdom ocean. So you can visualize yourself performing activity in this way, to imbue your work with wisdom and love, and to awaken your mind to the fact that there is only one doer—Shiva. At the same time think that he is in your heart, pronouncing Om Namah Shivaya, flooding you with blissful peace, to imbue your thoughts with inspiration and wisdom, and to awaken your mind to the fact that Shiva is your Consciousness, creating, maintaining and dissolving your thoughts. Shiva can be realized in the heart through love of others and through devotion (love of Shiva).

As a sitting meditation, visualize yourself the same way as above, only sitting in lotus position within a stainless white-pink lotus on a turquoise-blue lake on the top of Mt. Meru. Recite Om Namah Shivaya aloud, think that you are flooded with blue light (tinged with gold) through your crown, purifying you completely. If you wish to help beings through the power of thunder, think that winds blow, storm clouds amass, Garudas appear out of the clouds, lightning and thunder pierce the sky above and all around. This awakens your mind and triggers a rain of blessings to fall to liberate all sentient beings from suffering. These two forms of Shiva are Cities of Lightning, both exist, I participated in them and wish to share them with you. They exist continuously and are means of attaining enlightenment. When you've completed a session dedicate it to liberate all sentient beings.

Shiva is always present, but we must cause recognition of this. Ordinarily our nature is unclear, our inner light of love is clouded, so we need to purify it. When our mind becomes pure and clear, tranquility and peace govern. When our intentions become pure and clear, bliss and love govern. When we purify the ground of our heart—Consciousness, we purify intentions or thoughts, since they arise as light from the

Consciousness. When we purify our intentions and actions, we purify the Consciousness from which they arose. Therefore the methods of purification which Shiva has transmitted purify our total being. He teaches us to practice self-less service and meditation together. We can either meditate directly on the nature of Consciousness, or we can use sound and imagery to do so. This exposition obviously focuses on the use of imagery and sound. Shiva has developed or created images and sound out of his light of love to liberate beings from suffering. Because we are unable to absorb ourselves for very long in the Absolute, Shiva gives us images and mantras. By concentrating on the images and sounds we are meditating on Shiva—the Absolute. Some teachers think that meditating on the space or breath is supreme, that mantra and nada (sound) is lower vibration and lesser practice. But actually this is not the case. The quickest means to attain recognition in this yuga is mantra yoga. Shiva has said this. One should use the mantra and image to make the heart tranquil, then dissolve the image and sound into space. Even if you continue the practice without cessation you realize that the mantra is sound-emptiness or silence, and the image is light-emptiness or luminous space. Like I said the mantra and image of Shiva is Shiva. We are accustomed to thinking sounds disturb the mind. But actually subtle sound sets the mind at peace, subtle light heals the mind. In mantra yoga (and nada yoga) you focus on sounds to dissolve into perfect tranquility—samadhi. The result is you experience all inner sound as void-tranquility. With mantra yoga we think of ourself, the mantra and Shiva as one. They are one, totally indivisible. Therefore through the mantra (and image) Shiva awakens and purifies our awareness so that we might recognize that we are Shiva—Om Namah Shivaya.

To achieve this tranquil state, we become Shiva. All of Shiva's images represent it. Those who achieved themselves through Shiva become known as Rudras, or Shiva. When Shiva arises out of light into visionary appearance, into spheres of star lights, into clouds, into lightnings, into giant deities and brilliant yogis, into the cosmos, and our very own thoughts and feelings, we call this multiplicity—Rudras. It is said that the beings he first created appeared just like him, there were so many they filled the 14 realms. In some forms, such as all Thunder-beings, he has recognition of his infinite nature, and is free of suffering, in other forms, such as innumerable transmigrating beings, he puts on a play and gets lost in it, he chooses the play and forgets his infinite nature. Shiva includes all beings and things, which are one wisdom-light and sound, one tranquil space and dancing electric Self—Nataraj. It is the destination of all beings that they will return to Shiva, that they will be awakened. Even if they do not choose Dharma, there is a fierce yet natural form of dissolution or pralaya called Mahakranti, in which Shiva destroys the multi-universe with fire. Our destiny is what we make for ourselves.

Our pure intention to help beings is Deity's pure intention to help beings. To return to the state of unity with Shiva's mind we must simply live according to Shiva's Dharma and practice awareness of ourself as Shiva. The unchanging aspect of our mind, which is the same from beginningless time is the Deity we arise from, it is the Shiva that we're projected from. It is this Mystery which projects, maintains and dissolves our appearance. We have the appearance of an ego because the light of the Mystery becomes sound (ideas). We have the appearance of a body because the light of the Mystery becomes particles (atoms).

To return to the state of Shiva we require two things—one is the grace or light of Shiva (all achieved beings) and yoga or meditation. Both cause the dance of worlds within to cease, so luminous space (peace) shines. Luminous space is Shiva, the creator of internal worlds, we seek to recognize this, to know who we truly are, and what everything is. When the cycle of internal worlds ceases, the cycle of rebirth ceases.

Shiva provides the grace of this recognition. It is not a personal attainment. The light to refine our nature or awaken it is beyond us in a sense. All forms of worship and devotion are methods of invoking Shiva's grace—which for us is necessary to bring our minds to rest. Since he is our supreme guru, he provides the path and the light of the path, to awaken our heart to its natural state of Shiva. He provides the grace to end continuous rebirth. Because our minds are not at rest, then our soul cannot come to rest, but it seeks to fulfill all its thoughts, it does so through the body. When Shiva brings your mind to rest he brings the cycle of rebirth to an end. He melts the cause of rebirth—which is lack of awareness of our true nature. Our true nature is Shiva, and has complete control over the mind. If we have recognition of it, this Shiva can control or will to come here or go somewhere else, its will acts out of love, always. So it can choose freely to come here to earth in a body for the welfare of others, or to work through unseen light and guidance. Because Shiva is totally free he chooses to be innumerable hearts, he chooses to close or sleep, to be unaware on the surface. He makes an illusion of separateness. This illusion causes us to desire the things of the world, which in turn causes us to return here to fulfill our desires. So Shiva causes our un-awareness, our desires and our rebirth in the world. This means that the antidote—Shiva (light) is in our ignorance, all our negative states, our mind—fully. We contact Shiva through our mind, in the midst of all internal states, to awaken our true nature, to de-stroy the illusion of separateness, to stop the cycle of rebirth. Ignorance, or the illusion of separateness causes sensory existence, the body, and it causes us to think that bliss and tranquility, the state of Shiva can only be attained through the senses, through attaining beautiful things. But these only bring temporary joy, and suffering. So eventually, in the midst of suffering or joy, we throw our hands up and decide to seek out the causes of all joy and suffering, to stop suffering and bring about an unbroken state of joy, delight or bliss. We seek out Shiva because Shiva causes the root of suffering and bliss. We seek out what is be-yond us and what is within us. (In this tradition we do not necessarily say that Shiva has a specific reason for causing suffering and rebirth, but rather it is part of the natural cycle of things. Shiva simply arises out of space into embodied existence for a time, then returns to complete space again. He is embodied, yet always remains beyond all forms—as their formless state. The formless state (Shiva) is responsible for all bliss, goodness, love in the world, the form is respon-sible for suffering, only the limited form suffers. Through this experience, it is lead back to Shiva beyond suffering. Because Shiva is wisdom, we might say that wisdom is the cause of all suffering, because it forces all beings to seek it out as the antidote to all ills. It is lack of understanding which causes people to think that Shiva must be cruel to cause suffering, but remember it is US, We chose this, not somebody else, not some external sky-god. Shiva is Us. We are free to choose, Shiva is this freedom, no-one outside us chooses. We each choose. We can choose to live here in ignorance and suffering or in great awareness and luminous blissful samadhi—free of suffering.

Look and marvel at Shiva in all beings—it is quite miraculous. All these minds are one thing—Shiva, all are interrelated by wisdom and light, Shiva-shakti. Because we were free we each chose life for ourselves,

and we chose rebirth. It is full of suffering, but indi-vidually we were free to choose it. The law of the universe created by Shiva ensures that we will return to Shiva, it ensures that goodness must be our ultimate aim, because only good acts cause bliss and peace. If Shiva were actually cruel, the universe would not work this way, and our nature would be the opposite of what it is.

Shiva means "good" or "auspicious." Lord Shiva is essentially the inherent goodness of universal exist-ence. Things in their natural non-dual state, the Reality of the universe is inherently good, not goodness against bad or for some religious end, but as the force and root of all positive transformation in the universe. We can focus on the suffering within and around us which is generated from forgetting our true nature, or we can focus on our inherent nature, in our hearts. Shiva is the root of the cycles or existence, of transfor-mation which is happening through energy. Shiva is the energy and what precedes and controls the energy. The word Shiva has another meaning: Sh means per-manent bliss, i means primordial male energy, va means primordial female energy. So Shiva is the bliss which comes from the balance of Consciousness (male energy) and energy (female). Shiva is the bliss-ful state of the mind that is balanced as well.

Shiva is the display, its energy transformation and he is what is beyond them. He is the state of our minds behind energy-display, before suffering, therefore Shiva is the liberated state. This state is our inherent goodness. It is the primordial nature of all things as self-illumination. As the universe this self-illumina-tion is in the star-lights and in our eye-vision which sees reality by its own light, as our minds this self-illumination is in our thought-lights, our inner vision which sees its reality by its own light. Reality, outer and inner is Shiva's illumination. Shiva is the inher-ently perfect state of the universe and all minds. It is already perfect yet our mind fixes it in its limited vision, and causes that we should witness imperfec-tion, suffering, energy in three qualities: sattvas, rajas and tamas, positive, neutral and negative. In reality, Shiva is gunajit, beyond qualities.

There are two aspects of Shiva (Infinite Con-sciousness): the Unmanifest, Eternal Tranquility, Un-differentiated Absolute (anuttara), and the Void of the Void (shunyatishunya), and its manifestation, the beautiful, quiescent sphere of nature, the universe of 118 worlds and seven realms. These correspond to Shiva-shakti—space and primordial energy. Through an ocean of primordial energy, of sound and light, Shiva arises into the forms of all things. Shiva is in the hearts of all beings—he is our awareness. Through the heart he manifests. First Shiva, Immovable Void, develops through his perfect sovereignty (shakti: power) in the hearts of all beings into the will, then knowledge (vision or ideation), then activity. The first shakti (iccha shakti: will) is said to be like a "throb in the belly of a fish" (matsyodhari). From this subtle flash of will within perfectly-free, blissful space arises a vision. Through this vision or knowledge (jnana shakti) arises activity. This happens in the hearts of all beings. Shiva is the inherent freedom of all beings. Through will, knowledge and activity Shiva arises into form, into the universe, into any of six states.

Another way to view this is that Shiva arises into very subtle sound (throb or pulse) through his will. This sound is the mantra Om Namah Shivaya. This then develops into a flash of light (a vision), then the vision develops into activity, of perceptible form, of sounds, lights, colors, smells, and so on. The first and subtlest forms to arise are sounds—mantras. These are pure will or intention. The will-power of Om Namah Shivaya is to create, sustain, and return all beings to Shiva. From these sounds arose Deity's—visions of Shiva. The first light-form corresponds to Om Namah Shiva—this is the form of the creator, sustainer, destroyer of all worlds. These are the forms illuminated below—the great yogi, the 18-armed Svacchandanath, and so on. These sounds and images are the Source of the universe. The five syllables na ma shi va ya are the five aspects of Shiva: Consciousness, bliss, will, knowledge and activity. Through bliss, Consciousness creates, sustains and destroys all manifestation.

Practically speaking the Unmanifest Shiva is our deep heart-nature, Consciousness within consciousness, and is perfect unmoving tranquility, equated with stone, vajra, and space. It is our clarity and openness as well. In our mind, thoughts (sound and light vision) arise out of a living cognitive space, they live for a time then return to that space. In the same way all external phenomenon arise out of space, exist for a time then dissolve back into it. The space is Unmanifest Shiva. The manifest form of thoughts and external phenomenon like our bodies, all sentient creatures, stones, water, fire and air are the sound-light display of this living space. The space and its display are one living harmonious Spirit. But beings don't perceive their true nature as Shiva, they feel cut off from the Source. It is natural for all beings to return to Shiva after undergo-

ing the cycle of the universe. By practicing Dharma, beings are liberated from this cycle. Through the vehicle of Dharma beings are able to reconnect with their Origin, to return to the Origin.

Shiva is our true nature—limitless and immovable (eternal)—and shakti (the sound and light of our awareness). Shiva is our thoughts and body. Therefore in Tantra we worship our heart and body as Shiva. By worshiping mind and body this way, our awareness awakens to the truth of this view, we realize this view. Shiva's grace enters our five bodies, electrifying them, purifying the mind (cittam: unconscious).

Because we have spent our lives directing our consciousness through the senses we have forgotten the state of Shiva within. We are the Origin and its manifestation at once. This is the lingam, formless meeting form. There is no separation between our infinite heart nature (Shiva) and the light manifesting from it thoughts, body. To cause this is the goal of yoga. This goal is demonstrated by many siddhas actually disappearing, dissolving into formless Shiva.

We are the wisdom-display and play of Shiva, our limitless unchanging nature. If you listen within by meditating you'll hear space as stillness. When awareness is stabilized in this space, immovable like stone, totally undistracted or unagitated—this is yoga, union of awareness and space, manifest Shiva and Unmanifest Shiva, union of consort (shakti) and Shiva, our body and Shiva. In Tantra, sexual embrace can symbolize this union—particularly since it causes great bliss. Because awareness is light, this state is full of bliss, the way the air around a rose garden is permeated with the scent of roses. So when thoughts arise as the display of Shiva we should think of them as shapes of bliss-light, translucent like rainbows, none other than Shiva.

Because Consciousness is all-pervasive, awareness stretches everywhere, it is what is beyond us and is focused as a ray constituting our present awareness and our bodies as a bundle of light-fibers. Our bodies are shifting particle light-projections of Infinite Consciousness. Shiva is one continuum which stretches itself out from its subtlest inexplicable Source (heart) to its grossest phenomena display (universe). Even though the entirety is Shiva, until we can recognize this fact, we generally consider Shiva to be the subtlest category of existence which is always behind the others. We worship the subtlest Shiva in order to recognize ourself and universe (manifestation) as Shiva. In Tantra this is outlined in the 36 tattvas, or categories of existence, which are the stages by which Shiva flows out from the uncontracted state of Undifferentiated Reality through primordial energy down to the gross elements. It is a ladder by which all individual sparks flow out and ascend back into Eternal Shiva (Sadashiva). It is a confluence, a circuit or cycle, an emergence and re-mergence. Shiva is the all-conquering Void, the emptiness which both produces all transformations from Eternity to space to solidity, and absorbs all transformations from solidity to space to Eternity. Shiva becomes atomic existence by changing the frequency of energy. Atoms are particles of Consciousness displaying a rainbow of elemental qualities—like a pearl. The samadhi experience of this Eternal Void is called sayujya samadhi.

To return to our Source, to become absorbed in the Eternal Tranquility we need to control our minds, to cultivate awareness, to destroy the root of poor mental and physical habits. We can achieve this through any yoga, but primarily this exposition is concerned with Tantra, the use of mantra, image, and yantra. Concentrating on mantra and image destroys the root of bad habits, creates good habits, increases awareness, compassion, inspiration, gives us control over our life and reality. Mantra-image-yantra are one thing, just different manifestations—sound, light and geometry. These exist at the Source of reality—they are the Deity's in our body and the universe. Through mantras one can become these Deity's, become Shiva, thus controlling ones thoughts, body and universe. If one possesses control over ones mind, then one has control over rebirth. The state of Shiva transcends the universe. Shiva's grace is the means to attain this state.

Mind can be controlled through any absorption, on inner sound (nada yoga), mantra (mantra yoga), breath (kriya yoga), energy circulation (Tantra yoga), devotion (bhakti yoga) and so on. The quickest means is to incorporate aspects of all yogas into one practice. The Siddha yoga practice(s) of Tantra do this. The practice of Om Namah Shivaya unifies all practices, and results in the goal of all yogas, but much quicker. Haidhakan Shiva says you can attain enlightenment in one life through it, but you must use it all the time.

Om Namah Shivaya is the quintessence of Shiva-shakti, of Shiva's grace—anugraha shakti. This grace takes the form of all mantras and images through which people might return to Shiva. The greatest distillation of anugraha shakti (light of grace) is the panchakshrita (five-letter mantra). Shiva's free expression or manifestation through shakti is grace or love. Because Shiva is love there is revelation—imagery and divine activity. Shiva's manifestation in images expresses the infinite multiplicity of Shiva, his perfect sovereignty to be in a billion places at once, instructing and guiding beings.

Shiva is Consciousness (cit), what we are, what everything is. He exists as our hearts, through our heart we can know Shiva, who we truly are. It is by paying attention to our heart, our inner space that we recognize our original nature as Shiva. By paying too much attention to the display or manifestation we have forgotten Shiva—the Source of the display. Shiva is Eternal, beyond or before time; when he generates the appearance of separateness in the space of our Mind (Infinity), he generates the appearance of separateness in the space of his Eternity. This produces time and space. Shiva is the Wheel of time-space (Kalachakra).

Unmanifest Shiva has two aspects, the originating Consciousness, utterly transcendent, and the energetic or light. The seed state or heart of Reality is utterly transcendent, beyond all minds and comprehension, eternal, empty and spacious. The other aspect, through which the universal manifestation arises, is energetic. These two are not distinct, although it is suggested that from Transcendent Shiva (Parameshvara) arose Transcendent Power (Parakundalini or Mahashakti), the power through which Shiva manifests universes, within inner and outer space. To symbolize this unified continuum, Shiva sits in sexual embrace with his consort. This posture suggests to the mind that inner and outer worlds are created through the friction between consciousness and energy, it suggests that creation arises out of bliss. It suggests that the child Shiva gives birth to—is his own light. The universe is light, our body is light, our thoughts are light. It is an illusion not to perceive Shiva as all things, so we invoke Shiva, who is a light of Knowledge (vidyut shakti: lightning) to destroy this illusion. One possesses this light of supreme infinite knowledge is Shiva.

Because Shiva arises into all phenomena through light (energy), all beings necessarily return to Shiva through light. By ingesting it through mantras and Dharma practice it enlightens us to recognize our inherent nature as Shiva. In this system our return to the state of Shiva is a natural process or cycle, and therefore spirituality or Dharma is what is natural for us. Nandi (Bull), symbol of this practice, implies both the Dharma or means of causing joy in our life, and the body, the vehicle of Shiva, the vehicle which Shiva takes as the forms of all beings, the vehicle which

Shiva takes to go through the universe in four seasons (four legs) and return to space. Nandi is represented in the stars as Taurus. His four legs are the four yugas or seasons of the universe and all beings; his crown is the Pleiades through which Dharma arose with our ancestors. The constellation Nandi implies that the practice of Dharma returns us to the star-system from which human civilization arose. First the souls arose from Shiva's crown into the stars, then the souls descended to earth, to live out four seasons, then return naturally to the stars and to Shiva's crown (the Undifferentiated). Nandi is also the entrance to the stars, to the crown of Shiva—our home. To fail to adhere to Dharma means to continually be reborn on earth or in the lower realms and to live in suffering.

Manifestation can be divided into subtle and gross. Spiritual reality and imagery are subtle manifestations. We use the subtle light to reach the space it arose from. The universe of phenomena is a gross manifestation. Shiva is the phenomena-Source, the root of all manifestation. Shiva is displaying all these distinct forms, and they are a vision. Vision is the same as awareness. The same wisdom light in our minds is in our senses and objects of sense. The light makes an electrical circuit from the heart through the senses to the external world. They are one thing endlessly connected. Vision implies light-substance. There is only one substance-light, such is why we call it one Being—Shiva.

What a glorious expression of Shiva's majesty—to cause the appearance of separateness within Undifferentiated Eternity. Undifferentiated also implies one homogenous Consciousness which precedes substance-light, which we experience as Eternity. The yogi literally sees and experiences the universe as one mass of blue-gold-light—Shiva. (The hiranyagarbha "golden egg," the "Face of Glory," and the Nataraj "Cosmic Dance" are various modes of this experience.)

The forms of the universe are the waves on an infinite ocean. The ocean is Shiva, the waves are shakti. The ocean is in the hearts of all beings, the form a being takes is projected as pure vision light from this heart. When we recognize Shiva within we recognize Shiva in all beings, we recognize Shiva everywhere. Shiva is the blissful open heart within which the universe throbs, flashes, pulses, dances, ebbs. The word heart (hrdaya) is used extensively in Tantra to refer to the Origin of things, for three reasons: 1. Because it denotes pure love, bliss, pulse of life. 2.

Because the heart is the beginning and origin of our perception and thought; our will, vision, and activity of projecting, maintaining and dissolving the universe. And 3. Because it is within our heart that we might experience Shiva and his universal play. The siddhas dissolved the bindu (drop) of their heart into the ocean of infinity then described the universe through their infinite Vision. They achieved this through the perfect light of knowledge of Lord Shiva.

We are creators. Our vision of reality has created something after our own hearts. Deity's created nature out of lightning—this was their perfect unimpeded creative freedom. If our mind is clear our creative ability, the freedom of our mind will result in perfection. The siddha is able to create perfect emanations of himself to be in multiple places at once teaching dharma to multiple students. Obscured vision of reality can only create what is mutable, having beginning, middle and end. Whatever we create is an extension of ourself. The creative motivation exists in the hearts of everyone. When it is chosen as subtle law or Dharma, the creative transmission of ideas through the heart, beautiful things are produced which are in the image of the Creator which bring a flow of bliss. If we ignore our inner creative motivation, whatever we attempt will blow away. Such is why Shiva has repeatedly said that Karma Yoga (selfless service) imbued with the light of japa yoga is imperative as the sole method of attainment in this yuga. Japa or mantra repetition clears awareness so that creative expression will shine with perfection.

Through time we have misused our energies (mind), our sacred powers to will, know, act, preserve and destroy. We have forgotten our nature, mistaking the physical world as our home and the only thing worth possessing. Having generated craving for the world, we bring ourselves back here again and again. Having generated immoderate desires for the world, inner obscuration is perpetuated. Ignorance has limited Shiva's five energies of consciousness, bliss, willing, knowing and acting, which become limitations (kanchukas: coverings) which become negative emotional states. Shiva caused this. Shiva chose this as my choices. Having generated habitual craving for the world, which only brings a portion of divine beatitude (fulfillment), we require a means of purification, of returning to our Shiva-nature. Thus Shiva maintains the Sanatan Dharma, Tantric and Yogic sciences, the means of restoring our omniscient nature by living naturally and contacting his subtle life, the means of transmuting the five powers that limit our Vision into Shiva—the five powers of Infinite Vision. (In this yuga Shiva has maintained Sanatan Dharma through singular mahasiddhas such as Mahavatar Shiva Babaji, who retains an immortal light body in the Himalayas until the end of this eon, and who retains unbroken lineages of siddhas to ensure existence of Sanatan Dharma. From time to time he emanates out of a light in Haidhakan, so is called Haidhakan Babaji.

Siddhas represent the body of Shiva, so we say they were born from the bones, organs, hair or eyes of Shiva. It simply implies they were pure from the start and never departed from their perfected state. Such people can be distinguished by siddhis or miracle display which causes us to listen to their wisdom, by aura and halo which transforms their environment and disciples minds into a mandala or city of light. We distinguish them by the feeling of bliss and spacious tranquility we receive in their midst. From having continually sacrificed themselves for others, their minds feel like space. From having generated the intention to help others their minds feel like love, and from actually having helped countless beings, their mind feels like bliss. And if our minds are open we might see their wings, crown, robes of light and Wisdom-deity appearance.

Shiva always teaches a way to recognize our inherent nature—Shiva. Shiva is best thought of as a state of our unagitated mind. We can see Shiva in the tranquility of our mind, in clarity as opposed to confusion, since Shiva is the clear state. Therefore the Shaiva yogis teach us to focus in the space of our mind, between thoughts and breaths. We can see Shiva in the insightful wisdom or knowledge of our mind, as opposed to ignorance, since Shiva is the state of infinite knowledge. Therefore it might be suitable to think of Shiva as the knowledge we possess which arises to assist others beyond suffering. We can see Shiva in our bliss and positive states, as opposed to negativity, since he is the state of limitless bliss. Therefore we choose bliss and to act according to what brings bliss. The result is like uncovering gold hidden in the earth. We can see Shiva in our selfless acts of love, as opposed to selfish ones, since Shiva is the self-less state.

If you look at this self-less wish, at every thought suffused in Shiva's vision-light, you will see that it is spontaneously or naturally arising. Love is what is natural for all beings, it is the substance or light of the ocean of Infinite Consciousness. It is the light which unifies. It unifies through its willing, knowing and activity. Therefore love pervades all manifestation, every thought which begins with a movement, a throb of light within the space of our heart. The limitless self-less ocean shines through every heart. We simply must choose it. If we choose it, then its qualities such as tranquility and bliss will arise, the natural state will consume us. Eventually the wisdom ocean drowns the island of the ego. This is the goal because the ego only creates a hell for itself, a barrier for the ocean. We want the ocean to roll free. Love is the movement within openness, the surging of the ocean, it is the movement to envelope and transform suffering at its root.

Our thoughts and inner states belong to Shiva, as his adornments, they are his intangible light display of wisdom on the screen of Eternity. Ignorance is this wisdom. Once we know that it is Shiva, we look for Shiva in it. We bring the light of Shiva into it, into every state. We take the lamp of Om Namah Shivaya with us in our exploration of ourself, our inner states. If we are angry, it is Shiva displaying the face of anger, if we're sad, it is Shiva displaying the face of sadness, it is Shiva projecting this illusion like a shadow or cloud over the light. It is actually the activity of the light and is thoroughly controlled by Shiva. We must begin to view all of reality as auspicious, that Shiva is the belching thunder-clouds and the bar-b-que which follows, the incandescent meteor and the forest fire which follows, the seething volcano and the desolation which follows, the burning desire of millions of people, the rumbling anger and agitation of innumerable people. If in the face of this we can be at peace we save ourselves much suffering. And if we're at peace, then insightful wisdom can shine through the heart to help those who suffer in the face of difficulty. All beings suffer, we know the cause and the antidote which are the same—so we tell people. Shiva's Mind is omniscience and truth, nothing can dispute its perfection, it is incomprehensible. We cannot judge the left hand of the Lord, nor the right. What we experience is akin to a dream, because it is intangible light and sound, shifting particles of Consciousness. There is only one subject, according to this Tantra, one knower and doer, one Universal Mind. If you look within you will discover an ocean, this is certain, and this ocean is Shiva. This subject is the heart of reality; everything within and without is the organization of five lights of one substance projected by Shiva from this heart. Shiva is emerging as the flow of shakti into reality. The heart is the medium between Infinite

Consciousness and the finite film display of this Consciousness. The space between and before thought is the mind of Shiva, the pure awareness and light, the source of thought. The thoughts are actually the radiating and pulsating activity of Shiva. In purity we are each a unique aspect of Shiva. Our Consciousness does not belong to the universe but precedes it immeasurably, and is not separated or limited but by a forgetfulness of our essential nature. This too is being projected by Shiva: the ignorance which causes attraction-repulsion, fixation to our mental states. We think this state is me, so is this one, yet in reality those are only adornments, illusions of the master magician. We chose them, the illusion, so are consigned to live under the illusion of separateness and physical limitation. Because our mind takes the form of whatever it thinks or holds it has presently taken the form of this body. It thought it was a separate "I" and by thinking repeatedly this way, it created the condition and karma to be in a body on earth. By forgetting its expansive Shiva-nature, its unity with all-pervasive space, it took a body on earth. For as long as we forget Shiva we will take a body. There are more and less limiting states or places to be depending on our degree of openness or recognition of Shiva.

In Shaiva Tantric view we consider everything a play of Shiva, controlled by Shiva. Play (lila) implies perfect freedom of expression. It is a unique view of this tradition that Shiva causes ignorance, birth and liberation from rebirth. As practitioners of Tantra we believe that Shiva creates our obstacles, and gives us the ability to overcome them. These are symbolized by Ganesha, the elephant-headed son of Shiva, and the elephant demon (Gajasura) which Shiva destroyed. If we view all obstacles as created by our Lord guru, then we will draw wisdom from them, we will supplicate our Lord to remove these obstacles, and we will have perfect faith that they will be destroyed. That Shiva intentionally creates suffering in the universe is really not totally accurate with this view. Each of us has freedom to choose. Shiva is our freedom to choose, which is the activity of spacious awareness. Shiva goes to sleep in our heart, becomes ignorant or closed as a natural or spontaneous process. (We arise out of the Undifferentiated). Shiva controls this process of becoming separate. And Shiva controls the process of our liberation through intangible light. But our choice to take or to give is our own. By choosing to take for ourselves, we choose inadvertently suffering and limitation. By choosing to give for others we choose to become unlimited. In truth, pain and suffering are in the world because we have chosen it. Out of ignorance we have chosen activity which causes suffering. Only the potential for suffering exists in Shiva and Shiva controls our intentions to cause us to return to the Source. If Shiva has done this because ultimately it results in wisdom, everything we do results in wisdom, to see this we only need to become more aware, to awaken Consciousness. Shiva closes it, like when the trees and earth close for winter, then he opens it. This is the grand cycle of all things. All minds begin fully awake, We are Shiva. They close because it is the cycle or way of things, of the universe which Shiva is creating. We must close for a time, Shiva says, then we will open and We will see it was never closed, We were projecting this illusion and were always awake behind it, above it, through it. We took the appearance of being contracted and limited in space and time, but it was Our joke all along. This grand vacade, play or illusion is called Maya, "inspiration-expiration," because the nature of things is to arise for a time then dissolve into their Source. Maya means the cycle of space-time and its many levels from minute to vast.

Shakti performs two things in an infinite manner: it acts as maya, the faintest veil which permits individual existence, and it causes these sparks to be seek and attain unification. The illusion creates suffering, so we seek to transcend it. We look to Shiva, and he provides us the light of knowledge to do so, to pierce the illusion, to see self and Reality as they are, as Shiva.

We are related by essence, to God and each other. The illusion which Shiva displays is in our minds. When we say we chose the activity which caused the mind to darken, to appear with doubt and fear, we also say Shiva controlled this. The minds illusion causes us to see illusion in the universe, to see something other than Shiva. Doubt and fear cloud Shiva's Vision of himself within. Shiva casts the illusion like a spell, then dissolves it to reveal the Reality, the Truth of things. If you view that Shiva creates the illusion of separateness then you can see him destroy it easily and quickly. When the lamp of Consciousness, of spanda (pulsation) radiates from the heart, through our practice, the shadow of maya recedes—here we see that Shiva was projecting it. So Shiva's dance we're so familiar with is the dance of the cycle of space-time, the dance of illusion, of Shiva's wisdom-display and the dance of destruction (Tandava) in which the illusion falls, in which we remember who We are. If the mind chooses the illusion of reality, the illusion of a limited consciousness capable of being hurt or damaged, a dualistic view, the result is suffering. Because people choose fear, doubt, desire and hatred, Shiva manifests as a destroyer. He is known as destroyer not because he bar-b-ques cattle in lightninbolts, but because he bar-b-ques egos in rapid illumination. Afterward he smears himself with the ashes to symbolize his ability to conquer egos.

Nature is Shiva's Vision Body. Like him, its three-qualities are auspiciousness, beauty and truth. Our collective karmic vision is our adherance to the illusion of separateness instead of wholeness—the state of Shiva, Truth, Reality. Our ignorance of Shiva-nature, our immoderate desires, mental opacity, fear, laziness, sadness and discontent, wars, pollution, viruses, stinging bugs and diseases, nuclear waste, killing machines and bombs all belong to Shiva inasmuch as he allows them for the sake of wisdom. Very often suffering causes us to seek out wisdom to end it. Suffering causes us to return to Shiva, to grow, so a measure of it remains on the earth. We have chosen suffering by exercising our destructive quality over our creative motivation. The universe teaches balance, because suffering is the result of destructive behavior. And suffering leads to bliss through wisdom. So even if we choose suffering unknowingly, we are choosing bliss. So every thing Shiva is choosing through us returns us to our Origin. Shiva owns the potential for all activity, but his motivation is to illuminate, therefore he wishes to see people choosing what is good. If he didn't his vehicles would be methods of destruction, advocating immoderate desires, vulgarity, etc. Besides when you experience his loving nature then you know his motivation and function in the universe. If there's any doubt about Shiva, use his name and leave yourself open. He provides that good and is that good. Shiva would not have made the universal law if he didn't want people to choose the good, because cause and effect always ensures that things work themselves out. We must eventually choose good. Because the nature of the universe is this way, we can see that Shiva is ultimate goodness. We can stay under the spell for only so long, then must wake up to imbibe the Truth, to choose to follow our bliss, since this returns us to Shiva. Shiva is our goal as the fully awakened state. Even though we achieve this by his grace, we still must choose it, he chooses through us.

* * *

In Tantra the evolution of Consciousness into matter is known as nimesha, "closing the eyes." Shiva conceals his complete self-illumination. Consciousness (citi) assumes four forms for appearing as limited individual life (citta), these are: cetana—intuition; manas—ideating mind; pranashakti—vital energy; and atma—ego. These four are varying frequencies of kundalini. Citi descends from the pure uncontracted state of Consciousness to become citta. Citta's four forms are said to be formations of maya, the veiling activity of kundalini shakti, for carrying on individual life. In Shaiva view, it is taught that as humans we're in the greatest position to attain Shiva-hood or remergence with the Undifferentiated. Some beings are simply at the beginning of their descent into cyclic existence or rebirth. We should not be cultivating the negative or animal states because we are on the arc of ascent of consciousness back into the Godhead. Shiva's clock ticks backwards; we are dissolving. All souls are reborn and grow in wisdom through Shiva's illumination, until they attain human rebirth and eventually gain the wisdom of the Unborn, as Lord of the Wheel. So as humans, if we adhere to this view we can see that we're in a supremely precious state, and if we know about Shiva, and seek to practice with Shiva's grace, the opportunity we have is like that of finding a pearl in the sand. If we use Om Namah Shivaya, Shiva's grace will break the wheel of rebirth, and we will become a Lord of the Wheel, a Lord of the universe.. Shiva's mantra burns up all negativity in the mind, all negative karma which causes our rebirth. When the mind is thus controlled (by wisdom) rebirth is controlled. When the mind is controlled, the body can be controlled. When mind and body are controlled, then the universe or matter can be controlled, rebirth can be controlled.

Spiritual cultivation entails purifying the cittam, the awakening of the unconscious, the expansion of consciousness, the dissolution of the veil or limitation of our nature. The cosmic process of evolution into Infinite Consciousness is known as gradual unmesha "opening the eyes" because our awareness is like an eye and is being expanded. This is our gradual remergence with Shiva. Human life is at the arc of ascent, of movement into Infinity. Our eye of primordial awareness are gradually opening. Shiva is unfolding in the lotus of the heart.

The Tantric tradition speaks of seven hierarchical grades of souls known as pramatas "knowers." These correspond with the seven chakras or unfolding consciousness and the seven heavens or lokas. Spirits contract from the Undifferentiated state and evolve through the earth from the grossest and simplest state to the most subtle and elaborate state. First it closes then unfolds by Shiva's grace of illumination.

In Tantra, Shiva is the sub-atomic field emitting light and crystallizing into form. The image of emanation is Shiva projecting the universe as light through his eyes. He has eyes which are everywhere, that is Consciousness has an inherent quality of Vision, knowledge or wisdom. He is the emission of his heart through his eyes into the space of the Void. (His children, Rudras and Thunder-birds emit lightning in the same way, traveling through their eyes, projecting their wisdom, their vision of reality into the universe and mind. In a like manner, the light of our heart is emitted through our eyes. It leaves its residual impression wherever it has alighted.)

When Shiva opens his eyes to project his play (lila) this is called unmesha. He projects his nature outward and a dream takes place. All minds undergo a seemingly real process of exile and return, at which time one recognizes there was no separateness to begin with, that it was a joke of Shiva. He was presenting himself with a very monumental joke (a joke because of the substancelessness of reality), through which Shiva was bursting into bloom and decay, smiling, crying, raining, thundering, howling, burning, laughing, clowning, living, growing, suffering, dying and liberating himself through primordial energy. Because his display is the dream reality it is a joke, a play, and all states are adornments, like nagas. The only reality is our Shiva nature. The dream happens in order to recognize that the process, all the transformations were not real, lacked real substance, but simply a field in which Shiva experiences his multiple selves by concealing and revealing. He conceals or limits himself for fun, and to display his inner beauty and gradually disclose his wisdom-nature. In truth Wisdom governs the entire process of spiritual evolution, which is the dazzling Wheel of Consciousness dancing, pulsing and flashing.

The universe is projected as pulsating illumination from Shiva. The Thunder-bolt is the converged form of Shiva, prior to manifestation, which veils its complete illumination by gathering clouds around it and descending to cast blessing-lights upon the hearts of people. This is what happens when good people call upon Shiva with an open heart. We gather together in a circle, and he descends in a circle to bless us and release us from suffering. If we do this consistently our circle becomes a City of Lightning, so we erect a temple in the shape of Shiva's mandala, with an awakened image in the center. The image is none other than Shiva. If we're practicing alone we think of our bodies this way, which become transformed into the City of Lightning at the heart of which is Shiva emanating light outward to transform the universe.

Shiva emanates as a spark, a soul, then magnetically attracts that soul which was emanated. But the magnetism, our desire for Shiva is a property of our spirit and body. There is certainly a part of Shiva which is beyond us which we're longing for. It is all Wisdom-beings, and yet is even beyond them. So you can see this Reality must be very profound, difficult to even call a being, since we define being by the lives and minds of humans. Shiva cannot be defined by anything but our individual experience. Because this is so we worship human-like images. To animals Shiva is each particular animal, to spirits he is each kind of spirit, to stones, Stone, and so on. . . .

I hope that you will go after him. He's coming after each of us. That's the magnetism, the love. There are only benefits in this love-affair. We apply this power, which is love or bliss, toward our transformation into subtle bodies of Shiva. So that eventually we will join his unified body, and come to represent him in the universe. That is the perfected state known as samadhi. We are going to awaken our minds with the power which creates and destroys worlds. We are going to be destroyed and re-created in order to emerge into Eternity radiantly blissful, shining with a light not our own. Shiva's power is so attractive, it is blue, gold mostly, purple, white-black, green, red, pink etc.. It calls out to us and produces our growth, like plants which align themselves to the Sun. Our method of alignment is the mantra and image. Shiva is a great star, like the Sun as witnessed at dawn. Shiva's five energies can be condensed into two modes: concealment and illumination. These are the gates out of and back into Eternity. Shiva goes to sleep then wakes himself up. The arc of ascent is the arc of reversal. Shiva illuminates us like spring thunder awakening the earth, he brings us back to our beginning. He brings us through the Eastern gate by absorbing us, by dissolving us.

Shivahood is the definition of our return to the original state which we possessed before our earthly lives. Shivahood is our potential for a blissful mind—samadhi. Shiva demonstrates this by appearing in icons as tranquil and blissful. Shiva is the samadhi and the means or energy to attain it. It might seem absurd that Shiva-hood be pursued, since we are already Shiva; it's like looking for a piece of hay in a haystack. Nevertheless, if our mind feels imprisoned by impurity and if we cannot live together because of this, these are indications that our true nature is obscured and that veil needs to be burned away in wisdom-fire; that some restoration needs to be effected in order to actualize and live a state of unbroken bliss. The heart must be brought to rest before it can rest, mind-training needs to be embraced. We only use the view to bring us closer to our goal, so close we see we're right on top of it all along. Because our perfection happens spontaneously, our enlightenment can happen instantaneously like lightning. We're on top of the bomb (Bom Shiva), the power. We just need to detonate it. It's a bomb which brings all beings to rest. Shiva is this bomb, he creates peace and beauty through it. Haidhakan Babaji says Om Namah Shivaya is more powerful than an atom bomb. It is destructive so how is it different than an atom bomb ? It removes us from suffering. It evaporates our negative states. It turns our ego into ashes. It illuminates its target. It makes a wide open valley. It makes a hole in the clouds. It makes a space in the universe. We must become as empty space. This continuum of empty space is what unifies all hearts and minds.

To achieve our goal we start from the view or base that we are already Shiva, "worshipping Shiva as Shiva." Shiva is the immutable ground of the mind, the witness or eye of consciousness. In this way we begin by shifting our view, from limited to infinite. We train in the result. We begin by identifying with Shiva, and by applying Shiva's methods to refine our energy, to dissolve into pure states. We become visions of Shiva by creating bodies of Consciousness and light. We don't have to appear externally like the image of Shiva, but begin to naturally embody Shiva in the reflection of internal transformation. Because this transformation is a dissolution of gross energy, Shiva is called destroyer. Because this transformation causes all positive growth, Shiva is called Creator. Everything which grows is actually dissolving, burning upwards with a fire and the life of that fire. The etymology of the word Shiva denotes fire and water, positive and negative, creation and destruction, up and down. Shi denotes fire, wisdom-flame, the tongues of lightning, of awakenment in the sky of mind, and the sparks of Consciousness clothed in a vision of congealed en-

ergy. Shi is the internal solar wind of the right channel, Shi is the ascending, the triangle pointing upwards. The va denotes amrita, the bliss aspect of eternal beatitude, it also denotes the cooling moon (amrita comes from the moon) the left channel, the water, the magnetic pole, the capacity of consciousness, the Mother. Together the two, represented by lingam and yoni, by Blue Star (of David), are the combined poles of existence. So Shiva means non-dual Reality. Shiva is the soul. The soul is wisdom-fire and wisdom-water. Shivoham "I am Shiva or Reality" means the indivisible Consciousness within me perceives it Self. To take this view, one develops humility and self-lessness—since in that is Shiva.

Shiva is the fabric of the universe and its root, the Weaver. The thread he uses is the shakti, the loom is the free state of the mind (to express itself), the quilt of the multi-universe is his own body.

Shakti: The Lightning-bolt Flashing in the Space of Eternity

Shiva is the Lightning-bolt in the Space of Eternity. "Shi" is Shiva, "va" is shakti—this is what Shiva is, union of Shiva-shakti, union of bliss-light and space. Our naked awareness is completely awake as a lightning-bolt of self-illumination. All yoga is designed to bring the mind to rest. Form yoga or images and mantras uses light-flow, shakti, Shiva's illumination, to bring about rest. Om Namah Shivaya is a flash or flow of light which brings the mind to rest. Perfect rest allows us to perceive the natural unity or yoga between our self and God-Self. In perfect rest our awareness sees itself clearly, it sees its luminous Self everywhere. Once Muktananda, a great Tantric siddha, said to a gathering, "I love all of you very much, as my very own Self."

The nature of God is Consciousness. Infinite Consciousness is the God of nature. This Consciousness is everything which we know and see, it is the underlying substance of the universe and what is beyond or within the Lotus Heart of all things. On the surface it is transient. Its deep nature is self-existent, it neither rises nor sets, and requires no cause or support. It is beginningless and endless, the Origin of all beginning and end, which are simply gates for entering and leaving Silence. It is always there as potential space, emptiness and energy. Shiva is eternal space and radiance (shakti) taking shape as all things right at this moment. The nature of omniscience is simply unbroken awareness as Shiva within the heart. Shiva expands through our hearts. Omniscience is this expansive condition of the heart, the awakening of the heart to its infinitely spacious state. It is the unveiling of the intuitive faculty (receptivity) and our minds creative freedom .

Shiva can display anything he chooses. This power of freedom is called svatantrya shakti: sovereignty. Our hearts are totally free, unless we believe they are not, in which case we give power to an illusion, since we have the power to create our reality. We manifest it through our dimension of pure awareness. This supreme siddhi is called Shiva-hood, the omniscient state of unlimited bliss. The eight mundane siddhis arise as Shiva's five capacities, the ability to cause transformations of reality at will. To achieve our goal we have to return to the heart of things when our mind is just a spark in Eternity, a branch of the Lightningbolt. This means becoming fully aware of who we are, dissolving all limits of awareness, the illusory ideas of what we think we are, our limited view of ourselves, so that Consciousness can flow back into its Source like water into water, or the merging of two flames. Viewing ourselves as Shiva means viewing ourselves as limitless and tranquil as space, bearing all of Shiva's qualities. Viewing ourself this way creates a pure vessel for the descent of illumination.

Shiva projects and withdraws worlds like sparks in an oven. This happens on an overt level and within. Think how quickly our thoughts dart in and out. They are flashes of light. Only the space before them, in which thoughts arise is unchanging. Just as atmospheric lightning comes from the Sun, in the same way, all minds receive their power and autonomy from Shiva, Eternal Light. Our thoughts are merely flashes in space, like lightning dancing in the sky or stars twinkling in space.

In Tantric doctrine the universe exists within the spine. The inner and outer universe are the theater within which Shiva is going to display his grace, Vision, bliss, and illumination, to awaken all minds. We invoke his grace and mix it with mind, vital energy, cells and atoms, until they reflect this grace. Our cells then form a shining body of Grace, the body becomes the mandala of Shiva, its cells become his dancing flashing limbs—Deities.

As the pure power, the Lightning-bolt is the mahaskakti, also known as parakundalini "transcendent serpent power," from which Shiva brings the universe forth. It is a branching tree of lightnings, an amorphous and homogeneous sea of thunderbolts. It is called serpent power by virtue of its movement, of shooting and darting. It reminds one of the Rainbow Serpent of the Australian aboriginal dreamtime who contains all creatures in its womb (and who was said to move along the earth, clearing out river beds, canyons, making caves and mountains). Parakundalini cannot be experienced during a persons earthly life because the body would perish before it. One can only gain its full experience at the body's dissolution, in the Spirit. It conceals itself in order to reveal itself because nothing manifest can stand before it. So it is robed in cloud. It stands concealed within the manifestation, within the heart of things. When it functions to conceal itself, it is called mayashakti, creating a dance of illusion.

The experience of inner kundalini (energy) represents a portion or branch of parakundalini that dwells in all bodies. Within us it functions as the dance of inner world sparks, and sustains the activity dance of our bodies. It is called kulakundalini, and exists in various states from subtle to gross. Our kundalini comes from the sun, like the lightning. The Blue Sun behind the yellow sun is Shiva, which shines through all things. We invoke the subtle Blue light to purify our mind and body so our inner kundalini can rise in our body like a lightning to unite with Shiva (the spark of Blue Sun at our crown).

The universe of 118 worlds is inseparable from Shiva: it is his creative circle or City of Lightning. Shiva is shining through everything. It is only our minds which fail to see this. It is within this body that we can realize Shiva. This body is the temple which Shiva creates around his heart. It is like the space and stars. The Pole Star is the soul, Pleiades is the crown, sun is the heart, and so on. Just as our spirit is a seat of dharma in our life, the Pole Star is the seat of dharma within the universe. Shiva is the center and circumference, of atoms, cells, body-minds, solar-system, universe, all galaxies.

Shiva and shakti are one and the same just as thunder and lightning are one and the same. Shiva takes the form of the universe through his shakti(s), his power of will, his power of knowledge or ideation, and his power of activity. These are the levels of all creation, from a plant to a thought. The will, vision and activity, exist simultaneously with the Void and its parakundalini. The Silence exists within and throughout the symphony of nature. From a relative standpoint we say that there is a "continuum" Tantra, where Void exists first, energy second. Through energy, Shiva develops into will, vision, then activity. Each arises from the one before it. Where a thought comes from we cannot really see, we might feel the flash of arising in the heart, the motivational will-power, but the silence before this we do not see. To look into this silent space is to look into ones self-nature, Shiva, the witness and creator of thoughts, of our life-being. We're seeking to set our hearts at rest in this space, to stabilize our awareness on this space. When our hearts look upon reality through the senses we see the universe of our Self. If heart is unclear, reality is unclear. If heart is clear—Shiva, the reality is perceived clearly as Shiva. Shiva's vision is light (vid) which is shining everywhere, from the hearts of our being.

Shiva conceals himself like lightning in the clouds, then reveals himself (in the mind) like a lightning-bolt from the clouds. We call him Megharaja, King of the Thunder-clouds. Thunder means beginning. It is Shiva's word (vac) made vibrant—visible. It is Shiva opening his eyes to illuminate himself. Nature is Shiva's Vision or the revelation of himself. Light(ning) is Shiva's thought made visible. Thunder is Shiva invoking himself, through sound. Sacred language such as Sanskrit and enlightened language mimics or reflects language of the Thunder-beings which is first language. Thunder is the first language in the universe and on earth. The Voice of Thunder always expresses the Truth, Eternity, what is already of past, present and future. So what Shiva says comes to exist—such is the meaning of indestructible speech.

The Lightning-bolt has two prongs, one is protective, emanates, the other its reverse, dissolves or withdraws. Shiva's power and function is self-illumination. In order to awaken that which has fallen into the sleep of illusion, that which has become exiled from its Source, something must be withdrawn and something new infused. So we call Shiva Hara. Ha means to remove suffering, Ra means to infuse new light (Ra or Da is equated with the creators voice of thunder). In the Spirit or Mind-sphere what is withdrawn is ignorance and the energy arising from it as negativity; what is infused is pure Wisdom and its energy of bliss. The two-prongs of white-light and dark-light is a Vision of ebullient love; it arises as a beautiful, quiescent universe, and destroys causes of suffering. It is electromagnetic, positive-negative, presence-absence, awareness-emptiness non-dual Consciousness. When

it becomes limited and distorted in the mind, it becomes attraction-repulsion, it becomes the dualistic or broken vision of reality. Non-dual Consciousness means attaining unlimited Vision of Reality by dissolving minds barriers of fear, desire, anger. When the pure Consciousness experiences reality through a contracted or limited vision, it sees reality as broken. The energy surrounding the heart is broken, so the heart looks through it and experiences reality as broken, one way OR another, hot OR cold, pleasure and pain, good and bad, etc. Reality becomes a source of suffering and pleasure. Whereas in truth Reality is a Source of pure bliss. It shines within us and in all things, so every time the mind meets reality through purified senses, bliss is experienced. When the mind is not able to see Reality clearly in its mirror, then it thinks this is bad, that is good, this causes suffering, that causes pleasure. So this dualistic mind must be purified or liberated. When this energy or awareness becomes liberated, the Consciousness (Shiva) experiences reality as it is, as its very own wisdom-display. Shiva experiences hot in cold and cold in hot, fire in water, water in fire, space in solid and solid is space, presence in absence, absence in presence, darkness in light, light in darkness, silence in all sound and sound contained in silence, time in Eternity and Eternity in time, changelessness in the mutable and the mutable in the changeless, doubt in trust and trust in doubt, purity in impurity and impurity in purity, etc., etc. Consciousness in its primordially unified state is experienced in this way.

Lightning doesn't appear out of nothing and it doesn't become nothing. This lightning arises as the Spirit and power of the Origin. Its two prongs, one protective, one destructive corresponds to Shiva's activity of revealing and concealing, projecting and withdrawing, creating and destroying—white-light and dark-light. He is absolute freedom to create and destroy because his Mind is Void, unobstructed emptiness and unstoppable power. His autonomy is displayed in the Lightning of the Spirit and the atmosphere. His activity of self-illumination arises from Void into flow through the intermediary of energy. The energy has three essential phases, again: will, knowledge and action. Thunder signals this transitional phase, as spring signals the beginning of birth on the earth. In Tantra it is spoken of as a billows, a slight throb in the belly of a fish, a flash. It is a radiant pulse into a wheel of ebullient bliss. This is the beginning of the universe and our mind. It doesn't mean we have to hear thunder and lightning, but that same subtle power is weaving our thoughts from that same silent ground of Universal Mind. The visible universe and thought are the revelation of Shiva, the sign and signature of the Mystery. The universe and thoughts are the orchestra played by the hands and winged-hearts of Eternal Tranquility. It arose out of silence and will inevitably end in Silence. But who knows how many numbers He has queued up for us. The idea is to recognize the silence emanating the music of life as ones own consciousness. Look for the silence and rest in it. Use the music of life to dissolve into silence—Om Namah Shivaya. Om Namah Shivaya contains all other sounds. Its luminosity creates all forms. It is a vajra or thunder-bolt. It creates everything out of space in a flash, and in a flash it destroys what was created. It is a great potential like an atom bomb. It is the secret origin of all things, the cause of their appearance and disappearance.

The spontaneous pulse of the Uncreate is the pulse of Shiva (flow of phenomena) from the womb of Undifferentiated Space. This creative potential space is our heart and is symbolized by the Cloud of the Mystery. The cloudy cloak of the Undifferentiated is unzipped and you see phenomena, the universe. So vajra stands for this revelation of Eternity. Vajra denotes Shiva's Eternal Reality, his invincible nature as Void. Vajra is likewise his revelation, his flash out of space. From the standpoint of phenomena, the vajra is a revelation of Ultimate Reality: the cloak of the universe and the heart is unzipped for a second and you see God. You feel the power. It is throughout the spheres of mind and existence, it gathers together and flashes forth to awaken and nourish the mind and earth. Shiva manifests as power because beings forgot inherent space heart-nature. Shiva manifests as forms because beings do not recognize limitless light within them. Shiva manifests as mantras because beings do not recognize the subtle soundless resonance of space.

The revelation of Shiva as shakti, power, light (imagery) and sound (mantra), is the vajra. It has two functions, to dissolve the dark and leave behind a light, to take away what obstructs space and to enhance the light of awareness. The shakti is the cause of our enlightenment. One of its shapes is lightning, another is a Blue Sun, another is a limitless ocean, another is Shiva's image and mantra. Om Namah Shivaya is the sound-light of the shakti. It is the first utterance of shakti, its first sound. When we utter it, this shakti dissolves us into space. We're uttering Shiva and shakti, space-sound-light, so we become Shiva-shakti, space-sound-light, tranquility and bliss. We ingest the nectar of God's name and we become that nectar, it fills us up and empties us out. It fills us with bliss and removes all suffering.

Shiva is our indestructible heart-essence, silence and its flow. By paying attention to the silence we can become that through and through. By paying attention solely to the flow we have become that, but it is not who we are, it is only the sign of who we are. By paying attention to our infinity we become omniscient. This heart is the root of our lives, the beginning of the pulse of consciousness and body. As the pulse of the body initiates its throb and flow (transformation), so the pulse of the mind initiates its throb of inner-transformation.

The primordial power polarizes into positive and negative. The power is controlled by Shiva, by the controlled Mind. The two poles come together producing friction and bliss and is represented by the friction of the union of Shiva and his consort shakti. From their sexual union a third is created, tangible energy, a flash. The geometric diagram of this development is the triangle (trikona), the yantric symbol of Shiva.

The function of Shiva is to illuminate, awaken and reveal. He conceals his Self, manifesting the appearance of different forms, the appearance of something other than radiance. Shiva actually casts a veil in the heart of all beings. The reality of the universe is nothing but Shiva—blue light. Primordial energy permits Shiva's experience of his infinite nature, the one become many And it is what yolks him to himself, so the many become one, they yearn for this. We arise from our uncontracted state as Shiva, auspicious, omniscient wholeness. We ferment in the universe for a time, then return ourselves through Shiva's grace, which is in our own yearning, to our original state. Primordial energy is the vehicle or fuel which takes us into the universe and which returns us to our Source. Tantra is the means of generating this energy to achieve our aim. Because Shakti is an indispensable part of Tantra, the female consorts of Shiva are worshiped. Because Shakti is an integral part of Tantra, sexual yoga is performed. Because Shiva's shakti is embodied in the female form, we combine worship of shakti with sexual posture to achieve the highest aim.

Shakti is luminosity dancing in the Eternal field. It conceals and reveals, makes things contract and expand, which is the foundation of cyclic existence, of birth, growth, decay, death. It can be depicted in many ways, as the trident, the nagas, the kundalini, the Divine Mother. The adept seizes hold of this current in order to electrify the mind. The method to achieve this is in the power, which develops into sound (mantra) and image (murti). The nature of mantra is the arising of Infinite Consciousness through sound. You are hearing the sound of the kundalini, which is figured arising from the divine mouth or heart. Shiva displays shakti as lightning.

Shiva puts the lightning in the universe to awaken things to see minds expand rapidly, heal rapidly, learn rapidly, liberate rapidly. The shakti in whatever configuration of light, whether sphere or lightning, sound or image is the gate into Infinite Consciousness, our primordial state. With the power of thunder Shiva initiates the flow of creation and the return of things back to their timeless Origin. Therefore Shiva's grace (shakti) is represented by the Lightningbolt. Through primordial energy (shakti), Shiva demonstrates his quality of flowing and gathering. Shiva is the space before the universe. He flows outward as light displaying the universe, he reabsorbs that universe as part of its natural cycle, thus exemplifying his forward-backward, creative-destructive capacity. Shiva's object is to absorb us and in fact this is the longing of our hearts. The veiled heart perceives many flames, many desires because it doesn't remember the experience of Shiva which is fulfillment, so it ignorantly seeks Shiva in many things. And Shiva shines through the world of mundane experiences. But his full beatitude is only in him, the super-mundane, in dissolving in him. When the heart is unveiled it reveals this singular urge. And it is Shiva shining in that urge. The basis of Shiva's sadhana is to seize hold of the primordial power of the universe which both projects and absorbs all things. We do this through sound (mantra) and light (image), these are the manifestation of Shiva and his Primordial Power of anugraha shakti.

Supreme Grace (anugraha shakti) is responsible for our achievement. It is the three shaktis in one—the trident of wisdom. The first shakti (will) causes creation, it causes a light to arise in the mind. The second is vision, it is the insight or knowledge which arises out of this light. The third is the activity which removes ignorance and suffering. These are the functions of Shiva's grace in the universe. The sound of this grace is Om Namah Shivaya.

Om Namah Shivaya: The Holy Mantra Garland of Five Letters Which Illuminates Consciousness

Om Namah Shivaya is Shiva's essential mantra of accomplishment. Om Namah Shivaya is the supreme invocation of Shiva's illumination, it is the supreme heart-essence of Shiva, and the supreme path to liberation. Lord Shiva initiated civilization and was the first teacher of Sanatan Dharma. Just as he sustains the universe, so he sustained Dharma through Rama and Krishna in the intermediate yugas (Treta and Dvapara). In the Kali yuga he incarnated as Haidhakan Shiva in order to remind people about the dissolution of the eon and to teach practices suitable to this time. Om Namah Shivaya is the most suitable practice for people in this yuga, because it purifies the mind. It causes inner mahakranti (dissolution). Shiva's going to destroy the universe, he's going to destroy our illusory vision of something other than Shiva. Haidhakan Shiva teaches us to destroy the cause of suffering in our life, so that this cause (ego) does not destroy us. Shiva's going to bring us back to rest through purification. Through Om Namah Shivaya we're purified. Through it we are enlightened. Through it we're protected.

Haidhakan Babaji said: "The energy of Om Namah Shivaya shall destroy all contradictory energies of hydrogen and atom bombs and will protect you. There are proofs in the scriptures, that it was the great Gautama Rishi who created the atom energy, and he has said clearly that the only thing that can conquer the atom energy is the Om Namah Shivaya mantra, by itself."

Haidhakan Babaji has taught that repetition of this mantra will lead to total union with God. When we gather together in groups to repeat it, Shiva actually comes down and opens the path of quick transformation to all. Everyone comes under his protection and is liberated from suffering. When we repeat his name in silent, our mind returns to its natural wise state. Shiva inspires the heart, opens it, uplifts it, clears the mind, makes one tranquil and joyous.

Babaji urges his devotees: "Always repeat God's name. Whatever you do, wherever you are, repeat the name of the Lord. . . . Om Namah Shivaya is the original mantra . . . it is like nectar, feed everyone with this nectar. . . . When mahashakti, the Primordial Energy, first manifested, the words she uttered was the mantra Om Namah Shivaya." We should use it continuously. When eating, sleeping, driving, bathing, meditating, we repeat it internally. This is a way of transforming life, of bringing worldly activity onto the path, of realizing Shiva or intrinsic freedom, of transforming ones body and environment into the mandala of Shiva. This japa acts as a stream to purify the mind, to awaken its inherent nature. As a meditation one should recite the mantra on the in-out breaths. This causes wisdom-light to enter through the heart, travel via two channels to the lungs and circulate through the 70 million nadis, purifying body of toxins, and mind of negative karma. Because virtuous activity also purifies negative karma, one can fully neutralize all negative acts committed by engaging in this recitation while performing self-less activity. This causes body and mind to be fully purified.

Shiva is a fire of Wisdom, a Lightningbolt which destroys what obstructs the tranquility and hearts free sovereignty or bliss. This mantra is the light-sound of great dissolution; he burns us up and wears the ashes. This means in essence we become liberated into Infinite space adorned in the universe. When the heart is revealed as Shiva it perceives reality as Shiva. Shiva's purpose to illuminate all beings is achieved by revealing himself as the root-essence of ones nature, the creator of inner worlds and what is beyond them, watching them. Through his luminous revelation we recognize Shiva as the witness to ourself, an eye watching itself.

Generally all Thunder-beings are purifiers, but specifically the practice of the 5-letter mantra is the greatest purifier on earth. This mantra is a force of purification. Through it Shiva provides a light which removes the root of suffering. Through this practice Shiva's grace of illumination rapidly dissolves negative energy and emotional states. This mantra destroys what obstructs the clear-light and space of the mind. It can be used to purify anything, person, place, situation—instantaneously. The result of this purification is peace and harmony. Om Namah Shivaya is just like lightning and thunder. It takes something away which causes suffering and leaves something new, light, fresh, vibrant. It heals, uplifts, turns things over so new growth can occur. Lightning turns whatever it touches into itself—same goes for Om Namah Shivaya. It turns our mind into Shiva—as quickly as lightning. It heals us and returns us to perfect tranquility and bliss, perfect inner freedom. To accomplish the 5-letter mantra is to become Garuda, whose flight is the hearts

perfect blissful freedom. Garuda is the transmuted body as well—vehicle to the stars. Shiva is the samadhi of our natural infinity, and Om Namah Shivaya is the means to attain it—the lightning yoga.

To use it now breaks the wheel of existence and closes the gates of lower rebirths. To use it when you die attracts Shiva who will release us from suffering into his sphere. To use it now causes supreme bliss and full awakening of the heart. To call upon Shiva this way causes him to appear as intangible light all around us and within us. Our internal circuitry will be blessed, our channels, our mind. Our mind will become like Shiva—tranquil, awake, blissful, luminous. Our body will be healed, the original state of the organs, bones etc., will be awakened, causing healing. Om Namah Shivaya heals all ills. Even though it appears as sound, it is actually light. When we say it, Shiva is saying it. We might visualize ourselves as Shiva to receive this descent of luminous blessing and as a reminder of who we are. By thinking of ourself in the image of Shiva then we're reminded of the pure qualities of Shiva. Also the light that arises when we intone the mantra is filled with trillions of tiny images of Shiva. It is full of Shiva's enlightening quality, it is full of tranquility and blissful love. So we might not visualize anything, but simply nurture gold intention for all beings.

Om Namah Shivaya awakens pure qualities in us, it awakens us to our natural tranquil and blissful state. If you wish to heal others, send up your heart-prayer on the wings of Om Nama Shivaya and your prayer will go to achieve its target like lightning. Or you might say the mantra and visualize Shiva over the being you want to heal, and visualize blue light descend into them. By visualizing this you cause it. The blue coloration is very important for healing, but the essence of the light is harmonious consciousness and loving intention, and this is what truly heals.

The mantra is sounding in the heart of all beings, which you can imagine as having five faces and 18 arms, as tranquil, effulgent etc. Through this sound Shiva is creating all thoughts, the body and the universe. By intoning the mantra we awaken to our heart-nature, and realize the view that we are creating, maintaining and dissolving the universe through sound. So a Tantric sage (aspect of Shiva) received this transmission because he realized his heart, body and universe was Shiva. Then he passed the mantra down with the view as oral transmission. The mantras literal meaning developed later as a result of ordinary conceptualization, the need of students to understand the mantra. The literal meaning views Shiva as separate, "I bow to Shiva", and was developed for those students who are not ready to view themselves as Shiva. But the mantras will take the practitioner to the point were they can realize themselves as Shiva. This mantra takes us to the goal. It invokes Shiva as blessing- light, bliss, love, righteousness, pure positive, celestial energy. So when we use the mantra we immediately experience this light, of bliss, love etc. We absorb this light and it awakens the light of our nature resounding in our hearts, it awakens our bliss, love, goodness, and so on.

Mantra invokes the subtle radiance of Shiva to arise through the heart and descend through the crown. The subtle light rides the vital breath (prana) which circulates throughout the body. The subtle sound moves from the Undifferentiated subtlest state (Shiva) through the heart (mind) to the prana (via channels to the lungs) into the blood which circulates through the 70,000 nadis (channels) to purify the entire body (of toxins) and mind (of negativity). It has the effect of speeding up the vibrational rate of atomic existence to produce awakening, to deepen and expand awareness. Light enters the atoms whose gross constituents (5 elements) are dissolved into their wisdom-source (Shiva). Mantra causes the gross atoms to dissolve into energy and the energy to dissolve into mind and the mind into pure uncontracted Consciousness. We are spiritualized and re-created in such a way into the subtle existence of the universe, so we dissolve into Shiva's Vision, which is Ultimate Non-dual Reality. Our energy is refined to the point at which it reflects Shiva. Shiva penetrates the mind as mantra, so the mind and body become Shiva. Mantra is the vehicle which takes us back to the subtlest formless state. This state is called samadhi or absorption or dissolution and is the necessary state for perceiving the universe and mind as a pulsating, scintillating bliss-body of Shiva.

In the light of this grace, and by the force of our concentration on the mantra, recognition takes place of ourselves as Shiva. By our inner thoughts (language) we create reality; if we tell ourselves we're afraid we give power to that fear so that we become fearful, if we tell ourselves the truth about ourselves that we are Shiva, then we give power to that truth to become Shiva. When we have afflictive states we alter our body and mind in a negative way. For example, when we're afraid the fear makes us cold and darkens our nature. Our body might actually shake. With this in mind think of what fear generated over one or many lives can do. It can cause illnesses and great suffering.

It must be cut off at its root. When we're angry, the anger makes us hot and darkens our nature. Our body becomes hot and we might loose control and sting, kill or harm others. Over one or several lives of generating anger, this will cause illness, calamity, hell. All of the five afflictive states can be looked at this way, they all result in temporal suffering. The root of them is in the heart, the beginning of thought. When we use Om Namah Shivaya, the root of the five afflictive states is liberated or purified. Therefore the root of all suffering and lower rebirths is sealed off. OmNamah Shivaya is the root of eternal or unbroken tranquility and bliss— positive states.

Om Namah Shivaya is the light of knowledge that purifies and dissolves the root of all our bad mental habits. Poor mental habits are the root of harmful activity. So if we create the habit of reciting mantra, we will express this naturally in our activity. Our activity will not be governed by ignorance and aflictive states that arise from it. Our activity will be governed by the Infinite Spirit shining within, by peace, love and harmony, truth, simplicity and perfection.

Repeating the Name, we become the Name. Since the mind is a mirror it reflects whatever sphere we turn it to, it reflects all the thoughts and activities that arose from it. Those trace-impressions color the mirror and transform it, they settle on its surface or clean that surface, the very surface which Shiva peers from, and creates from. The Name clears these traces to reveal the unstained surface as Shiva's own Mind. The mirror of the heart is purified in the radiance of the mantra, so the nature of things as reflected in it are perceived clearly as one pure essence.

Om Namah Shivaya is Shiva's primary mantra and can be used to contact any aspect or energy-body of Shiva, such as peaceful, fierce or wrathful forms, or masters like the mahasiddhas or ones own guru. The mahamantra (great mantra) was extended by Lord Shiva thousands of years ago through a mahasiddha, and comes to us through unbroken lineages of siddhas. It comes to me through Haidhakan Babaji and Shiva. It is the initiation mantra of Siddha yoga, Shiva's vehicle of identification. Shiva arose as Primordial Energy and its first utterance was Om Namah Shivaya. Through it creation was initiated. It is written in the foundation of the universe and mind. So by repeating it, it invokes the subtle Emissional Power which is causing reality. To seize this power is necessary to return to our Origin. Through this mantra alone we can achieve this. When we repeat it we should take the view that Shiva, the mantra and ones mind are one—

Shiva. You are bringing Shiva into your mind (as sound) to make a light so you can recognize Shiva (as mind).

Om Namah Shivaya can be understood in five deep ways, which are interwoven. If you want to think of this mantra by linear meaning, then you can think that in ancient times, our ancestors, Deities and dakinins who served Shiva proclaimed this mantra out of their shear devotion and actually bowed before Shiva, their guru as Shiva and Shiva's mind-born images. By doing so they were blessed by Shiva's hidden grace. We use this mantra to bow to Shiva as all-pervasive Consciousness and receive grace in this way. So through Shiva's blessings we are enlightened, awakened to the fact that Shiva is everywhere, and by repeating the mantra we awaken our inherent love for our Self. It means "I bow to Shiva" so it implies that a sacrifice is being made so that we can literally be awakened within to see we are Shiva. Second, it means "I do the will of God," so it opens one to the subtle rays of will and righteousness (appearing blue and yellow like the stars and Sun), which is the wisdom which destroys negativity, heals the mind, and provides well-being. Repeating the mahamantra awakens us to the wisdom-light that is all around us, that is who we are. It clears the mind and causes our recognition of limitless Consciousness. It magnetically attunes the mind to God, who arranges ones life energy around the powerful nuclear center of the heart, like filings arranged around a magnet. It magnetically attracts Shiva's power to us, which we gather and which erase all the karmic imprints (of negative thoughts and activities) stored in our mind. These imprints cause suffering and desires and bring us back to earth time and again. So this mantra ends suffering and transmigration. Shiva becomes imprinted in the mind, revealed there actually, and is beyond the universe, beyond time. It causes God to take a seat in your heart, and that creative energy to radiate as bliss, inspiration, love. It causes body-mind to dissolve into Shiva to become Shiva, auspiciousness, beauty and truth. Thirdly, the mantra is the first thing God uttered in the universe, it is the breath of God, the Will, Vision and Activity, the Consciousness crystallizing into form. It is the sound-symbol of the trident of 3-shaktis. So it is the fuel that propels us into existence and brings us back. It is the initiating sound, the Voice of Thunder echoing from the heart of Eternity. It brings our thought, our mind or energy back to rest in its Origin, so it brings our soul-spark back to rest in its Origin. It leaves us thoughtless so we are mindful. It strengthens memory as it clears the mind. It is the sound of reversal, it brings us and all those within our radiant field, back to our tranquil and joyous state. Fourth, it is the Name of God, his-her sound resonance, the sound of Infinite Consciousness whelling up in its heart, like a tear (Rudraksha). It is the name of the nameless, the sound of the soundless Void. The name is the key to the silence. As an eternal-spark, it evaporates the gross body which belongs to our parents and the universe, and which is a cause of suffering. Our living-death makes us truly present, as open and empty as space, as present as lightning. There is only ever the slightest membrane remaining, like a fragrance or film surrounding a bead of dew, or the particles which create rainbow coloration in a singular light substance. There is a new body created from the mantra and sustained by it, an immortal body of bliss—Shiva. This body is born of mantra, so it is the sign of the mantra, its Vision. For this reason as well, the mahamantra can be called a mother mantra. It is both the mother and the child, the child is symbolized in icon as the blue-baby Shiva.

The fifth meaning is in the individual letters. Sanskrit is a living, radiant language or body of sound. This body is called Maitrika Shakti. Each letter represents as aspect of Shiva where the resonance and meaning are the same. Shiva uttered these sounds, so they are eternal, alive, they have inherent wisdom and power. The meaning of the letters can be known by reciting the mantra and tasting the light in the heart. They correspond to Consciousness, bliss, will, knowledge, activity. These are the Source of the five elements. In the same way each wisdom-element corresponds to an aspect of Shiva's image-bodies. Na corresponds to earth, solidity of the image; Ma to water, fluidity of the image; Shi to fire, heat of the image; Va to air, mobility of the image; Ya to ether, spaciousness of the image. Om is Shiva, the totality and immutability of the image. By reciting the mantra, the five elements dissolve into their wisdom-Source, denoted by the six syllables. These sources might be figured as dakinis or rays of Mahashakti. Repetition of this mantra can cause transformation of all elements of ones life-being, ushering the breakthrough into spiritual reality. It liberates the heart. Because it destroys self-cherishing, we cannot help but be filled with love.

Shiva is creating the universe through sound, speech or mantra. His initial speech is paravac or "beyond speech," it is alive, precedes vibrational frequency, and is felt as an infinite depth of tranquility—Void. Shiva's voice or sound initiates and becomes the display of the universe; it is there as something, as pulsation, yet it is Absolute Tranquility—a mirror. Paravac is not produced from the collision of any two things, it is "unstruck," subtle or eternal sound (shabdabrahma), the Sound of pure Consciousness. Language is produced from the collision of any two things, two winds or electricities. Paravac is substanceless tranquility erupting into subtle sound. Subtle sound then develops into light by friction. This friction produces all forms of illumination from thought to star-light to vegetation, like when crystals are crushed there are tiny flashes. This friction is known as spanda "pulsation" and is bliss radiating.

The process of Shiva radiating into sound is delineated in 3 levels corresponding to the 3 shaktis of will, vision and activity. A spark of light issues forth from the will or paravac. The spark contains Shiva's idea or vision, of a world. It's like a bubble within which is a world. It makes a sound, as lightning makes thunder. And within that sound is stored all language, as within thunder there is language. Generally this sound in most language systems is Ah, the first letter. This spark of sound-light develops into gross appearance, "visible speech," pashyanti vac.

Sound is the power to create the universe. It remains eternally at the substratum of the universe. Keep in mind the universe was not created at some point in time, but is being created as a film in Eternity. Sound or pulsation is at its root. The Consciousness, bliss, will, ideation and activity of the universe all exist simultaneously. Pulsation exists eternally at this very moment and can be heard in the heart as the utterance of Consciousness, Shiva's sound-body, name, wisdom and primordial power. From this power infinite letters and syllables arise. The letters are the light form of the sounds. In Tantra these give rise to all inner and outer worlds. They are maya; they arise, are sustained for a time then fall away. What precedes them, threads them and weaves them is Consciousness. Consciousness creates them as a language, a dance of sound and light, of multiple sounds and lights, pulsating music and imagery.

Mantras arise before visible speech, as subtle sound, out of intuitive experience, out of a transmission from Shiva. They exist in potential or seed form in the Undifferentiated drop, which is the Heart of Shiva. In the body this drop exists either in the heart, a blip just below the heart-drop, or a drop just below the navel. It is both emptiness as unstruck sound (OM) and bliss. The seed of all (70 million) Sanskrit mantras is

Om. From Om, Consciousness develops into Om Namah Shivaya, which becomes the womb of all other mantras. Therefore it contains the functions of all other mantras, can be used to contact the deities and spheres designated by all other mantras, including those within the body, such as the deities of the organs. Thus using this mantra awakens the deity's of the body to heal the body. Likewise this mantra can be used to awaken the deities of nature, such as people, animals, and spirits, to converge harmoniously on earth. As a vehicle of one's heart, mahamantra acts as a vehicle or radio-transmitter to receive revelation from any sphere or deity. This is so, because it is the very wisdom-nature of all minds. It is considered a mother mantra for this reason, and because it is the mother (maitrika shakti) of the universe. Therefore it is taught that the Mother as primordial energy (mayashakti) utters this mantra as the first arising in the creation of the universe. Om Namah Shivaya corresponds with the wisdom-root of the 5 elements, or the amorphous energy-womb of the universe prior to branching into element-qualities, which is the Reality of the universe. It is actually the sound of the phenomena Source, of the 5 wisdom-lights. This Reality is Shiva, he and his sound are not different, thus it carries us to our Origin. The universe is a homogeneous mass of blue-light, "Face of Glory." All the souls in the universe and the universe itself dance as this blue-body of light which is Shiva Nataraja, the Cosmic Dancer. The blue-drop of our soul exists at our crown, in the center of its wheel (Chakra) and is called the Blue Pearl. So mantra, especially the 5-syllabled-Shiva invokes the blue radiance of the universe which comes through our soul and heart which are magnetically attuned to it. It connects us to the Transcendent Spirit and our Self—Inner God (which are one). Illumination is the substance of the universe; we perceive reality by virtue of this inherent radiance. Because Shiva's mantra is resonating at the root of the universe in the heart, it can be used to transform the universe. So as Shiva, you can use it to prevent wars, stop famine, cause weather changes, heal.

The five faces of Shiva gave all transmissions of Tantra. The ultimate origin of Om Namah Shivaya is the five faces. Each mouth uttered each of the five letters. The sixth letter Om is the root vibration that pervades all sounds, from which all sounds arise. The five letters are the expressions or variations of Om. Om is Shiva. Shiva has five principle shaktis and five activities. Each energy performs an activity. Each letter or sound invokes each shakti to perform the activity.

When the name is repeated internally, it is good to concentrate on the sound with the knowledge that Shiva is uttering it. It exists eternally in the heart as the Source of the five elements and the beginning of language. All the letters (sounds) of the alphabet come from the five. The mantra takes us back to the beginning of internal language (thought) which is silence. This is what we listen to—the sound of Eternity. Because it echoes eternally, at a certain point one may notice the sounds arising simultaneously. Repetition acts like a stream to purify the mind and awaken it to its inherent nature of bliss. It invokes Shiva's grace to descend as a blue-light, which heals, stills and uplifts the mind. (It corresponds with subtle blue lightning, the Mystery). When externally uttered, one should concentrate on the respective image, leave oneself open or concentrate on what you wish to achieve for others. We should nurture or cultivate an altruistic motivation to liberate all beings from suffering since this is Shiva's objective.

When you chant the mantra, in order to fully receive these blessings visualize yourself as Shiva (or at least think of ourself as Shiva). Our mind will take the form of Shiva. This represents our natural samadhi, so will cause us to recollect our natural state.

Shiva's image comes from vast inner space, it rides with his grace-waves, which bear his pure qualities and attributes, which are inherent in the image and mantra and our pure ground of awareness. His images and mantras are his continuous subtle body of sound and light. Shiva assigns multiple images and their mantras a certain function. They are living reality, he is the life of their life. The mantra and image raise the consciousness by causing the minds frequency to vibrate at a higher rate. Mantra and image are bridge to subtlest reality. Applied properly they turn the ordinary mind back to subtlest reality. They have the power to bring us to Eternal Tranquility and Bliss. The image and mantra are used to awaken or illuminate, to remove ignorance and to bestow wisdom, together they are like thunder and lightning. Like lightning and thunder they re-establish harmony is the spheres of mind and existence. Through the image and name Shiva enters the mind for the benefit of those who fail to recognize him in their mind. They are woven out of shakti (creative blissful energy) and wisdom. They are the gate by which Shiva reveals himself as formless Absolute, by which we enter Shiva-hood. The image

and name are the guru, the grace of Shiva concentrated into our field of vision which guides the mind from (gu) dark to light (ru).

These symbols are not static just as Shiva is not static. The symbol is the living dynamic force of Shiva and pervades reality unseen in the subtle threads of light and sound. To embrace the practice is to awaken to this reality which contains all Deities, images and mantras. Shiva works through these practices to bestow grace, siddhi and Shiva-hood.

As you chant Om Namah Shivaya visualize Shiva in front as follows: Shiva sits peacefully upon a tiger skin in full-lotus posture, his white skin smeared with the ashes of cremated egos. He has a blue throat or bluish-hued skin to symbolize his power to destroy the poison of the ego. When I saw this form, he had skin the color of blue sky to symbolize that he is the sky-like nature. He wears a tiger-skin of fearlessness and is surrounded by effulgent light. He is three-eyed (these are equated with sun, moon and fire (agni), denoting the three channels and internal lunar, solar and fire energies in those channels). He makes the Shambhavi mudra with his eyes. This denotes that he is ones state of highest realization or samadhi. He is two-armed. He makes the mudra of bestowing peace. His jata are coiled on his head and they hang freely down his back. The coil symbolizes the fruit of cultivation of wisdom, pure knowledge (brought forth from the ascent of kundalini shakti to merge with Shiva), and the ascent of the jiva to Shiva. From his crown a spray of sparks emerges and cascades to earth as the river Ganges. The outer meaning of this is as follows: the pure starlike souls arise from the Undifferentiated state into the galaxies of stars and descend to earth into bodies. The inner meaning is as follows: the state of Shiva implies that the channels are totally pure, the Ganges denotes the purity of the sushumna nadi or central channel. Because the Ganges is purifying, it also implies the stream of Shiva's grace. The free hair can also denote the descent of blessings into the world. The crescent moon is by his forehead which symbolizes the ambrosial result of contemplation, immortalizing nectar (amrita), and the birth of a new immortal body. It could also stand for the internal lunar energy of the left channel retracted up the central channel. Sometimes the Sun is by his neck which would symbolize the retraction of solar energy in the right channel. On his forehead, neck, arms, chest are the tripundraka (3 yellow bars of ash) and tilak (red essence) these are his three shaktis, three activities, three gunas and AUM.

So too, For each line there are nine deities in our body. The red tilak is the Shiva Netra—eye of primordial awareness. This is actually a sign of attainment of Shiva—awareness radiates from the forehead and body in as these bars. Through this awareness one gains control of the universe.

He is adorned by Rudraksha seed malas, which symbolize his compassionate activity to liberate beings. Rudraksha means "Shiva's tears," it is said that, looking upon suffering beings he cried, were his tears of compassion landed, these plants grew, so he prescribes their use as a rosary. He is adorned with nagas symbolizing shakti and control of inner and outer electricity. On his left is the trident which symbolizes the three shaktis, the illumination which creates, maintains and dissolves the universe, the light which causes us to recognize our inherent nature. The three prongs of trident are also sun, moon and lightning, the various methods Shiva uses to awaken beings and the aspects of our natural wisdom which are devouring like fire, cooling like the moon and water, and the two combined as lightning. The two lights, dark (moon) and light (sun) are combined in our hearts by which we know, in our eyes by which we see, in the luminosity of the universe by which we live, in its cohesiveness and fluidity, ability to congeal and disintegrate, in all elemental qualities. The elements themselves are this singular light, branched into five qualities.

Shiva projects, maintains and dissolves the universal vision through his energetic connection to things. Shiva is never disconnected from the universal display, people only forget their unbreakable link to Shiva through energy. Shiva projects and sustains us through energy, so consequently we connect with Shiva to dissolve through energy. The image of this energetic connection is the trident, the three-pronged Emissional Power. It is the umbilical chord or umbilicus mundi, through which the fetal universe and the Tantric adept grows, is sustained and dissolved. The trident is the Emissional Power and Baby Shiva is being conceived and born. In Tantra the trident arises from Shiva's navel. It is the primary tool of Shiva and his vast retinues. It is the three activities of creation, maintenance and dissolution. Three lotuses blossom on it which are the three powers corresponding to the three activities: willing, ideating and activating. These are like a flash of lightning, the trident is the thunderbolt scepter. It is the one power of Consciousness through which all forms blossom and return to their Origin. It is the Source and life-line by which all

energy renews itself. It is the power of Shiva to remove obstacles to the omniscient state, to remove suffering and its source-ego, to awaken minds and nourish all life. It opens the gate to the Mystery. It is illumination. Hanging on it is a horn and the damaru or double-headed drum, which together are thunder and lightning, Silence originating into sound and light that blossom into manifest worlds. It is the power to completely transform consciousness. To wield a trident is a reminder of Shiva's sovereignty in our lives, of our inseparable link to him-her.

The damaru opens the door to the Mystery, so we use it to invoke Shiva. Sometimes Shiva holds the damaru and a conch. We use both to invoke Shiva. The damaru and counter-clockwise spiraling conch symbolize respectively the creative sound (pulsation) which gives to creation and bliss, and the sound of dissolution which returns us to Infinity.

As you visualize Shiva, think that blue-gold light pours into you from him, and that you become purified, that you become Shiva. So arise as Shiva, think too that he is within your heart. Visualize yourself being flooded with blue-yellow light, which purifies you and destroys afflictions of body-mind. Once saturated visualize the light radiating from the Shiva in your heart like a Blue Sun, going out to liberate all beings.

The accomplishment of the mantra is called mantra-siddhi, and is denoted by the ability to say the mantra and have the image of the mantra appear before your very eyes. Haidhakan Babaji said that when we say the mantra Shiva should appear before us this way. This image is the subtle body of Vision which arises out of Om Namah Shivaya. It is an iridescent blue-light body, it is the ocean of Primordial energy. It is the body which we will take upon reaching the self-perfected state—Shiva. We think of his image when we practice because it is not different than our subtlest energy, our Inner Wisdom, it evokes our subtlest essence, its tranquility and power to come to the fore as a guiding light for ourself and those around us. According to our alignment, when we gain recognition of our Self-nature, when we gain the vision of the Blue Pearl at the sahasrara chakra, it will take the form of our cultivation. The vision of each of the four bodies (koshas) happens consecutively, from gross to subtle. As the body becomes purified, the eye of vision, mind becomes purified. First the physical sheath is seen as red light, then the subtle body is seen as white light, then the causal body is seen as black light, then the supracausal body (Blue Pearl) is seen as blue light. With the Five-syllabled mantra it will appear as Shiva. It will appear according to the method we embraced and the grace that comes through it. The highest attainment is that all four bodies dissolve into Shiva. You will actually see all phenomenon as Shiva. You are pervaded with Shiva, so all things are pervaded with Shiva. There is no more inner and outer, subject and object, only Shiva. You recognize your Self everywhere. And you love that Self everywhere.

The highest accomplishment is to be able to appear as Shiva bearing his qualities and five activities, free of all impurities. Because Om Namah Shivaya is the essence of the scriptures, of Shiva's instructions which arose through the intuition of the siddhas, by accomplishing this mahamantra one becomes the source of all instructions, of Sanatan Dharma. As Shiva one maintains the two systems of instruction, and demonstrates them in body, speech, mind. By accomplishing this mantra one becomes the heart of all Wisdom-beings, and the embodiment of Shiva's stream of blessings. Therefore one becomes worthy of self-worship and worship by others. The efficacy of worshiping devotees of Shiva as Shiva is presented in the Puranas. To worship oneself sustains recognition of ones continuum as Shiva.

Shiva-hood is not instantaneous, it is a gradual process of growing recognition caused by flashes of illumination, which are caused by Shiva to destroy negativity and uncover insight or wisdom. Insight only metaphorically appears like lightning, but it is self-appearance, and is not bestowed from someone outside us.

Because Shiva is behind our minds, all beings have no choice but to evolve, to dissolve. Haidhakan Babaji says, "there is no saint who was not a sinner and no sinner who will not become a saint." Our Consciousness is always unfolding itself into higher more liberated and spacious forms. Life is seeking unconsciously or consciously to liberate itself, to return itself to the Unborn state from which it arose. All our desires, all the individual flames of passions are one heart-flame seen through a broken glass. The heart is burning to unveil itself. By misinterpreting its language, by not paying attention to the essence, we forget the essence (what we're after) so desire ceaselessly. We desire many things thinking they will bring us to Shiva, to fulfilment. Not so. We must go through many bodies, many robes before we realize the naked state is the one we're after. We're after what we are,

like the shell and the nut. We're the nut but think we're the shell. We must train to realize we're the nut. Then we become truly nuts.

Let Om namah Shivaya be the prayer through which you offer yourself and activity to God to liberate all beings from suffering. This mantra is the sacrificial fire which burns up our negativity at its root, and burns up the negativity of all beings. It is the flames that surround active forms of Shiva, the flame that he holds in dancing images. The flames are the mantra, the grace-shakti of Shiva, Shiva is the dhuni or fire-pit. We offer ourself into the flames. It turns us into flames, into mantra, into Shiva-shakti. It turns us into a fire of great attraction, of love. This attraction causes beings to seek one out, to listen to wise-speech, to follow ones example. This fire causes beings to be warmed, to be pacified and happy in ones midst. It causes those close to be cooked, refined, dissolved, absorbed. Om Namah Shivaya is the sacrificial fire, the means of making life sacred. Offer everything into it, self or mind, heart, knowledge, virtue, body, wrong-doings, the universe, everything. This wisdom-fire burns up negativity, it causes nature's transformation, it leaves earth body and mind pure and clear and peaceful. At the end of a kalp it turns everything into ashes, at the end of a cycle of existence it turns us into ashes, vibhuti. The meaning of the word for ashes is "essence," the essence of what is burned up. Out of the flames of Om Namah Shivaya we rise up like smoke, we return to the Source, to space. Our essence, and that of the universe is Shiva-shakti, space and luminosity, infinite Bliss-Consciousness. The ashes Shiva wears after burning down the universe are simply the essence, Source or foundation of the universe, the mandala of Infinite Consciousness—Mind or Self. These ashes are Shiva's adornment, just as the universe, our body and thoughts are his adornment. Om Namah Shivaya causes our awareness to see that the essence or foundation of the universe is Shiva, that our nature is Shiva, and that our body is his manifestation. Namah is infinite manifestation; and Shivaya is Infinite Consciousness, or Omniscient Knowledge. These five letters are contained within the sound Om. Om is both Absolute and its manifestation. It is said that Om is the sound of the universe, resounding in the hearts of all beings. It is called nadabrahma or shabdabrahma, "sound of the Absolute." The letter Om has three parts, these are denoted by AUM. These are the three phases of anything: creation, maintenance and dissolution, the three shaktis which cause the three activities, and the three Deities which govern the three phases—Brahma, Vishnu, Rudra. When you say Om this way, you trail off into space, into infinity, it sets you at peace. When it unfolds in the hearts of all beings, the heart of the universe, it becomes Namah Shivaya. Through Namah Shivaya, the activity of the Absolute, of returning beings to peace is increased manifold. Om Namah Shivaya is the wisdom-sound of the Absolute, of the Lord of Thunder-beings, so, as his Thunder and Lightning, he causes the transformation which returns all beings to peace, to his nest. He causes the storms in nature which bring about seasonal transformation, and he causes the storm that creates, maintains and dissolves the universe.

Most Mahasiddhas achieved themselves through one essential or root practice. Many achieved themselves through Om Namah Shivaya. It is not necessary to do the visualization with the mantra. If you want you can just pay attention to the sounds with the sense that Shiva is uttering them. You can visualize any image of Shiva since they're all the same nature.

There is an amazing story which illustrates accomplishment of this practice. A great Siddha known as Sananda accomplished himself through the 5-syllable mantra. When it was his time to leave earth Shiva came for him. When they were ascending Sananda noticed black smoke coming from the nether realms, perhaps he also heard cries. He expressed his desire to go there, but they told him he hadn't said the proper mantras. He insisted, saying that if he couldn't go there, he would refuse to go to Shivaloka. So they took him there. Because his thought, his mind had become Om Namah Shivaya, when he arrived and saw the suffering he uttered Om Namah Shivaya! (As we say "O my God!") All the beings there were liberated by its power.

Om Namah Shivaya is in the Bible as Shiva is the God of that scripture and the practice of that tradition was "calling on the names of God." The Hebrew name given to Moses from the "burning bush" is Yah Vah Shim Ommen, in which the letters of the mahamantra are reversed. In some cases we reverse the letters and the power of purification is increased. But because Haidhakan Bababaji was Mechizedek we can trust that Om Namah Shivaya is the backwards and proper form to repeat since this is what he taught.

By accomplishing the practice of the five-letter mantra, you will be on the same level as Shiva. The heart, body and universe will be perceived as one living Self or Mind, a luminous awareness-space without boundaries. From ones infinite-heart arises this universe, as a projection of light in the formation of a wheel with spokes (Dharmachakra) or a spherical linga. This Wheel of Consciousness also has a particular image. This five-faced image is the eternal origin of Om Namah Shivaya, of the universe and of the original Tantric transmissions.

The Wheel of Infinite Consciousness and Its Eastern Face

Included in the above visualization (of yourself as Shiva), you can think that Shiva is in your heart with five faces. Each face peering out to the directions resounds a letter of the panchakshrita mantra. These Faces together uttered Om Namah Shivaya, and individually and in combination uttered the Tantras.

In Tantra, according to Trikasara lineage, it is Shiva Svacchandanatha who creates, protects and dissolves the universe of 118 worlds through his eighteen arms and five powers (faces). Each face or energy peers out to the five directions of space and each utters the 164 Tantras. In the Tantra-rahasya, the Face of the East is pearl-like, three-eyed, crowned by the crescent moon; the Face of the South is yellow, three-eyed; the Face of the West is that of freshly-formed cloud and is associated with destruction. The North Face is blue, three-eyed and is associated with grace. The upper or central Face is the Illuminator of Consciousness and is white or crystalline. Its name is Ishana. The names of the other faces are Vamadeva, Sadyojata, Tatpurusha, and Aghora. The central face corresponds to Consciousness, space and is the foundation of the universe. The other faces correspond to the shaktis: bliss, will, knowledge and activity. Each Face predominates over a cycle of four yugas or a Mahayuga (manvantara), at the end of which is a dissolution (mahakranti). Yugas represent both the cyclic existence of the macrocosm and microcosm. There are four yugas representing the four stages of life, happening on all levels from the minute to the vast.

The Solar System revolves around the Pole Star, the Divine Star-seat of Universal Consciousness. (Just as there are geographic arisings of pure Consciousness or piths, and psycho-physical arisings or drops, so there are cosmic star drops). When the Sun is nearest this star the Dharma governs through love, because it is a powerful magnetic pole, a Thunder-power. Most Wisdom-traditions suggest we come from the Pleiades. It is the crown of Nandi, Shiva's white Bull, (Dharma). Because his four legs are the four yugas, Dharma is definitely governed by the revolution of the solar system. Dharma has its origin in the crown, the seven stars of Nandi and our own crown where our spirit (Shiva) abides. Our body is a mirror reflection of the universal body of Shiva. Just as there are stars out in space, so there are stars, wheels of light in our body—together with bindus (drops), winds, channels, these are mind. From these lights arise Dharma when our mind is clear, unagitated. So the crown Chakra(s) are the crown of Nandi or Shiva. Our awareness is Shiva's third eye, our spirit is the Blue Star at the crown, the root of internal worlds is the heart, and so on. All the stars and 118 external worlds are in the body, the universe is in the spine. Our cells unfurl like pearls, like stars. Atoms unfold like galaxies—by spiraling.

Since the Pole Star changes every several million years, the divine star-seat must change, and perhaps certain aspects of the Dharma also change. Each form of Shiva presides over a kalpa (1000 yugas). So the five forms of Shiva are great electro-magnetic powers, or aspects of Shiva functioning in the universe, earth and all minds. The 19th kalpa called Shvetalohita was presided over by Sadyojata; the 20th kalpa called Rakta is presided over by Vamadeva; the 21st called Pitavasas by Tatpurusha; the 22nd called Shiva by Aghora; the 23rd called Vishva-rupa by Ishana. We are in the 23rd kalpa presided over by the central aspect of Shiva, the totality of all aspects. The 1st Mahayuga (cycle of 4 yugas) of this kalpa was governed by Ishana, the 2nd by Vamadeva, the 3rd by Sadyojata, the 4th (present) by Aghora, the final by Tatpurusha, the Northern dimension, the place of absorption. The final eon governed by Tatpurusha will end in dissolution and return to the Undifferentiated.

From each face Shiva emanated deities to function in the universe through the attributes, the predominant power of that face. The Face that is related to the emanation of Thunder-powers is the Face of the East, which is called Vamadeva (in this Tantra, in others it is figured as Tatpurusha). He is pearl-like, white with rainbow-hue. The pearl-like is dawning, the pearl symbolizes beginning. The soft morning light is pearl-like. The Face of the East is Omniscience, Vision, Wisdom.

Vamadeva represents the Eastern dimension of awakening and the Rudras—Thunder-beings. Vamadeva as the Eastern Face emanated Wisdom-beings that would be in charge of initiating and closing the fourfold cyclical life of the universe, of protection, restoration, keeping balance. Through Vamadeva, Rudras were emanated, "howlers," the thunder-power and star-beings. From his body as Vamadeva he discharged thunder and lightning, which tells us that this power is with the beings born of Vamadeva, the Eastern dimension. Shiva takes the form of Rudra to come out of the East bearing the power of thunder and lightning, the initiating wisdom of Vamadeva. Vamadeva also emanated Garuda(s). The Garuda is the revelation bird who carries the "winged word," or wisdom to restore things to order. Garudas are related to Rudras. Rudras have the ability to become Garudas, or bird-men with flashing eyes etc. When Thunder-beings (Rudras) descended to earth, they fought large snakes whom they would continue to battle. The Garuda Tantras and Bhuta Tantra, which are revealed by Vamadeva, teach how to utilize this Garuda power as the Thunders had used it and continue to use it, to remove snake poison, to exorcise etc. Garuda Tantras are also concerned with recognizing oneself as Shiva Garuda.

Vamadeva revealed these Tantras and Vama Tantras as well as Karma Yoga. Vama Tantras are concerned with pacification of malevolent spirits, the acquisition of siddhi and performing pure acts. These are not the same as Vamatantra or left hand practices, to my knowledge they do not derive from Thunder-beings. Vamadeva taught Karma Yoga. It had its inception on earth with the Thunder-beings, the ancient creators who worked self-lessly carving out geographic features, subduing monsters and creating animal life. Karma Yoga is the pure activity of Shiva, Dharma. For us it brings about re-union (yuj, yoga, yolk) with Shiva.

Vama means "left," deva "god." Vama means "contrary" and "beautiful woman." This dimension referes to the entrance to Shiva: grace, illumination. These are the powers which initiate life and which restore life, the power which melts the frozen energies which obscure our heart-nature. Our entrance to Shiva is through control, awareness and the awakening of kundalini, inner potential. Shiva reveals this power through Thunder-beings. It is Shakti. Shakti is associated with the left and with the Mother. The left hand side of Shiva (as Ardhanareshvara) is female, the right male. It symbolizes the shakti, the fuel to reach our goal, the dynamic fluid essence of the Mystery, the maternal energy that gives birth to kindness. This is fully embodied in the Divine Mother—Durga, who also has the coloration of the pearl.

Wisdom is a "beautiful woman," she holds up a mirror which is the capacity of the mind to reflect. The union of lingam and yoni, of Shiva and the Mother is the primordial union of Spirit and energy. She is the beauty within Reality, Shiva's beauty, that of our heart. She is the blessing of life, and life giving freely of itself. 1000-rayed, 8-armed Ardhanareshvara is the rain-maker, the non-dual Reality expressed by left red-female, right white-male. The beautiful face refers to the lightning, the shakti flashing to illuminate all minds. Vama also refers to the moon, as the left side of Rudra's chariot of the universe.

Vama means "contrary." It is the power or reversal, the Spirit which goes counter to the normal coarse of things—the sun-wise mundane world cycle of birth, growth, decay and death (satyuga, treta, dvapara, kali). Usually the moon is a symbol of this, but so is venus the "contrary planet" and the lightning spirits. Shiva is actually this power which breaks the wheel of cyclic existence. He causes the state of moksha (liberation), immortality, emergence or return to the Incomprehensible. The goal is symbolized by the full moon, the power to achieve it is the lightning-grace of rapid illumination. Shiva reverses the passage of time to before or beyond time. He causes us to be born back into the Unborn by taking us back and back and back. By taking us back he takes us forward. For us to evolve we must dissolve. Shiva is a clock which goes backwards, a Time which goes in reverse. He re-establishes the primal harmony of the eternally youthful state. He brings you back to your true "beautiful face," to the state when things are just a flash out of space, a slight throb in the belly of a fish. Through the Unborn spark, the Thunder-beings restore original state of things. They are bringing things back in time to before they fell out of harmony, to before the slightest veiling of the Original Mind. Thunder-beings are the Victors of Time, so Shiva is called Mahakala, Great Time, or Transcendent Time. Shiva has always stood for the reverse evolution of the universe, the dissolution of things into the Origin. Even the universe is a clockwise spiral. Shiva's power reverses the universe to its seed or spark state. From his Will arise manifestation and dissolution. Manifestation is related to the Sun, it is centrifigul, a movement from within outward. Gradually Shiva "closes his eyes" devweloping into inconscient matter. Absorption is related to the Moon and is centripetal or counter sun-wise. Gradually Shiva "opens his eyes," illuminates himself to himself, reveals himself to all minds. This is the state of return to rest out of movement, the state which all spiritual practices strive for whether Tantra or Yoga. It is indicated by the crescent moon by Shiva's head, the crescent-moon-eyes of one of the Thunder-birds, the moon between the two horns of Thunder-bird Isis and the Chief Thunder-bird. The trident symbolizes the waxing and waning moon and the lightning, these are symbols of the shaktis of reversal, the fuel which takes us back to Eternity. The lightning is the power of reversal because it changes the direction of energy, the direction of a path of movement. If we're moving according to samsara, when Shiva touches our life, we will soon be moving in the opposite direction, toward the Truth beyond time. Shiva is the natural synthesis of the power to project and withdraw. He functions to close the eyes and open them simultaneously, he measures out a time for everything, a time to enter the universe of cyclic existence and to break out of it. We must recognize that the human arc is an arc of ascent back to Shiva. This is what he designated, like the signature of the rainbow in the sky. We must embrace the centripetal movement of phenomenon back to its center, or you might say it is time to ride the Garuda to the summit of Meru. All the unnecessary troubles we have are generated from not flowing with this natural confluence of light back to its Origin. The Siddha path is the return of the exiled spark to Shiva.

In the Matangatantra, the word Vama denotes the mystical, the guhya or "secret." Guhya means "cave" too, so it is residence of Shiva in all beings' heart. It is synonymous with the word bhaga which means yoni, womb-door and womb. So it is the entrance to Shiva. When in the Tantra sexual imagery is used, it very often, depending on the context, implies this entrance, or grace. The union of Shiva and shakti denotes Nondual Reality, the symbiosis of polar opposites. It is a secret because it cannot really be communicated, it is even unthinkable. Nevertheless it is found within the cave of our heart. Its profound reality can barely be hinted at. Tantra uses sexual imagery to communicate bliss. Shiva uses thunder and lightning imagery to transmit its function to awaken bliss.

Rudra: The Howler

Rudra is the initiating and dissolving Wisdom of Shiva. He was born from Shiva's heart (while Brahma, Vishnu were born from his legs). He has several forms, eight of which are central and correspond to the elements. Some are four-armed with attributes others are two-armed without. One of the primary eight is known as Ashani, and is the Primordial Thunder Lord. He flies out of the East in the midst of a great Thunderstorm. This signifies initiation, the dawning of the clear-luminescent Consciousness—enlightenment, and dissolution into the state of Shiva. After a long night of the sleep of ignorance, Consciousness dawns with its morning thunder, the thunder dissolves us back into Shiva. He rides among the storm-clouds. He has a man's body to reveal that we are Shiva and he is our potential as Cosmic Man (Tatpurusha). He is a giant, with such a body he perhaps walked the earth in ancient times. He is naked, symbolizing that he is Reality unadorned, naked Consciousness, non-dual. He is pure white, as white as the clouds he travels with and the lightning he controls. This symbolizes his immaculate purity, freedom from bondage to ignorance, pristine awareness, unobstructed Vision. He has black hair which falls to his shoulders and a black moustache. He is the black and white lights of the Mystery. He has a fierce expression. He teaches us how to utilize our aggression for the purpose of attaining realization and awakening others. Anger and joy are the same energy experienced at different levels of awareness. The awakening of anger brings a power of bliss, its original state. The Vision does not mean Shiva is angry. Rudra has no attributes besides the thunder and lightning, which are his ability to pacify negativity and enlighten the mind. Rudra dissolves all the ills of life, the root of death, so his sadhana has this function. In the etymology of his name, ru stands for ruk "disease" and dra stands for dravi "melter," "dissolver." He is also called Howler. He roars thunderously, the vibration and mysterious activity of which dissolves negativity, it heals. His power is a great medicine. His voice is the divine will announcing the Wisdom of the Absolute. It dispells negativity by penetrating the mind with its Mind. He mixes his Mind with ours by penetration, and awakens it thus. He uses sound and light to achieve this. His howl is the HUM, the symbol of Mind. Simultaneously he raises his right arm and shoots lightning from the tarjani mudra which he makes by pointing with the forefinger. This is the threat gesture symbolic of overcoming hindrances or obstacles. The lightning which he shoots is one streak with no forks, it is pure Wisdom-light, pure Vision. He is giving diksha, which generally means initiation and specifically means to remove darkness and provide insight (inner sight). Rudra connects with us so we can connect with him. When it strikes it shines in the mind as a brilliant white light. It literally saturates a person with the clarity of immutable awareness and bliss. It is kundalini. It heals magnetically, the power of love brings the pieces of scattered energy back into harmony, so the mind-body is made whole. It recreates the minds energy-body, reorganizes it into the configuration of its own enlightened Wisdom. It awakens the same Wisdom within as an inherent state of harmony. This is Shiva's luminosity descending into the finite or gross vision of reality. This shakti is known as anashrita shakti. It is a protective-destructive power. Just as it destroys all negativity when it strikes the target, so the yogi who absorbs himself in it through the sadhana, brings about the destruction of all sins and receives protection. That is why in the Tantra it (Shiva) is spoken of as the one true place of pilgrimage or refuge: kshetra—ksha is from kshapana, destruction of all sins; tra is from trana, protection. This place is the heart-mandala of Rudra, his Wisdom infused in the heart, his City of Lightning.

Rudra has arisen in the universe and yet you see him flying on currents of light as silent as thunder as loud as space. He is the electric body of Shiva, the Lightningbolt in the shape of a cosmic man. His flight is the emergence of light from the heart of reality. He is the Lightning-bolt at the center of the wheel of Eternity and he is clothed in wisdom-image and sound. His illumination takes us back to Eternity. His flight is our remergence, our emergence into Light. His flight is the emergence of omniscient Vision.

This form of Rudra is called Vidyut Ashani Rudra, which means the Howler with Lightningbolt Illumination. Ashani is related to the word to illuminate, perhaps also to meteoric iron or thunder-stone. Ashani refers to Lightning and is a word related to his names of illumination, like Isha, Ishana, Ishvara. Ashani is clear luminous Spirit, because of its electric existence we can experience it. Ashani refers to Rudra's power to cause dissolution. It is the power of Universal Destruction. It is very beautiful. In the Veda, Rudra is the name of Shiva as Destroyer. This is the form that Shiva takes at the dissolution of the universe and mind. Vidyut means lightning and is related to the root vid or ved (as in Veda) which means "to know" or "see" and is related to our root vis: vision, visual, what is seen. Vidyut is therefore what of God is seen. Vidyut implies revelation. Vidyut is the light of Consciousness which makes things internally visible as our awareness is its spark, and externally visible as our eyes contain its light. It is the light of knowledge, of insight. The

Vidyut-Ashani is the same as the vajra (above). The vajra denotes the heart which is spontaneously flowing into a sound-light texture of inner or outer reality. Vidyut-ashani designates the actual illumination. So you have Rudra, his heart, and its revelation. The deeper interpretation of his name is The One who Destroys Sins with the Power of Universal Destruction (Ashani) and Protects the Soul with the Power of Universal Creation (Vidyut). On the deepest level, I feel vidyut denotes white-light, ashani denotes dark-light. Together they are his indestructible power, his capacity to remove obstacles. His power clears a path to Recognition. Our vision is cleared, knowledge or Vision replaces ignorance. Low frequency energy which prevents our unlimited clarity and blissful radiance is awakened. His Will, Vision and Activity frees us within. It is expressed in his Voice of Thunder.

Rudra stands for initiation; he initiated the cycles of the universe, he awakens through the power of Supreme Illumination. White is his color which stands for awakenment, awareness, light, enlightenment. Rudra's power corresponds with his whiteness, or Absolute nature. His white is hot like snow, cold like fire. Elements at the level of Shiva are metaphors for various states or attributes of Consciousness. These are various flavored lights of one substance, one taste, like flavors of ice-cream. Ether is a metaphor for his limitlessness and clarity. Air stands for his apparent mobility. Fire stands for luminosity, what makes things visible. Water stands for fluidity and cohesiveness, earth for solidity and immutability. They are naturally inherent in the image, our infinite vision and all phenomena.

Rudra is the image of Primordial Thunder Lord, the Lightningbolt of Eternity. He is one white Lightning emitting sparks of the souls of 350 million (Rudras) who dance as his white-star body of inner space. This is Rudra's City of Lightning. Shiva's is blue. Both are dancers, bodies of lightnings, shooting, darting, striking, bodies of souls. Infinity contains all the Cities of Lightning or Wisdom-spheres like drops of nectar, indivisible chemical light-compounds. We arise from these Wisdom-spheres.

Rudra's atmospheric manifestation mirrors his mystical lightning-body (City of Lightning). The Ashani is all-pervading electric energy (tadit-shakti, vidyut-shakti), the nature of cosmic and animal life. The lightning is sympathetic to all nature of life. Shakti is the green organic light, fire and water. The lightning-bolt of the atmosphere is a gross-vision of

Rudra, which gathered invisibly. Ashani is the spark-of-universal-destruction (vaishvanara-agni), made of protective and destructive elements. It is Shiva's power of manifestation, preservation and dissolution in one—the trident and vajra of 3-prongs. The lightning of the Spirit and atmosphere serve the same function on both sides of the universe. Rudras serve this function, they are many and yet One. Their Origin and totality is Rudra or Maharudra; they are his transformation bodies. Many have arisen on the earth in the bodies and some are here now. Many are in the upper sky and make storms. 350 million are star-beings, an invisible-visible cosmic body of Rudra. Stars are the doorway to the higher lokas, of which Shivaloka (sachikand: 7th heaven) is the highest or subtlest. There are eight main aspect-Rudras and innumerable emanation-Rudras, which together form one mandala. Usually Shiva-Rudra's children arise into the universe through his third-eye of omniscient Vision. They are Rudras many Visions. Mythologies reveal Shiva becoming fierce and shooting lightning-bolts from his 3rd eye electric lamp. When the smoke clears a wrathful child stands there, ready to perform a function. In one such myth, a terrible monster wanted Parvathi, so Shiva became angry and opened his eye. When the lightningbolt hit the earth it became a lion-headed being hungry to devour this monster. This is a reality, there are beings which Shiva emanates to eat evil spirits, I have witnessed it. The monster pleaded with Shiva, so Shiva told his bhairava to eat himself instead. In which case he began with his feet and devoured himself, leaving nothing but a face. Shiva called it the Face of Glory because he was very pleased, and said whoever failed to bow to this Face could not reach Shiva. The idea is that without self-control and mind-control one cannot realize Shiva within. Therefore this Face is placed at the entrance to Shiva temples in India.

Mythologically the Rudras have arisen from the thrashing of his locks (jata). They arose from collision which produces a sound like cracking a thunder-whip, and which produces a flash like the light which arises when a crystal is crushed. The jata are their Mothers, writhing energies, shaktis. Each lock is a bundle of singular rays or dakinis. The jata are his channels, currents of light going out into the universe. The Rudras may also be related to pranas "breaths" in the earth and perhaps mind. They appear like Rudra-Shiva: they're white, have jata, three-eyes, weapons and sometimes chariots that gleam lightning. They can take bird form, and their glance can kill. They are Shiva's Thunder-birds, the Garudas.

The basic sadhana for invoking Rudra and for purifying and dissolving into Consciousness is called the Shri Rudram. The Siddha Yoga lineage practices this text and I do as well. Since it may be rather hard to come by, it is sufficient to use one of the most significant mantras from the text, which is as follows: Om Namo Bhagavate Rudraya Vishnave Myityur Me Pahi. This mantra is very ancient and sacred, it provides mind-protection and protection from death. It invokes the white-light image of Rudra to arise and destroy the causes of decay and death, it envelopes the mind in the armor of Rudra. He can be visualized as above. For silent japa: visualize Rudra in the heart and hear the mantra as his utterance arising from the image. For chanting japa: visualize Rudra at the crown while repeating the mantra aloud. Next we supplicate him to descend and to unite his mind with ours. Thenceforward we visualize ourself as Rudra, and feel like him. In order to feel like him you must have received an initiation. Therefore who-ever practices this should visualize him at the crown, until Rudra gives the initiation. This practice stimulates recognition that one is Rudra, it destroys and recreates us as a luminous fully awake bliss-body.

He brings about our dissolution, an end of a cycle of ignorance and the beginning of expansion of awareness. He unfolds us like the light of the sun acting on a lotus. He truly reverses the process of decay and death, bringing the jiva-spark back to its original Shiva-nature. He "opens the eyes" of your vision with his brilliant white light. Just as when a storm passes the earth is refreshed, vibrant and peaceful, full of white light, so the mind becomes calm, refreshed, mixed with white light. The cittam is purified, returned to its state as Citi (Universal Consciousness). It is clear and newly born (wisdom-ether), free to radiate (wisdom-air), bright and vibrant (wisdom-fire), flexible and calm (wisdom-water) and immovable (wisdom-earth). Rudra awakens these qualities as the Phenomena-Source, Infinite Consciousness.

(Scholars have speculated at the similarity between Rudra-Shiva and Osiris, the Egyptian deity. There have been several parallels both in terms of iconography, mythology, ritual etc. There seems to be some definite link between star-beings associated with Sirius, namely: Osiris, Dionysius, Shiva, and perhaps Blue-star Katchina and Tlaloc. They often have bull-imagery, and are blue or white. There are

icons of Osiris that are nearly identicle to Shiva, with bull-mount, trident, lingam and consort. From the highest perspective Osiris would by definition be considered an emanation of Shiva. When you experience them the scope is so vast you cannot see the whole because it is always beyond view. To be sure, one has to reach the same state as the deity in order to see for oneself. They arise as the same Absolute, yet each feels slightly unique. Mystically they appear very similar, I mean the way they appear in Vision which is the way they appear in this book, as oppose to the way they might appear in artistic rendition. When Osiris appears with thunder and lighting he has a crown of lightning, yet his beautifully fierce face is remarkably similar to Rudra's, with round pupils, bearing fangs, white skin. Osiris' body is swollen like thunder-clouds and he is winged like the Herukas of the Vajrayana pantheon. Both Rudra and Osiris wield the white lightning and fly amongst the white Cloud of the Mystery.

There is also iconographic similarity between Rudra and Padmasambhava, the Vajra Guru of Tantric Buddhism. Guru Rinpoche, as he is known by his primary image (presented above) shares great iconographic similarities to Rudra, like the white-skin, black locks, moustache, wide-awake stare, trident, Hum as seed syllable, 8 forms, and his function on earth as Thunder master, supreme vajra-guru. Some practitioners say Guru Rinpoche came out of a lightningbolt that fell on a hill. To the Nyingma he is the absolute truth, the image of the primordial Wisdom Mind. In other traditions he is an emanation of Chenrezig. The Shaiva lineage of Natha Babas (in Nepal) worship Chenrezig as Shiva alongside Buddhist practitioners. In fact, in Nepal Shiva and Chenrezig are considered identicle in the form called Triloknath, Lord of the 3 realms. Chenrezig also has pure white skin, black moustache and black hair. This is an unmistakable resemblance to Shiva. Another strong link concerns the fact that the Lotus Buddhas, like Amitabha-Chenrezig are responsible for descending from their pure realm of clear light and initiating the present civilization. In Shiva Tantra which is much older than Buddhist Tantra, it is Shiva who initiated civilization. Both traditions say things began at Mt. Kailash. Perhaps the Natha Siddhas have more profound evidence, after all, the Mahasiddhas of the Shaiva Tantra were often practicing Mahasiddhas of the Buddhist Tantra. Certain of the original 9 nath siddhas were mahasiddhas of Buddhist Tantra as well.

By definition all Deities have the same ultimate nature, we can call it Shiva or Buddha's Wisdom Mind. Once Haidhakan Shiva- revealed himself as three-faced: Buddha, Babaji, Christ.)

Kundalini Awakening

The primordial energy of the universe is known as kundalini, "coiled female-serpent." It is the luminosity through which Shiva reveals and conceals the Spirit. Kundalini dwells in all bodies. When the Spirit enters the human body its kundalini separates and dwells at the spinal base.

Shiva's sadhana entails the awakening of kundalini-shakti which dwells in the psycho-physical organism, the awakening or refinement of internal energy which rises of its own accord. It also implies the awakening of the layers of consciousness as this rising electricity pierces them. These layers in Tantra are thought of as wheels, with a hub and spokes.

To awaken the mind, the kundalini must be awakened. But the aim of Tantra is not necessarily the kundalini experience of having a lightning shock rent your spine, but is actually the awakening of kundalini and its mergence with Consciousness at the crown. This re-union culminates in omniscient realization precipitating supreme bliss, and it is this state which is the aim of Tantra.

When the jiva enters the womb in a flash at conception, the kulakundalini enters. I heard it enters first to prepare the womb. It remains separate until which time as spiritual cultivation is embraced to raise it. It remains coiled at the spinal base in 3 and 1/2 coils symbolizing the three gunas (qualities of energy) and gunajit (the state beyond them). They also denote the three states of waking, sleep, deep sleep and turiya or the Transcendent state of Consciousness. The coiling symbolizes potential power, the potential for an awakened mind. Its like in Winter when the powers of life go into the earth and freeze. So the awakening of kundalini is like the awakening of the earth in Spring, when the power of the earth comes out and things become strong again.

The complete transmutation of all gross energy which obscures the mind, into subtle energy, in this tradition is referred to as the awakening of kundalini. There are multiple ways to awaken kundalini; since this text deals with mantra-image method I will speak of this path. In Shiva's mantra-murti sadhanas we learn to invoke his luminosity and mix it with the gross energy (prana-shakti) which it awakens. Actually he mixes his Mind with ours. It rides the currents of vital energy and diffuses throughout our life-being. It increases the vibrational rate of the energy of the elements. Impurity is destroyed or awakened and new light replaces it, for this reason Shiva is called Hara, Ha, "to remove," Da "to bestow." The gross impure elements are awakened to reveal the pure display of Shiva as Reality. They dissolve into their Wisdom-Source. In Tantra there is one specific practice to achieve this (Bhuta-shuddhi) and yet any invocation practice will do. The elements dissolve, earth into water, water into fire, fire into air, air into space and space into Consciousness. This is the same process which happens at death. Such is why spiritual cultivation is a dissolution, a death and re-birth. The light increases the vibrational rate of the elements and they dissolve into light simultaneously. We come to identify with higher and higher rates. The frequency of the mind produces its states. Our awareness is expanded, the mind cleared. Dormant layers of the mind are aroused by Shiva's light coming in through the crown and heart. The light comes in through the chakras. It refines the energy of the body and mind. From the heart and chakras it travels on the vital winds in the channels. The refined energy begins collecting magnetically at the fields or chakras. I feel it is because that is where the high frequency light is coming in. It also collects in the spinal column and brain.

The kundalini is a reservoir of energy coiled at the pelvic base. It is very much electric and, like atmospheric lightning, is derived from the Sun. The kundalini is also equated with lightning by virtue of its powerful electric experience of zapping up the spine and illuminating and awakening the mind. The power which we receive from the Thunder-beings is something like their kundalini. The kundalini is related to refined sexual energy called vajra (thunder-bolt), no doubt because its awakening is like a lightning-charge, and because when the refined energy moves to pierce the heart and radiate through it, it awakens the adamantine nature. When kundalini sleeps it is inactive in the lower energy field. It is like the life-force of a tree in winter which rescinds into its roots. So when kundalini sleeps ones life is not quite the same as when it is awake. Our unconsciousness is not our natural state, the natural state is when the energy flows up the spine to the head. And Shock ti!! To be restored to our natural blissful state, kundalini shakti must be raised. Because in doing so the wheels of consciousness along the central channel are activated, and wisdom awakened. Because in doing so the kundalini melts the bliss-drop at the crown and rains down nectar throughout the body. In the first stage, prana-kundalini, the energies of the glandular secretions, vital energies for organ and muscle functioning, etc are refined and awakened. The next transmutation of the kulakundalini is called nada kundalini, the awakening of the mind, or the energy which has collected at the heart. Nada means sound. The sound here is the radiance of the heart as thought, and subtle sound. One comes to identify with this state of consciousness. With the opening of the heart comes the shift from self-cherishing to compassion.

When the mind has attained a certain tranquility the kundalini might rise to the head with a shock, ascending the central channel in the spinal column. Kundalini tradition also prescribes multiple practices to achieve this end. This experience is indeed a focal point in the kundalini tradition (Tantra). The experience culminates in indescribable bliss. Again it can be brought about or it can happen as a natural reflex of a still mind. It can happen all at once or it can happen gradually. A charge like lightning shoots up the spine to the crown. Since the spine contains the universe, kundalini's ascent can be likened to a charge of kundalini in the atmosphere. The body is a miniature replica of the universe. As embodied Rudras the kundalini can be used to benefit others, to heal for example. When the body is thrown off, this power can be used to gather thunder-storms. When kundalini rises it causes ones vision to expand, and the mind to become clear and enlightened. The kundalini is hot, it melts a drop of white nectar above the crown toward the forehead; the nectar of this drop flows throughout the body causing bliss. It is a drop of beatitude, of immortal juice, of ecstacy. In mythology the Thunder-beings drink a related substance—soma, which intoxicates them, giving them pristine qualities. In Mythology Garuda journeys to the heavens and takes this amrita (nectar) perhaps from the crest of Mt. Meru, the cosmic mountain, and brings it down. This reminds me of the kundalini rising to the head to melt the drop. The melting of this drop is like all heavenly blessings, especially the rain which follows the lightning. In Tantra this bliss is said to be produced from the friction of Shiva and shakti's union, and is depicted by sexual union. It is called siddha-yogini, which refers both to inner unification of Shiva and shakti, and to outer unification of adept (siddha) and consort (yogini). The highest transmutation of kulakundalini is called bodha or citkundalini, and is essentially the original blissful

state of Shiva in union with kundalini. Cit (Consciousness) in union with kundalini (energy). When the re-union of Shiva and shakti is stabilized through continued practice, the Eternal beatitude flows forth inexhaustibly, the Siddha radiates bliss from the spiritualized cells. The Siddha becomes the Wheel of Blissful Radiance (Shiva), and like a Star nourishes those in his midst. This is the state of recognition, liberation or samadhi, and is achieved in varying degrees of stabilization, the highest of which is nirvikalpa, the fully unified and stabilized state of Bliss Consciousness, the true "nest of the highest." This is also called sayujya samadhi and sahajavastha, "natural samadhi." It is the state of perfect omniscient realization.

In the awakening of cit kundalini within the body, the four koshas are perceived consecutively. Thus the yogi experiences first the red light, then the white, then black, then eternal blue. Accompanying these lights are subtle sounds, smells, tastes and visions of Deities. The sounds heard are bells, flute, drums and divine thunder. The divine thunder corresponds with the vision of the blue pearl at the crown. One may hear thunder while perceiving all-pervasive blue light and seeing the form of Shiva. This form which abides continuously at the crown center will give one teachings and as the primordial guru, will teach through ones heart. This state, once attained, does not cease. One has achieved the samadhi of Shiva. Shiva Megharaj thunders at ones crown in the form of the nila purusha "blue person," whose form is presented above, two-armed, with golden jata, crowned by the cranial crescent, adorned in rudrakshas, and so on. He is our eternal soul, the same for everyone. He is the witness Consciousness and the creator of universes. He pervades all things. He is the Eternal One displaying the Dance of multiplicity and transformation. He is the five elements, the five winds, the five senses, the five viscera, the four koshas, the 720 million nadis, the five shaktis and their activities, the 36 principles, the five main deities, all deities of the body and nature. All things and beings are Shiva shining. Our original experience, Shiva's experience is one of perfect unquenchable bliss. Shiva's image represents the fundamental nature of all things—empty, tranquil, blissful, clear, luminous.

The function of Shiva is to illuminate. The function of illumination is to reveal what was concealed, to awaken the Mind. It might achieve this by a shock or otherwise, to make a space in the mind, between the creation of any two things. Tantric dharanas (practices) seek to achieve the state within the adept, by concentration on inherent space which is between thoughts, breaths and actions. Tantra also utilizes shock such as when one sneezes or is suddenly startled. Ordinary consciousness gets a shock, a jolt and a space opens up immediately; within that space is spanda or pulsation of deepest Conscioousness, the Source of ones being. So this position can be taken hold of during shock or by concentration in the space between two things, between the creation and destruction. Shiva is in this space, he emerges there in bliss. It is said that when the mind is clear like this, the body or mind will heal itself.

Kundalini can be experienced through this space as well. Out of the sky the vidyut-shakti collects and presents itself as a lightning which the eyes see and body feels. Out of the sky of the deepest Consciousness, the kundalini shakti gathers and presents itself as a lightning-like charge which can be seen with the mind and felt with the body. The eyes of nature open, of plants, animals, earth, as vidyut kundalini flashes in the sky-theater, as the kundalini of Cosmic Man (Rudra). The eye of primordial wisdom opens as kulakundalini flashes in the sky-mind and body of microcosmic man (Rudra). Kundalini awakens the earth, restores the earths original face. The kulakundalini restores our original state where Shiva and shakti are joined. Consciousness adorned with kundalini pervades the three realms. This is represented by Shiva wearing nagas. They stand for the ability to control electricity at any level. The body is such an adornment of the soul. Thought is such an adorment of the mind. The universe is such an adornment of Light and space.

When anugraha-shakti (pure energy) replaces ones own limited energies, then this nectar creates a "bliss-body of Consciousness." The Soma which creates the "bliss-body" is both Shiva's grace an the light of the melted-drop which have saturated the body in bliss. This body can be related to images of intoxication. Intoxication is what brings Shiva to dance the universe. It means our natural state of intoxication. The Dancing Skeleton is intoxication. As the Nataraja, Shiva is figured with a Datura flower in his hair, it is a symbol of this Transcendent Ecstasy, a symbol that the state of Shiva-hood is one of God-intoxication. It is in the bliss-drops at certain points in the body that when melted produce this state. It erupts like a flower at the crown, makes our hair stand on end and spirit dance.

The Datura flower (and soma, charas and madhvika wine) are symbolic of Shiva's beatitude. Purifica-

tion brings God-intoxication, which comes through Shiva's hair or branches. Shiva and other Lightning gods are associated with a hallucinogenic sacrament and a powerful dance which follows. The dance and the sacrament are the same. Indra gets drunk on Soma (from Garuda) and dances in lightnings. Mahakala gets drunk on madhvika wine and dances before Kali. Dionysius gets drunk on his vine—he is the Vine. In Tlaloc's rite (Meso-america) sacred mushrooms are used which have an electric nature—they dance. There is a "fabulous fungus" in China and a dance in the thunder-rites. These are images of heavenly ecstasy-fruits. This spirit-dancing is produced by kundalini electric crackling-power descending from the Spirit of Bliss in the sky, ascending to the Spirit of Bliss at our crown. It makes the yogi drunk on the rasa "taste" of the self-effulgent state (samadhi). The physical sacrament is mostly a reminder of the bliss which radiates from Consciousness. (Although certain substances are keys to blissful states, if this were not so Shiva would not have communicated these symbols to remind us of inherent bliss, the image is in a language we are capable of understanding).

To emerge as Shiva is to have become immortal, undecaying, blissful and omniscient, the Lord of the Universe and Cyclic Life. This "bliss-body" is a subtle body of pure Vision, Light, Infinite Consciousness. In the lineage of Siddhas known as Siddha Siddhanta, of the millenia B.C., many of the masters attained this and remained on earth for hundreds and thousands of years, such as Boganathar who flew to China where he spent hundreds of years compiling the immortal sciences as Bo-yang or Lao Tzu. Lao Tzu was responsible for gathering all Taoist sciences together. His Indian student Mahavatar Shiva Babaji is still on earth in the Himalayas, where he has been for thousands of years. He is responsible for gathering the yogic immortal sciences together and transmitting them. Haidhakan Babaji, whose grace is greatly responsible for this work is none other than his appearance or play.

Sadhana is the practice of gaining control over shakti on ever finer levels. The essence and goal of practice is mind-control. Yoga Tantra are sciences of controlling the mind. The controlled mind is relaxed in its natural unified state. Kundalini is abundantly illustrated in Tantric texts as nagas, because they symbolize the mind of shaktis refined, balanced and brought under control. All the minds energies must be swallowed, digested and refined. The power to achieve this corresponds to the vajra, because it fulfills the same function as universal lightning to renew and restore the original nature of nature.

In Shiva sadhana one learns to swallow negativity by swallowing negative states. If the negative state is not swallowed it is perpetuated and results in suffering. Others may suffer around us by being stung, and certainly we suffer by living with the limitation of bliss. Swallowing the negative state gives us power over it, and it liberates it. Shiva demonstrates the importance of this in the fact that he has a blue throat or blue skin—which symbolize his activity of swallowing the poison of the root and effect of time, by swallowing the poison of negativity of all beings. In a split instant, as soon as one chooses, one seizes hold of the pure power of the mind (vajra, enlightened wisdom) and with this tool goes into the face of whatever negative states are arising. The vajra is cast symbolically into the heart of the matter, and when it hits the target it explodes a space in ther mind, it absorbs or removes what negativity was there and it leaves something positive there, a seed. This is how we can apply Shiva's vajra internally on a very practical level to awaken us. So it is not something remote from anyone. Anyone who chooses not to radiate negativity in the world uses the pure power of Consciousness. This means going into the face of anger, confusion, fear, desire, hatred (wild nagas) and bringing Shiva, Om Namah Shivaya. The pure power awakens the impure. In such a way our life-being can become transmuted. Garuda eats the serpent. Shiva eats our internal negative states, and ultimately he eats us, our egos are devoured by Wisdom—and it turns his throat blue.

There is a beautiful myth repleat with mystical symbology depicting this process. The celestial Rishi, Kavya Ushanas, a Thunder-power who had created Indra (Thunder gods) vajra, had fallen to become king of demons. I guess he liked to wreak havoc like the demons. He went to Kubera, Lord of the City of Alaka on Mt Kailash, entered him and stole his wealth and freedom. Kubera went to Shiva, his Father, and explained what happened. Shiva became terrific—Bhairava, swelling blue-black like thunder-clouds, wrathfull, darting eyes, spitting fire (similar in appearance to Vajrapani—above). He took up his lance and went after Ushanas, who hid on its tip. Shiva bent it into a bow, the rainbow, symbol of protection, divine Will, the firmament and the display of Reality in elements. Shiva swallowed Ushanas and then undertook millions of years of austerities. Negative emotions are to us what Ushanas was to Shiva—a piece of

energy out of harmony. Shiva arose from the waters of absorption and wisdom and saw that Ushanas had benefitted greatly from being in Shiva's belly—he was shining. Ushanas wanted out, but Shiva closed all the outlets but his semen passage, the vajra-linga "thunder-bolt symbol." Shiva shot him out into space, restored by the power of Thunder. He went up to become Venus, he became known as Shukra—"shining," "semen," "Venus."

Being swallowed by the deity is being swallowed by grace, by Super-luminal Light, Supreme Love and Supernal Bliss. There is a real mystical experience of being swallowed by the deity. Other examples include the swallowing of the mahasiddha Minapa by a great fish Shiva, the swallowing of Jonah by the whale Yahveh, the swallowing of Padmasambhava by the Wisdom Dakini, and the swallowing of a Kalachakra adept by Mother Tara. It is a symbol of complete transmutation (digestion) and gaining the wisdom of the subtle inner workings of the universe, seeing things as a true "insider."

The story of the swallowing and transformation of Ushanas symbolizes the tranmutation of gross energy which as the myth attests was originally pure energy (vajra). Regenerative energy is vajra, it has an electrical quality as it is related to water and fire. It derives its light from points with the subtle body and brain which provide us joy. Because of misuse, the energy becomes depleted and we rob ourselves of our potential for joy (wealth). Therefore Shiva teaches self-control and natural sex or sex which raises or retracts energy. (Only misinformed teachers of Tantra would teach masturbation). Shiva extends his grace to transmute gross energy. The subtle-energy of Consciousness comes down as a "live-wire" through the crown, the summit of Kailash, to devour gross energy which obstructs our development, our freedom, our free-radiance bliss. Once Ushanas was digested in Shiva's inner luminosity, he shone like lightning, like Venus on the firmament. The shining fruit which we give birth to through such fierce inner practice (tapasya: generation of inner luminosity) is called ojas, "vital lustre," it is a distillation of seminal energy. It is responsible for good health, strong memory and longevity in everyone. It exists as radiant yellow fluid (like Venus) in the bones and spine. Because it is distilled from semen naturally, one result of immoderate sexual activity is brittle bones and reduced lifespan. The result of retention is the opposite. When semen is refined into ojas it goes to the head to collect (the same goes for menses in women, so an achieved woman will stop having her period). The ojas acts as a transmitter and a magnetic power enabling the yogi to perform feats of controlling mind and reality. I think it is also possible to interpret the myth as a kundalini story, because the urdhva-linga of Shiva symbolizes retraction of internal energies (semen) upwards and the ascent of kundalini.

The vajra in either case is Shiva's penetrating illumination. The belly is the place of rapid dissolution of the ego and gross energy. The belly of Shiva is the place in which we die and are reborn as a shining gold subtle-being—Siddha (Perfected One). It is the domain of Mahakranti—Great Dissolution—the end. The birth which takes place is the birth of Shiva, it is reminiscent of being born from a mystical thunder-egg, being eaten by Thunder-bird and born from his Voice, being eaten by Shiva the Great Fish and then spit out, being struck by Lightning.

Mahakranti: The Great Dissolution

The result of spiritual cultivation is that it returns us to space. We rest our hearts in the unchanging tranquil state of space. This is the space that uncountable lives ago, we arose from. It is through purification and enlightenment that we return to this state. It represents our natural dissolution into Shiva. We might call this final arc or process of breaking through illusion, mahakranti. When the wine vessel of a yogi breaks, the wine spills out everywhere, and results in lightning, clouds, rainbows, weather changes. When baby thunder-bird hatches from his egg (body) there are cracks of thunder and lightning. When the egg of the body-mind is dissolved into wisdom, Spirit, the sacred bird within is free to leave the nest.

The natural end or transition between any two cycles of existence of a kula (a family of units: a cell, a thought, a person, civilization, world or universe) is called Mahakranti. It refers to the dissolution of the manifest universe by Shiva, and the dissolution of the ego, the limited vision of ourself and reality, by Shiva. As an internal process it signifies the destruction of impurity and the melting of the heart into Shiva. It refers to annihilation of the false view we nurture of ourselves as separate, less than divine chemistries. Mahakranti is the dissolution of the gross categories of existence into the subtlest category—Shiva, thus it is called "dissolution of the elements," and occurs

through sadhana by the increase in vibrational frequency of consciousness. To project the dream of limitation, Shiva changes the frequency of shakti dancing on his surface. He appears to get lost in the dream, which is the whole idea, not to be imprisoned, but to be lost in pure enjoyments—life, sex, eating, drinking, sleeping, working, clowning. Because Shiva is the nature of who we are, this ensures that We will recognize our true Nature. Shiva's energy and Dharma are the inherent means whereby remembrance takes place. All beings are inherently radiant and beautiful by virtue of it. All activity is inherently good, because Shiva is fully within it. Shiva keeps causes of suffering in the world, because we can only know Reality and Truth by its opposite. Suffering is the effect of not realizing that Shiva is the knower, the creator and doer, of thoughts and activity. If we feel that what we have done is our own, then we must take responsibility for it. What we intend is reflected in the universe through our actions. The mind creates all its states (from hell to heaven, the 7 lokas are the seven knowers, the 7 chakras) by choosing. We say the appropriate mantra and it gets us to the 7th heaven. Our intentions remain with us as traces. Good intention and good acts purify negative karmic traces stored in the unconscious (cittam). Those traces made us appear on earth in bodies of gross-vision and when that residual veil of ignorance is removed, destroyed by Shiva, then our gross-vision body is removed. In this way we die, such is the Mahakranti. Then we recognize that Shiva, the pure mirror was acting all along, reflecting his many lives on earth. But this is not without purification and work. The force of love, devotion and concentration burns away the veil of ignorance. Ignorance is the cause of the body, so the body is burned away as well. Understanding this intellectually is as useless as the jewel on the serpents crown. One cannot abstain from taking the path and hope that, because Shiva is in control of everything, one will, without effort, become liberated. Base metals are not transmuted into gold without a firing process.

In the context of the relative world, the dissolution of worlds at the end of the final Kali yuga, a Mahayuga (four yugas) and a kalpa (1000 yugas) marks the pause between grand symphonies, the pause that the Creator takes before beginning a new note or a whole new song. For the souls of ordinary people, this time implies a negative dissolution into which the soul falls into unconsciousness, latency. On the earth, my guru saw the Mahakranti and told people about it, and I'm sure acted to avert it. He was Shiva, so He saw the storms coming, the Thunder-beings who usher in the purification, and the purifiers. He told us about the previous civilization which detonated nuclear bombs, and told us to use a much more powerful bomb (Om Namah Shivaya) to annihilate the ego, because if we don't engage in the internal mahakranti, then the external mahakranti will overwhelm the earth.

Mahakala Bhairava takes the active form of Kalagni Rudra, the "Fire of Time, Melter of Worlds," and burns down the universe by danceing. His Dance is called Tandava, Dance of Destruction, the Dance of Parakundalini, the Great Lightningbolt withdrawing the universal vision into Shiva. The film comes to an end, so all you see on the screen is Light. Shiva becomes absorbed in himself "Beyond Time," beyond the universe, so the gross Vision stops, its burned up, it melts into the subtle space and the space into Light and the Light into Void. His luminosity reverses time to the prenatal state of the universe, this state is depicted in the Eternal Baby Shiva and the Undifferentiated Space—Mahakala—"The Great Black," "Victor Over Time."

This outer Mahakranti is Shiva lighting up the whole universe, exposing himself. No physical form can stand before this Power and live, so everything perishes. When Moses wanted to see God, he was told he could not see the Face and live. God instead revealed his "back," a fraction of his Power, and this disfigured Moses as though he'd been struck by lightning. So the Mahakranti might be like the universe being penetrated by Parakundalini, like the greates shock imaginable, great enough to stop the heart-beat of the universe. In the space which follows Shiva-shakti exists alone, nothing else but Void the deep nature of all Minds. It is said that even the Parakundalini (Light) is absorbed into Shiva. When the rest is complete, the process reverses itself and flow returns. Shiva begins dreaming, drumming up ideas—a restored universe unfolds from latency. In this way the Lightningbolt of Eternity initiates the end and beginning of a cycle of great existence. The fall of Lightning occurs in Shiva's boundless delight and madness. To those who didn't follow the law, it will be a dreadful event. If there is inner darkness it will burn. The outer Mahakranti is echoed by the prophecies of medicine men and mystics of the world traditions. I too have seen it and it is a "laughing sword." Only holy minds will be led to safe ground, the rest will perish. The four legs of Nandi (Taurus) represent the four successive

yugas. Each yuga is dissolved by a mahakranti. The Kali yuga, according to tradition and Haidakhan Shiva is nearing its end. We can wake up, start practicing karma yoga, kindness, generosity, service and Om Namah Shivaya. Individually this will lead us to the shakti yuga (age of luminosity) through mahakranti (enlightenment). Ask Shiva to destroy you and put on your ashes, or to saturate you with immortalizing nectar and help you to help others. Have faith and be inspired!

The inner Mahakranti happens by Shiva's initiation. It is a glorious process. Bhairava removes obstacles by shock, attracting then paralyzing us, opening up the space between thoughts which allows Shiva to shine. Although the goal is glorious, the process can be difficult. Nothing guarantees all circumstances will suddenly turn over, but the ultimate result is positive, a breakthrough into Infinity, mind merged with space, a heart liberated from suffering, a constant recrudescence, spring, emergence.

In Tantra there is a practice where one cultivates the inner Mahakranti. One views gross energy, impurities being burned up by Kalagni's fire (which rises from the big toe of the right foot, via a channel) while intoning this mantra: Om Ra-Ksha-Ra-Ya-Um Tanum-Dahayami Namah. Afterward we imagine the entire world being enveloped and burnt to destroy impurities. In this way we bring about our Mahakranti, our dissolution and emergence as Shiva and we help to destroy negativity in the world. We become absorbed in anashrita-shakti and this frees us from thought-contructs, allowing Consciousness to shine and kundalini to rise. When we become absorbed in Shiva, it is Shiva who is becoming absorbed or dissolved. He dissolves our obstructions to the omniscient state. He causes the film, the illusion of being something other than Shiva, to end.

When Rudra's cloak is off, the Mahakranti is upon you. Eternity presents itself as Reality, Ones urge in the beginning was to consume everything to avoid our consummation, to take and not to radiate. Finally having given up to the Loving Destroyer, having stripped everything away from the skeleton, the heart is left raw, recrudescent, always new, and fresh like spring. First we go after our abode. Then our abode approaches us. God is coming after us. We can only give up to the trident, pray and prostrate until we see those are Our Lotus-feet.

(Several people have actually expressed fear of Lord Shiva, and do not embrace his practice because they feel they are going to lose everything. Perhaps Shiva might take everything away which prevents their full omniscience. I suppose anything is possible with Shiva. It is true that the fear of God is wisdom. But there is no real reason to fear losing everything. Losing everything could liberate one from this world, it could teach impermanence, especially if what we possess is obstructing our realization. If Shiva takes everything, then he shows us that our permanent state (abode) of Shiva is the only thing worth pursuing. One thing Shiva will never take away—is love, ones capacity to help. He always bestows blessings. Even if we fall into calamity and lose everything precious to us, if Shiva caused it, then it is for the higher good. Our wisdom and compassion (Shiva) is what is truly precious. Shiva bestows these and removes suffering. He removes the root of suffering. Use Om Namah Shivaya and you will know this. Because our Shiva-nature is wisdom, it ensures perfection, growth, awareness, bliss, as the ultimate result of Shiva's activity. If we find ourselves in a situation of great loss, then pray that since Shiva caused it, then may the perfected state of Shiva dawn, may luminous awareness and love be awakened like lightning.)

The Skeletons of Infinite Consciousness

What remains once we dissolve all our material existence into subtle elements, once all the sinew, muscle, blood and brains is gone, once the finite view of self is gone and we're able to give freely everything we have, there is only Shiva. Shiva radiates bliss unobstructedly, and this radiance is the compassion or unconditional giving that we must cultivate. The skeleton means that there's nothing we've reached the bottom of the barrel and now there is only radiant space. It means we never stop giving, we keep digging until the treasure of diamonds is found, then we give and give and give. The diamond heart is an inexhaustible wealth. There are diamonds for everyone, wisdom to nourish and guide all beings.

Shiva reveals himself as a Skeleton to teach this, and to show the utter nakedness, bareness of the fully awakened state and Reality. The Nothing-but-Shiva, no adornments Reality of the universe. Shiva eats us so we can achieve this Skeleton-state. A Thunder-bird eats his children so they can become his body, one of his voices. Kali eats her children too. The Thunders want to eat their children to enlighten them, to make

them happy, resounding with the music of their Father-Mothers Light. We look for our previous state of bliss. We devour the Light and the Light devours us. We give of ourselves and the divine gives of itself. When you're fully devoured you become full again—fulfilled. And that's it, that's our true accomplishment, our continuously abiding accomplishment. The death that makes a Skeleton is a continuous birth and emergence into Infinity. It is returning-to-the-Source, the path-is-the-goal, and the only way to get there is by giving of oneself. This is so because it is the nature of Shiva (Bliss) to give. Following this way is following bliss.

Dancing Skeletons appear in Shiva's great retinue. They symbolize self-control and awareness as the path and delight as the fruit or goal. They are our Infinite-nature. Shiva projects them just like a living-film or play. Having self-control means letting Shiva take the helm of ones life; he's going to ferry us across the ocean of suffering to our abode of Pure Delight. If we practice awareness it means we're going to gain entrance to Shiva's inner abode. What we're not aware of brings suffering, robbing us of natural freedom. Awareness is freedom or bliss. They obviously symbolize impermanence and the need for mind-control, awareness and kindness.

The Skeleton is the nature of our refined and restored Consciousness. If you see their song and dance you will know they are a Vision of pure Delight, what is rightfully ours. As desireless bliss they dance the ego to its grave. Their lightning is the Awakening-lights. It reverses us to our pure Skeleton state.

In Tantra there is a practice for achieving bliss-Consciousness, called Karakani Mudra, (Skeleton Gesture) whereby one visualizes oneself as a subtle skeleton of ether, then one visualizes the world as a skeleton of light.

The Skeleton image teaches generocity and self-sacrfice. It teaches that our nature is to give of ourself. Self-control is a sacrifice of that which put the mind in bondage. Our true inner state of beatitude is not being sacrificed, rather one renounces that which has caused the loss of joy. Liberation is leaving behind a view that caused suffering for one which causes bliss to shine in all thoughts and acts. Only through self-sacrifice (love) and awareness can Shiva be attained.

Another Shaivite myth describes this ultimate sacrifice. It is the origin myth of thunder-bolts. The Rishi Dadhici practices intense austerities and was granted the boon of having thunder-bolts for bones from Lord Shiva. So he received great power and sovereignty.

The other deities needed his bones for some urgent task, nothing else would do. So Dadhici made the ultimate sacrifice for the welfare of others—he gave up his bones—his very Immutable Self. The highest sacrifice is that of our self-awareness.

Universal harmony is maintained by God sacrificing himself for himself. The bones of this self do not belong to a limited ego, but are part of the Light. The bones are Shiva. The bones are a way of pointing out what cannot ever be pointed out. Our responsibility, function or duty is also Shiva. Our activity is our radiance, what we give and do. Shiva radiates dharma-light endlessly in the form of insight, truth and love.

It is through sacrifice or giving, kindness and creativity that our duty is fulfilled. It will always be the greatest passion in our hearts because we know that it will bring the greatest bliss. The Skeletons sacrifice everything and since there's nothing left they dance and sing to bring delight. The ultimate surrender is made by Dadhici, not even the bones remain. To surrender to God is to surrender most of all our bones to benefit all beings. The actual state of affairs from the beginning is that we own nothing, we inherit nothing, we are no-thing. And this No-thing is Shiva. So while there's a body and mind give of oneself. This is cultivating the heart for Shiva. This brings the ultimate joy, the revelation of the Skeleton-of-Infinite-Consciousness.

The Thunder-beings are the Origin of this activity. The Dharma is their radiance. It is Love; it motivates them to nourish the earth, and motivates all people to take care of one another. Love is what makes the Thunders dance in delight. Love is Bliss and it's a Live-wire, it makes us dance because it tickles the heart, like a mother tickling her baby. The universal fabric is an electric ebullient-light dance of Shiva. He makes universes dance like fire-flies, or sparks bursting from lightning. His illumination makes all beings dance, often literally in exaltation. It intoxicates, causing us to rise up in wonder and delight. It touches the heart and dissolves us, it keeps destroying us until there is only a bliss-body of Infinite Consciousness—Shiva.

Durga: Queen of Lightning, Remover of Difficulties

In Sanatan Dharma there is a strong tradition of Mother worship called "Shakta" referring to worship of Mother Divine. If we're just doing Shiva practice then we might be inclined to think Shakti is the luminosity aspect of Shiva. But in Shakta tradition Mother is the Sacred Source, the Primordial Wisdom which gives birth to all other deities, and all beings. Mother is womb of all beings and she is those beings male and female which arise in this womb. Mother is the unique feminine essence, the Absolute as Feminine Wisdom-reality. Mother is all things. She is the Supreme consort of Shiva, as expressed in most mythology. Shiva's many consorts can be said to be emanations of Durga. All her aspects, or forms are avenues to Her. Usually they were female wisdom-beings who walked the earth. Durga is the first, primordial Mother. She walked the earth and acted almost exclusively to subdue negative forces. In her main practice of the Chandi it says that she is the aggregate energy of all the gods, and relates how she is created out of a mass of their light to destroy incorrigible demons.

Tradition relates that the Mothers were on the earth around 50—75,000 years ago as the ice age was receding. Durga fought to subdue fierce demons. She would emit lightning emanations from her third-eye, who were increasingly wrathful forms like mahakali, kalaratri, chamunda, chandika, varahi. The myths denote her ability to tame all minds, to destroy inner and outer obstacles. In the atmosphere She sports as lightnings, rain, clouds, rainbows etc., in the inner sphere she sports as thunderbolts of illumination, clouds of wisdom, rainbows of bliss, rains of nectar.

In Hinduism, She creates all inner obstacles or illusions of limitation and for this reason she should be invoked to remove these obstacles, to dissolve the illusion of limitation of what is truly unlimited. She is the cause of our basic ignorance (which allows us to be born on earth) and is the cause of our freedom from rebirth. She is the essence or light of dharma, if we adhere to it and we invoke her we will be free of suffering and will not be reborn again and again. By her Thunder-bolt of Illumination (her wisdom-light) she breaks the wheel of rebirth by destroying the obstacles preventing realization of Infinite Consciousness. She is the ultimate power to tame our minds. We supplicate the Mother because She tends to respond more quickly to our hearts plea. Although there are many mothers, they're all together Durga, her emanations. Durga is the power of illumination which causes our return to the clear, tranquil state through the removal of obstacles and confusion, sources of misery and suffering. Durga is called Remover of Difficulties,

Confusion and Obstacles. She is the cause of igno- rance and birth, and the cause of liberation from rebirth. This means that we're emanations of the Mys- terious Mother, who, looking upon the immense suf- fering of beings, generated the intention to help them by incarnating. This also means that once you attain liberation from ignorance you recognize that she caused it. But when you're ignorant you don't see it. If you train in the fact that ignorance and negative states are her adornment or play, and use her mantra, then she will subdue or awaken those states. She will reveal her true face in us. Just use her mantra and think that she is behind your life. She is causing or creating you now, your thoughts and external functions. All is Her.

She is the Mother Eternity, the intrinsic change- less nature of all minds. If you look at things from her perspective then you see that all deities and beings are her children, all states are her adornments. She is everything that Shiva is in the key-note or fragrance of the Spirit and Power of the feminine. She is the Creatrix and its first emanations. The multiple moth- ers known as Durga, from the nine primary forms, to the 10 mahavidyas, to the numerous emanation-bod- ies, are one unity. And yet beyond these there is still the Primordial Undifferentiated Eternal Mother—Maha- durga or Parameshvari Mata.

Often when people refer to Mother they think she is solely Mother nature. She is Mother nature in the sense that the five-lights which form the fabric of the universe are hers. They are totally subordinate to her. She is their projector. She is Projector, projection and the film. Nature is alive, she is the capacity and the creative arising. She is the five elements (nature) and their Source.

Durga is the feminine origin of thunder-powers, the aspect of the Mother who lives with thunder and lightning and brings it into the universe. Her name carries a couple of meanings, one is "difficult to approach." One must be humble before her, and have good clean thoughts. The etymology of her name points to her ability to remove obstacles. She is the Reliever of Difficulties. Perhaps it is related also to the word durjaya, "invincible," and dorje. Durga is the potential enlightened state and the power to remove obstacles to this state. She is a great warrioress, she controls the power to subdue demons; her thunder- power is war-power of universal good, the power of love that wins all hearts. One myth tells that she destroyed a demon named Durga, and that she took its name (and weapons) to signify her victory in battle.

Durga appears as a beautiful goddess amidst crim- son lightning. She is emitting an effulgent pearl-white halo, electric light tinged with gold, green, pink, red, blue. She is white in color, has long black hair and wears a gold crown. She has a joyous expression and roars fiercely like thunder causing the earth to shake and all negativity to dissolve. She has eight or more arms and holds a variety of weapons: bow of determi- nation, discus of revolving time, thunder-bolt of illu- mination, club, sword, trident, conch, lotus, bell, drum, shield etc.. These weapons are aspects of her power to protect us from external and internal en- emies. Her Lightningbolt came from Indra, and Indra received it from Shiva. She wears a red and green sari. She rides a tiger which roars. This stands for the unpredictable electric shakti, the power which she controls. The power of the Mother is the greatest protector that exists, it is displayed in her crimson lightning and symbolized in her tiger mount. It is love.

The red lightning is love, it attracts us, then de- stroys our igorance. With Durga it is obviously protec- tive, divine-energy. It is her subtle life-essence, like blood, her enlightened vitality. Durga is sacrificing her electric life-blood for you and the earth. The red lightning are her arteries pulsating in the sky. They symbolize fire, the dimension of full growth, the earth and minds' unobstructed upward movement to yield its fruit and bloom. In Durga Sapta-sati it says her nature is as fire. Her crackling fire is destructive of all obstacles to the radiance of the mind and vegetation. In her sadhana these obstacles are symbolized by de- mons. Her fire burns them up at a glance. Although her destroying of demons is a fluent theme in mythology, this is just one aspect of her function to establish harmony on earth.

Surely her power is related to transmuted passion as well, to the awakened inner energies. Her image demonstrates the female potential to transmute menses or sexual energy into vitality, into spiritual power, the universal potential for life. The new trans- formation-body of Durga Consciousness is pure inde- structible life. Vidyut-shakti is her lightning; vid is the light in our hearts, the light of consciousness and light of our eyes. Deity creates ideas in our heart through this light, and lightning in atmosphere through this light. Transmuted sexual energy is electric bliss, a power to cause life or restore life, wholeness, har- mony. Mother and father cause life with lightning. With hearts desire we can heal with it. But it must be refined by applying self-control and awareness.

Durga's tiger symbolizes this mastery over lower energies—their liberation. For us the tiger is sexual power. For her the tiger is the thunder-power she controls perfectly. She rides this energy on currents of light through space. The tiger suggests her connection to the earth also. That what is of the earth can be refined to take off into space. Tigers appear as Thunder-beings both in South America (Ccoas) and China, where they emit lightning, rain and hail from their eyes and tail. In the Five Tiger mandala, I was told, two are associated with thunder-power. Thunder-deity Dorje Drollo rides a tigress (see above). Durga has several mounts, she might also be seen riding a lion, a garuda, a swan or dancing on Shiva or in union with Shiva. Specifically the nine basic forms ride tiger or lion, the three emanations Mahasarasvathi, Mahalakshmi, Mahaskali ride swan, lotus, Shiva—respectively.

Shakti assists all growth, fertility of the earth and mind, a good harvest. She is the sun, the various forms of cold and hot, water and fire which nourish the vegetation. She is the green power of the earth, so Durga worship (Navaratri) coincides with the birth of Spring, the sowing of seeds, and the harvest of crops in the fall. She is all the sparks (jivas) of Consciousness in the universe, which are arising out of the earth, which are flowing through the seasonal transformations of birth, growth, decay and death. She is their beginning, flow, and return to rest, their liberation. She is Silence—Undifferentiated Space and its creative flow. She is lightning flashing in space. She is rainbow lightnings to reveal the wisdom-root of the elements and her beauty in brilliant rays: pink, red, gold, green, pearl-white. She is the female lightning. She is our heart-power, Love, which ensures the growth of bliss and truth. She is the non-dual taste of Reality. She is especially gentle and nurturing, the slight roundness of her body suggests this. She is also fierce, hard to approach. She attracts us and zaps us simultaneously.

To align with Durga we repeat her mantra, wave-lights (aarati) and practice the Durga Sapta-Sati. Her mantra for removing difficulties is Om Hring Shring Dung Durgaya Namah. It can be recited silently, or aloud while visualizing her image. The effect is to clear obstacles and increase our capacity for kindness and nurturing typified by the Mothers methods. One can pray for anything, such as healing or rain with this mantra as well. She bestows joy on all beings and is the Source of liberation—so with her mantra one can attain the awakened state. Her practice also balances all internal energies, such as masculine-feminine

shaktis. Haidhakan Babaji told his Western students to do Mother puja in order to balance the masculine-feminine shaktis. Western traditions have been dominated by the patriarchal view of Divinity as male, whereas Divinity has no such boundaries, it is both Mother and Father and yet beyond them altogether. Shiva and Durga are just symbolizations for our comprehension of the Mystery and for our use in bringing about inner harmony and balance. We use mother practice because when masculine energy and patriarchal view get too strong people lack nurturing motherly qualities. History has shown that there can be much destruction in patriarchal cultures. Much violence and lack of compassion can be attributed to this imbalance in people. Men fail to respect women because of this imbalance. People in general fail to respect mother earth and her children because of this imbalance. Therefore it is supremely efficacious in these degenerate times to embrace Mother practice. If we wish to cause true inner peace, to awaken true wisdom and compassion then we should embrace Mother practice. This means practice in which by invoking Mother in the heart, sacrificing ourselves to her, we arise as her. When we offer ourselves to the mother with good intentions, she accepts that offering with light that saturates us. Becoming Mother means being fully saturated with her. We need to get a sense of what it feels like to be the Mother. This is much more important than what it looks like to be her (clear visualization). Because being saturated with her means that she will act through the heart, she will inspire ones life. If you can feel like the mother by invoking her and sacrificing ones limitations to her so that she will be there as you, then you can feel like the essential love in the hearts of all mothers and respond to the sufferings and needs of all beings as your own children.

Durga relieves us from misery and is the grace, the door (yoni: vagina) by which to return to Eternity. She is the Womb of Reality, the heart which conceals and illuminates. She is the beautiful wisdom that entices you then dissolves you. She is not merely shakti—energy. She is in the urge to return to the Origin and the power to do so. Absorption in her means viewing reality tinged with the light of her Consciousness and overflowing with the experience of her blissful heart

She becomes fierce when there are fierce obstacles to destroy. From her third-eye, She sends out a bolt, when the smoke clears it is her wrathful form, Mahakali or Kalike. Kali appears dancing on the corpse of Shiva. (Kali is the force of Shiva's activity, Shiva is the space from which she arises). Black, wrathful, her anklets sounding the musical rhythm of blissful destruction (of suffering). She has three roving blood-shot eyes, wears a mala of skulls, holds a trident, flaying knife and skull cup of blood. Her hair stands on end from the electricity blast, and she sticks out her blood-reddened lolly tongue. She laughs ferocious dakini-laughter as she cuts out hearts (ego's) and devours her children. She is the bliss-energy aspect of the Mother.

Kali provides the luminosity to attain the Absolute. Kali devours demons to open them up. She devours the ego to open it to its deathless state symbolized by the corpse of Shiva. In Mahakala's mandala she is the entrance to Bhairava's mandala, so she may be figured astride a supine Shiva is sexual embrace. She ushers aspirants through the gate (vagina) and takes them to the center. In such a way she devours our negative inner states. When we invoke these powers of rapid illumination, the rays destroy our confusion. She teaches us to stand up to all obstructions, to be a fearless warrior. She awakens the warrioress inside of our heart, which is the strength to penetrate negative states to control the mind.

It is often taught in the shakta tradition (of Vama Tantra) that the Deity (Kali-Mahakalbhairav) is grateful upon receiving our offerings (which sometimes include animals), and our practice. Wisdom-Deities are happy with our self-sacrifice symbolized in Tantra as the slaying of animals and in mythology by the slaying of demons with animal form. Mothers are happy with the effect self-sacrifice has on us and innumerable beings, not with the offering itself. She is happy with the heart-essence that goes into it, as opposed to the extravagance or quantity of the offering. She is happy as a mother is happy when her children are kind and giving. It is the motivation that will bring us to the goal. They are only happy with this sacrifice because it makes us happy immediately and makes us clear so the Wisdom-deity can be on earth. Mother is the light inside all beings, so she would not advocate causing pain to animals by killing them!!

This is a cause of obstacles for us, and a cause of suffering for numerous animals every year during Kali puja. The Mother is happy with our selfless service, with all yoga.

Another reason why there are practices for sacrificing animals in Tantra, such as with the "gayatri of release," is because it is devised by high yogis of the past who were able to recognize that by taking an animals life, the animal soul would be liberated (to a higher state). Other than realized yogis no-one should take the lives of animals. Killing is responsible for the shortening of life-span of animals and people. People should be able to live 120 years, but because we have killed we reduced our life-span. We should not take life. If we have already killed an animal then we can pray to the Mother to release the animal to a higher state. Our yoga frees us from causes of suffering. The Deity indicates her happiness by blessing us. The blessing liberates us and encourages us to adhere to the Dharma of virtue and practice.

(The nine main forms of Durga function solely through Sanatan Dharma tradition, the mandalas of Shiva and Vishnu, although her quality of wisdom is similar to that of other primordial mothers, like Isis and Vajra-yogini. The manifest rays of coloration of these Mothers are similar: red-pink, green-gold, blue-white, and their quality of wisdom is also similar. One of Durga's main forms is called Varahi "Execellent Desire of Union" in which she manifests with the boar. One of Durga's main forms is Mahakali who appears nearly identicle to the Buddhist Dakini Kalike. Another, known to yogis is Rakteshvari who appears red, dancing, naked like Vajra-varahi. Another is Sarasvathi who appears in Buddhist tradition as the white form of Vajra-yogini—Sarasvathi. Yet another is the form known as Chinnamastaka, the "Severed-headed." She is worshiped in an ancient Nepalese temple by Buddhists as Sarva-Buddha-Dakini (Vajra-yogini). In addition, the shakti piths that were geographic arisings of Durga's wisdom have been converted to piths of Vajra-yogini (Vajra-varahi). So there are many similarities.)

BOOK THREE

Lei Kung: The Primordial Thunder-bird

Yuan-shih T'ien-Tsun, the Celestial Venerable of the Primordial Beginning, Highest Divinity, according to China's ancient tradition, transmitted the vast body of teachings of the Way (Tao), spiritual reality, and the practices by which humans can return to this Source. The earliest teachings during this eon were transmitted to shamans from various Deities who are subordinates to Yuan-shih. Among these teachings were Thunder rites. These practices for controlling the power of thunder, were transmitted through Lei Kung, Lord of Thunder, who was patron to these shamans.

The first people to be instructed in the Way were known as Fang-shih, "master of prescriptions." They were the shamans and sages of ancient China, the earliest descendants of the Deities which gave birth to humanity on earth. They lived in the North East coast of China. They were the precursors of Taoist sages, immortals and priests. The teachings they received were essentially the same, only differing according to time. Fang-shih were proficient in astrology, astronomy, healing, prophecy, divination, geomancy, dual-cultivation, prescriptions for attaining immortality or shen-hood, and Thunder and rain-making rites. The vast body of practices that exist in Taoist lineage to this day have their root in the practices which were developed and transmitted by the Fang-shih. They viewed all of nature as sacred and alive, each aspect being an extension of an unlimited existence, Tao. The cosmos was controlled by Deities, by an Unmanifest Origin. The veneration of these Deities, of nature, was an essential part of life. Spirits controlled everything, therefore gaining control over the spirits meant gaining control over nature. The female wu (shaman) danced and invoked the spirits who exist in the four

directions of space, particularly the Thunder-beings and star-beings of the Big Dipper who were our original ancestors. They danced to bring down the powers to dissolve obstructions and inert energy, so energy could move freely, in the earth and mind. Congestion of energy meant drought or illness. They controlled the elements by living in unity with nature by living in unity with the Origin. The Origin is nature's primordial unity. By dwelling at the beginning of things, the shamans were masters over hot and cold, fire and water, Yang and Yin, the organization of which produces the universal manifestation.

All Deities were recognized as our ancestors, Yuan-shih gave birth to all shens, who took root in nature to control nature. The early people recognized they were extensions of nature, of something that developed out of the influence of the stars, moon and earth. They recognized their relatedness to Thunder-beings, who existed in the Pole-Star and sky. So they called Thunder god, Lei Kung, Grandfather or Ancestor Thunder, and they called his consort Thunder goddess, T'ien Mu Niang Niang which means Mother of Heaven. Lei Kung has been referred to as the prototypical Thunder-bird by scholars who think civilization began in China and therefore the first Thunder-bird must be Lei Kung. In actuality he is the archetypal Thunder-bird, one image of the Primordial Thunder Lord (Yuan-shih) which was revealed to the sages of ancient China in ancient times.

The people aligned themselves with the Thunder-beings to perform Thunder rites. They used the images and names, dances, invocations and gestures that they were transmitted. Some masters aligned themselves with the Thunder Lords and gave birth to themselves as children of Lei Kung. Lei Kung is one Thunder-bird and yet many.

Thunder rites implied alignment to Thunder Lords and specifically Lei Kung, their chief. Thunder rites mirror his own activity; they are used to influence the weather, perform exorcisms, purify the mind, heal illness and save souls. It is one power which belongs to Lei Kung, he puts it on the earth with his children, his transformation-bodies, to serve his function. The Thunder specialist becomes a conduit for nature, the power and illumination of the Tao. They teach the Tao, the Origin and its flow as nature. Their vision is natural wisdom. Spirituality is not something supernormal or unnatural. For those who live naturally there is no need for perfection or self-cultivation, service therefore can be fully offered to benefitting others. The illumination which we learn to control is for others—it gathers above the head only when our intentions are virtuous. So the original tradition of Tao in China was simply a way of flowing with nature, of living naturally in harmony with people, earth, animals, sky, moon, planets, stars, deities and their root—Highest Divinity or Tao. If you abide at the root of things, the Source of harmony in the universe, one will naturally live in harmony with all things. Abiding at the root implies having a clear heart, since the heart is the root of our life, it implies intuition. Through our heart the subtle law of Tao, transmits itself, as Te, power or virtue. Once people fail to adhere to their inner nature by living virtuously, they loose their place in nature and require a means of returning to Tao, or at least returning our heart and energy to the pristine state where the activity of Tao is inherent. This constitutes the state of things prior to birth, when energy is harmonious, radiant, blissfull, pliant, vibrant. This is the state we must return to; Tao is the harmonious Way of nature, it is primordial balance, the unified state of energy, of earth (gross energy, yin—body) and Heaven (subtle energy, yang—spirit) through mind. Or you might say on a deeper level it is the balance of white light, or ultra violet light and black light or infrared spectrum. These are in the eyes and make vision possible, they're in the heart and make thought possible, in the spirit and allow for revelation. They have something to do with the cooling of stars as well. Originally the Great Ultimate was depicted by a circle, the principle of light. Capacity-space and radiance was depicted through the yin-yang circle, but the colors were violet and red (as opposed to black and white).

Thunder-bird Lei Kung is a revelation bird and has transmitted the teachings on Thunder rites. The sha-mans worked under the Thunder-bird to clear out negative energies in the earth which cause suffering, disease, drought and disasters. The Thunder specialists dances to bring down the powers and dispatch them to heal, exorcise, clear out obstructions of impure yin energy which in Thunder-bird iconography is symbolized by the serpents. Thunder-beings teach his children how to use his power. The practitioner, as well as supplicating the Deity to descend in the subtle or gross lightning, can ascend to the Divine Abode, transform into a Cosmic being or shen, and descend to function as the Deity on earth.

The Deity's image is the means whereby wisdom could be transmitted to people, and it is the means whereby the people can contact the heavenly shens, to heal and control nature. The image is the means whereby the Deity descends and ascends, it is the vehicle of the deities subtle and gross revelation; to see it appear out of lightning is to see it appear out of Deity's spacious Vision. Cosmologies and iconographies developed both out of descent and visionary transmission, and ascent of the human messenger spirit to deity's abode. Both descent of the Deity and ascent of his embodied transformation body, are symbolized by flight. The word for immortal in Chinese, shen or shien, implies flight.

Lei Kung gave initiation into his rites through visitation in visions and dreams primarily. Early on he was viewed as a great Owl. Other Thunder-beings have taken owl-form. Shiva became an owl to transmit a specific doctrine, Indra also has an owl form known as Uluku. The owl certainly denotes wisdom, for its penetrating sight. The owl is a light in the darkness; Lei Kung is a lightningbolt in space. Lei Kung's sight or vision, like that of an owl is bright and penetrating. Primarily the owl features stand for the light of knowledge. Owls are excellent hunters, ridding the land of what often times brings disease. The same is so of Lei Kung, he is a powerful warrior and exorcises malevolent spirits, he acts to cleanse the waters of energies which cause disease. The great horned owl hoots to signal Spring. Lei Kung comes out with thunder, beating his drums. Owls are fearless, as is Lei Kung; both are destroyers of snakes. Owls clack their beaks together as a warning, similarly there is a practice of biting ones teeth which arouses internal deities, both as a preliminary to practice and when there is danger or malevolent spirits around. There is some relation of owls to magic, most likely because shamans could shape-shift into an owl. Lei Kung was also the root of secret magical practices. The shamans were called wu, which means wizard, witch or wise one. The owl also has some relation to the dead, the ancestors, the after-life and abode of spirits, which was symbolized by the moon. This is not just symbolic, the owl transmits messages that it receives from the Spirit. In many cultures the spirits of those who die go up to become Thunder-spirits, messengers who can appear as skeletons or bird-people. It is traditionally taught that all shens existing in the subtle realms had to go through the Womb of the Mysterious Mother, the manifest universe, by taking bodies. It is the Way of the universe for life to arise from Unmanifest Void, evolve through this realm, then return to the beginning—Void.

Highest Divinity Yuan-shih is primordial, while all subordinate-deities are its emanations, who incarnate on earth, ferment for a time, and return to Heaven after living a life governed by natural wisdom. The shens inhabiting the highest realms (subtlest states) are the ancient developed people who were on earth in previous eons, before the present civilization, like many Thunder-beings. For example Highest divinity gave birth to Yuan-shih, Ti, Yu Huang (Jade Emperor) and Pan Ku in ancient China. They were beings that incarnated on earth as giants and lived long long lives. Ti was the original ancestor of the Shang people, so became known as Shang-ti and worshiped with the stature of Supreme Being. Later, Jade Emperor took the place of Yuan-shih is Taoist cosmology. They form the deities of the Three Highest Realms of Purity. Lei Kung is likewise an ancient one, but takes a subordinate position in the cosmology to the Jade Emperor or whoever Highest Divinity happens to be. Nevertheless he is the vehicle of the Mysterious Source, of its revelation as thunder and lightning. He is Mysterious Divinity's function and image.

The Divine Ones are our creative ancestors. This tells us that we as humans can become like them—Immortal Spirit and pure creative energy, and in fact this is the aim of the Taoist tradition of the Immortals. For the ancient gods on earth, there was nothing to become; when they left the earth they ascended to Heaven and continued to function as nature, extensions of Tao, the Sacred Origin of the universe. Their heavenly nature remained undefiled, they never lost their pure connectedness to their beginning, to the Unborn state. We are all part of something very profound, which is always functioning through our lives in ceaseless transformation, this is the Tao—the Spirit, the Mystery behind our lives.

In the ancient Chinese tradition this Source was called T'ai-i, and Yuan-shih t'ien-tsun or simply Tao.

It is the root, stalk and bloom of total universal existence. It is the Spirit manifesting through pure, creative, generating energy. It produces all beings, and at the same time is above all beings and realms. All beings from the subtlest divinity to the manifest reality constitute its body. He was said to dwell even above the highest of the three pure realms, and the 36 heavenly caves. His seat is associated with the Pivot of the Pole Star, which is highly significant in Thunder rites, as an origin of celestial lightning and thunder-power. The Five Thunders (Lei Kung), and the thunder soldiers of their Court had their celestial abode in a "Jade Bureau", Jade Pivot, or Jade Mountain, which are synonyms for the Pole Star Pivot. Lei Kung is considered Jade Emperors subordinate, carrying out his decrees on earth. The 9 stars of the Big Dipper, 7 visible, 2 invisible, were considered the origin of Chinese civilization. The earliest descendants were generally considered shens that descended from the realm of Purple Tenuity, surrounding the Pole Star, and are worshiped as the Taoist pantheon. There are approximately 36,000 Deities in the pantheon existing in 36 heavenly caves or realms beyond time and space.

There is a myth which relates the incarnation of Thunder Lord on earth, and his re-ascent to heaven. Mythology records that Lei Tzu (a 3-eyed form of Lei Kung who rides a black unicorn traveling the speed of lightning), incarnated as Wen-Chung T'ai-shih in the first millenium B.C. He fought in a historical-mythical battle called the Battle of Mu or Battle of the 10,000 spirits. He was defeated and retreated to Swallow Mountain (Yen Shan) where he encountered Ch'ih Ching-tzu who flashed a yin-yang mirror at his unicorn mount, overpowering it. One of Lei Tzu's sons, Lei Chen-tzu, struck the animal with his staff, splitting it in two. Wen Chung escaped but was confronted by another known as Yun Chuung-tzu. Yun made lightning with his hands, surrounding Wen Chung with 8 columns of fire which charred him out of bodily existence. Prior to hearing this story I saw Lei Kung in the form of a man who was all blackened and charred (from the lightning). The myth relates how he incarnates and is re-absorbed into lightning. After the battle Yuan-shih gave Wen-chung direction over thunder, clouds and rain. He became one of Lei Kung's lightning-body.

Most schools of Taoism understood that their teachings could be traced back to the shens, either earthly shens (achieved ones) who developed practices (especially which mirror the movements of animals), or heavenly shens who transmitted practices to earthly shens. Thunder rites are among such practices. Some schools claimed direct lineage stemming back thousands of years to the beginning of the eon. One example of this was the School of the Magic Jewel which existed around the time of Christ and claimed lineage stemming back to the beginning of the eon, 12,000 years ago. The revelation they followed was highly significant, it was called the Scripture of the Magic Jewel. It came into being at the beginning of the world in the form of golden signs written on tiles of jade. Their meaning is communicated by Yuan-shih to subordinate deities at the beginning of each eon. These Deities then transmit these teachings on the multiple Taoist sciences to earthly emanations, such as the Taoist Immortals, sages and Fang-shih. These teachings formed the basis for several schools of Taoism which use practices given by the celestial shens. (The origination of these teachings is virtually identicle to the transmission of Torah. According to the Kabbalah, Yahveh spoke the Torah to Gabriel who in turn gave it to Adam. The Torah through oral lineage became the basis for the development of Judaism. We might also consider the transmission of the decalogue tablets, inscribed by YHVH's finger, given to Moses on Sinai during a 7-day thunder-storm. Another such parallel concerns the Emerald Tablets of Atlan, the tablets recording the mystical teachings from Atlantis inscribed in gold, brought to Egypt, and possibly hidden in the Sphinx.)

Although Lei Kung emanates as many Thunder-spirits, his main capacity is to emanate as Five Thunders, known as Wu Fang Lei Kung, Ancestor Thunder of the Five Directions. They are utilized in multiple rites and incantations which request purification. The Five Thunder, who appear as Thunder-birds nearly identicle to Lei Kung, are ultimately guardians of the earth, warriors of negative energies in the universe, great healers, as well as aspects of our own inner electrical power and wisdom (Inner Divinity). The five are one natural power, one totality of wisdoms, split into five configurations, dimensions and directions. They each control the thunder-power which exists in the direction they govern, and the thunder-light in certain parts of the human body, namely the 3 tan t'ien and the mysterious portal (ni wan), as well as other drops in the shoulders. They are the heavenly wisdom that was put on earth at its inception to maintain balance between dark and light forces, to see especially that suffering does not overrun the earth. They are the pure heavenly yang that each person has inher-

ited from the Mysterious Source. This heavenly essence is responsible for our inherent positive virtues and our connection to the subtle law which produces positive transformation in our lives and which governs through our lives.

Although Mysterious Divinity takes shape, it is still formless, as the deep amorphous nature of all minds. Each shape and being expresses its different energy formations and functions. The egg or sphere is its Unborn shape, symbolizing its wholeness and unity, the cohesiveness and magnetic quality of light. The egg is the true shape of the universes beginning, indicating the subtle Tao, or Original harmony. The egg is the symbol of the convergence of the Tao; it is the tai chi of Spirit, symbolized by yolk or the precious middle, and Energy (chi) through which Spirit takes shape. It was known as Yuan-chi, "primordial energy." First it ascended in a pure state to become Heaven (Yang, creative energy), then became clouded or congealed and descended to become earth or solidity (yin, dark). It is inner luminosity (yang) and has the quality of flowing and gathering (yin). It is yang within yin, light within dark, the male seed within the mysterious female, heaven within earth, heart within body. It is the primordial qualities of fire and water, metal, wood, earth, the life-force of the 10,000 things, and the spiritual vitality of all Immortal Beings.

To describe the state of the universe, the Source, before its convergence, the tradition calls it hun-tun, which is usually translated as chaos, but means "luminous cloud." In Chinese mythology, the hun-tun was a four-winged bird spirit. It is a diffuse, undifferentiated potential Space or field. The "luminous cloud" begins to shoot forth rays from itself; within, it aroused thunder and lightning. The thunder awakened it, awakened its potential, its flow. It is like a sleeping dragon in Winter, its spirit-force scattered. In Spring when it awakens, it gathers together and forms a powerful thunder-spirit, attracting clouds of vaporized water all around it. The "luminous cloud" is pregnant like the clouds in Spring. Naturally it gathers into the shape of an egg or cloud. It begins as an egg or pearl and unfolds like a conch spiral, a thunder-storm. It congeals into the 10,000 things—an uncountable multiplicity of forms. Each spiraling galaxy is a being which mirrors the image of Primordial Divinity. Each celestial body is a being which mirrors the image of the Primordial Divinity. Each person is likewise a universe of beings, whose reality, mirroring the Primordial Divinity, is spirit (yang) within and yin (form) without. The Primordial image of Divinity is mirrored by virtue of the continuity of spirit and energy from the minute to the vast. The law of energy transformation is likewise the same on all levels, from the universal to the sub-atomic. The image of Tao as Cosmic body is the Self of the universe, figured in the images of Jade Emperor, Yuan-shih, Pan Ku on their thrones of glory and Lei Kung on the Jade Mountain, the axis of the universe.

The Void gives birth to solidity. The power of the Void is with the Thunder-beings, their Mind is the Void. This power is with nature, the elements. It governs the elements from within. Everything is radiant, and this power to make things visible is with the Thunder-beings, it arises as lightning out of the clashing elements. It is the essence of life, the same energy clashes to produce life and our thoughts. When we control our thoughts, we control the clashing of lights, just as the Thunder-lords control the clashing of their lights to produce lightning. Nature is their mind, the thunder-storm is their heart moving across the sky and stationary in Eternity, the lightning is their thought or self-illumination. To control our minds is to control internal energy, our thoughts are a radiance, our self-illumination. When we act upon creative energy, then we mimic the Thunder-beings to create powerful symbols to illuminate and awaken all beings. Our creative thoughts and acts are like lightning, the creative activity of Thunder Mind.

The Mystery arouses thunder from its being. Thunder-bird arises as the Vision of the Thunder. He lives with Lightning from Eternity to Eternity. He is always Unborn or primordial and yet gives birth to himself here occasionally, in the sky and on the earth. To denote their state and birth out of that state as a first emanation of the Source, they reveal birth from a thunder-egg—an egg which hatches amidst thunder and lightning. His Mind becomes the universe and his power is that of growth, life, and dissolution. His power is that of positive transformation, it produces movement from dark to light. The process of unfolding signified by the thunder-egg is the return of all things to their beginning, to the Unborn state—Tao. The Tao converges, contracts or congeals, then opens, unfolds from within outward like a lotus, until it reaches the fully opened state from which it arose.

The Primordial Beginning has enormous potential power within it. That power is its first manifestation, as thunder and lightning. So the hun-tun could be referred to as the first thunder-egg. This Primordial Beginning is a Spirit—Yuan-shih, and when it reveals itself amidst thunder and lightning, it is Lei Kung. The egg opened up and the Thunder-bird came out and initiated the flow of the universe, the earth and human civilization. The space opened up and there was a lightningbolt. The earth opened up its middle and there was lightning and thunder, then all life was born. A person converges his essence into a strong, luminous, immortal being, and when the spirit arises from its energy-egg there is radiant sparks, rainbows, pearly clouds, lightning and thunder.

Within the heart of reality is its essential nature or Origin from which it arises, the beginning of the universe is with us now, and we will dissolve into it according to our aspiration. The Origin polarizes into positive-negative, yang-yin, heaven-earth. Yang is the subtle energy of everything, the true essence of all minds. It is the original energy of pre-manifestation, the light of the Thunder-beings. Yin refers to that same energy congealed into the material plane. They are two sides of the same reality—Tao. Yang is the subtle, unmanifest Tao, yin is the manifestation of Tao.

Light (yang-chi) is the subtle essence of things, the essential nature of the Universal Mind, the spiritual reality of all beings. Youthfulness describes this nature, the fetal state describes it even better. Birth and life are a movement away from this center or beginning. Things in the womb are closest to the Unborn state, which is heavenly and mirrors the divine integrity represented by the sphere, egg, drum and mandala. Things evolve from their subtlest state to their grossest, then from their grossest back to their subtlest. The universe comes out of the subtlest energy that exists, known as Tao or Highest Divinity or Spirit, evolves into its manifest form, then returns to its Source through refining back into its subtlest state. This is the Tao, Way or circle of all things which is viewed in the cycle of seasons, day-night, moon phases, orbiting planets, solar systems etc. The human fetus evolves in the womb in the same way, its pure yang energy in the eyes gives root to the organs, and a body is formed. The eyes are very important because their energy always remains pure (even being yin, they are pure). They are like seeds. They are a reflection of the original spirit, the vision of the heart. The spirit is wise and sees things automatically, its knowledge is vision. Consciousness itself is vision, an eye that looks through all our senses. Our eyes contain the lights of the Spirit with which we see reality, the heart contains the lights of the Spirit with which we know reality. The eyes are a pure reflection of the spirit. The heart is like the lotus blossoming from the seeds of the eyes. The light of the heart travels through the light of the eyes, via two channels. The heart becomes the window or transmitter to the Divine, so it is related with sound as subtle vibration and radiance (which are the origin of thought. Thunder Lords heart and eyes are thunder (thought) and lightning (vision). The two in reality are one. Though you see lightning coming from his eyes, he emits it from his heart.

The original fetal or Unborn state of our mind is sustained through yang energy. If it has been lost this medicine-power is held by the Thunder-beings to re-establish it, they are known as the greatest healers in the universe. Yang governs the healthy harmonious flow of life. This automatically infers that where yang exists purely in the universe, in subtle space, there is unlimited life, peace, joy. It also implies that, because it exists in our body as our pure heavenly inheritance, that it can be gathered and increased to gradually replace the congealed energy which governs the cycle of decay and death. Normally yang governs the first part of life, and slowly is depleted unless it is being gathered from the universe, until it is gone and the body perishes. Yang and yin are also in this sense the phases of energy-transformation. Thunder-beings embody the yang energy, it radiates from them. They carry the power of the harmonious order of things, of the universes birth and growth. They carry the power of life, and with it illuminate the earth, and with it set things on fire, and with it set our hearts on fire, and with it dissolve negativity. It is a crackling fire, it can cause life where there was none, and can kill because the charge is so great. Thunder-dragons, lung, were used as symbols to denote yang energy. They can produce, lightning, fires, winds, hurricanes as natural beings aligned with heaven and earth. Occasionally dragons will appear before someone or a group of people, the thunder-dragon will actually set down on the earth during a storm and people will see it. The same is true of Thunder Lords, if you pray to them diligently they will come to you.

The tiger was used as a symbol of yin. Certain Tigers can produce storms as well, but in this image the tiger is strictly symbolic of pure yin. The union of dragon and tiger, yang and yin produces natural growth, from vegetation to our growth into spirit. The clashing of poles produces lightning in the atmosphere, and it produces our return to the Origin. It produces a balanced, controlled mind which integrates spiritual energy from heaven and physical energy from earth. It is the mind which reconnects with its Origin and is illuminated. The Mystery (Tao) polarizes into positive and negative whose collision produces friction which develops into wind and then sound. In the atmosphere thunder and lightning are the result. In summer the balance of polarized energy is indicated by thunder. In the microcosm, the balance of polarized energies, of spirit and body, produces thought, equilibrium, inner peace and harmony.

Yang is the energy which supports the shens immortal existence, yin is the energy which supports earthly existence. Yin allows shens to descend from the stars and take bodies. In order to return to the Origin it is necessary to contact and gather pure yang energy which is embodied in the shens and made visible through stars, lightning etc. Because the amount of yin energy in the body far exceeds the yang energy, it becomes necessary to gather this power. In most traditions the pure energy is embodied in Highest Divinity as One or multiple aspects of One, thus it becomes efficacious to venerate Celestials to gather positive energy in order to return to the Source.

Yang governs our return to the Origin, which is a reversal of the process of decay, a replacement of the limited yin energy with yang in the body. To keep this natural way in harmony, the powers of reversal, Thunder-beings function in the universe. Thunderstorms are a movement back to the Origin, a re-establishment of the Origin on the earth. Thunder-beings are the activity of the Origin, of pure yang controlling yin, the elements. We can learn something from this, from nature, that when yin rules, decay governs to produce illness, when the body governs the spirit, illness and death are the result, when spirit (heaven) governs the body (yin) unlimited life is the result. Thunder-beings bring about a transition from dark to light. If dark begins to rule, decay and illness lead to death, and for people to spiritual opacity. The Thunder-beings spontaneously reverse this process. They are constantly working to bring harmony and balance back to the universe.

Yang is identified with the sun (and stars). Yin with the moon (and earth). The sun energy is associated with being and doing, the moon with resistance to the sun, and is produced by reflection. When the two symbols are integrated, the meaning is medicine. An actualization of yang and yins fusion is the lightning or thunder-storm (of fire from the sun and water from the earth), the electrical balance which nourishes the earth and produces spontaneous external and internal growth. Therefore we refer to thunder-power as a medicine and to rain as a blessing.

Their power appears to be contrary, the clashing of opposite poles, but in truth, it is a natural fusion; Thunders express through their energy and activity the underlying unity of things—Truth. A chief Thunder-bird of the Lakota pantheon, Haokah, cries when he's happy, when he's hot he shivers, and so on. The Spirit of Tao embraces all nature, nothing is contrary to anything else. Two things rubbing together produce a spark—that's it. The degeneration of our mind, our ignorant behavior are the only contraries from the perspective of the Truth, the unified state of things. Truth (Tao) is the only all-pervasive reality.

The nature of Thunder-beings' power of reversal appears contrary, its Mystery is the natural primordial union of poles. What to us appears as opposites are complements, we merely fail to see the whole picture. The reversal that they cause is the movement from dark to light, illness to well-being, opacity to radiance, chaos to harmony, yin to yang.

The lightning is luminous concentrated life-force (chi) in union with Spirit (shen). This synthesis is called ling—spirit-force. Thunder-birds wings can symbolize this unity, one representing Spirit, the other Energy. Thunder-birds control the pure ling of Highest Divinity to benefit the universe. To preserve the harmonious operation of nature, the lightning, "power of reversal," has two prongs and functions, one to remove what is old, the other to bring new life-light. That makes it a tai chi or electrical balance of positive and negative. Since the combined symbols for yang and yin form the symbol for medicine, the power of reversal is a medicine. Lightning is the earths medicine. It can cure illness because it is living power, a live-wire that initiates life and renews it continuously.

One light we equate with destruction, the other with creation, but in truth there is only awakening and its simultaneous transformation. When yin dominates, energy becomes old, brittle, out of balance, so the Thunder-birds function to awaken it to its primordially youthful state (Tao) by presenting it with a glimpse or Vision of the Origin, its very own true essence. They give us a look at our Origin in the lightning. It jogs the universal memory bank into recalling its Unmanifest, or pre-manifest, original state. Before there were animals there was vegetation, before there was vegetation there was fire and water, before fire and water there was solidity, before solidity there were two energies, before the two energies

there was Void, formless Spirit in union with Energy (Tao). When there is lightning and shock the Tao naturally returns to rule with radiant light. You are seeing the Tao in the sky, and it jogs all minds back to their radiant beginning in the Void.

The shens energy is the light of Tao which neither rises nor sets. Thunder-power reverses the process of decay by awakening the impure energy to its Original unlimited, pure state from which it arose. The image of the activity of the Thunder-beings is the Thunder-bird flying counter-clockwise around the sun, or the sun and moon following reverse orbits from sunset (yin) to sunrise (yang, light). The Thunder-beings bring the universe back to its dawn again and again. The End and Beginning are one. The Origin is the end to which all things must return. Thunder-beings control the power of transformation which brings everything back into itself just as it produced it. Everything returns to the still point between creations (Tao). It is the Silent Space (Void) before and between the arising of any two things. It is pure capacity and potential energy. Because yin's true essence, the true essence of the five elements and nature is untainted light and empty space (Tao), nature is beautiful, radiant and alive. That unobstructed luminosity in all its transformations is the heart of the universe—Tao, the shape of which is Thunder-bird. He stands for all of nature, from T'ien Tsun (subtlest state) to the earth (grossest), the top of his head to the pit of his belly. The yang essence is symbolized in alchemical terminology as gold. It enables base metals (yin, the body) to be transmuted into gold (true nature, spirit).

When the universe was young shens came forth into it. They took root in the subtle realms associated with the star-systems, the palace and seats of heavenly existence. The illumination we equate with God, shining from heaven is the same light as that which shines as stars. Illumination is the nature of all minds and the universe, even space is an illumination. Out of the pure natural Spirit arose human spirits. Humans are potential shens on earth. Like the stars and Thunders, we shine naturally with the heavenly-light inheritance of our Creative Ancestors, whom we venerate as natural deities or God. God is the gold of our primordially undecayed nature. God is also the essence of the elements, their true nature. Therefore when the physical energy-form of the body is awakened to its yang-essence, our life takes on an undecaying electrical-light quality whose heart is like white jade, and whose capacity for kindness is undiminishing.

Unstained purity is our true essence, symbolized in Taoist alchemy as thunder, or a bright pearl (which dragons roll to cause thunder). The word for shen (immortal), in ancient Chinese script means thunder and lightning. Shen means "spirit" and "an extension." The shens are an extension of the Subtle Source, as its first emanation. They are eternally existent as the Subtle Source, in converged unity prior to the universe, emanated into various subtle realms (36 heavenly caves) and constellation form realms, once the universe is born.

Originally, when shens took bodies on earth, they remained pure extensions of the Source, therefore we say the gods walked the earth—those people were form-gods. Immortals initiated this cycle of human existence around 12,000 years ago, following the melting ice of the last deep freeze. They descended spiritually; the idea of the metallic space ship is a recent human development, which is based on limited perception of reality. The shens can shape-shift, taking whatever form and color they want. They can be seen riding dragons, unicorns, horses, tigers, Thunderbirds, cranes, wheels, and chariots, of unique spiritual coloration where all the colors are inherent yet distinct, where the vehicle is an ebullient super-luminal life. Their spherical light-bodies are the vehicles made of out gossamer subtle-life-particles. They are very holy and wise beyond reckoning.

Generally the human populace in early times remained as pure emanations of Spirit en-robed in matter, like their ancestors. Most followed nature and lived simply. They were wise and learned, they were not primitive or like apes. We have developed a taste for technology, comforts and a complex life style, calling this evolved while it goes against nature (Tao) and as such creates unnecessary troubles. At the same time Yuan-shih transmitted teachings (which they do at the beginning of each eon) to assist humanity to live natural lives in harmony with the energies of the universe, and to return as shens to the subtle realms. It is essential to understand that each person is potentially a shen, that a shen is a perfected being, a person who has adhered to the subtle law of nature through virtue and who has cultivated wisdom to the extent that it governs ones entire life. Each of us originally was shen, a pure extension of heaven, and we certainly can return to this state. What makes us heavenly extensions are lights of varying frequencies, pure yang-essence, within our body.

Our life-being arises from the Void (hsu) as Hsing-ming, nature and life. Hsing stands for the root of spiritual consciousness, the source of the mind, and ming stands for the substance of life, the source of chi or energy. Hsing is the source of spirit, ming is the source of energy. This primordial energy at the moment of birth separates into hsing and ming, or spirit and energy (like Shiva and kundalini). The aim is to return to the original wholeness, void, by uniting energy and the root of the mind into a spirit (shen). This is only possible through spiritual-cultivation.

By virtue of heaven existing within us, as Spirit (as fire in the head and the three tan t'ien), we are related to all heavenly beings. By virtue of earth within us, as physical energy (water in the abdomen), we are related to all earthly beings. The natural synthesis of the two is the mind (in the heart) which makes us human. The harmonious order is for the spirit to control the body through the mind, its mediary. The mind is the meeting of spirit and physical energy. So many people do not allow their spirit to rule their body, but rather follow the physical impulses through glandual secretions. So the body comes to control the spirit through the mind. And the spirit becomes imprisoned in the world of the mundane impulses. This activity causes our nature to become obscured, the light to become darkened and depleted. The possibility of giving birth to ourselves as shens with unlimited lives can only be brought about by reversing the activity where body controls spirit, to where spirit controls the body. This is a preliminary to all spiritual paths, and very often entails renunciation and self-control. We went so far to this physical extreme, now we must go to the opposite extreme to correct the problems, to balance our energy. We are really seeking to balance our energy (yang-yin) by balancing our activity, because activity gathers energy from the universe. If we are non-virtuous, then the effect will be a subtle darkening, and if we're virtuous, the effect is a subtle lightening.

Shen-hood comes about when we have gathered sufficient yang energy from the universe to sustain an unlimited existence. This state comes about through refinement of dark energy of the body through practice of self-cultivation. When all the dark energy is replaced by light, then we become shen, free of suffering, not governed by the physical universe, a conduit for the subtle powers and law of nature. Because we are a mirror of the Origin, because the 36,000 Deities exist within us until we die, we have complete potential for restoration of our self as shen, a joyous and still natural spirit. It is through our internal pure energies that pure energy is gathered, they attract one another, they are love. We are attracted to the shens through devotion, they are attracted to throught compassion. Eventually we meet.

Just as the Thunder-Mind brings this harmonious state about in nature, so they assist us to bring it about in our mind. They assist us to make the transition from dark, limited energy to expansive, positive light, from suffering to beauty. They bestow two things: one is light which they continually diffuse into our hearts and lives in order to gradually awaken our minds, the second is teachings or guidance which enables us to awaken more quickly by plugging into their socket to transmute the body of consciousness to give birth to spirit. They give practices (Fou Jou) which we can use to achieve ourselves, to refine our internal states, to widdle ourselves down until there's nothing left but the tool in a chest of empty space, and the realization that we were never widdling anything to begin with.

Our purpose is like the Thunder-birds—to reverse the process of decay and death by removing the negative energies. Once one achieves a balance within ones life by gathering clear-light, by refining ones yang-essence out of yin, then one can shift ones emphasis onto guiding others onto the path. When one has achieved a certain degree of perfection, then the Thunder-beings give you a higher duty to fulfill for them, perhaps one may become a Thunder specialist, a piece of Thunder spirit functioning on the earth, waging war against beings who have fallen out of harmony and who prey on the weak and defenseless.

Thunder-bird represents the energy and path to achieve this state which potentially resides in us. They act to assist us to enlightenment, their energy takes us back to the dawn of our mind, back to hsing-ming. Achievement means replacing all the low-frequency energy with subtle high frequency energy, when we're 100% subtle, then we're perfect—Yuan-shih's first emanation.

The ancients aligned themselves with nature, because nature, the stars, sun, moon, thunder, clouds and spirits are windows through which the pure creative energy of the Unmanifest Tao, the Tao that cannot be seen, shines. Thunder-bird is an immutable expression of this Tao, a clear mirror a cloud of blessing-lights. Those who achieve themselves through the power of thunder become great healers and sages—Thunder specialists—shens. Certainly we know only about a few who were written about. Although there are some on earth presently, I'd like to make mention of Yu the Great for two reasons; first his work on earth echoes the ancient work of the Thunder Lords, secondly,

because Yu's transmission figures prominently in the Thunder rites.

During the 2nd millenium B.C. there was a great flood, one of two recorded by Chinese writers. A divinely appointed ruler known as Kun was trying to dam the rising waters of the deluge by plugging river outlets with mold. Kun was executed and his son, Emperor Yu the Great was appointed by God. Yu arose like thunder, from the belly of Kun. Yu was a shape-shifter and powerful Thunder specialist. The waters were rising toward heaven. Yu worked with the powers of thunder, the work of thunder is the work of yu. Yu carved out river beds and dug holes through mountains, no different than the Thunder Lords had long before. Yu got to know the names of the gods and spirits of nature. He gained assistance from them to drain the waters into the sea. Through his use of invocations he set the stage for the Thunder specialist to heroically achieve divine accomplishments, specifically to recycle negative stale energy on earth by contacting pure energy (shens) and dispatching them. He also transmitted the "step of yu" as a bird dance practice in the Thunder rites. Yu used it to counter disaster. The Thunder specialist mimics Yu's dance, which he observed in birds trying to crack open stones by stepping on them. Clearly this is a transmission from Thunder-birds who set down on the mountains. This step in also called the Ho t'u. This ritual used for controlling natural disasters, controlling thunder and lightning, driving out evil from a community and stopping armies.

Generally it is taught that Thunder god created the deluge. The Chinese myth relates that a certain man became angry with Thunder Lord and actually imprisoned him in a cage. The man's two children freed Thunder Lord by giving him a glass of water (power). Then Thunder Lord favored those children, and when he created the deluge, put the two in a gourd and floated them to the next world to initiate it. So avaricious people caused a drought, and a deluge.

Thunder-birds birth does not signal the birth of calamity, but rather the birth of subtle law which rules wisely and judges fairly the activities of human-kind. His egg-birth signals life and new-growth as well as judgement. It ensures that suffering be curtailed before it reaches its zenith. It is the birth of wisdom, the medicine which people need to create harmony on earth. Thunder-birds birth from void, egg, cloud, is in the form of a lightning issuing from an egg, or thunder from a drum. Lei Kung's birthday is celebrated as the 24th of the 6th month of the lunar calendar. One myth tells that Thunder god was born from an egg revealed by a dog. The birth of the Uncreate is its first emanation, its first rays, its first convergence and most powerful bursting forth. It is the birth of storms on the face of the earth, at the beginning of time, at the beginning of Spring, at the dawn of our subtle life, for his egg birth is the archetype of our own birth into spirit since we have the potential to fly in the Void, to become shen.

Thunder-birds in universal iconography are seen in the act of subduing serpents in their talons, eating them, and especially Bar-B-Q-ing them in lightnings. The serpents are yin energy rays, they cause decay, illness and death. They are impure energies. The Thunder-birds, out of compassion for living beings, battle and subdue these and all other malevolent monsters. They were the first exorcists. They give this power to their earthly messengers. (In fact it is not really we who dispatch them through supplication, but they who dispatch us to supplicate them.)

The main schools of Thunder rites which flourished in the Sung dynasty (960-1278 a.d.) Trace their origin to the slaying of a serpent by a Thunder specialist using the power of thunder. His name was Hsu Hsun a Confucian administrator and Taoist master who was assumed in 374 a.d. A huge snake demon was attacking people under his administrative jurisdiction. With his 12 followers he confronted it and destroyed it. Thunder specialists utilizing the power of thunder, transmute their body into Thunder-bird and battle the yin energies of nature, spirits that dwell close to the elements, and snake demons under the control of black magicians.

The Schools which trace their lineage to Hsu Hsun are as follows: the Mao-Shan or Hun t'un Thunder sect; the Ching-wei Thunder sect which descended from Mao-Shan; the Sanskrit Primordial Breath Thunder sects, which included the Ling-pao sect, the Shen hsiao Thunder Magic and the Tai-i sect; the Yu-fu sect and the Chen-i Heavenly Master Thunder sect; the Pei-chi Pole Star Thunder Magic sect and the Pole Star sect. Of these, the Ching-wei, the Fire-Master Thunder Magic, and the Shen-hsiao continue their lineages.

At the level of the microcosm the serpents are the causes of our illness, they are impure negative energies which obscure essential nature of our pure spirits of the three spheres, body, mind and spirit. According to the Inner Deity Hygiene school there are "three worms", yin energies that exist in the three cinnabar fields (tan t'ien). The three worms try to shorten life

and prevent immortality. They are cause of diseases. The adept tries to rid himself of the three worms.

Thunder-birds control the universe and mind, so their power defeats the serpents of internal energy just as well as those of the cosmic sphere. The energies are really the same acting in one sphere, deemed the Mysterious Mother. The thunder essence is within us as our purest divine inheritance—ling. It is concentrated at certain places within the body, the most notable being the point between and behind the eyes—the mystical pearl or mysterious portal. As the Five Thunders are stationed in the five directions as guardians over the earth, they are also protectors of each person, stationed within the body in the four directions and center (along with the Three Pure Ones of Highest Divinity in the upper, middle and lower cinnabar fields). With this in mind it enables us to see how Thunders can arise within us from vast inner space, how they can respond to us immediately, how they can touch our hearts and burn from within.

Because everything is the Tao, the external universe and its cycles of transformation are mirrored perfectly in the body and life of each person. The Tao is one complete field and unity. The 36,000 deities that control the external universe abide also in our bodies where they control the inner universe. The Inner Deity Hygiene school allocated deities to parts of the body and organs. Being in the body is a prerequisite for life, when the deity leaves, the body perishes. They are our protection. By means of right nourishment, virtue, invocations, visualization of deities, and meditation, these deities are contacted and induced to protect the body and assist in attaining immortality. Contacting the deities causes radiant light to appear from their abode. For use in transmuting energy into spirit, it is gathered in the body. When it is gathered throughout the body, or circulated, it has the effect of harmonizing all internal states, and driving out potential or manifest illness (three worms).

The Five Thunders, whose totality and Chief is Lei Kung can be invoked within the body to grant protection. This practice is called "Protection of the Five Thunders." The seed syllable of thunder is HONG or BONG, which are the Chinese equivalents to the Sanskrit HUM and BAM. This practice is utilized to protect a Thunder person from evil spirits, or any practitioner from calamity and harm. With the right hand, fold the thumb across the palm and fold the fingers over it, to make a baby-fist mudra. With the first knuckle of the second finger: touch the mysterious pass between the eyes and pronounce HONG; touch the left shoulder and pronounce HONG; touch the right shoulder and pronounce HONG; touch the heart and pronounce HONG; touch the throat and pronounce HONG. Repeat the invocation five times.

This practice invokes the powers of the Five Thunders in the microcosm. It awakens the Five Thunder Mandala in the body. (Similar practices have been transmitted in the other Tantric traditions, the one I'm aware of is called Nyasa and invokes aspects of Shiva or other Deities in the body, at crown, heart, eyes, forehead).

Because some of the essence of the Thunders is inside the body, the adept can become Lei Kung by continually gathering his wisdom-essence (ling) through practices of visualization, invocation, mudras and offerings, and eventually when there is sufficient ling, cause a response from the outer force of Lei Kung to cause rain, lightning, heal, drive out evil spirits, or manipulate reality. Lei Kung's image is used primarily in these rites (in the Thunder Magic schools), along with his name, invocations, gestures, dances and offerings, to contact his ling and apply it where needed. Although it should be understood that the Thunder-beings are beyond form, you can feel them first, you can taste them through your mind, they make your hair stand on end and your spirit dance. Their ling arouses the spirits of all life even before it reveals itself in sound and light.

Thunder and lightning, image and name, are just symbol-vehicles for the subtle formless state of the Thunder-Lord. The iconography and invocations are recorded in registers (lu) which are transmitted to a Thunder specialist or Taoist priest upon ordination. The lu gives a complete list of spirits and Deities over which he has dominion. In these scriptural texts, the iconography of the deity and aspects are provided with the heavenly register of names.

Lei Kung and the Ministry of Thunder

In China the pantheon of Thunder-beings is known as the Ministry of Thunder. There are 80 Thunder-beings in the pantheon, the chief among them being Lei Kung a.k.a. Lei Tsu—Chief Thunder. Lei Kung means Grandfather Thunder, and has been used to denote the entire pantheon of Thunder Lords; they are many and yet one. Traditionally he emanates into the five directions of space, as wing-flappers like

himself. He is their totality, what each is through and through. They seem to group in pairs according to their axis: East-West, North-South (such was one way I saw them). Lei Kung is worshiped under the names Chiu T'ien Lei Tsu, Wu Fang Lei Kung, Lei Tsu Ta Ti and Kwantung. Chiu T'ien tells us he is Highest Divinity; Lei Tsu and Lei Kung designate his stature in the hierarchy of heaven, that he is Grandfather and Chief among Thunder-birds and shens; Wu Fang tells us he's the Thunders of the five directions; Ta Ti tells us he's a great warrior. Lei Kung is translated often as Ancestor Thunder, as opposed to Grandfather Thunder. We are descendants of the heavenly Wisdom-beings. When they walked the earth, they lived as pure manifestations of Tao, following subtle law (as virtue) within. We can follow their example and become shens and Thunder-beings. We can align with their spirit-energy and utilize it to attain the immortal state. Master Ni Hua-Ching says: "This stream of eternal spirit responds to the divine way of self-cultivation whereby one can refine one's energy to become the same quality as that of Heavenly Immortals" (199 Hua-Ching Ni, Workbook for Spiritual Development).

Lei Kung possesses the universal Thunder-bird iconography. He has a man's torso, beak-like face, wings and talons. If the human attributes symbolize the descent of spirit into the earth, the base from which we will begin, then the bird attributes symbolize the ascent of the spirit back to heaven (as shen). If the human attributes symbolize the archetype of the human family, the bird attributes symbolize the field from which we are born. If the human attributes symbolize the earth, then the bird attributes symbolize the subtle realm to which we can give birth to ourselves. Human and bird attributes symbolize the spiritualized, immortalized state of the body. As lightning, Thunder-bird connects heaven and earth. The human torso means that mind (the sphere of which is the heart) is joined to spirit symbolized by the bird's head and wings. The 9 spirits, 3 corresponding to the body and lower cinnabar field, 3 to the mind and middle cinnabar field, and 3 to spirit and upper cinnabar field, are converged into one unified spirit—shen. Lei Kung is our fully spiritualized angelic state—a representation of shen-hood. His wings symbolize the freedom of spirit, the ascent of the spirit to subtle realms, but also the freedom of the heart bathed in the pristine quality of spirit and energy. They symbolize the motivation of this heart, to extend itself (shen) to awaken all beings (through luminosity). So the wings symbolize descent of ling to earth as luminosity. Very often the flapping of wings produces thunder—the activity of their heart produces awakening. Ling is the "winged-power" which Thunder specialists learn to direct in order to cause heavenly accomplishments on earth. The wings are the force of emanation, the original tai chi of spirit and energy, the first arising out of Void, the first revelation of formless Spirit. Lei Kung is the vehicle which carries the Unborn Tao, the Sacred Mystery into the universe. Their revelation is the Light of the Unmanifest Tao. Lei Kung is the potential for our achievement, the force and activity of our achievement.

Lei Kung is electric blue, like the blue lightning from the sun, dressed in a loin cloth, standing in an active and protective posture. He is blue to symbolize the unlimited and free state of spirit—omniscience, and energy—omnipotence. Blue is the color of the protective, Lei Kung is a great protector. He protects us from evil, calamity and suffering. His posture and color reflect his gesture of love. He is one of several beings who keep watch over the earth. His activity is for the restoration of the universe and mind. He brings us back to the Tao within, our inner stillness and luminosity. His posture means he is actively helping beings to attain shen-hood, and that we must do the same in order to attain his state. He carries a string of drums over his shoulder, in his right hand he holds a wooden mallet to strike the drums, in his left he holds a magical dagger. His drums are the sound of thunder which arouses the universe and the power of thunder to awaken all minds. Thunder signals the beginning of natural flow from Tao, and its flow back into Tao. So it symbolizes our return to Tao. Thunder awakened the egg of the universe. It signals the beginning of movement within the earth, the beginning of growth each Spring, the first stirring of love within the heart. It symbolizes the complete turning of the heart, our complete awakenment and breakthrough into the limitless Void state. Thunder awakens the internal spirits through initiation. Thunder is the Sound of a connection being made, between heaven and earth, yang and yin. It is the fusion of two sparks, one light, one dark. The spark emitted by his drum is the lightning. His drum is the drum of the sky. Drumming was a way of mimicing thunder, of melting into Lei Kung. So the Thunder masters would adorn themselves like Thunder-bird and drum and dance to bring down the power to heal, to rain, to awaken the earth, to drive out the evil sha (spirits). Thunder specialists learned to use thunder-power invisibly for healing and visibly for causing explosions. A charged pearl or magic bowl could be applied to destroying temples of malevolent spirits and subduing those spirits. Later fire-works were developed to mimic thunder as heavenly sound.

The drum and egg are interchangeable metaphors for the energy sphere of the universe, earth and human. They represent energy fields created by the polarization of positive and negative, which form around solar systems, stars, planets, storms, and people. These fields emit light from the friction of charges in the egg or drum. The beating on heaven emits light which awakens the earth. It also represents our return in a clap of thunder to the great emptiness of Tao. The thunder brings about the transition from dark to light. It is the hatching, completion and birth of the shen into the spirit realms. Thunders children come out of an egg or gourd into the next world to begin unlimited life in subtle space. The egg or drum is the energy-sphere within which we complete ourselves, within which we jam and unite yang and yin, within which the friction of yang or thunder-essence with yin produces our awakenment and rapid illumination (lightning). The sound which issues forth from the egg is alive, self-luminous, it is the spirit or baby shen. Thunder-birds' voices are his many children. His lightnings are his children.

On the surface, Lei Kung's magic-dagger is the visible counterpart to the drums, the lightning. The popular religion interpreted his dagger as a device of retribution (he was said to have been ordered to punish the guilty). Although the power of Judgement or Truth is born with the Thunder-beings (they're stern disciplinarians), no retribution is practiced by such heavenly beings. Death by lightning happens by the law of universal response; because the energy of the universe and oneself are the same you receive an echo for every voice you send out. When one has acted virtuously, the Tao has been adhered to, and the results are positive. To harm others is to infract upon the Tao, the pure energy of the universe. The effect will be the same as the cause, perhaps in a different shape. There is a subtle darkening of the light. The frequency of the act reflects the cause of it, creating a vicious wheel. So the person naturally attracts his own doom. From the standpoint of Thunder people, it is non-virtuous people who are the real contraries, because the true law is broken time and again. The dagger of the true law (Tao) of spiritual government which breaks the wheel of suffering, of negativity. The dagger is the power which cuts through negative states like a flash of lightning, which liberates minds like a bolt out of the blue. The dagger is Lei Kung's pure ling, with it he magically subdues and destroys negativity, he pins it down and cuts it up, he severs the root of all suffering. His dagger is the same as the phurba of the Vajrayana Deities like Vajrapani. Lei Kung rains it down on our enemies, our negative states, to sever the root of all delusions. Lei Kung pins them down and cuts them open to liberate their heart. The heart of all demons is Tao, light of silence. The heart of our internal negative states is the light of Tao. The power (dagger) makes a light in our mind, it is Vision or wisdom and replaces our ignorance, the root of all suffering (inner demons). It is brought forth in the atmosphere as the power to subdue outer demons. And it is brought forth from the subtle space of Tao to refine our gross internal energy into vitality and pure spirit. It is the power of awakening in no matter what sphere.

Lei Kung has a family. His consort is named T'ien Mu Niang Niang and is a goddess of lightning. Her name means Grandmother of Heaven (with Lightning), and she is a Goddess of the Ladle. When taken together, Lei Kung makes thunder while T'ien Mu makes lightning with two mirrors. She holds them above her head. As thunder and lightning are the same so are Lei Kung and T'ien Mu, they are two aspects of the same reality, such as masculine and feminine, flow and capacity (rest), nature and Tao, energy and Spirit. Her mirrors could be taken to represent the divine waters in which the lightnings are reflected. Her mirrors suggest that she's reflecting the sun (or Tao). Her mirrors suggest the receptivity of our awareness, the capacity for shen in which the alchemical process is going to take place. T'ien Mu has been figured wielding lightning in her hand. She also has 10,000 golden snakes which flash electricity throughout the universe. Those serpents are lightnings, the gold alludes to the yang-essence, the realm of gold purity, one of the mothers primary rays. It alludes to the sun and the movement of electricity through space. Such electricity could be said to be at the root of life, as the pure life-force which is absorbed and transformed by all beings. Electricity is said to be a gift from the Thunder-beings, that without it nothing could live. In this way T'ien Mu is the aspect of the Mysterious Mother related to growth and fertility.

She stands on a cloud, like other Mothers, symbolizing celestial vitality, her heavenly purity. She is fierce like other lightning mothers (Durga, Kali, Vajravarahi, Trolma, and those in meso-merica, where the degree of violence of a storm corresponds directly to the degree of violence of the rain-mother who created

it). She is the female lightning, the female rain. She embodies the maternal energy and Spirit of the Sacred Mystery. She also, and most importantly represents the capacity for woman to become a Thunder-being, to become Lei Kung (T'ien Mu). The females who achieve themselves through Lei Kung's Thunder method (Tantra) become T'ien Mu. Symbolically the Mother stands for the root of kindness, while Lei Kung is the root of wisdom, or selflessness, the necessary condition for spiritual achievement.

Another way of looking at these symbols is as follows: yang represents flow, movement, while yin is the capacity for this movement. She is the receptivity and openness of the Spirit (Tao), while Lei Kung is the energy which flashes in her mirrors. She is the pure awareness, the clear-light is Lei Kung. So although Lei Kung and T'ien Mu are actual Wisdom-beings, multiple Thunder-spirits residing in subtle realms and mysterious pearls within our body-mind, they can be viewed as universal forces, currents and their fusion which produces thunder phenomena in the atmosphere and which produces electrical stimulation and shen within the Thunder adept. Thunder-bolts arise from the fusion of yang-fire from the sun, and yin from vaporized water, positive and negative. The fire is the seed infused into the womb of the Mother producing a thunder-egg (cloud) and a beautiful lightning-bolt child.

All people given yang and yin from the Creator, yang being our heavenly endowment, yin being our earthly inheritance. The fusion of yang and yin produces creative electrical energy, a powerful current that runs through the body and gathers in the lower cinnabar field, not unlike lightning running through the body of the sky. A master who has joined the fire and water in the abdomen can use the new power to heal, cast out demons, magnetically attract storms (Thunder-beings), start fires and give shocks which make the mind smile. This is the inner meaning of the dagger, the outer implement is just a reminder of the inner power. Lei Kung's dagger is his spiritual essence, which we invoke and mix with our own energy. When the quality of our energy becomes like his, then, lo, we look and in our hand is Lei Kung's magical dagger, and our body is blue and our experience of reality is flavored with Lei Kung.

In the microcosm the thunder is a symbol of the awakening of ones spirits, ones original yang-essence, which underwent refining from gross to subtle. It is a symbol of the gathering of pure energy like the gathering of thunder-clouds, the lightning is the pure shen which follows—the lamp of Tao—a true baby Thunder-bird.

The similarity of birds to Thunder-birds is astounding—they are related but not the same. They arise from the same Source. The Source originates this sacred iconography, not people—it doesn't come out of the imagination. Thunder-bird image is bestowed out of the Heart of Primordial Spirit, and the Subtlest Energy in the universe; it is Immortal spirit—bird, wind, sky, rain, lightning, space, thunder, stone, earth are just adornments. Young Thunder-birds act like young birds. This is metaphorical. Young birds must undergo a real training, a maturation. They have to be trained in order to leave the nest, to fly, find food, etc. Their training is as natural as their instinctual behavior, so these cannot be separated. We must also undergo a real training in order to mature into a spiritual being—that is if we're interested in an unlimited life of pristine qualities. If we remain true to our nature from the start, true to our heart, then our training will be natural and intuitive—spontaneous. Otherwise it may seem like work at first, like discipline. But this work bears true fruit, fruit the taste of which liberates minds, it leads to ecstasy, to the ability to fly, for the spirit and transmuted body, to take off from the nest of earth into the emptiness of Tao.

The Immortals were called "bird-men," because they could fly, and be seen covered with a coat of feathers. The Chinese pictograph for shien, Immortal, meant rising, ascent into the air. The crane, phoenix, dragon and Thunder-bird are symbols of immortality, heavenly energy and unfathomable wisdom. Immortals were often seen riding such beings to heaven. The Thunder specialist and priest has been called yu-jen, "feather-man." This flight first denotes the ecstatic freedom of the heart, of ones energy, since this is our first attainment and the goal more quickly attainable. Secondly it represents literal flight and assumption into the clouds of heaven.

Lei Kung has children as do many Thunder-birds. His children act like young birds, clumnsey and mischievous. The young Thunders are said to kill accidentally, while the elders, the Lei Kung, are very wise and never kill. The elders make the big thunder claps, while the young make the rumbley thunder which follows by mimicking their parents. Thunder-birds are usually hatched from eggs or from one giant egg, or they might arise from Thunder-bird's voice. If you see these eggs in the dwelling of the Thunder-birds (the nest in the Tree or Crag of Eternity), it symbolizes the womb of heaven from which one is reborn into a spiritual plane, it is our energy-egg out of which we give birth to ourselves through spiritual cultivation. The earth is called the womb of the Mysterious Mother, it is a transitional realm in which to cultivate and grow. The body is the same as this womb since it came out of the earth. Within it the process of transmutation from gross to subtle, dark to light is undergone. This womb is the thunder-egg, the energy-egg of our life-being which includes the inner universe and the outer auric envelopes. It is an egg of reversal, its hatching is only possible by a reversal of the activity and thinking which put the mind in bondage. The egg is the gateway to the Uncreate. Thunder-birds are Lords of this reversal, they are the grace to achieve it, so they are called Contraries. Most Immortals were viewed as sacred contraries because they embody the Tao of non-dual Reality and express the opposite of the mundane view.

One of Lei Tzu's sons is named Lei Chen-tzu; he was hatched from an egg after a thunder-clap and found by soldiers of Wen Wang. This King gave the child to one of his sons of the Clouds, Yun Chung-tzu, to rear. Wen Wang was taken prisoner by the opposing forces. Lei Chen-tzu found two apricots and ate them, after which wings grew from his back, his face turned green, his nose became a long beak, tusks came out of his jaws and his eyes shone like mirrors. He then rescued his adopted father Wen and flew him home on his back. This is a story illustrating the attainment of a Thunder master (apricots), the becoming of an immortal Thunder-bird.

The remarkable feature of the myths concerning Lei Kung are his children's likeness to young birds. One has troubles taking off, another gets caught in the cleft of a tree, they always wind up annoying somebody with their thunderings—some mundane minds do have real problems with contrary behavior. I think we can see in the behavior of the Immortals the young freshness of Spring, the empty mindedness of the Unborn state, the clashing and sparking of hot and cold and the vibrant flow of the Tao. We can see a pure motivation to awaken minds. We can see the childlikeness of the spiritual baby of our wise elders. The Immortals are undecaying, so their complexion retains the glow of a child, of a fresh sprout and young flower.

Hatching an Alchemical Bird

In the ancient Chinese practices, the process of internal refinement or transmutation is referred to as internal alchemy. Within us, spirit is essential nature and vitality is eternal life manifesting or masquerading as generative force. Immoderate desires cause the energy to flow downward into its reservoir, the abdomen. It remains separate from the spirit (in which case we remain separate from our Original state), unless the energy is refined. The three spheres of being are located in the microcosm thus: spirit in the head, mind in the heart and earth in the abdomen. Within the person of mundane desires and activities, vitality, like water, seeps downward, while spirit, like fire, flies upward. If they're not unified, at death, what belongs to the earth (by adhering to the ways of the earth) returns to the earth, so the energy scatters, and the spirit either remains in a stupor (without the body to control it) or seeks to clothe and fulfill itself again. Therefore it is said that water and fire must be joined.

The Immortal embryo is formed by a threefold ascension, generative force (jing) is refined into chi or vitality in the lower cinnabar field (cauldron) of the abdomen. The heavenly yang-essence is brought in through the heart and crown, or inhaled directly from the first storm. This energy is mixed to refine the gross energy of the body. Thunder-power can be stored in the body for later use, such as making talismans and performing exorcisms. The fire is said to vaporize the water, turning it into steam. Generative energy is electrified, refined into white or silver light, vitality. It flies upwards to the brain (sometimes with a shock), enlightening its path. The stage when sexual energy has been electrified and transmuted into a crystalline substance gives rise to the experience of bright silver light called the Silver Flower. It likewise liberates the mind of limited energy which was imprisoned by the urges and emotions which accompany the gross energy frequency.

The eternal life-spark of the heart has the potential for new spirit (refined energy) within it. Yet there is nothing within it that has not existed since before heaven and earth. The light that emanates from the heart must be cultivated and the grosser energies of the body refined in the heavenly luminosity that Taoist practices awaken. The process creates spirit out our grosser energy being. The shen becomes an extension of the heart, like a house or especially like the bloom of a lotus.

In the middle field of the heart, vitality is transmuted into the immortal fetus. The refined energy rises upwards of its own law to the brain to link with spirit. It is the reverse flow of energy in the body, and for this reason is called the "backwards flowing," and the "Wheel of the Law." It is the way things are supposed to be—energy is supposed to flow to the head to nourish us with joy, peace and inspiration. It is like the reverse orbit of the Thunder-birds around the sun. In this case they stand for the reverse of mundane activity which causes energy to flow down and out, it also stands for the resistance to the sun, the clashing which causes their power. The moon is also a relevant symbol of this resistance, and a prevalent symbol in Thunder-being iconography. It is also a symbol of immortality, of the birth of spirit at the crown brought forth by the resistance and integration of inner fire and water, sun and moon.

In the upper cinnabar field, spirit is nourished so that it can merge into the golden emptiness. It resides above the crown. The experience of golden light denoting this stage gives it the name—Golden Flower. At this point the mind is fully liberated, the heart is set free to expand (fly) in space, like when pollinated flower seeds leave the bloom to create a new sprout.

In alchemical terminology the yang-fire transmutes the base metal lead of low frequency yin energy, into silver by gradual firing, and through further firing, into golden elixir. This gold has the same property as the heavenly yang that we invoked for refinement. In the center of yin is yang. The base metal is truly yang all along. We're returning the state of energy to its original configuration. The ling of the Thunder-beings penetrates our own energy because of its subtlety. It awakens it to its inherent nature (golden elixir), which is always undefiled at its center. The energy naturally begins collecting at the heart center, an indication of this is increasing love and joy, and the fact is—you can see this as wings that sprout out of the heart (as wisdom and kindness) and grow from the back. The energy that collects in the heart is awakened through further mixing and refining. When energy, symbolized by fire and water or sun and moon) are unified, returned to their original state, they form a medicine bird, a mystical embryo, a spirit. It is formed in the head (the realm of inner heaven). This spirit can be used to travel and can be multiplied at a certain point to make ourselves increasingly available.

The highest transmutation of the spirit is the Thunder-bird. The complete restoration of our being as shen comes about in the fusion of subtle elements, gathered into the mystical embryo within the thunder-egg of our total life-being. First arise in this way as a form spirit or deity, then through ultimate realization, emerge as formless (by merging with formless Tao), with the capacity of taking numerous forms.

Thunder-bird is the alchemical bird. The hatching from the egg is the birth of the Immortal fetus or Red Baby into the Wisdom-spheres. A thunder-storm is the gathering of energy into a powerful convergence brought about with a Mind, Lei Kung. It is egg-born. The birth of the shen is similar, spirits are refined and converged into a powerful spirit, brought about with the mind, and the grace of Lei Kung. The shen can fly and looks like a bird. The birth of Thunder-bird is the specific transformation utilizing thunder-method or Taoist Tantra to mix the Mind (ling) of Lei Kung with ones own. It can be invoked and gathered directly from the deity and from the thunder-storms.

Lei Kung and the Ministry of Thunder have given their earthly messengers or emanations specific teachings and practices for utilizing the pure subtle energy that Thunders control -ling. These Thunder rites called Fou Jou, the science of Talismans and Invocations, entails drawing mystical diagrams and writing and reciting mystical words to make contact with the realm of Thunder-beings—Lei Kung's assemblage.

One specific practice given by Lei Kung is called "Calling on the Five Thunder Lords." The functions of Fou Jou are the same as Thunder-bird's, to control weather (thunder, lightning, rain, wind, mist and snow), to subdue malevolent spirits, and to heal. Fou Jou is the science of gathering the yang-essence known as ling and utilizing it for transmutation. Thunder-birds gather the same energy through their hearts in order to cause storms and battle negativity. Thunder-bird applies the yang-chi to restore the natural state of the earth. Analogously, we gather this thunder power using invocation and visualization and apply it to restore our own energy, or to redeem another persons. In Thunder rites the yang chi can be gathered directly from a thunder-storm, or the Thunder-beings all pervasive Spirit, as a catalyst and stimulus in the process of refinement. Any vitalizing practice which gathers yang-chi is termed "fiery dragon." It expresses the inner meaning of Thunder-bird battling serpents, rapid transmutation of inert yin into something which nurtures our spirits. The new spirit is gathered through the expansion of inner luminosity which envelopes and refines gross energy beginning around the heart.

The gross energy serpents become the golden, rainbow or lightning snakes of the Mother, the shens natural divine vitality, and his magical dagger.

In ancient times, the use of spiritual discipline was a natural part of life, so language and incantations could be used to enhance ones pure power, to communicate on deeper levels with nature, to effect transformation of the elements to produce storm phenomena. These practices are even more relevant today in directing us back to the center of our being, in healing broken disharmonious energy of mind and body. Today, although people think it is something extraordinary, it is a necessary natural part of life to practice spirituality to integrate the self with the universal Self, to return to flow with the Tao, naturalness.

In order to connect with Highest Divinity, the embodiment or expression of Tao, there is an effective practice which anyone who resonates with this tradition or simply wishes to align with God as Primordial Unborn Spirit can embrace. One should face East around sunrise and intone: Jiu Tien, Ying Yuen, Lei Shang, Pa Hua, Tien Tsun. You can actually practice this at any time or all the time. The meaning is as follows: "Highest Divinity of Universal Love and Thundering Response." It is a way of aligning with the root of all Thunder-beings—God. Ancient practices like this have been passed down through lineages and the deities continue to impart them and renew them for the benefit of achievement.

Language was at one time organic, a reflection of nature. The first word was thunder. So words were based on mimicking nature, thunder. The first written script in China and elsewhere reflected nature and internal phenomenon. Invocations and incantations could be used to commune with them, to be able to gather and control their power, to use it to serve the same function on earth which Thunders serve in the sky. The Thunder Lords voice is thunder, it awakens the earth, illuminates things, carries the Spirit-force on the sound as its winged-vehicle. To understand the language of the spirit which all beings share, and through which we live, it is necessary to listen to the heart, otherwise we only hear multiple languages from thought to cricket up to thunder. It is necessary to be able to feel what is being said behind the words. Words can never fully express the Truth behind them of our life, certain languages are developments of this intuitive experience, like Chinese, other languages are adulterated and cannot express but fragments of the Reality, like English.

Thunders give their winged-power to the Thunder specialist, through initiation in dreams and visions. The Thunder specialist uses the ling (word) in the same way as the deity. This achievement is called "voice of thunder," its basis is a pure heart and energy. Language could be used to perform great accomplishments (like Yu), to make storms bringing blessings to earth or to divert harmful storms, to heal . . . to always create a positive environment through the vibrancy of ones pure language. In this way we can bring their activity to earth, of enlightening minds. The Thunder person is a conduit for Lei Kung, one of his many voices.

Through Fou Jou, Thunder-beings have taught people the thunder-path through which they achieved themselves and through which they continue to live and work. First it presents the path of internal alchemy as a preliminary and preparation for restoring ones life. It calls upon the assistance of those giants who have risen up before us out of the earth and made their way into the clouds and stars, who have passed through form into storm and formlessness. They layed the foundation for our development into the incomprehensible. The internal alchemy is also a necessary preparation for practices of exorcism and healing by gathering the ling to accomplish this. A preliminary knowledge of internal alchemy is necessary for mastery of Thunder rites.

In the Ch'ing-wei tradition, the Thunder specialist must complete preliminary meditations called the "Yellow Court" meditations ("Yellow Court canon"), before he can control thunder power. The power of thunder is gathered and stored each Spring out of the first thunder-storm. The adept faces the direction of the storm and inhales the electrified air while using the proper mantra and mudra. The power is circulated through the organs (with visualization) and stored in the gall bladder. It is used later to light the alchemical furnace in the lower cinnabar field. The refinement begins thus: the vapors of metal and water are joined together in seminal essence. The vapor of metal is white, and stored in the lungs. The vapor of water is black and stored in the kidneys. Both are circulated upward and mixed with saliva in the mouth. The mixture of saliva and breath is sent down to the lower tan t'ien and refined into vital essence, by firing. The ultimate product is seen as white vapor, and personified as the Tao-te Heavenly Worthy, the 3rd in the Taoist Trinity of Upper and Inner Gods. Next, the vapor of earth is brought forth from the spleen and mixed with saliva in the mouth. Inhaling through the nose and swallowing saliva, the mixture is sent down into the furnace and refined into yellowish vapor, the symbol of primordial spirit. From the yellowish vapor is seen to congeal the Ling-pao Heavenly Worthy, the 2nd in the Taoist Trinity. Finally, vapors of wood and fire are joined to form primordial breath. The vapor of wood is drawn from the liver, and the breath of fire issues from the heart. Both are mixed with saliva and sent to be refined in the furnace. The product is a green-blue vapor which congeals into the Primordial Heavenly Worthy, the inner counterpart to Yuan-shih, Highest Divinity. In the final stage, the adept stops breathing and visualizes the 3 primordial breaths ascend upward to the central void, (Yellow Court), a space between the kidneys and heart. A cinnabar pill is formed by joining the three primordial breaths, original spirit and vital essence into one—thus forming the Thunder baby. The adept sees himself in the presence of the Eternal Tao. Now the adept has completed the preliminary and can control the power of thunder.

Meditation for gaining control over thunder is preceded by establishing the monthly position or finding the "gate of life." This gate is at the position pointed to by the handle of the Dipper. Thunder must be summoned from the direction of the Pole Star. According to certain invocations, the Pole Star is one great origin of thunder powers. The month, day and hour of Thunder alchemy and Thunder rite is determined by the Pole Star. Power of thunder is likewise summoned from the organ in the body which corresponds with the direction of the Pole Star—since the body is the microcosm of the universe the organs correspond to constellations.

The power of thunder, once infused in the body can be used to make talismans, to heal, to exorcise spirits, to control the sun rays to heal, to protect against sorcery. Fu lu is the particular practice of using talismans. An image in mystical writing is inscribed on bamboo, metal or paper. This writing is a form of "cloud writing" (Yun-chuan), which resembles the imitation of clouds and is used on amulets and talismans, imbued with powers to cure sickness and ward off evil spirits. It is very likely derived from mystical vision and mystical phenomena from the clouds themselves, taking shape as the writing of Thunder-bird, which is read through our heart. Thunder-bird can create cloud formation just as easily as he can direct the lightning. One use of the talisman is to wear it because it protects against illness and malevolent spirits. The older use of talismans entailed making a contract with the deity which was written on a small piece of paper or metal. It was split in half. One requests something, and one gives something. One requests purification, healing, rain, victory over evil spirits, and promises to do something creative. The deity will heal that person and the Thunder specialist will accomplish something beautiful. It is like a thunder-dream. Through such a dream Thunderer sacrifices himself (literally), he puts his subtle sparks in the person. This sets the mind at peace; he grants us our request, and he asks us to fulfill something creative for him in return.

Masters in Thunder rites are the worldly extensions of Lei Kung. The Thunder master becomes possessed by his power. This power belongs to the Thunder Lords, they give it to those who are worthy, who they want to receive it. Culture is not a limitation upon who receives subtle wisdom, but unvirtuous activity and impurity is. Thunder-beings protect all their teachings and power so that it can't fall into the wrong hands. Only those who are pure of heart can gain a good response from Thunders such as ending drought and clearing a community of disease.

The Thunder master is enlightened by the beings that brought him here. He acts in the very same capacity as the heavenly Immortals. His achievement is the City of Lightning. He is given ling by the Thunders, so that part of them can be on earth, while most remains above. As the lightning links heaven to earth, the Thunder master links heaven to earth through the mind. Thunder-bird represents the development of the human state, its growth into wisdom. Great energy can be manifested within this new open space, like lightning flashing in an open valley. An electronic field is created from having fused yang and yin. It gathers around the Thunder person. In the heart it is love. The heart-spark has a thunder-clap of awakening in it. It attracts and radiates. Thunder stands for true essence. It resounds in the golden middle, the heart of ones new spirit. Shen is perfectly free from the limitation of the material realm and personal suffering. This achievement is called uniting with the beginning of the universe, and is the hatching of the egg of reversal. The pure unconcealed nature of the heart acts through the ability to create multiple transformation bodies, the ability to assume whatever form one wishes, the ability to travel anywhere within the universe or vast subtle realms, the ability to come and go as one chooses, to be infinitely small or large.

Our emergence as a shen is referred to by the passage through the mysterious gate, portal or eye, and is signalled metaphorically by thunder and lightning. This gate is also called the "gate of life," the gate of the stars, the gate of the ni-wan or Inner Heaven and dwelling place of God. The birth of Thunder-bird is the birth of lightning above the clouds, and the convergence of the adept with the Tao. The thunder-egg is the locus of our energetic convergence as spirit, as our body-mind-spirit it has arisen from the Mysterious Mother T'ien Mu. Our mergence with Tao through Thunder rites, happens through Lei Kung and is our birth from his egg into his City of Lightning. As the baby Thunder-bird one is free to fly within the Eternal Divine Body of Undifferentiated Unity (Tao). According to our cultivation, our new energy formation, we return to the subtle realms beyond space, to our home in the nest of Lei Kung's City of Lightning. This nest is likewise the station of our heart merged with Tao. In esoteric Taoism this place may have been called the Mountain of the Bird-man. It is the abode of the Immortals, highest reality and the state of perfect tranquility and illumination.

To speak of our deep unity with all things we refer to it as Sacred Origin, Mystery, Source and Tao. It is not possible to define Tao as God without redefining God in terms of experience not dogma. God is our true essence and our responsibility to converge our energy or internal spirits into that original essence. In Thunder rites a date-wood vajra is used. It will always remind us of our true nature, of God whom we know through the looking-glass of hearts. He is the Valley Spirit of the Tao, the Spirit and energy flying as if through an open valley. He is our inherent limitless openness, absence and our energetic awareness, presence. He is the completely refined and alchemically spiritualized state, symbolized by the shen, bird-man. All such perfected beings have risen to the same level of formless Spirit and Energy.

Countless perfected beings assist us in the restoration process. They are responsible for every movement toward the divine state. They shine in the space of our selflessness. They control the mind through our freedom to love. They work through our positive heroic virtues, through the hearts inherent clarity. They are the light of heaven shining in the depths of the earth, the spirit and light in the heart of reality, symbolized by thunder-clouds pregnant with light and sound, and by the cauldron of our being within which we transmute what is poisonous within our body-mind into immortal medicine. Thunder-method teaches us to reverse time, decay to the state when the mind was pristine, eternally youthful, natural, harmonious and beautiful. This is the Tao as goal and path. This is also called Thunder-bird trail, the orbit he makes around the sun, out of the clouds, and the one we train in which reverses our internal energy flow to the crown. The Thunder power of Lei Kung is the ling which reverses time. His egg is the reversal of time egg, like being swallowed by the Deity. It refines what has fallen into decay, to what is undecayable, the immortal state prior to birth. The ling keeps reversing time, destroying it until one has gone back through the animal states, vegetable states, crystalline states, mineral states, fire and water states, until one is the simplest, subtlest, most unthinkable yet profound substance one can think of—Spirit, whose revelation is thunder and lightning and whose heart formation is Lei Kung.

Conclusion: Prophecy and the Spontaneous Play of the Lightning-bolt

We are eternally related to the Thunder-beings. Just as we are connected to people, events, places, spirits with chords of light, so we are tied to this Subtle Mystery as if by a rainbow chord or a lightningbolt. Our indestructible tie is with the Deity of our heart. It seems we're going after them in our life, but in reality they're coming after us. They're bearing down on us like a whale swiftly moving in on small fish to devour them.

Traditionally Thunder-beings manifested in the prepared mind, speech, body of the yogi or shaman. People like Moses were the sole recipients of this profound wisdom, most people require purification to become truly intimate with Wisdom-beings. But our intimate devotion will cause our purification. We become intimate with Wisdom-deity by becoming inseparable from his name and image.

It takes a wisdom-image in our dimension to express our capacity for achieving the enlightened state. The image represents our inherent nature and the method of our achievement. The image is the symbol of the heart of our Consciousness. That heart is inner divinity. The image we embrace as our tutelary-deity becomes the very image of the angelic light body we are going to give birth to. Even if we choose to arrive at Silence through silence, the symbol-body of our god-parents will remain with us, along with their wisdom-quality.

Each of the three Oriental wisdom traditions has essentially the same ultimate goal or fruit, and that is the birth of a new spiritual body crystallized out of the former gross energy and body. It is a body of light and vision, wisdom and supreme bliss, a body of pure Consciousness through and through. To reiterate: in Vajrayana that body is called the "spiritual body" and the attainment is called Buddhahood; in Shaiva Tantra that body is called "bliss body" and the attainment is called Shiva-hood; in Taoism that body is called immortal body (shen) and the attainment is called the union of Tao and man. The universal symbol of this is the Garuda, who can be an angel or Thunder-bird or man depending upon which Ancestors crack the egg. The wings grow from the heart, literally as emanations of spirit and light. They symbolize our development of wisdom and compassion. They grow through a persons back and can be seen there. The higher a persons development, the greater the wing span, so those called archangels or creatures of the Throne or Garudas or Herukas or Thunder-birds are first emanations of the Mystery. They have given birth to themselves into that level of development, they have created their spirit through alignment with the Primordial Wisdom-beings. Those of a lesser attainment, who retain a form body of an angelic being have a smaller wing span and function under the tutelage of the Wisdom-beings and ultimately must return to this realm or one similar in order to complete their attainment. Though there are many varied states, the level of highest attainment or Great Perfection, is the same for all achieved ones.

Our potential or primal purity has not completely been lost to us, nor can it ever be lost. Wisdom and love will be with us eternally because it is our very nature. Each of us stands before the great Wheel of powers and is sustained and nourished by that Origin which is projecting us as a bundle of light fibers. The blessings of Thunder-beings are raining unceasingly on us. The perfect atmosphere is there, we simply need to leave our houses, our heads, to open up, to think of all others. Nevertheless, no-one can deny that our divine inheritance of pure energy (inherent goodness) has degenerated, that, as a result our clear-light mind has been partly eclipsed, that our nature is in dire need of the wisdom-medicine of recognition, the sacred wisdom vehicles, and a reversal of the activity which produces suffering in our life. This work is the revelation of an elaborate City which exists concealed within the heart. This work is an unveiling of what is integral and true and which robes us in space, cultivates flight through the hatching of a bird-person through the growth of wings from the heart, and crowns us in sovereignty. This work is a reversal, a dissolution into empty space. This work is an unlearning, a refining; we widdle ourselves down until there's nothing left but the tools and the realization that we were never widdling anything to begin with.

The clear heart is the Heart of the City of Lightning. It is Cloud yet sunshine, electric yet static, Thunder yet Silence, lightning yet space, presence yet absence, rainbow yet blue sky, awareness yet emptiness, impermanence yet eternity. We're perfect mirrors reflecting the Eternal, echoing its dance of emptiness-light and sound.

Just as it is the work of the Thunders to fasion bolts above the clouds to give birth to storms to renew the earth, so it is our responsibility to work on this collection of winds (mind), to hammer it out to fasion it in the midst of flame in the divine furnace of the heart, to transform the lead of heavy inner states into the pure gold of enlightenment, "coppery jiva into golden Shiva."

The Awareness-being is the City of Lightning which travels on immutable light currents, East and West, North and South. Our work is to awaken our pristine heart-nature, to realize our non-difference, our relatedness. The work of the lightning is to clothe itself in image, the work of the thunder is to clothe itself in its name to manifest blessings.

We are an accumulation of energy, like a cloud, the results of activity since beginningless time. Our cloud is body and mind. Virtuous and wise activity yields a cloud of wisdom; ignorant, harmful, and self-serving activity yields a condition of suffering. The Thunder-beings are an accumulation of wisdom, generated out of compassion. Their minds are infinite space. Their bodies are clouds of luminous compassionate wisdom-mind. We have this potential to accumulate wisdom and compassion, to give birth to ourselves into infinite space, and to benefit others by spontaneously appearing in the body of thunder-storms.

The work of cultivating wisdom, according to the Oriental traditions must be embraced at some point in our total existence. With knowledge of cause and effect, we can clearly see what a future existence might be like; each of us is building our future life. No-one can afford to waste the opportunity of human life. With knowledge of cause and effect we can clearly see what a future society might be like, together we are building a future vision of the world. Based on our insight into the present circumstances of the world we can easily project the future of our society. The lamas say that things are not going to get better, at least not until far into the next world system.

It is overwhelmingly obvious that the world is in need of wisdom and love to fulfill our lives. Many Westerners are becoming increasingly aware of the Tantric view and some are aspiring to practice. Some lamas feel that this surge is like the last and high flicker of a candle before being extinguished, that the Vajra vehicle will dissolve until the next world system when it will be renewed by Maitreya. Other masters feel that we're gradually going to explode into a new shakti yuga or era of divine electricity.

The Kalachalera Tantra predicts the coming of a golden age in about five hundred years which will mark the end of this present kali yuga. It is said that a global battle will ensue between forces of negativity and goodness. Harmful forces will invade from outer space and the warriors of Shambhala will come out of their secret land identified with Mt. Kailash, the geographic seat of Samvara and Shambhu (Shiva). The warriors will win the battle and initiate a time of global peace, a new cycle of yugas. Then, according to Lord Buddha's prophecy, the Dharma will completely die out until the coming of the Buddha Maitreya millions of years in the future.

Even though times may be getting worse, the lamas encourage us that the Tantric practices generate more merit now than ever, and that practices such as the Guru Rinpoche sadhana will actually gain in strength as times worsen. They also teach that in the next world system only Vajrayana will exist, lesser vehicles will simply not have any sway over the obscurations of future minds.

If we die without undertaking any cultivation, without having lifted a finger for others, we risk having to return again until we sow the conditions of an enlightened human existence. This entails establishing some connection to wisdom through enlightened beings. The human family risks having to return here again and again until we sow the conditions of an enlightened society, otherwise unbroken life in subtle inner space is not possible. If we establish or have previously established some connection to Wisdom-beings, if we have lived according to virtue and kindness, at the bodily dissolution the form of that Wisdom-being will present itself. In such a way this book might be instructive. To someone related to Thunder-beings, they are bound to appear at death. The Mystery extends its grace unceasingly. But I certainly didn't write this book to tell people this is who you might see when you die. It is better that we connect with the Wisdom-beings during our life, the importance of this I cannot stress enough. They are there to give us assistance, without them the goal cannot be reached. It must happen through the guru-deity, through his transmission vehicle and through his blessing-lights. Even if we do not reach completion in this life we will still have auspicious links established, to attain ourselves at a future time, either by entering the Mother-luminosity at death or in a future life. And if we are good practitioners of the Deity, then they will most likely take us into their Subtle Enjoyment Realms at death. Some practices, like transference into Pure Realm are geared entirely for this.

As humans we have the greatest potential to achieve enlightenment. Only as humans can highest achievement be made. It is usually taught that even form-gods yearn for a human body, since only through such a body can the accumulations of merit and wisdom be completed, yielding enlightenment.

In Sanatan Dharma the simplest way to attain this is the joint practice of karma and japa yogas. Selfless service completes the collection of merit when it is empowered by mantra and devotion, and mantra completes the collection of wisdom when empowered by service and devotion. I mention this because it may be difficult to gain initiation and practices of Highest Yoga Tantra or Kriya Yoga or Dzogchen which lead quickly to high realization. But Haidhakan Babaji has said that in this yuga, the above practice yields enlightenment. Any of the mantras provided herein can be employed for such purpose, they're each highly blessed. As a basic meditation train to visualize the Deity at the crown when singing the mantra aloud. When doing silent repetition visualize the image in your heart and the sound of the mantra arising there-

from. Or absorb oneself in the sound. Enthrone the Deity in your heart and think that his grace-waves envelope your body and reach all sentient beings, just as when you place a crystal in the sun's rays, rainbow-light is cast throughout the room.

It is very important to nurture altruistic motives, to always pray for others first, otherwise it is possible to cut yourself off from the Deities. When we continually dedicate our work and prayers, then light gathers at the crown. When we seek to draw light or anything to ourselves for selfish purposes, the light will not gather. It is unconditional, yet controlled by Sublime Beings, their activity or light is obstructed when we operate through self-serving attitude. Eventually, when it goes too far, when it begins creating calamity, Thunder Lords will clear the obstruction to their light.

I feel it is this self-centeredness which makes the Thunder Lords disappointed with humanity. They are waiting for us to open, mostly they want us to see our sublimity and true face. We are already primordially awake in past, present and future. Mind is unconditioned. They are reminding us. Each of us is being called to act from wisdom and love—self-lessly. When the mind is clear it will turn naturally and the spirit will guide through the heart spontaneously through intangible light and sound, through intuition and thought. There are no real set of rules, we simply must choose a certain attitude or way of acting, the actions themselves will not adhere to a set of rules but are based on what is right in the moment. This is called Dharma or Tao.

None of us with smarts can afford to let life slip through our fingers without doing what we can to leave the world a little bit better than we found it. This entails not empty repetition, but dedicating the mantra, breath, heart, life, body, awareness to liberating all beings from suffering.

We practice so infrequently, yet the Sublime Deities are prompting us for our true benefit and to establish a chain to fulfill their aspirational light which seeks to release beings from suffering. They use every language to communicate, no matter how imperfect. The perfect language of the spirit is a silent whisper, even the thunder is no longer understood. So they use vibrant and outrageous beauty, they use symbols we can understand, they make things clear, so there's no question of what's right and what's not. They use the raw energy of life to communicate Dharma through our hearts, to liberate us. Every thought is magnificent in their light. We only need to think of them and they're there. When we see them, their sublimity and profundity, we make them our ideal. To shift our ideal off of material habits which obstruct our tranquility, onto Wisdom is the path. They developed many methods, many things that we can use to think of them, of God. Our minds are used to thinking of things, instead of abiding in the natural ease of emptiness, so the Deities give us beautiful things to think about, which unconditionally awaken us and bring us back to our natural ease. Since our mind is used to fixating on things, they give us something which by fixating on it, we become non-fixated. The method of fixating on Wisdom-deities ends all fixation. Fixation or attachment causes us to fear, desire and hate. This energy brings us back to earth magnetically or it may cause us to descend to lower realms of greater suffering and limitation. So negative intentions draw us back here to fulfill that energy. Primarily desire brings us to earth. Positive aspirations draw us back to earth to fulfill that energy—to help liberate beings. Only through positive aspirations are we able to control our future rebirth, to choose it. Perhaps we'll choose not to return here, at least we have the freedom or mind-control to choose. But since we're here now, we must do everything we can to help others, we have to get out of our heads, and we have to get to really know ourselves. We should pray continuously to the Deity-guru we hold most dear in our hearts.

As Thunder-people we pray under the sky canopy of storms. We pray under the stellar Wheel of powers. We pray under Cities of Lightning, to enter Cities of Lightning. As Thunder-people we pray under lightning sky canopy because it has the power to awaken our heart treasure of unlimited bliss and awareness. We pray under the storm canopy of sky because in those clouds stand the Thunder-beings, and those Deities are happy to see us working to help one another, to become better people. By praying under the storms, we're praying under Thunder-beings, we're praying under our Grandfathers, those responsible for all beauty and goodness in the world, all wisdom and joy in our hearts. So they give us wisdom and joy. We pray under them whether its storming or not. We invite them to the cloud seat of our crown and heart. They're the winged-vehicle of our prayers. Even if we just pray with their name in our hearts that name returns to its Source, bearing our prayer, just like an eagle returning to its tree-nest. In this case the name returns to its nest in the Tree of Life, the sound-spark of lightning returns to its Eternity Lightning root. We pray under the storms because the Source of our prayers is potently there. The Source abides at our crown when we live

virtuously, and responds to us in the same way with a rain of wisdom. In ancient mythology this was depicted by Garuda returning from space to Mt. Meru (Sushumna Nadi: central channel) with heavenly nectar. Thunder-bird returns to his nest (crown-wheel) in the Tree of Life (central channel) with food for his children. We all need to gather together and pray to our personal divinity. Whenever we use the name or mantra the Deity arises around us and within our mind-stream—as awareness-light. This light awakens us and transmits our heart's prayer to rain benefits on all sentient beings. This light radiates outward from the crystal lamp of our heart, liberating all beings from suffering.

The light(ning) is a transmitter to broadcast our hearts gold intention to transform the universe, to liberate beings from suffering. There will be a time when all people have no choice but to lift up their hearts to Thunder-beings. Most people will be utterly bewildered and senseless. To prevent this, pray now continuously, sacrifice oneself for others continuously, remember Wisdom Deity of your heart continuously. If there is inner purification for you then there will not be outer purification for you, your mind will be protected. If there is inner purification for all people, then there will not be outer purification for all people—all virtuous golden hearts are protected by Thunder-beings.

Know that even if Purifiers come down as Primordial Thunder-bird and surround the earth with lightning, inexhaustible power of fire and water, it is because people failed to purify themselves and instead chose to adopt bad habits and poor quality energy, to harm others and pollute the earth. If the civilization destroys itself as has occurred previously according to tradition, then it will have to return to this realm. The realm corresponds with a state of spiritual development. The meaning of this body is endurance, which is the name of this world in Buddhist cosmology.

I think we can at least strive to be a little bit better person than we were before, to take after God's honey bees (the heavenly who do not sting, only produce honey). By refining our life outwardly and inwardly we increase our capacity for kindness (which determines our future state) so we increase our potential for a brighter happier future. We can cultivate with the method and light of the Wisdom-beings we were born from, and gain re-birth into that City. This is the way things are supposed to be on earth, otherwise we remain exiles from our true abode, our true omniscient state.

In the span of earthly existence our human family has given birth to many spiritually enlightened beings, it did not happen without natural living and compassion. The present civilization has degenerated and we are coming into that time which prophecy accords the great purifiers are going to restore natural harmony on earth. It is based on cause and effect, the earth's response to peoples energy and activity. Wisdom yields balance, ignorance and selfish behavior yields imbalance. Thunder-beings are the Mind of nature and judge our activity based upon whether we've given or taken. They are very disappointed with humanity because we have more than enough to create beauty. They control nature, to cause floods to destroy the causes of disease and restore harmony, or alay disasters to prevent suffering. What we as people have made out of our life will rise up to support our life or destroy us. Wars and human conflict cause future disasters. What happens is based on our will and activity, our use of the powers we're given.

The Sacred Mystery has shown me that he is very disappointed with people and if we do not wise up, extend ourselves to each other, live creative truthful lives, then he is going to annihilate everything. He showed me how this would happen, how it would come like a bolt out of the blue, with no external warning, how the entire sky would erupt into lightning, how the fiercest winds and rains would decimate everything. That Vision was a whip that jolted me wide awake. Each one of us has to do our part, has to work together, has to choose with a selfless heart. If we don't do it this very moment we'll slip closer to the Divine dissolution.If we don't choose inner Mahakranti to melt the frozen heart, the outer Mahakranti will set upon us and devour us by melting reality. We cannot save ourselves alone, we cannot slither into a hole in the earth, nothing will escape this destruction except those who were truly virtuous in their lives, who were aligned with Wisdom or divine hierarchy, who extended themselves unfailingly to benefit others. The Wisdom-beings will guide their awakened children to safe ground. I cannot say what will become of the other souls. I pray that compassion is sparked in all hearts before the dissolution fire is sparked in Transcendent-heart.

I pray that all minds possess sufficient awareness to embrace the cultivation of love and peace in their lives. It's really up to each person to choose to follow path of bliss or path of tears. We need to have faith in our masters, but we need to understand that no-one is going to carry us. Our masters will light the flame of our hearts to guide us in right action, to unfurl unlimited potential, to open heart meridean, to embody stream of Deity blessings, to guide all sentient beings to the state wholly free of suffering. Pray to Thunder-beings since they're the supreme Omniscient Ones who bring about creation and dissolution of worlds, that they will avert disaster and Devouring-fire until all hearts are awake and unified.

After I saw this Vision (of great dissolution) I was sick at heart so made offerings and dispatched many Thunder-beings to awaken hearts so the Thunder Mind wouldn't have to decimate everything. It rained for days without cessation then there was a double rainbow over the village. In the Bible, after the last flood when the patriarch Noah made offerings, YHVH made a rainbow to symbolize the covenant that he would not annihilate civilization again. The rainbow is also a symbol of unity and compassionate-bliss.

Thunder-beings maintain the harmonious peace of the earth. They are going to preserve the way of nature. They are the greatest power in the universe. They are going to fulfill the subtle law which controls the universe through the hearts of natural deities. They tolerate our activity and send us the vehicle and fuel necessary to live according to the subtle law. It's our responsibility to choose that creative force to work through our lives, no different than the natural deities. We do this by always acting creatively and compassionately. In such a way the subtle law controls the universal manifestation from within. Divine mercy has been with us since the beginning, it has allowed our society of ways to continue to this point. We do not want to see the other side of the Mystery!!

The Thunder-beings want to see heavenly universal good on earth which manifests spontaneously through a selfless heart of positive inherent qualities. The Thunder-beings want to see things fresh, radiant and beautiful. They put their Vision on earth in the lightning. They put their will on earth in the thunder. They put their wisdom on earth in the messenger— yogi or dakini. That Vision, will and spirit is a tool of creation and cosmic renewal. This process happens naturally, the law of the universe (karma) is the universe, it cannot be escaped. If people are interested in renewing their energy and the society through individual spiritual work, it is possible to avert the purification. We have to put our hearts together. Whatever we choose, we also choose to live with.

The Thunder-beings are among the great purifiers; if they don't see positive behavior on earth, people using their light to do good, to build a creative evolving human society, they are quite naturally going to re-establish order. It has happened before, it will happen again if we don't turn our hearts toward that Light. There is a rainbow which unzips the covenant rainbow that shoots across the entire firmament. It will happen if people continue to infract upon the way of the universe and heart, since the way of the universal heart is the real covenant.

Positive activity or love has its origin with the Mystery, with all enlightened beings. It sheds light continuously as the subtle law which governs the universe from within as Truth or Dharma. Because of immoderate craving, emotional afflictions and habitual thoughts, the mind fails to hear this subtle message which is transmitting. So at the start it takes a little bit of faith in the masters, the view and techniques. But even this is based on what feels right in our heart. Eventually, practice yields that one can feel and prove the spiritual reality since the heart faculty is uncovered. The mind must become purified—the heart is the seat and seed of the mind. Since the Mystery shines or loves unconditionally, if we open ourselves through the name and image given us, we can be transformed.

If we are gathering good energy, we will be protected and won't have to worry about purifiers, hurricanes, twisters, lightning—they will go around us and make a space in the clouds for the sunshine. But most importantly they can completely transform us in the fire of their love. Use the names, they remind us of who we are and where we're from. The nectar of divine resonance is the light of recognition by which we become extensions of divine substance and energy on earth. That our inherent nature is divine destroys all karmic impurities because we recognize that the Deity was the knower and doer all along, that this is their stage, mask, dream or dance of dark-light and white-light. This is the reality of identification of oneself as a divine extension and ones indestructible heart-drop as the City of Lightning. The Presence exists deep within us as the 7th heavenly degree and the great emptiness, so we have to relax our minds into this originating space. If we experience ourself as the Awareness-deity it is by their light. Everything becomes suffused in that light, we can literally see everything we ever did as naturally good, as an unfolding of wisdom, a spontaneous expression of Deity's unfathomable Mind. We see what is present as an illusory crystal palace that Deity creates out of bliss.

They're working on us by working through us. To be created or emanated from Wisdom-deities, means that we embody them on earth, and that we have in our hearts the intention to help beings, and that we have the potential to realize ourself as Wisdom-deity. So where are the qualities of Thunder-beings manifest in people today? First and foremost they are revealed in our inherent goodness, our compassion, our protectiveness and self-sacrifice. They are revealed in our dharma, our creative endeavors to re-establish harmony in this sphere. They're rarely apparent in our speech except when we chant and speak kind truth to mimic speech of Thunder. They're rarely apparent in our silence except when we meditate one-pointedly to reflect Thunder-mind of stone-like space.

This book might be useful to whoever resonates with the images they see, with thunder and lightning, with Wisdom of the three traditions, with nature. If so I suggest pursueing these traditions and praying to these Deities. Actually I suggest everyone pray to them, they are what we are and what gave us life. They are the Omniscient God and there is none higher. There might be a time in ones life when it is highly efficacious to do so. Actually that time is now, not just when there are storms or decimation by floods, volcanoes, famine, war. There is a storm raging in the human heart, a confusion, a longing for what has been partially forgotten, for what has become intangible, too minute and yet too vast for the fragmented, kaleidoscopic view of a broken or veiled heart. Wisdom-method is preventative medicine and antidote. Attunement is the solution, while wisdom-method is the key, the medicine to heal the broken heart, the tongues of fire with which to burn away the veils limiting our mind.

Thunder puts things back together, lightning reassembles. The essential wisdom of the Thunder-beings in the Oriental traditions reveals our inherent connectedness to pure energy and substance. Each person is responsible for spiritual development, for returning to our Origin by living natural lives on earth. We can only say God is responsible if we recognize that. The Thunder-beings have provided more than sufficient wisdom to achieve this. They bear the Truth because they are the Truth. The Truth which happens to present itself as Dharma is the way which all beings are urged to live. The Truth which presents itself as Tantra is the way which all beings are urged to view reality. When the desires are controlled and liberated they reveal this singular urge, Love or enlightened energy. It seeks to free itself and all other beings from suffering. The Truth is in our fire; when refined it appears as creative-bliss arising from wisdom-void, a flash in empty space. The Truth is our indestructible heart and its arising. The Truth is the formless Absolute and its Lightningbolt. If we're remote from our inner spark we are remote from its Source-bolt. We deceive ourselves consistently until we embrace the training which leaves a passage through which divine electric current can spark as self-illumination, in which emptiness mixes with emptiness, Wisdom with wisdom, Mind with mind.

The fruit can never be unknown by its Tree. The energy around the heart, appearing with limbs, hands, feet, head, either supports the heart like a crystal refracting sun-light and fathomless beauty, or it darkens the heart like a veil. Our object in traditions where wisdom serves as a method of spiritualization, is to sacrifice our life-being, all the energy revolving around the heart and the heart itself to the divine ideal who has been invited to take a seat in the heart of life and govern from there. This means simply offering body, speech and mind. All the sacrifices we ever make, all selfless spontaneous acts are a sacrifice by a benevolent divine being, of the Self or Self-less Heart of the universe. We are training ourselves to see that we are truly divine bodies evolving through earth, sharing one blood, one spirit. Our activity is caused by the originating spark of primordial light (God) and the result is the same, a revelation or unfolding of wisdom, a spontaneous flash of insight, a pearl of awakening, the utterance of thunder. Yet enlightenment or natural wisdom does not unfold without self-less service and cultivation: Truth, Simplicity and Love. This is the direct inheritance of my lineage through Mahavatar 1oo8 Haidhakan Wale Babaji—Shiva. "Ishvarovacha Phuro!" Shiva says: Be Inspired!

Lightning returns form to emptiness. The shock is so great that after the smoke clears there's nothing but an empty space and a pair of footprints. Those who cultivate with the raw power of thunder, according to Thunder-beings' grace, dissolve back into the City of Lightning—the space from which we arose. We must die first to the clockwise world to live with God, the Clock which reverses time. This does not imply we're out suicidally looking to get blasted by lightning; the love affair we have is with its Spirit, since that Cloud is our Beloved. We long to have everything which stands between us and God annihilated so that only Mind shines. This is the inner meaning of the Destroyer and apocalypse, the revolution necessary to return us to Infinity. Its work is always quick, and it hits the mark. When the smoke of intense cultivation clears, there's nothing left but an empty space and a pair of footprints—an empty space in which We live. Empty space is the indestructible foundation of the Cities of Lightning. All traditions have arisen from the Living Cloud of Primordial Thunder-beings; the bolt is the revelation and its play is to awaken its Presence within our heart and life. The spontaneous play of the lightningbolt is the activity of Thunder-beings' immeasurable blessings.

Iconography is central in the practice of the Thunder-beings, which utilize image and name to invite the Deity to take a seat in the heart and awaken his City of Lightning around it. We create ourselves in their image—a lightning-bolt of bliss, a Diety awakened.

Cities of Lightning is the efflorescence of the unique and compassionate nature of the Thunder-beings. What Truth or treasure can be distilled from this exposition derives from them, what error derives from this human mirror.

May this treatment of their rare and precious imagery and wisdom enhance the bliss of sentient beings and Deities.

May these ideas serve to awaken and inspire wisdom in all hearts. May Cities of Lightning benefit all sentient beings.

May the wisdom of the Thunder-beings fly out to the directions of space like a Wheel of Lightning.

Closing Verses

Om Namah Shivaya
To all Thunder-beings throughout Infinite space I bow.

Thunder-Lord, take us back to before we were born, to before we conceived of I and mine, to when we were lightning flashing blissfully in the womb of space.

Thunder Lord, take us back to the root of our being, to the heart of ebullient stillness and ecstatic joy.

Thunder-Lord, take us back to the Cities of Lightning, to when our hearts were merged in self-illuminated awareness, to when we were shooting stars playing and dancing in space, to when we were rainbows in the sky of the mystery.

Thunder-Lord, take us back to when we were as simple as the "Dew on the Grass," as profound as the ocean of the mystery, as luminous as a crystal lamp, to when all beings were unified in one City of Lightning.

Works Cited

Blofeld, John. *Taoism, The Road to Immortality*. Boston: Shambala, 1985.

Blofeld, John. *The Tantric Mysticism of Tibet*. N.Y.: Penguin Books, 1970.

Chatterji, J.C. *Kashmir Shaivism*. Albany: State University of New York Press, 1986.

Chogyam, Ngakpa. *Wearing the Body of Visions*. N.Y. Aro Books, 1995.

Edou, Jerome. *Machig Labdron and the Foundations of the Chod*. Ithaca: Snow Lion Publications, 1996.

Gold, Peter. *Navajo and Tibetan Sacred Wisdom. The Circle of the Spirit*. Rochester, Vermont: Inner Traditions, 1994.

Govindan, Marshall. *Babaji and the 18 Siddha Kriya Yoga Tradition*. Montreal: Kriya Yoga Publications, 1991.

Gyaltsen, Khenpo Konchog. *The Great Kagyu Masters, The Golden Lineage Treasury*. Ithaca: Snow Lion Publications. 1990.

Hughes, John. *Self-Realization in Kashmir Shaivism*. Albany: State University of New York Press, 1994.

Lame Deer, John (Fire), and Richard Erdoes. *Lame Deer, Seeker of Visions*. New York: Washington Square Press, 1972.

Landaw, J. and Weber, A. *Images of Enlightenment*. Ithaca: Snow Lion Publications, 1993.

Lodo, Lama Rinpoche (trans.) *Garden of All Joy*. San Fransisco: KDK Publications, 1994.

Mathieu, Ricard. *The Life of Shabkar*. Albany: State University of New York Press, 1994.

Mishra, Kamalakar. *Kashmir Shaivism*. Portland, Oregon: Rudra Press, 1993.

Ni, Hua-Ching. *Tao, the Subtle Universal Law and The Integral Way of Life*. Santa Monica: Sevenstar Communications, 1979.

Ni, Hua-Ching. *The Taoist Inner View of the Universe and the Immortal Realm*. Los Angeles: The Shrine of the Eternal Breath of Tao, College of Tao and Traditional Chinese Healing, 1979.

Ni, Hua-Ching. *Workbook For Spiritual Development of All People*. Santa Monica: Sevenstar Communications, 1984.

Ni, Hua-Ching. *Internal Alchemy*. Santa Monica: The Shrine of the Eternal Breath of Tao, 1992.

Saso, Michael. *The Teachings of Taoist Master Chuang*. London: Yale University Press, 1978.

Satyeswarananda Giri, Swami. *Babaji, The Divine Himalayan Yogi*. San Diego, The Sanskrit Classics, 1984.

Shyam, Radhe. *I Am Harmony*. Crestone, Colorado: The Spanish Creek Press, 1989.

Singh, Jaideva (trans.) Abhinavagupta. *A Trident of Wisdom*. Albany: State University of New York Press, 1988.

Singh, Jaideva. *The Yoga of Delight, Wonder and Astonishment*. Albany: State University of New York Press, 1991.

Thirumoolar, Siddhar. *Thirumandiram, A Classic of Yoga and Tantra*. Montreal: Babaji's Kriya Yoga and Publications, Inc. 1993.

Trungpa, Chogyam. *The Sacred Path of the Shambhala Warrior*. Boston: Shambhala Books, 1988.

Thunderhorse, Iron, and Donn Le Vie, Jr. *Return of the Thunderbeings*. Santa Fe: Bear and Company Publishing, 1990.

About the Author

Samudranath is a Trantric adept, student and teacher of the three Oriental traditions—Buddha Dharma, Sanatan Dharma, and Taoism. He has done extensive research on these three traditions. His root gurus are Guru Padmasambhava, Lord Shiva Megharaj and Venerable Lei Kung, the Wisdom-sources of the three Oriental traditions. It has been through their grace and blessings that *Cities of Lightning* arose for the welfare of all sentient beings. Samudranath received profound instruction in dreams and pure vision, and was asked to write *Cities of Lightning* as a vehicle for the wisdom of the Thunder-beings. Samudranath is a Thunder-specialist who gives instruction in Sanatan Dharma and Shaivite practices to individuals and small groups. He is a pujari (priest) and student of Haidhakan lineage under the tutelage of Mahavatar Sambasadashiv 1008 Haidhakan Wale Babaji. He is also an adept of the Karma Kagyu lineage of Tibetan Buddhism. He presently resides at Karma Triyana Dharmachakra monastery in New York state.